COOK·off

COOK·off

RECIPE FEVER IN AMERICA

AMY SUTHERLAND

VIKING

VIKING

Published by the Penguin Group

Penguin Group (USA) Inc., 375 Hudson Street, New York, New York 10014, U.S.A.

Penguin Books Ltd, 80 Strand, London WC2R 0RL, England

Penguin Books Australia Ltd, 250 Camberwell Road, Camberwell, Victoria 3124, Australia

Penguin Books Canada Ltd, 10 Alcorn Avenue, Toronto, Ontario, Canada M4V 3B2

Penguin Books India (P) Ltd, 11 Community Centre, Panchsheel Park, New Delhi – 110 017, India

Penguin Books (N.Z.) Ltd, Cnr Rosedale and Airborne Roads, Albany, Auckland, New Zealand

Penguin Books (South Africa) (Pty) Ltd, 24 Sturdee Avenue, Rosebank, Johannesburg 2196, South Africa

Penguin Books Ltd, Registered Offices:
80 Strand, London WC2R 0RL, England

First published in 2003 by Viking Penguin,
a member of Penguin Group (USA) Inc.

10 9 8 7 6 5 4 3 2 1

The recipes included in this book were taken directly from their respective sources and printed as is. Neither the author nor the publisher tested them.

BAKE-OFF® and the Doughboy are trademarks of The Pillsbury Company and use thereof does not indicate endorsement of this book.

LIBRARY OF CONGRESS CATALOGING-IN-PUBLICATION DATA
Sutherland, Amy.
    Cookoff : recipe fever in America / Amy Sutherland.
        p.   cm.
    ISBN 0-670-03251-4
        1. Cookery, American.   2. Cookery—Competitions—United States.   I. Title.
    TX715.S9537   2003
    641.5973—dc21   2003050169

This book is printed on acid-free paper. ∞

Printed in the United States of America
Designed by Carla Bolte

For Scott, the love of my life.

For Joan, who taught me to love life.

For the cooks, who make life worth living.

CONTENTS

ACKNOWLEDGMENTS

The talents, knowledge, and patience of a long list of contesters made this book possible, notably Diane Sparrow and Roxanne Chan. These two ingenious cooks and creative spirits were the central muses of this project. They changed the way I think about cooking and everyday life for the better. Thanks also goes to contesters Pat Harmon, Edwina and Bob Gadsby, Norita Solt, Barbara Morgan, Kristine Snyder, Janet Barton, Liz Barclay, Camilla Saulsbury, Susan Runkle, Janice Elder, Ruth Kendrick, and Shirley DeSantis. Their exuberance informs every page of this book.

I owe big thanks to Bob Plager and his crew, Kathleen Tolbert, Dixie Johnson, Bob and Doris Coates, Allegani Schofield, and Johnye Harriman, who all graciously tutored me on the ways of competition chili. My guides at the Memphis in May World Championship Barbecue Cooking Contest included Janet McCrary, the Gifford family, the entire Airpork Crew, the Pink Ladies, Don McLemore, and MIM staffer Lynne Doyle. Wally Taillon put up with unending questions while he tried to win a jambalaya cookoff, as did Tootsie Gonzales and Byron Gautreau.

This book also would not have been possible without the guidance of Arlette Hollister at the Iowa State Fair, Diane Kirkbride and Sherry Hill of the National Beef Cook-Off, Beth Duggar at the National Cornbread Cook-off, Richard Lobb at the National Chicken Council, and Peter Cicarelli at the Great Garlic Cook-Off. Marlene Johnson at General Mills helped me throughout this project, from when it was merely an idea until I was proofing the edited manuscript.

I relied heavily on Cooking Contest Central, the website created by Betty Parham. I also found myself repeatedly turning to Sylvia Lovegren's *Fashionable Foods* and Jean Anderson's *The American Century Cookbook*.

Jan Longone, curator of American culinary history at the Clements Library at the University of Michigan helped me enormously with research on early contests, as did Sarah Hutcheon and Barbara Wheaton at The Arthur and Elizabeth Schlesinger Library at Harvard University. I also owe my thanks to the periodical desk librarians at the Portland Public Library, who repeatedly had to show me how to use the microfilm viewer as well as fetch stacks of worn issues of women's magazines for me.

Writing your first book is a task so overwhelming that it can bring on hives, insomnia, even dementia. That's why I owe special thanks to my agent Jane Chelius, who not only made this project possible through her expert advice and hard work, but whose soothing encouragement brought me in off the ledge many a time.

I am forever indebted to the wisdom of Ray Roberts, who not only made this project the best it could be but also put up with the daft questions of a first-time book writer with grace and good humor. He made me believe in myself by always treating me like an author. Cliff Corcoran at Viking attended to the nitty-gritty details that made my manuscript, with its various fonts and wild spacing, a book.

An endeavor of this scale could never be accomplished without the help of family and friends. My mother, Joan Thomas, worked as researcher, holing up in the reference room at the Cincinnati Public Library, and proofreader. Andy Killinger, my brother the computer whiz, coached me through various crises and, most important, backed up my files.

Michael Sanders, Sara Corbett, and Michael Paterniti, all remarkable writers and generous souls, saw a book in this project before I did. They not only gave me key encouragement but also showed me the ropes. A core group of cheerleaders, led by Dana Baldwin, Jessica Nicoll, and Ray Routhier, kept me going through the rougher patches with their enthusiasm. Friend and neighbor Diane Davison helped me in innumerable practical ways, from taking care of my beloved dogs while I criss-crossed the country to braving a frigid winter day to take my photo for the book jacket. Steve Greenlee, a great boss and friend, got me a month's leave to first develop my proposal, cheered me on along the way, and then managed to read my manuscript in between his job and caring for his young family sick with the Norwalk virus. Aurelia Scott and Michaela Cavallaro, friends and writers, squeezed proofreading my manuscript into their already word-heavy schedules at a moment's notice.

My Australian shepherd Dixie Lou and border collie mix Penny Jane kept me sane by insisting on walks, thus untethering me from my desk twice daily and reminding me that you should never let a day go by without smelling the sweetness of the world. Many books, even the greatest literary accomplishments, would never have been written if it were not for dogs. We writers and readers alike owe our steadfast canine companions a great debt. Here's to you, girls.

Finally, how do you begin to thank a soulmate? My husband, Scott Sutherland, encouraged me from the start and never for one nanosecond flagged in his enthusiasm for this book, even when he found himself in a remote corner of Texas without his luggage and in a motel straight out of a David Lynch movie. I could have no better companion on this great adventure known as life. ✦

COOK·off

START YOUR OVENS

I had hardly turned my calendar to January 2000 when a hefty envelope from Pillsbury thumped on my desk at a newspaper in Portland, Maine. Inside was a voluminous press packet on the upcoming 2000 Pillsbury Bake-Off® contest in San Francisco. Since going through my mail methodically was my preferred means to procrastinate writing, I had at it.

Pillsbury had sent me this weighty missive because for the first time since 1984 Maine would send a contestant, a career postal worker who in her spare time had invented Cheesy Potato Corn Cakes using a box of Hungry Jack mashed potato flakes, a can of corn, and a pile of cheese, among other things. That brainstorm meant that Mary Jones, the single, fortyish mail handler with straight black hair down her back, now had a shot at winning a life-changing grand prize of $1 million. Jones's brainstorm gave me, a fine arts reporter who wrote about food in between penning thumbsuckers on Van Gogh or the Byzantine workings of museums, an official invite to the Pillsbury Bake-Off® contest.

It took a while, about one extra grande latte with two shots, to get through the Pillsbury press materials. As I paged through the recipes, making gagging noises at the horrifying ones, such as the meat loaf with a jar of El Paso salsa mixed in, and read over the descriptions of the one hundred contestants—there was a junior high school student, a harpist from Hawaii, a cookbook collector, a funeral director—I was struck that this publicity event cum Americana refused to die. Rather, here we were in a new millennium when women are CEOs and American cooking had finally begun to get some respect, and cookoffs not only had endured but were actually thriving. National amateur cooking contests were born in an era long before Title IX and jogging bras, before a Mrs. could be a Ms., and before Sandra Day O'Connor had become the first female Supreme Court justice, albeit with a '50s housewife hairdo. Cooking contests came long before cilantro became a pantry staple, before food processors, espresso makers, and bread machines crowded kitchen counters, before fusion this and that, before Julia, for God's sake. Why hadn't cookoffs gone the way of Tupperware parties, kid gloves, and pigs-in-a-blanket? How could any self-respecting woman or cook deign to enter such an anachronism?

Off I went to find the answer.

〜〜〜〜

I joined a small army of reporters and editors from around the country that converged on San Francisco to follow the 2000 cookoff contestants for three days as they ate, yakked, toured, and battled it out at the stoves for the million dollars. I, a thoroughly twenty-first-century career woman who also knew what to do with a chinois, arrived with an eyebrow arched, ready to make fun of the entire event like many of my colleagues. Instead, I quickly got caught up in the breathless excitement of the contest, the closest thing to sports that I had ever covered. I began handicapping with the contestants. I listened intently to the creation stories of their recipes. I, who had not sunk my teeth into a Pillsbury crescent roll in twenty-five years, began to think up a few recipe ideas for the baton of dough myself.

Not that there wasn't a comic side to the Pillsbury Bake-Off® contest. That first afternoon I hovered as contestants giddily lined up to have their official photos taken and introduced themselves as their dishes

("Hi, I'm Chocolate Pudding Cake" or "I'm Hawaiian Corn Salad"). They passed around their contest cookbooks, scribbling "Best of Luck" and their names in the margins by their recipes like graduating high school seniors. They buzzed about the legendary Tunnel-of-Fudge Woman, the 1966 second-place winner whose cake had sparked Bundt-pan mania in this country. Rumor was that she was here in San Francisco. "Really!" someone in line squealed. No one could say for sure, though. No one knew what the Tunnel-of-Fudge woman looked like despite her celebrity.

I quickly realized what the contest meant for these contestants. These were everyday people who, thanks to an often thankless task, cooking, had had something *big* happen to them. From the confines of their kitchens they had catapulted to a national stage. Reporters pumped them for their opinions on fresh garlic versus powdered. TV crews crowded around their stoves. Company bigwigs toasted them. Most of the contestants had reached that age when you begin to wonder, glumly, if you will ever make your mark, if anything thrilling will ever happen to you again. Well, it had. Their dreamy smiles said so.

By the time I went to the press orientation that first Sunday afternoon, I was completely taken with the cookoff. Consequently, I was surprised by how blasé so many of my colleagues were. It turned out that many of the reporters, if not most, had been there before. They were here primarily to soak up Pillsbury's considerable attentions, including breakfast in bed. I struck up a quick conversation with a brisk food editor in cowboy boots, a contest veteran who made it clear that she planned to spend as little time with the contestants as possible. "You're going to meet a lot of trailer trash," she warned me.

I really hadn't expected trailer trash; I had expected stereotypical midwestern homemakers galore. The first surprise was that California supplied most of the contestants, followed by New York. I found an amazing cross section of Americans, given that most of the contestants were white, middle-class, middle-aged women. I talked with an airline flight scheduler from rural Pennsylvania who told me on the contest floor, as she calmly swabbed mustard sauce on a triangle of crescent refrigerator dough, "This is nothing compared to the blizzard of '93."

I met a type-A video producer from Washington, D.C., who was decked out in black and bent on winning the big bucks by sending his mayonnaise-lathered chicken Waldorf pizza in dead last to the judges. I interviewed a paramedic and mother of three teenagers from North Carolina who doused some leftover squash with Italian dressing and threw it in a sauté pan, thus planting the seed for what became Fiesta Veggies, her winning entry. What if she won, I asked her. How would she spend the money? She wasn't sure, thought a moment, and said, "My husband's car just came out of the shop and mine just went in."

So many different roads led here. I met Tracie Ojakangas, a nurse from Missouri with an Elizabethan forehead, fair skin, red hair, and a lilting northern midwestern accent. During the two years prior to the contest, Ojakangas had endured Lyme disease and then breast cancer. Her mother-in-law, who won second place in the 1958 Pillsbury Bake-Off® contest with Chunk o' Cheese Bread, encouraged her to enter to distract her from the rigors of chemotherapy, which had roused the Lyme disease. Despite nausea and exhaustion, Ojakangas came up with three recipes, including Mozzarella and Pesto Crescent Tarts, a big hit with her two young sons and her winning entry. Fate, however, was not finished with her. During the few months leading up to the contest, doctors spotted the shadow of a brain tumor on an X ray, benign but in a bad spot. Two and a half weeks shy of the competition, Ojakangas's tumor was zapped with gamma rays for thirteen hours.

She arrived in San Francisco with her husband, fatigued yet exhilarated. Ojakangas couldn't help reading her cooking conquest as a sign, a sign that a rip tide of bad luck may have turned because of a can of Pillsbury Refrigerated Crescent Dinner Rolls, two tablespoons of bottled pesto, two medium tomatoes, one small red onion, one to two teaspoons of fresh rosemary, a half cup of shredded mozzarella, and a quarter cup of shredded Parmesan. If you could get Lyme disease, breast cancer, and a brain tumor all in a row, why couldn't you win $1 million for a recipe?

I met Millie D'Elia, a stylish if shrunken seventy-three-year-old retired secretary who arrived at the contest with a prepared sound bite. "I feel like Susan Lucci," she repeated to reporters, Pillsbury execs, and, at times, no one in particular, referring to the soap opera star who was annually nominated for a daytime Emmy, only to lose again and again. Compared to D'Elia, though, Lucci got off easy. "She only did it eighteen times," D'Elia cracked.

D'Elia had entered some thirty-five times, only missing a few when her two children were young. She still had an entry form from the original 1949 contest, now a collectible, she told me. That year D'Elia was a twenty-two-year-old bookkeeper for Singer and was still living in Westchester County with her seven brothers and sisters and widower father. By the time the hand of Pillsbury chose her as a contestant, D'Elia was living on Long Island in a mother-in-law's apartment in her daughter's home.

The only problem was that this Italian-American cook had been picked for her least favorite entry, Creamy Parmesan Broccoli, for which she smothered frozen broccoli with a white sludge of Parmesan cheese, sour cream, and mayonnaise. She added toasted pine nuts to the quasi-broccoli-cheese casserole for a "gourmet touch." Broccoli would never win the grand prize, and D'Elia knew it. After her long wait, all she could hope for was a $2,000 prize. What's more, she couldn't demonstrate her substantial Italian-American cooking chops with her broccoli dish. The longed-for experience of a lifetime had proven a bit anticlimactic. She even had trouble getting a relative or friend to accompany her.

Then I stumbled upon a subculture: the contesters. This group of about two thousand cooks, mostly women, makes a serious hobby if not a near career out of cooking contests. They put in long hours researching trends and winning recipes, and, like mad inventors, they endlessly tinker with their creations. Their time and effort pays off. Their names figure prominently on winners' lists of all kinds of national cooking contests.

At the 2000 competition there were ten contesters of various levels of seriousness and experience, including Diane Sparrow, a tall, kinky-haired Iowan who in four quick years had emerged as a formidable presence in the cooking contest world. She had won a prize in the hard-to-crack Gold Kist chicken recipe contest four years running, capped by the grand prize in 2000, a trip to La Varenne in France. She had gone to the National Chicken Cooking Contest in 1999 and to Bay's English Muffin contest in 1998. In a variety of contests she has picked up five KitchenAid mixers, $1,000 worth of cookware, $1,000 worth of knives, an electric smoker, a ceramic cooker, and a complete set of new kitchen appliances. She had recently won a year's worth of sauerkraut.

The Pillsbury Bake-Off® contest had become a point of pride for Sparrow. Even though she'd cleaned up at many contests, she had yet to crack the "big boy." So while other contestants stumbled upon their entries or entered as a hoot, Sparrow methodically went to work like a high-stakes gambler sizing up the racing form. First, she hit the cookbooks. She researched hundreds of recipes, perusing all the past winners. Quick and easy was a must, a touch of ethnic food was good, but, moreover, Sparrow concluded, the contest favors the most average American cooking. She'd have to dumb down her foodie instincts but somehow work in some ethnic flavors.

Her strategy in place, she decided to use El Paso salsa as a stand-in for a slow-cooked sauce. She came up with a sweet-savory combo, her signature kind of dish. She browned ground beef, added chopped apples and salsa to the pan, then dried cranberries, green olives, and cilantro. She spooned this culture clash of a sauce onto rounds of Pillsbury refrigerator biscuits, baked them—and Picadillo Pies were born. And here she was in San Francisco, a contestant at last. "I told my friends who are contesters that I've figured something out but I don't know what," she said.

What all these people had in common was cooking, a great leveler of class, age, and education. You don't have to be a genius to be a good cook, nor do you have to be a toned athlete or naturally talented. Neither must you be rich or young. That is what makes cooking contests so quintessentially American. All comers have a shot in this very democratic competitive arena where the common cook can make American food history and win as much as $1 million for a simple eureka moment in the kitchen.

Almost everyone knows about the Pillsbury Bake-Off® contest, but, as I quickly learned, it is just the sizable tip of the American cooking contest iceberg. There are a dozen or so national cookoffs a year, most offering substantial prizes, $5,000 to $20,000. There are even more recipe contests, competitions where winners are selected by recipe alone with no cookoff component. The prizes for these can likewise be very impressive, often $10,000 or more, sometimes all-expenses-paid trips to exotic locales. These contests are growing in numbers, as are the entries. That is largely due to the Web, which has popularized these contests by making them easy to find and enter.

Then there are chili cookoffs, barbecue cookoffs, Dutch oven cookoffs, jambalaya cookoffs, and chuck wagon cookoffs. These cookoff worlds are mostly unique to themselves and focus more on technique than recipe originality. They are also the cookoff arenas where men dominate. Note that they are all outside, and most involve a wood fire, not to mention piles of gear and a long list of rules. Boys will be boys. Oddly enough, there is typically far less prize money at stake in these contests, and winners vie mostly for bragging rights. Still, the same urge is at work—the urge to outcook your opponents, to show the world that you reign supreme in the kitchen.

Back in the pressroom, most of the reporters treated the contest as a quirky, funny story. To some degree they had to. The journalists were on deadline and so had to surface-feed. Obviously I had found that you didn't have to reach too deep to find material that could keep cultural anthropologists and food historians busy for years, from what cookoffs say about Americans' wacky relationship with food to how women compete. While the reporters tapped out their stories, I had my own eureka moment.

Thanks to the food revolution of the past twenty-five years, food has finally started to matter to Americans, or at least much more so than a generation ago. Cookoffs reflect Americans' newfound interest in food, and winners regularly include ingredients that just ten years ago were considered gourmet. On the other hand, these contests, with their emphasis on speedy recipes and processed foods, reinforce the most slovenly American food habits, the ones that foodies abhor.

Cookoffs lie at the intersection of two counter forces: the push for a respectable American cuisine and the devotion to the casserole aesthetic. At a pivotal point in the food revolution, cookoffs and their longevity are a gauge of just how far American home cooking has come and how far it has to go. Early indications are that the battle against Crock-Pots and cream of mushroom soup is far from won.

In addition these contests say much about Americans in general—our intense love of speed, ingenuity, competition, and fun. That's why, by slicing this phenomenon this way or that, you can get at so many different aspects of the current culture, edible and otherwise. As the food celeb Burt Wolf once told me, "Show me a culture's food, and I'll tell you about that culture." Clearly, I was hooked.

As for my original question—Why are cooking contests still with us?—this book is the answer.

CHAPTER 1

NATIONAL CHICKEN

Thousands of entries have been screened, a hundred or so have been prepared, and fifty-one dishes have been given the thumbs-up. The cooks have been telephoned with the news: "You're a contestant in the National Chicken Cooking Contest!" The chosen have crammed their dry ingredients, pots, knives, and timers into their carry-on bags and flown from points in every state and the District of Columbia to Sacramento, California, on this April weekend for the 2001 contest. They've checked into what the tour books say is the best hotel in town, the white Hyatt Regency, which looks vaguely like a Florida import. They have zipped across the street to the convention center to inspect the cookoff floor and their 10-foot by 10-foot cooking station, complete with their state flag. They've had their official photo snapped as they all yelled "chicken"; pawed through their goody bags of almonds, apricots, avocados, and turkey-jerky; devoured a dinner of California-everything in the state museum, where they glanced over the state constitution and met John Muir's ghost in between making cocktail conversation. And now, bright and early on the morning of the cookoff, they—five men and forty-six women—stand in single file like beauty pageant contestants, their red sashes emblazoned with their home states draped across their chests, waiting to walk the red carpet into the opening ceremony.

As celebrity hosts Cindy Williams, she of the poodle skirt on *Laverne and Shirley*, and Andre Carthen, a wound-up TV and Broadway actor who nobody has ever heard of, call out their names, flub hometowns, rattle off jobs and hobbies ("She has over twenty cats"), the contestants walk in one by one as a spotlight gilds them. Some look embarrassed, almost sheepish. They clasp their hands before them or grip purses like security blankets. The contestant from Alaska seems to sleepwalk. Others soak up the attention, flash big cheerleader smiles, and take long, easy steps. One chirpy contestant even waves and yelps "Woo-hoo." Halfway through the alphabet, at Montana, it becomes all too clear: The heavy hitters are here.

There are at least fifteen contestants, nearly a third of the entire group, who are cookoff veterans. Ten are alums of the Pillsbury Bake-Off® contest. Two have each been competing on the cooking contest circuit since the 1970s. One just won two grand prizes in national contests, including $5,000 for a rice recipe that used . . . chicken.

"Oh-sawge," Cindy Williams sings out, garbling Diane Sparrow's hometown in Iowa. Sparrow, unfazed, smiling, shoulders back, marches in the room like she owns it. She is back for her second National Chicken in a row. She was celebrity struck at the '99 Chicken, what with all the big-name contesters, such as Edwina Gadsby and Roxanne Chan. Now she returns, a name to be reckoned with thanks to a winning streak that hasn't given yet. Also, it didn't hurt Sparrow's confidence that the contest director pulled her aside at this morning's breakfast buffet to tell her she dreamed that Sparrow had won.

She has lugged a cupboard of equipment with her, including a ceramic pitcher that she had custom-made in Minnesota for serving her Sticky Sauce of Dijon Mustard and Maple Syrup. Her husband still fumes over all the driving to get the pitcher. It took two three-hour round trips to Red Wing, Minnesota. Sparrow didn't care about the gas or time, just that the pitcher perfectly complements the blue-speckled plate that the Maple Mustard Chicken drumsticks go on. She has also packed an outfit—navy pants and a yellow blazer, both linen—that matches her dish. She is not known as the queen of presentation for nothing. Add to that, chicken is her forte, and she has practiced making her dish as she never has before.

In saunters Bob Gadsby, one-half of the powerhouse contesting husband-wife team ("He enjoys restoring old fire engines"). His Montana ribbon drapes over his offensive lineman-like girth, cinching at his waist. He dwarfs just about everybody, except for a giant white chicken in a polka-dot dress who watches the proceedings, beak agape, from a dark corner of the room. As a customs officer who once worked the California-Mexico border, Gadsby doesn't break a sweat easily over cooking competitions. As he puts it, he's so calm, "acid could run off my back."

This is his first Chicken, as the contesters call it. Gadsby has switched roles with his wife, Edwina, whom he tagged along with to the '99 cookoff in Dallas. Edwina walked away empty-handed, but her husband roamed the cookoff floor, carefully studying what worked (organization) and what didn't (disorganization). In other words, he knows exactly what to expect, and that includes "being in the money" with his Tuscan Chicken Cakes with Tomato-Basil Relish. If he was to win, he would be the first man to do so since 1976.

Pat Harmon steps into the room, her penciled arched eyebrows giving her a slightly manic look. She strides down the red carpet nonchalantly. Harmon, a retiree and devout Jimmy Buffet fan, is one of the few female contesters who doesn't consider competition a dirty word. She embraces it, which is near heresy in the contester world.

This is also Harmon's first National Chicken. She's been entering at least one contest per week for the past several years and has the winning gift baskets and cookbooks to show for it. She has two Bake-Off® contests under her belt, but until now she has not been able to break into other major national cookoffs. Chicken thighs braised in tea and apricot nectar got her here. National Chicken marks a turning point for her as she finally competes with her peers because, as she puts it, the "who's who in cooking" is here. She is not intimidated, as usual.

Then there is classy Janice Elder, an executive assistant in Charlotte ("She'll use any money she wins for a dream trip to Africa"). National

Chicken was her first ever contest back when she was a kitchen-challenged newlywed. Her dish, chicken doused with canned cherries, looked like a leftover from a traffic accident. Since then she has honed her chops at about every cookoff you can think of and regularly scores in recipe contests, as does her husband, Larry.

Ruth Kendrick is relatively new to the cooking contest world but, as Carthen announces, "She was fourth runner-up at the last Chicken cookoff." What Carthen doesn't mention is that she is a crossover competitive cook from the ultra-tough Dutch oven world, which makes the likes of National Chicken look like a coffee klatch. Moreover, she won the 1998 International Dutch Oven Championship Cook-off with Salmon in Black and White Sesame Seeds and Raspberry Ganache Fudge Cake. And she did it over a fire in the desert using a cast iron pot. Obviously, she's no slouch.

They just keep coming. Barbara Morgan of California is the queen mother of contesters, having scored in more than six hundred contests since winning a much needed $100 for a meat loaf recipe with fresh spinach in 1980. In two short years of contesting, Claudia Shepardson of New York, who includes her grandson on her list of hobbies, has come on strong on the circuit, picking up grand prizes right and left. Liz Barclay, an assistant principal in Annapolis, Maryland, zips into the room like a filly eager for the starting gate. She regularly makes it to cookoffs and places in recipe contests, but the big cash prizes have eluded her. She hopes this cookoff will be different.

The rookies have no idea what they're up against. Some of them think the cookoff is a big hoot, "me, at a cooking contest." They've been carrying on as if they just won the lottery. They've been too busy quaffing free wine in the hospitality room, sucking down gratis meals, and napping on king-sized beds in their paid-for room to strategize or even think about the actual cookoff. To them their presence here is just a lucky break, a divine blessing that landed them an all-expenses-paid trip for two to California on this early spring weekend.

The contesters know differently. Sure, they figure fortune had something to do with it, but they know it's no fluke. Like gamblers, they are well acquainted with the fickleness of Lady Luck. But also like gamblers, they know the game and have played it for all they are worth. In short, they have earned the right to be here. They thoroughly researched past winners, boned up on current chicken trends, foisted innumerable poultry creations on their family and friends, and kept notebooks on their nightstands to scribble drumstick brainstorms in the middle of the night.

Having made the cut for the cookoff, they practiced making their recipes, carefully thought out their presentation, scoped out the competition, and planned what time they would send their dishes to the judges. There is $25,000 at stake. This is National Chicken, after all.

∿∿∿∿

There is no clear-cut annual season to national cooking contests, but there is a recognizable cycle, a kind of Triple Crown, dictated by the three biggest cookoffs, all biennials. It begins in the spring every other year with National Chicken. The National Beef Cook-Off with its $50,000 grand prize and twenty contestants follows in September. Then the Pillsbury competition, by far the biggest with its one hundred contestants and $1 million grand prize, rolls around in February. Once the hysteria of that contest recedes, contesters turn their attention again to poultry and National Chicken. The cycle begins anew.

In between are sundry annual cookoffs, not to mention a slew of national recipe contests such as Colavita's Better Than Butter Recipe with a grand prize of a round-trip for two to Italy. Most contesters fool with the stinking rose for California's Gilroy Garlic Cook-Off in July and then experiment on their backyard grills for Sutter Home's Build a Better Burger Contest in September in Napa Valley. There are plenty of smaller, regional cookoffs as well, such as the National Oyster Cook-off in Maryland, the National Cornbread Cook-off in Tennessee, and the National Dandelion Cook-off in Ohio's Amish country. And new cookoffs pop up here and there. During this cycle that I'm following, several have already appeared on the horizon: the Post Selects Cereal Brunch Contest ($10,000 prize), the Reynolds Hot Bags Foil Bags "In the Bag" Recipe Contest (a round-trip for two to the Caribbean), and The Great Australian Barbeque Cookoff, for which the finalists will be flown to Sydney, Australia, to compete.

National Chicken, as far as anyone knows, is the longest, continually running cookoff, just beating the Pillsbury Bake-Off® contest by months. However, National Chicken got its start as a regional event, and Pillsbury has always been a national one. The first chicken cookoff was held at the annual Delmarva Chicken Festival in Salisbury, Maryland. Delmarva is the squished-up name for the squat peninsula that Virginia, Delaware, and Maryland share between the Chesapeake Bay and the Atlantic Ocean. It is also the birthplace of America's commercial chicken industry. The year was 1949, when chicken was sold as a whole bird that home cooks dismembered in their own kitchen. This was before mandatory federal inspection of chicken, before chicken tenders or boned breasts, before Kentucky Fried Chicken went from coast to coast, before chicken's sound thumping of beef.

That first year the contest was open to all comers. Some 160 local cooks showed up, toting their own frying pans and wrinkled, stained family recipes scribbled on the backs of envelopes. The judging went late into the night. Out of a field of mostly fried chicken the judges made a bold choice: a broiled bird. Broiled Chicken Deluxe, submitted by Mrs. A. L. Keith of Salisbury, a dark-haired woman in a floral apron, called for squeezing lemon juice over a two-and-a-half-pound broiler, dusting it with a mix of salt, paprika, and pepper, smearing it with melted butter, and then finishing it with a sprinkle of sugar. Mrs. Keith won a custom-designed Westinghouse kitchen and $400 in cash toward its installation.

By the 1960s the Delmarva Chicken Cook-off had evolved into a national contest, with a contestant picked from each state and the District of Columbia. Entries were more and more expected to be original. Those early years produced recipes that are still requested, such as Sweet 'n' Smokey Oven Barbecued Chicken, a baked bird cut in parts with a sauce of equal parts catsup, cooking oil, and maple syrup lightened with some vinegar and mustard, and Sweet and Sour Chicken, baked chicken parts slimed with Russian salad dressing, dry onion soup mix, and a jar of apricot preserves. You can still find both recipes on the National Chicken Council's website.

By the early '70s the contest had become more work and money—what with a $10,000 grand prize and fifty-one all-expenses-paid trips—than a regional festival could handle. The cookoff was transferred in 1971 to what was then the National Broiler Council and renamed the National Chicken Cooking Contest. The competition left the Delmarva strip and became a roving event, moving from one poultry-producing state to the next with each contest. It remains the biggest promotion put on by what is now called the National Chicken Council, a national trade and marketing association in Washington, D.C. It also remains the only national cookoff where contestants represent their home states.

Although the National Beef Cook-Off offers a bigger grand prize, National Chicken has long been the big favorite of the contesters for two reasons. First, they love it for the deluxe treatment, which they consider only second to the attentions Pillsbury lavishes on its chosen. Each contestant wins a three-night, all-expenses-paid trip for two wherever the cookoff is held.

Second, National Chicken gives contesters the freedom to flex their gourmet muscles. While most cookoffs require the use of processed foods, all this cookoff calls for is chicken, plain and simple. In fact, recipes that rely heavily on processed foods rarely make it to the finals anymore. The Beef Cook-Off calls only for beef as well but limits the number of ingredients to six, including the meat, and literally holds cooking time to thirty minutes. These restrictions necessitate processed food. At Chicken there is no limit on ingredients. As for time, contestants must cook their dish twice in three hours, which may rule out wrapping up a galantine, but otherwise it is a leisurely, liberating pace. Simplicity does count in the judging, but in equal shares to appeal, appearance, and taste.

Consequently, at National Chicken most contestants actually cook rather than just heat. You find exotica such as peanut oil, coconut milk, fresh basil, shiitake mushrooms, Chinese five-spice powder, and even the hallmark of fine cooking, shallots. Sometimes the freedom goes to the contestants' heads, as with the cultural mishmash of Nuevo Cubano Chicken Kiev with Mango Mustard Sauce or the pantry of ingredients for Barclay's Moroccan Chicken Pie with Sweet Potato Polenta. Mostly the contest produces some genuinely interesting dishes and ideas, such as Roxanne Chan's second place winner in '99 that called for smoking chicken breasts in a wok and then serving them sliced over a sesame vegetable relish. That said, there is one recipe in the 2001 contest from North Dakota that calls for two cups of finely crushed pretzels and uses lemon Jell-O in the glaze.

〜〜〜〜

When the rules for the 2001 contest were issued, the contesters were understandably alarmed at what might seem like an incidental change to an outsider. For the first time cooked chicken, as in rotisserie chicken, could be used. To the contesters this signaled a seismic shift. They feared National Chicken would now go the way of National Beef, that ease of preparation would edge out taste. Rotisserie chickens today, frozen chicken fingers tomorrow.

Bob Gadsby was not bothered by the introduction of cooked chicken. Rather, it inspired him. Gadsby grew up in the San Diego area where he honed his acute appreciation for crab cakes crafted from the Pacific's sweet Dungeness crab. Since the U.S. Customs officer's transfer to Great Falls, Montana, he had led a relatively crab-cake-deprived existence. Good fresh seafood of any kind was almost impossible to find, and crab cakes rarely showed up on Montana restaurant menus. However, Gadsby tinkered with them in his own kitchen, sometimes using canned crab. He came up with Crab Cakes Italiano, which won him a trip to the '98 Bake-Off® contest, and Spicy Crab Cakes with Chipotle Aioli, which scored the $5,000 grand prize in the Sonoma Sun-dried Tomato recipe contest, his biggest win to date.

For chicken, Gadsby began turning crab cakes over in his mind during his primo creation time, his long drives to the small far-flung airports of Montana that he oversees. What if he used chicken and created a kind of far-inland non-crab crab cake? He figured a rotisserie chicken would pull apart easily and supply the meat. He pretty much applied a basic crab cake recipe to the chicken, adding jarred pesto sauce and roasted red peppers to give it a Mediterranean twist. He had to fool with the aioli because the chicken cake couldn't stand up to all the lemon. Thus, Tuscan Chicken Cakes with Tomato-Basil Relish were born. As his wife, Edwina, said, "Leave it to a man to take chicken apart and put it back together."

Gadsby wasn't the only contester to embrace the new rule. Janice Elder tore apart a precooked bird and riffed on an American classic, pulled pork. She piled her Pulled Chicken Barbecue on corn cakes that she fried in a pan, then topped the whole apparatus with a red-vinegar coleslaw concoction. Karen Shankles, a relative unknown from Tennessee but a Bake-Off® contest veteran nonetheless, used pregrilled strips to make a chicken salad with wild rice, dried cherries, and pistachios.

The precooked chicken wasn't the only change that caught the contesters' interest. For the first time National Chicken offered an extra grand to any winning recipe that used dark meat. In the case of the fifth place prize of $1,000, that would double the cash. The hope was that the bonus money would inspire some creative recipes using dark meat, the pariah of the American market. There was a time not too long ago when Americans favored dark meat, specifically drumsticks, for frying. That all changed when we began counting grams of fat. Now white meat, mostly in the form of pearly planks of boneless and often tasteless breast meat, sells by a two-to-one margin. Most of America's leg meat is sold overseas where the rest of world still favors these less expensive, more flavorful cuts.

The contesters bit as the Chicken Council hoped. Sparrow used thighs, and so did Kendrick, Shepardson, and Harmon. Sparrow rolled them in panko, the Japanese oversized bread crumbs. Shepardson plopped them atop a bed of shiitake orzo. Kendrick paired the thighs with Argentina's spicy chimichurri sauce.

The night before the cookoff, most of the contesters gathered in the hotel lobby. It was a subset of a subculture made possible by a website, Cooking Contest Central (recipecontests.com), which debuted in March 1998. Harmon, Sparrow, Kendrick, Barclay, Morgan, and others who regularly swap tips and report news of wins on the site's chat room posed for a group photo. Gadsby did not join them. As with a few other top-winning contesters, neither he nor his wife, Edwina, participate in the chat room, which is called The Forum. Everyone suspects that these contesters who do not participate are "lurkers," meaning they read the chat room but don't post messages, like eavesdroppers on a party line. The Forum gals can be rather clannish, cheering on "Team Forum." At times they get to resenting the lurkers. This creates a slight schism in the contesting world that cracks wide open now and again, but not here at National Chicken. The contesters are having a reunion of sorts. Sparrow and Kendrick haven't seen each other since the '99 National Chicken in Dallas where they met. They're right back at ribbing each other. Harmon visits with Shepardson in person for the first time. The two have developed a kind of mentor-protégé relationship via email. Barclay, at the cookoff by herself as usual (her British husband thinks this hobby of hers is a goof), hits it off with Margee Berry, also on her own. The two are athletic and outgoing. Like Barclay, Berry has yet to win some big money or prize.

That's another thing contesters like about National Chicken: They can count on being among their own. Finalists are picked state by state, which is why there are so many contesters. Competing within their state borders, the contesters vie in a much smaller pool than when finalists are chosen nationally. Contesters especially rule in the states with low population. That partially explains why one of the Gadsbys has represented Montana at the last three National Chickens.

There is a reverse effect as well. If you live in a state like California, a relative hotbed of contesters and good cooks, and only one contestant will be selected from the state, the competition is fierce. That is why every time National Chicken rolled around, Barbara Morgan joked that she would move to the small burg of Rhode Island. Morgan, one of the most veteran contesters, entered the contest over and over before finally getting the call for her Polenta Stuffed Chicken Breasts with Cranberry-Apricot Relish.

Not only can the contesters meet and greet, but they can test their mettle against their peers. That's why placing or winning at National Chicken is considered the mark of a talented contester, and contesters regularly place or win at this cookoff. At the last one, first and second place, respectively, went to contesting celebs Marie Rizzio, who was a finalist for her third time, and Roxanne Chan, who has won more than four hundred contests.

❦ ❦ ❦

After the botched opening ceremony, the cookoff gets under way at 9 A.M. sharp to the call "start your ovens." The contestants begin rinsing, peeling, and chopping piles of veggies in earnest. Washing slippery bits of chicken is no easy task because there is no sink, only a pitcher of water and a tub, like a campsite. A mob of food press, family members, and public is unleashed on the contestants from the get-go, and they wander aimlessly around the catacomb of booths. They ask questions like "Do you like to cook?" and "Are there any samples?" The contestants chat cheerily as best they can while cooking. In the middle of answering questions from a *Better Homes and Gardens* editor, Sparrow realizes that she doesn't know whether she put salt in her drumstick coating. She forgoes it, thinking no salt is better than too much salt.

Gadsby towers over his prep table, and his ingredients are well out of comfortable chopping range. He lowers himself into a chair and with rubber gloves begins to calmly rend a rotisserie chicken. As usual he is "disgustingly calm," as his wife puts it, losing concentration only momentarily when a camera crew zeros in on him just as he plops his crab cakes in the sauté pan. Edwina wanders aimlessly around the floor, at loose ends not cooking and worried that she'll make her husband nervous if she hangs around his booth. For lack of anything to do, she watches the demonstration of a new wonder refrigerator that will thaw meat and cool wine.

Barbara Morgan has become a darling of the media, who have been lapping up her funny quips and her compelling bio—a single mother who worked as a coal miner, ranch hand, and lobsterer. Morgan's husband, an engineer, read too many Ayn Rand books, used his retirement money to buy five acres atop a mountain in Costa Rica, and abandoned the family for the libertarian life. Four of the couple's five children, including her blind son, still lived at home. Morgan barely got by, each month weighing which bills could be put off. Contesting helped her pay the bills and afforded her much-needed vacations. More than that, contesting gave her hope.

She is also the oldest contestant at seventy-five, a reliable angle for reporters on a deadline, so there is always one or two hanging around her booth. As she entertains them, she starts hunting for the brown sugar that goes in her Cranberry-Apricot Relish. It is nowhere to be found. She panics. The rules are that no ingredients can be supplied during the cookoff. Morgan asks for sugar anyway. When she is told no, she leaves her station and arrives at Sparrow's nearly in tears. She is about to be disqualified, she wails. The contest relents, the sugar is provided, a scene is averted, and Morgan returns to her stove.

While the public's milling around and peppering them with questions rattles other contestants, Kendrick, a large woman with a naturally boisterous voice, is not flustered. In the harsh world of Dutch Oven cookoffs, contestants are judged on how much they talk with the public, not to mention the cleanliness of their cooking area. D.O. judges even check to see if the dishwater is hot. Compared to Dutch Oven standards, Chicken is like heating up a TV dinner for Kendrick. When the first dish is sent in to the sequestered judges around 10 A.M., Kendrick, who believes timing is key, is not far behind with her Chimichurri Chicken Thighs, keeping to her strategy of turning in near the front of the line but not right at the front

Harmon, who lugged an electric frying pan all the way from Pennsylvania only to find there was no outlet for it, has happily adjusted to the Calphalon pan the contest provided. As she cooks, a buzz runs through the crowd as Sparrow breezes by with a rattan tray packed with pottery, her drumsticks cinched with corn husks, and the whole darn thing looking like a photo shoot for *Gourmet* magazine. Harmon looks up from her prep table and thinks "whoa," and makes a mental note to herself, "Work on your presentation."

As at every cookoff, the clock hands seem to spin faster and faster as the contest winds down. No one is more aware of time streaming by than Barclay. Last night she wondered if this might not be her turn to finally win big. Now all she's hoping for is to get her dish in on time.

The first one already went in to the judges, but if she doesn't get the second version done for display, she'll be disqualified. She came off the blocks at a sprint and hasn't let up, chopping zucchinis, sweet potatoes, and red peppers at a clip, charging through the many steps of her Moroccan Chicken Pie with Sweet Potato Polenta. Now, as the second hand takes its last spins before noon, Barclay pulls her pie from the oven, garnishes it with parsley, and then hot-foots it to the display table as someone calls, "You go, girl." She is the very last one to turn in her dish.

~ ~ ~ ~

By the time the entries have been hauled back out for the evening's cocktail reception, they have taken a decided turn for the worse. Six to eight hours after their creation, many of the dishes appear to be suffering from an advanced state of rigor mortis. Sauces solidify like aspics gone wrong. Parsley garnishes wilt and lay prone across chicken thighs. Vegetables pale and shrivel. These waning casseroles, stir-fries, soups, and salads are set one after another on a long linen-covered table. The effect is something like a forgotten buffet or church dinner, one where the diners mysteriously vanished and the only clues left are these tired chicken dishes. The presentation doesn't always help. One contestant plopped her chicken salad in an Easter basket. Another served hers on a terra-cotta saucer, the kind you slip under a potted houseplant.

The contesters, showered and gussied-up, pace the table, sizing up the competition, working over in their minds what dishes rate cash. Kendrick clasps her contest cookbook in one hand, a pen in the other. She notes her picks next to the recipes. She marks Gadsby's recipe and Sparrow's. She marks Spicy Chicken Cutlets with Three Pepper Slaw, the Oklahoman's dish, as well, but as a distant pick. Kendrick, losing her earlier confidence, rules herself out of the running. Her presentation, balancing thighs atop red and yellow pepper rings, just doesn't cut it, she decides.

Walking the length of the display table, Sparrow is convinced that hers looks the best hands down, that those long drives to get the custom-made pottery paid off. Alas, her recipe is too simple to win, she thinks. Morgan has a shot, Sparrow thinks, because she has been the media darling. She doesn't think Gadsby will win, if only because his chicken cakes don't look that good. Harmon thinks the same. Gadsby disagrees. He comes away from the table feeling his is the most innovative, that he will win something. Edwina agrees. She thinks he'll place. What she doesn't say is this: She doesn't think his is the grand prize winner. None strike her that way.

After a voluminous, five-course dinner that starts, surprisingly, with halibut, albeit Pacific halibut, and concludes with a mini white chocolate state capitol, its dome pushed askew by a rising mound of chocolate mousse—pretty but not easy to eat, especially if you are distracted by a $25,000 check dancing in your head—the wait is over. The head judge goes on excitedly about all the cross-cultural dishes, Greek-Asian, Asian-Hispanic, that the winners have "broad appeal" (big contesting buzzwords) and are perfect for spring and summer. The contesters quickly read these tea leaves, recalculating their odds. There is not much time to think, though. The prizes are announced by state, with a corny drum roll, in reverse. Fifth place ($1,000) goes to a bespectacled blonde from Idaho for her Chicken and Black Bean Soup. Fourth place ($2,000), the second chicken cookoff in a row, to a surprised Kendrick. Third ($3,000) to Sparrow. Second ($5,000) to a stylish grandmother of six from Oklahoma for her Spicy Chicken Cutlets with Three Pepper Slaw. Each winner is handed her droopy dish to hold.

With all the places named, Edwina figures her husband is out of the running. She leans over to give his knee a wifely pat and whisper, "Better luck next time," but before she can lay a hand on him, he rockets out of his seat. Suddenly he's standing at the front of the room holding his plate of crab cakes. People rise and applaud. Edwina is flummoxed. She looks around. Then it sinks in. He has won first place. He has won $25,000. He has won National Chicken, the first rooster in twenty-five years.

〰 〰 〰

The next day breaks cool but sunny. The contestants are bused past fields polka-dotted with mustard and poppy blossoms to Napa Valley, where they tour a champagne cave, blend their own chardonnay at the Kendall-Jackson Vineyard, and quaff California's best. National Chicken is one of the few cookoffs that fete the contestants the day after the contest. Most cookoffs ship the contestants out as quickly as possible, like house guests who have stayed too long. At Chicken, contestants get a day to enjoy themselves without going over their recipes in their minds. The fight has already been fought. They can relax, except for Gadsby.

Gadsby feels very self-conscious, an unusual feeling for him. He is suddenly the guy with "a $25,000 check in his pocket." He exorcises some of the guilt over his newfound wealth by raising a glass of champagne at the cave and toasting his fellow competitors. It is a nice gesture, but it doesn't stop the clucking.

It isn't that Gadsby himself won. It's that rotisserie chicken won. That rotisserie chicken was allowed was bad enough, but giving it the grand prize, well, that only validates the convenience product. For some of the contesters this is a very ominous sign, a sign that Chicken may someday soon limit ingredients and limit time, that before too long the contestants will not be cooking but heating.

〜〜〜〜

Bob Gadsby from Great Falls, Montana, won the 44th National Chicken Cooking Contest with his crab cakes cum chicken cakes.

TUSCAN CHICKEN CAKES WITH TOMATO-BASIL RELISH

3 cups cooked chicken, shredded and chopped
1 cup Italian seasoned bread crumbs, divided
1/4 cup mayonnaise
1 egg, lightly beaten
1/4 cup prepared basil pesto
2 teaspoons honey mustard
1/3 cup finely chopped roasted red peppers, drained
1/3 cup finely chopped red onion
2 tablespoons olive oil
1 package (5 ounces) mixed salad greens
1/3 cup prepared balsamic vinegar and oil dressing

Golden Aioli (recipe follows)
Tomato-Basil Relish (recipe follows)

In a large bowl, mix together the chicken, 1/2 cup of the bread crumbs, mayonnaise, egg, pesto, honey mustard, roasted peppers, and red onion. Using a 1/3-cup measure, shape the chicken mixture into 8 cakes. Lightly coat each with the remaining 1/2 cup of bread crumbs. In a large nonstick frying pan, place the oil over medium-high heat. Add the chicken and cook until golden brown, about 3 minutes per side; drain on paper towels. Toss the salad greens with the dressing and divide among 4 serving plates. Top each with 2 chicken cakes. Drizzle with Golden Aioli. Top each cake with dollop of Tomato-Basil Relish.

MAKES 4 SERVINGS

GOLDEN AIOLI

In a small bowl, whisk together 1/2 cup mayonnaise and 2 tablespoons honey mustard.

TOMATO-BASIL RELISH

In a small bowl, mix together 1 cup seeded and chopped plum tomatoes, 1/3 cup chopped red onion, 3 tablespoons (drained) chopped sun-dried tomatoes, 2 tablespoons slivered basil leaves, 2 tablespoons prepared balsamic and oil dressing, and 1 teaspoon prepared basil pesto.

CHAPTER 2

A COUNTRY OF
COMPETITIVE COOKS

If amateur cooking contests, especially cookoffs, seem quintessentially American, that is because they are. These contests are not totally unique to the United States, but no other country squares off at the stove on the scale we do. Most any weekend American cooks somewhere are sharpening their culinary competitive edge.

There may be on average only ten national company-sponsored cookoffs like the National Chicken or the Bake-Off® contest a year, but Americans cross spatulas at approximately more than 1,300 such competitions annually. By far the majority are small local events. Chili alone accounts for more than 750 cookoffs nationwide. In Texas alone a chilihead willing to travel—and there really is no other kind of chilihead—has his or her choice of a half-dozen or more cookoffs most weekends. The *National Barbecue News*'s calendar lists more than 150 contests where you can park your smoker. Utah holds 250 Dutch oven cookoffs annually. Small regional cookoffs, typically part of summer food festivals such as the Louisiana Shrimp and Petroleum Festival, add another 30 or so. Add to the cookoffs the long list of recipe contests, about 75 annually, and the vast number of state and county fair cooking contests, and you have a country that seemingly cooks not to eat but to compete.

That is not to say that amateur cooking contests aren't a worldwide phenomenon. They are. The website Cooking Contest Central has listed contests in Kuala Lumpur, India, and Belgium, to name a few. There was a fried rice cookoff in Singapore at the city's annual food festival in 2002. A Dutch oven cookoff scene has caught on in Japan. In Manila celebrities were given thirty minutes to make a sauce using olive oil or tomato as the base. The winner, as reported by the *Manila Times*, included parsley, mushrooms, crab eggs, feta, onions, garlic, red wine, crushed walnuts, capers, anchovies, rosemary, and pandan leaves. In Dubai amateur cooks prepare a three-course meal for two to win the title Super Cook and a trip to London and Paris. In Australia, our culinary cousin, amateur and professional bakers gather in the small town of Ouyen to make six perfect custard-filled rectangular pastries in the Great Vanilla Slice Triumph.

So what is it about Americans that makes us such competitive cooks? After a year plus of thinking about this, I've found the answer to be surprisingly complex, one that speaks to our national character, starting with our deep and abiding love of competition in all things. That Americans like to compete is obvious, from the summer ritual of Little League, to the enduring popularity of TV quiz shows, which provide a vicarious form of competition for us viewers who lie supine on the couch while calling out answers to the deaf TV screen. Our passion for sports is proof enough, but our love of contests doesn't stop there. We dance competitively, throw Frisbees competitively, spell competitively, fiddle competitively, rope steer competitively, garden competitively, and even yodel competitively. There are beauty contests, sewing contests, eating contests, writing contests, and Scrabble contests.

Competition is one of our most innate democratic rights, the right to test ourselves against our countrymen whether it be bent over on a croquet green, hunkered over a chessboard, or dribbling down a pocked inner-city basketball court. Through contests we embody the founding fathers' ideal, that we are free to make of ourselves what we can through our own talents, persistence, and know-how. Even if you are stuck in a dead-end job in a dead-end marriage on a dead-end street, in America you can rise above your station and reign supreme at the bowling alley or the dog show or the poker table. You may even find the American dream of fame and fortune along the way. Certainly, some winners of the Pillsbury Bake-Off® contest have.

It is only natural that this national trait should carry over to cooking. Agricultural fairs were the first to channel this drive. Elkanah Watson, the wealthy, forward-thinking sheep farmer who dreamed up the American agricultural fair movement, bemoaned how few farmwives and daughters attended his early events in Massachusetts, according to an article by historian Linda Borish, a professor at Western Michigan University. Whether it was that the ladies saw enough of cattle and pigs at home or were too busy cooking, cleaning, and mending, women were essentially no-shows. One newspaper report wondered if female attendance was low because a fair in Worcester had been held on Monday, laundry day.

With his fairs Watson hoped to stem the flow of farm daughters and sons leaving for the city. He planned to do this by teaching more modern and profitable ways of farming at the fair. He would also extol farm life, making his fairs early PR vehicles. In that vein Watson and other farm reformers believed that what was good for the farmwife was ultimately good for the farmer. Watson added competitions for domestic products, needlework, jams, and baked goods, complete with prizes, to his 1813 Pittsfield, Massachusetts, fair, figuring correctly that few homemakers could resist the opportunity to strut their stuff. These contests not only lured women to the fair but also, by besting their peers, gave the undervalued farmwives some much-deserved recognition, maybe even from their husbands.

This was radical thinking at the start of the nineteenth century when women, given little education and barred or discouraged from most professions, were cloistered in the home. The only audience for their accomplishments was their families, which, like today, weren't always appreciative. Thanks to Watson their prowess in their private kitchens could lead them to public accolades. American farm women responded, and by mid-century female competition was a mainstay of the fair, as was female attendance. Consequently, many generations of American women have grown up thinking of cooking and baking as not just an end in itself but as a path to blue ribbons and personal glory.

❧ ❧ ❧ ❧

Cooking contests appeal not only to the American love of challenge but also to our strange food ethos. We like our food fun, fast, and novel, with taste far down on the list. Nostalgia even comes before taste. How else to explain the continuing fascination with dishes such as Jell-O and Spam? Like infants we prefer playing with our food to eating it. We want to eat with our mitts, munching anything on a stick, squirting yogurt from a plastic tube into our open mouth. We like food in bright, funny colors: blue margaritas, orange crackers, pink cotton candy, red hot dogs, green sports drinks. We are fascinated by potato chips stacked like a deck of cards and cheese that pulls apart into rubbery strings.

Across the ocean, the culinary mature, the tradition-bound French and Italians, take their foods seriously. Food is not a source of childlike mirth but of grown-up sensual pleasure. They value taste above all else and see little reason to experiment with what they consider the world's best cuisines, cuisines that certainly no freewheeling home cook could improve on.

Au contraire, says the land of the pioneers where ingenuity reigns supreme in all things. Food is no exception. The twentieth century has seen a long procession of American food inventions: the Caesar salad, the grilled cheese sandwich, instant coffee, chop suey, frozen vegetables, not to mention cocktails. The list goes on and on because we cannot leave well enough alone. Moreover, we like our change to bubble up from the bottom, preferring the inventiveness of the common cook to the expertise of a hoity-toity chef. We may soak up Julia Child in all her guises but then ooh and aah when a cook breaks with tradition and, say, makes candy with a can of Progresso bread crumbs—a brainstorm that won a home cook $10,000 in the last Pillsbury Bake-Off® contest. That's the kind of American ingenuity that makes Child want to hit the sherry.

Enter the giant, the American processed food industry, which lumbered into the country's kitchen at the turn of the twentieth century. This was a watershed moment in the country's food history. The early home economists, such as Fannie Farmer and her Boston Cooking School crew, had essentially wiped the kitchen counters clean by preaching the evils of America's culinary heritage of heavy, fatty foods and pointing the way to a modern, cool-headed approach to cooking that emphasized efficiency, cleanliness, and appearance. To these Puritan-minded kitchen reformers, how food *tasted* was of little importance.

Simultaneously, more and more middle-class American women who had never cooked, nor had their mothers or grandmothers, were forced into the kitchen as their maids bolted for higher paying factory jobs. Mary Drake McFeely writes in *Can She Bake a Cherry Pie?* that the number of servants diminished by one-half between 1896 and 1927. These new cooks needed help, a lot of it, and they quickly came to rely on the processed food industry, filling their cupboards with boxes of Jell-O and cans of Campbell soups, learning to cook from reading the recipes on the labels.

Consequently, the nascent food industry found that it had an endless need of new recipes to show housewives how to use their products. More recipes were needed to show how versatile the products were and to keep the housewife using them. The company test kitchen was born and was staffed with cheery economists who churned out idea after idea. These dishes went on the label or were assembled into pocket-sized, inexpensive brochures. Some of these recipes came from home cooks who regularly mailed their own creations and old family favorites to processed food companies. It dawned on a few early ad men that a contest might solicit even more of this homegrown fare and also work as a marketing tool.

Food companies borrowed the idea for recipe contests from newspapers, which ran them to boost readership and sell papers. These contests were also an inexpensive means to produce cookbooks, which the newspapers sold as well. In 1889 *The Press* in New York, "Largest Circulation of any Republican Paper in America," dangled one dozen solid-silver spoons in front of housewives to entice them to send in their "best methods of preparing staple dishes." As early as 1902 the *Los Angeles Times* began holding sporadic contests to produce a series of cookbooks. The *Los Angeles Times Cook Book No. 2: One Thousand Toothsome Cooking and Other Recipes* sold for 25 cents plus postage. As a later 1923 edition of the series explained in the foreword, creating this cookbook would have been prohibitively expensive so "it was decided to invite the cooperation of local cooks and housewives, making the undertaking a sort of partnership enterprise."

For food manufacturers, recipe contests encouraged cooks to purchase new items and, while they tinkered with them, learn how to use the products. In 1905 Knox Gelatin held a contest to entice women to buy their instant, granulated, and, as advertised, odorless version. In 1918 the General Chemical Company offered prizes for recipes using Ryzon, the Perfect Baking Powder; they were then compiled into a handy cookbook on how to make cakes, bread, and biscuits with bicarbonate of soda. The book includes what was then believed to be the first recipe for baba made with baking soda. In 1925 the Hawaiian Pineapple Company, now the Dole Food Company, offered cash for dishes using canned pineapple rings, hoping to give the new product a boost.

These early contests received an astounding number of entries. The pineapple contest drew some 60,000 entries. Eighty thousand arrived at the Postum Cereal Company for a 1925 Grape-Nuts contest. They gave the $1,000 grand prize to a bobbed California cook who threw the gritty cereal into an omelet. Minute Tapioca received 121,619 entries for its 1929 competition, including a meat loaf calling for three tablespoons of the starchy little pearls.

Women's magazines, such as *Better Homes and Gardens*, also got in on the act, running their own recipe contests as a way to increase circulation and help plug advertisers' products. *Sunset* magazine in California began running contests as early as 1929, the year Lawrence W. Lane, a former advertising executive at *Better Homes and Gardens*, purchased the magazine. In April of that year a Mrs. Lowell from Oakland won the $5 first prize for a fig conserve that used "1 flat can of sliced pineapple." *Better Homes and Gardens* trailed a bit behind, starting its contests in 1933 "because women everywhere have given tremendous thought and care and even genius to devising, adapting, and perfecting recipes in their own kitchens, and because there has been no suitable recognition in this creative art in the past." Winners were called "endorsed recipes." The prize was $1. A year later a monthly grand prize of $5 was announced. The first dish-of-the-month prize went to a fish loaf from a Mrs. Brachett of Estherville, Iowa.

Pillsbury took the core idea of a national recipe contest and blew it up into a prime media event with the First Grand National Recipe and Baking Contest held in 1949 at New York City's Waldorf-Astoria. Having gathered ninety-seven women and three men, installed one hundred General Electric Stratoliner Ranges (retail price $369.95) in the hotel's Grand Ballroom, and staked a $50,000 grand prize, Pillsbury created an event that major publications—*Life, Newsweek, Collier's,* and *The New Yorker*—couldn't resist covering. The contestants were no longer faceless housewives represented by bits of recipes. They were flesh-and-blood everyday Americans with tales to tell. There were dramas and mishaps. A woman, worried that her canned coconut had fermented, asked company president Philip Pillsbury to smell it. A great search went up for peppermint extract, which went missing in New York City.

The cookoff cost a lot more than a recipe contest. According to a *Newsweek* report, company officials estimated they had spent $1 million on the event, but as the reporter pointed out, the resulting "good will and publicity would show up on the balance sheet." The company, having planned the baking contest as a one-time event, realized they had happened upon a winning formula, one that continues to work today.

Who thought up cookoffs or where the first one was held in this country remains unknown. It wasn't Pillsbury, which was predated by the National Chicken Cooking Contest. Chances are it wasn't the original organizers of the National Chicken Cooking Contest, either. What the Bake-Off® contest did was spread the idea of a battle royal at the stoves far and wide. Still, it took a decade or two for cookoffs to really catch on. By the 1970s there were about a half-dozen national contests, including the National Chicken Cooking Contest, the National Beef

Cook-Off ($10,000 grand prize), the National Pineapple Cooking Classic ($15,000 grand prize), and the National Pork Cookout Contest (two-week vacation in Hawaii for two).

The Bake-Off® contest also gave birth to contesters, who evolved out of the women who repeatedly got into Pillsbury's then annual contest. Before the three-times-and-you're-out rule, some contestants went as many as eight times. As other national contests emerged, these repeaters entered them with the same doggedness and began winning those as well. Pillsbury also became the threshold contest where many women learned about contesting and got hooked.

When Shirley DeSantis, a grande dame of the contester scene, went to her first Bake-Off® contest in 1969 with Gourmet Chicken Wrap-Ups, veteran contestants instructed her in the world of contesting. They told her about newsletters and round-robins that passed on contest information. She learned about National Chicken and the Pineapple Classic. The next year she won $10 in a *Better Homes and Gardens* contest for a dish with manicotti and hot dogs. There were far fewer contests to enter then, but they were far less competitive. There were fewer entries, DeSantis says, and many more prizes.

The 1970s also gave birth to the great outdoor gathering. Whether it was rock concerts, neighborhood celebrations, or harvest festivals, Americans wanted to commune at huge outdoor parties. Cookoffs became entertainment events at these new festivals, such as the Gilroy Garlic Festival. Even a few old festivals added cookoffs. Arkansas' Wings Over the Prairie Festival and World's Championship Duck Calling Contest, begun in 1936, added a duck gumbo cookoff in the late '70s. Likewise, the chili and barbecue worlds turned up the heat, drawing men to the joys of competitive cooking. Tipton, South Carolina, claims to have held the first barbecue cookoff in 1973. Chili got off to a small start in 1967 in a remote corner of Texas and then quickly evolved into a full-blown circuit during the '70s.

Thirty years later there are many more contests and contestants and much, much bigger prizes. Neither women's lib nor the gourmetification of American food nor the much-touted death of home cooking have curbed our appetite for testing our culinary mettle. Cooking Contest Central typically has fifty contests listed on its website almost any day that you check it. There is an ever-growing number of company-sponsored contests for kids, a little league, so to speak. State fair contests have not only endured but thrived as city dwellers who wouldn't know a cow's teat from its tail have begun entering their home-cooked goodies. Chiliheads may be graying, but they have yet to falter. Barbecue just gets bigger and bigger. The Kansas City Barbeque Society reports a yearly increase of 15 to 20 percent in contests and contestants. Down in Gonzales, Louisiana, entrants at the International Jambalaya Festival are getting close to the limit of one hundred. Some year soon they may have to turn away some jambalaya cooks and their pots. At the start of the twenty-first century Americans are far from hanging up their kitchen aprons, especially when a prize is involved.

Maybe that is because cooking is going the way of archery. The day has long since passed when we had to know how to shoot a bow and arrow. Archery, however, persists largely through competition. What was once a practical skill is now an arcane leisure activity. Certainly the many inventions of the twentieth century, from TV dinners to microwaves, have made cooking, like archery, nearly an archaic craft. You once had to cook, or live with someone who cooked, if you wanted to eat. No longer. All you need know is how to heat.

Cooking has become a means not to feed ourselves but to show how cultured, rich, or creative we are. As a nation whose type-A work habits spill over into our free time, we cook complicated dishes on the weekends as if our next raise relied on it. We install bulky Viking stoves in our kitchens to wow our friends, only to leave them cold and unused during the week. As cooking becomes more and more of a hobby, there may come a day when the only remaining cooks are the weekend warriors at the cookoffs.

CHAPTER 3

THE GREAT
GARLIC COOK-OFF

Skirting off Highway 101 down an exit ramp to Gilroy, I roll down my window to inhale my first dose of fresh air after a cross-country flight topped off by two hours cooped up in an air-conditioned car. I exhale the stale chill and breathe deeply. My nostrils, mouth, throat, and lungs fill with the earthy aroma of fresh garlic. It is not the sharp kick in the nostrils that a sticky mound of minced garlic can deliver but, rather, the mellow fragrance of a bulb slow-roasted in the oven until the cloves are a dark, luxurious caramel. Yum. My mouth waters as if I'm eating the air. I sniff here and there like a bloodhound, tracking the aroma. It's no use. Every which way I turn my wriggling nose, I scent it.

Other than the appetizing air, nothing stands out immediately about Gilroy. It has the standard gaggle of boxy motels, gas stations with enough tarmac to land a jet, and low-slung, hyper-lit convenience stores along the highway. The effect is Anywhere, America, except for that smell. I pull into the Forest Park Inn, a kind of upscale motel with such niceties as flower gardens and a tennis court, where I ask a teenage clerk with a sleepy but polite manner about the garlic smell. She has lived in Gilroy her whole life, she says, but has never smelled it. She shrugs. "Do you know if there are garlic fields nearby?" I ask. She lazily wags her head no.

Outside under the withering sun, I hustle squint-eyed across the skillet-hot parking lot with the image of a five-story-high bottle of spring water in my head. I feel as if the entire top of my head is about to blister. In the Quick-N-Easy Market, I lean deep into the wall of fridges, pause to soak up the pool-like cool, and snatch a water. At the front counter I ask again about the garlic smell, this time questioning a middle-aged clerk who leans against a wall of cigarette packs with his arms contemplatively crossed over his chest. "It smells when the wind blows west during the harvest," he says in a polite but disinterested monotone.

The harvest. Such a modest term for what is going on nearby. Just south of Gilroy lie the flat, fertile plains of the San Joaquin Valley, the engine of California's powerhouse agriculture. Sandwiched between the scruffy Diablo Range on one side and the comparatively lush Santa Lucia Range on the other, the valley grows at least 80 percent of the entire United States' garlic. The Mediterranean climate, hot and dry in the summer, cool and moist in the winter, is perfect for the bulbs. In rare years rain close to the harvest renders the garlic an unappetizing black, which forces the growers to peel the bulbs at an extra expense. Otherwise, this is as close as it gets to garlic heaven.

Each fall, waxy white cloves are tucked into the dark earth where they gestate for nine months "just like a baby," as Don Christopher of Christopher Ranch, one of the region's largest growers and shippers, likes to say. In May, bent-over fieldworkers rudely rouse the garlic, clipping the roots and pulling the bulbs by hand into the light of day. Exposed, they are left to cure in the sun. They are then loaded onto trucks headed north to Gilroy's processing plants.

Gilroy may be known as the Garlic Capital of the World, but not a whole lot of garlic is actually grown here anymore, not since a white rot fungus silently crept through the fields in the '80s. There are only three hundred acres of garlic left in Gilroy, but the small city remains a major garlic-processing center thanks to the likes of Gilroy Foods and Christopher Ranch. Every day a million and a half papery bulbs bounce through Christopher Ranch alone. "It's like trying to fly east—you always go through Atlanta" is the way one local explains it to me. "If you're a head of garlic, you always go through Gilroy."

Trucks will haul in papery, bouncy bulbs until September, but the harvest celebration can't wait. This weekend the small city will celebrate the 2001 season with a humongous sun-soaked party, the twenty-third annual Gilroy Garlic Festival. Over the next three days some 120,000 visitors, mostly urbanites from the Bay Area, will descend on Gilroy to wolf down all things garlic, from fries to kettle corn. They'll even stand in unfathomably long lines in the 90-degree-plus sun for free garlic ice cream.

The festival sprawls across a public park on the southern edge of Gilroy, hard by paltry Uvas Creek. This year festival organizers are especially proud of the blanket of AstroTurf green sod that covers the park, which feels like freshly laid plush carpet underfoot. It's Friday, the first day of the festival, when the locals converge because the crowd is manageable. Even the lines for the coveted and generous pepper steak sandwiches are short.

I've come for a quick tour of the festival that gave birth to the Great Garlic Cook-Off, which will be held tomorrow. I jump into a golf cart with Cristin Reichmuth, a blond triathlete and former Garlic Festival queen, for a quick tour. As Reichmuth weaves the golf cart around stroller pushers and past the Moon Walk with the kids ricocheting around inside, she tells me this year's festival is BYOB, bring your own breath mint. Our central destination is Gourmet Alley, the heart and stomach of the festival. The alley is a temporary mess hall under a copious tent that churns out the garlic- and butter-laden munchies that the festival is known for: plumb mushrooms groaning with garlic, pesto pasta dotted with pearly garlic bits, bread smothered with garlic, and calamari panfried with its weight in garlic. Not bringing my own breath mints could prove a problem.

The army of volunteer cooks use brick-sized blocks of butter. They cook pasta in huge metal buckets, which are filled with garden hoses. They sop the pepper steaks with what looks like small mops dunked in a rosemary marinade. Blue propane flames buzz incessantly. Large, lazy bubbles break on the surface of a vat of viscous scampi sauce. It is as if they are cooking for Gulliver. Of course, given that all this cooking is outdoors and involves some substantial gear, men have commandeered the cooking while women ready the plates for the T-shirted masses. None of the males express their inner caveman with as much aplomb as the Pyro Chefs, a kind of cross between line cooks and fire-eaters. As generic rock music cranks, a line of deeply tanned men in ball caps, white aprons, and sunglasses pour long, arcing streams of olive oil into red-hot wok-shaped skillets. The oil crackles like a loose power line. Flames rocket out of the pans. The gathered crowd roars. Female volunteers boogie as they dish up the Pyro Chefs' freshly seared scampi and calamari. It is classic American cooking cum theater.

That is also the point of the Great Garlic Cook-Off. The contest is considered one of the festival's top entertainment venues. Festival organizers spend $55,000 to bring eight contestants from around the country to square off on the outdoor cookoff stage with original recipes using a minimum of six cloves or three teaspoons of minced or chopped garlic. The grand prize is $1,000 and a bulky crown of garlic bulbs. Now this is total chump change in the scheme of cookoffs, but many of the contest's 170 entries this year were penned by contesters from far and wide. They have been entering the contest since the 1980s. There are several reasons why.

Unlike other cookoffs with this size of grand prize, the Great Garlic Cook-Off pays for the contestants' airfare, hotel (albeit within earshot of Highway 101), and a rental car—in short, a nearly all-expenses-paid weekend in California. Now Gilroy itself is no top tourist destination, but it is less than an hour's drive from Monterey and sundry other picturesque California beach towns.

Like National Chicken, the Great Garlic Cook-Off likes the recipes long and complicated, which gets the contesters juiced. Unlike National Chicken and most other cookoffs, recipes using processed food or calling for the dreaded microwave are routinely chucked. This year's contestants will use wasabi, potstickers, Grand Marnier, duck, phyllo dough, and prosciutto. Contestants get a generous two hours to make their dishes. Half the recipes run to two full pages, a travesty in the world of quick-and-easy-obsessed company-sponsored cookoffs.

The cookoff has earned a reputation as being fun, mostly due to the down-to-earth, friendly nature of the organizers who are all local volunteers. Unlike other cookoffs, there is not a hint of corporate formalism—no suits, no lectures, no appliance demonstrations. The small purse eases some of the standard cookoff anxiety so the contesters can kick back and enjoy themselves. "It's just a big party," as one put it.

They may kick back a little, but the contesters still win regularly. They swept the 2000 contest. Camilla Saulsbury, a blond grad student at Indiana University and one of the youngest contesters, took the crown with a potato gratin fancied up with Gorgonzola, pears, pecans, and ten cloves of garlic. New Mexico's Sharyn Hill, her ever present, oversized Jackie O. sunglasses on her nose, won in 1999 with a cream of roasted garlic soup that included melted cream cheese.

This year's lineup of eight contestants includes two top contesters, the formidable Roxanne Chan and Diane Sparrow. Since placing third at National Chicken four months ago, Sparrow has scored more wins: $500 in a Blue Bonnet contest with a peach spice cake and fourth place in a *Bon Appétit* rice contest.

That is nowhere near the clip Chan collects prizes. She averages twenty-five to thirty a year. The self-taught cook started entering cooking contests seriously in 1984 at the urging of family and friends. Like many new contesters, Chan had beginner's luck. Within three years she hit her personal best. In 1987 she hauled in forty-seven prizes, practically one a week. Also in 1987, Chan miraculously gave birth to her son, Tai, at forty-four after being told for years that she couldn't have children.

This will be Chan's ninth cookoff in Gilroy, which is just a few hours down the highway from her home perched atop a hill in the Bay Area. She went three years in a row in the '80s when the dishes, she says, were lackluster. Entries were such home-style fare as forty-clove chicken. Her creations, such as Epicurean Eggplant Bake, a kind of savory baked

Alaska topped with a meringue of egg white and garlic, easily stood out.

That dish won her a second place in 1986, the only prize she has to show for her eight appearances at the cookoff. She mostly chalks up her poor showing to the fickleness of judges. In '92 she was told off the record that she had come in fourth, that the judges liked her dish but there wasn't enough garlic. She thinks her next entry, a garlic crostini smoothed with goat cheese, mint, and garlic, was too oddball. The garlic was sautéed in vinegar and sugar, which didn't sit well with some judges. In '97 she stuffed grape leaves with mushrooms, hazelnuts, and garlic, and doused them with garlic vinaigrette. Again, perhaps too oddball. In '99, the year her oven didn't work, she thinks it was the reverse, her Italian Ricotta Torta wasn't unusual enough.

This year's competition, to Chan's eye, does not look as stiff as in the recent past. She thinks she has at least a shot at placing with her Florentine Frittata Salad. She has used her standard Gilroy approach: using garlic in each element of the dish. She has used a quarter cup of minced in the frittata, which is sliced and served on a bed of baby greens topped with balsamic vinaigrette flavored with more garlic. The salad is garnished with a whopping cup of sliced browned cloves, making her recipe the most garlic intensive in the cookoff.

This is Sparrow's second crack at the garlic crown. She competed in 2000 with a cheesy pepper tart made with a flourish: a top of ruffled phyllo dough. She had picked up the technique at France's La Varenne cooking school where she studied for a week as the grand prize winner of the Gold Kist Farms chicken recipe contest. Here in Gilroy, Sparrow has once again returned to her strong point, chicken. This time she reworked the bird into the architectonic Asian Chicken Stacks with Wasabi Cream. She alternately stacks watercress, spiced shredded chicken, and pan-crisped potstickers and then douses the whole teetering contraption with pale green wasabi sauce. It is very pan-Asian-fusion meets tall food. Sparrow's stacks call for eight cloves of garlic, a pittance in the scheme of this year's finalists.

Sparrow doesn't know it, but there is a chink in Chan's armor that she can exploit. Chan is not big on presentation. She knows how to garnish a dish, but she's not going to knock herself out as Sparrow will. Presentation is half the fun for Sparrow who can get downright compulsive about finding what she considers the correct serving dishes, covering sizable geographical reaches in pursuit of chargers and salad plates. There are two kinds of shoppers: buyers and hunters. Buyers come home from every excursion lugging bulging bags. Purchasing is the goal for them. Hunters relish the search. Like botanists seeking a rare orchid in the rain forest, they meticulously scour store after store for sling backs in the right shade of lime green or paw through bins of bedding to find gingham pillow shams. Sparrow is an adamant hunter.

This persistence paid off at National Chicken, so Sparrow was back on the trail, this time for a dark-colored, square, Asian-looking plate. She started with Pier I and T. J. Maxx in Rochester, Minnesota, about an hour's drive from Osage. She went online, where she found plenty. Then Sparrow's contesting buddy from Utah, Ruth Kendrick, telephoned. She was standing in a Pottery Barn in Salt Lake City, where before her sat stacks of square plates in different sizes and colors, including purple. There were even matching chopsticks. Kendrick dug her measuring tape out of her purse, sized up the plates, and after further phone consultation, purchased six plates per Sparrow's directions. Kendrick had just gotten a few blocks from the store when her cell phone rang. Sparrow wanted the matching chopsticks. Kendrick went back.

It turned out that the plates did not fit on the tray the contestants are required to use for serving their recipes. So the night before flying out of Minneapolis, Sparrow swept through the epic Mall of America with her husband reluctantly in tow. She hit housewares departments in Marshall Field's, Macy's, and Nordstrom in record time. She told me later it was like falling out of an airplane and hoping the chute opens. She hit the jackpot at her final stop, Nordstrom, where she found the perfect purple-lacquered rectangular plate.

Chan and Sparrow have competed against each other only once before, at the '99 National Chicken in Dallas. Chan won second place with her Tea-Smoked Sesame Chicken. Sparrow, star-struck and intimidated, won nada for her Lemon and Dill Chicken Salad. Now you would think, as I did, that this cookoff might be a clash of the Titans between these two cooks, that each would consider the other her toughest competition. Think again. After looking over the finalists' recipes, neither Chan nor Sparrow considers the other her main competition. Oddly enough, they've each separately picked the same person to win: a newcomer and local boy.

Adam Sanchez is a local car dealer. He is thirty-nine, heavyset, and an extrovert. This is the first cooking contest he has ever entered. In fact, he's the only one of the eight contestants who has never competed before. He entered on a dare, a classic first-timer move.

Three years ago, after a lifetime of washing, painting, fixing, financing, and selling cars, he bought Al Sanchez VW/Mazda/Jeep from his father, Al. The dealership has a thirty-thousand-square-foot building and twelve mechanics. In a typical month it moves 120 to 140 cars. Sanchez works Monday through Saturday, sometimes Sunday. He likes to say he works half days, "nine to nine."

In his rare hours off, Sanchez couldn't quit thinking about his dealership. He ran numbers in his head. He thought of calls he needed to make. He needed a distraction badly. Golf, too frustrating, didn't do it. Cooking, to his surprise, did.

He was a basic cook but had always been an adventuresome restaurant eater, sucking down chicken feet and the like in San Francisco's Chinatown. Sanchez's rule is that if other people are eating a food, he'll munch it, too, even if he can't identify it. He began cooking the kind of complicated dishes he loved to eat in restaurants. To his surprise he easily made the quantum leap in the kitchen from grilling steaks to creating his own bouillabaisse. It was like sitting down at the piano one day and finding you could bust out the Rach Third. Not only had he happened upon a natural talent, but Sanchez found a weekend afternoon in the kitchen incredibly soothing. He pulsed away the week's worries at the food processor. He sautéed leeks to relieve stress. His wife urged him to relax on the weekend. "This *is* relaxing," he countered.

There is something inherently competitive about cooking. Serious cooks may not say anything, but they are always sizing each other up. Sanchez was no different. Just being a salesperson and a male, he was more verbal about it. At Al Sanchez VW he and his business manager baited each other constantly as to who was the better cook. Finally, they went pan to pan in a kind of mini cookoff cum dinner party. He cooked a rack of lamb. She cooked a spring pasta dish. The guests, however, refused to pause from hoovering the feast to vote.

The event ended in a draw but established a tradition of one-on-one cookoff parties where the guests always refused to vote. Finally, a friend suggested that if Sanchez won the Great Garlic Cook-Off, that might settle the matter. With car salesman bluster, Sanchez responded that of course he would win it. In fact, he never expected to make the cut for the eight finalists.

He created one recipe for the contest, the clunkily named Garlic Marnier Duck Pot Stickers. Sanchez marinated duck breast in the liqueur, orange juice, cornstarch, a bit of granulated garlic, and a pinch of salt. He sautéed the duck, minced it, mixed it in with a kind of garlicky mirepoix, spooned the mess onto potstickers, and pinched the packets closed. The potstickers were deep-fried and served with a simple dipping sauce of soy sauce and white vinegar. He used about two bulbs of garlic in total. He sent in the recipe and forgot about it.

When he received the call from cookoff chairman Al Heinzen that he was a finalist, Sanchez was convinced it was a joke, but he played along. He asked Heinzen for his phone number, then called him back, expecting that one of his buddies would answer. It was Heinzen's office. Sanchez was shocked. He still had his doubts. He asked Heinzen if they picked him because he lived in Gilroy, which saved the festival plane fare and two nights in a hotel. No, Heinzen assured him, a committee had selected the recipes without knowing the names or addresses of the contestants.

The import of the cookoff began to weigh on Sanchez. The festival is a huge deal in Gilroy. Some four thousand residents or, put more impressively, 10 percent of the city's population, volunteer at it. Only two other Gilroyans had won the cookoff in its twenty-two-year history, in '81 and '95. Sanchez was the hometown hope, the only local in the cookoff. He would also be the only contestant cooking in front of bleachers filled with his family and friends. The local paper, the *Gilroy Dispatch*, did a big story on him. He got to work.

On weekends he practiced making his potstickers; he recruited friends to time him, getting down to one hour and fifty-five minutes, just under the two-hour limit. He took photos of different presentations so that he could compare them. His friends and family complained about being guinea pigs. They begged him to quit making potstickers. He kept churning them out. If he wasn't selling cars, he was making potstickers.

〜〜〜

I find Sparrow on Friday afternoon pacing in front of Gilroy's spanking new grocery store, Nob Hill. In one hand she holds a three-by-five card with a shopping list neatly written on it. She is manicured and pedicured, and is wearing capri pants and a sleeveless turtleneck with a matching purse. She is model tall and, after a recent regimen of walking five miles every morning, newly svelte.

"I'm going in if they don't get here soon," she says to her husband, Jon.

They are a film crew for the Food Network, which is in town to shoot the cookoff. They are going to film Sparrow as she shops for her cookoff ingredients. Jon, bespectacled, a mellow yin to Sparrow's intense yang just now, wanders off into the gargantuan store to find the crew, the automatic doors whisking closed behind him.

It has been a meteoric rise from winning a state egg contest four years ago to having a national television show follow her through a grocery store. None of Sparrow's many skills and hobbies have produced the results that contesting has: a kitchen full of prizes, exciting trips, buckets of cash, and now, the jewel in her crown, fame. Only contesting has made this middle-class midwestern homemaker a star.

"I've never had to look cute to buy my groceries," she says, straightening her sweater.

Sparrow may technically be a homemaker, but the label doesn't quite fit. It's true that she hasn't had a career in the classic sense and has spent a good chunk of her life raising four boys. Along the way, though, she and her husband restored old houses and sold them. She has worked as her husband's assistant in his photography business. For a while she made sachets for bed-and-breakfasts. Sparrow is always riddled with self-doubts at cookoffs, but she is one of the most can-do people I've ever met. She quilts, wallpapers, refinishes furniture, and pulls candles. She has taught herself to tile, to make pottery in her own kiln, and to mat and frame. When she taught herself to upholster, the man at the fabric store told her, "Most people don't start with Queen Anne wingback chairs."

Sparrow grew up in farm country—her father inseminated turkeys—but she had ideas about working in fashion. She attended a two-year program at the "Denver institute of something. You can see how well I did." She eventually returned to Osage to help her mother run a dress shop. They sold high-end moderate knits, ordering only three sizes in each outfit because in a small town no one wants to be seen in the same dress.

Jon Sparrow moved to Osage to become news editor at the local paper. He never intended to stay. He was accepted at the prestigious photography school, Brooks Institute of Photography, in Santa Barbara, California. Then the couple met, fell in love, and married. Sparrow had her first son at twenty. She had three more boys, hoping each time to have a girl. Other than a brief sojourn in Duluth, Minnesota, the family has lived in Osage.

While the boys grew up, Sparrow poured most of her considerable creative energy into cooking, devising her own recipes to test on her four guinea pigs. She had been creating her own dishes since childhood, when she was thrown into the kitchen because her mother had heart trouble. Back then she would crack a cookbook and make a grocery list, and then her dad would drive her to the store. "It occurred to me pretty early that cooking would be boring unless you came up with new recipes."

A young mother, Sparrow became a young grandmother. Her first grandchild was born while she was still in her forties. For her granddaughter's baptism, Sparrow invented a wild rice and egg casserole. Af-

ter one forkful, a friend suggested that Sparrow enter it in the annual
Iowa Egg Council recipe contest. The next thing Sparrow knew she was
holding a check for $500. She had won first place. Emboldened, she
entered Gold Kist Chicken's annual recipe contest because she needed
a new refrigerator, one of the prizes. Soon it was making ice in her
kitchen.

In that first year of contesting Sparrow racked up $26,000 in cash
and prizes. She liked the loot, the recognition, and the competition,
the "outsmarting other people." And she liked the sensation which
contesting gave her, that something was always on the horizon.

Jon emerges from the store with two women in tow, one a faux
blonde in overall shorts, toting a home video camera. This is Erica
Wilner, a former TV news anchor who is now an independent producer. She instructs Sparrow to go about her shopping as she normally
would. Sparrow turns on her heel and charges into the store with the
small camera crew in tow. Jon, holding Sparrow's purse awkwardly in
one hand, and I trail farther back.

The store is a classic new American grocery store, soaring ceilings,
warm lighting that gives everyone rosy cheeks, and as big as the Pentagon. Everything looks beautiful in the air-conditioned chill, a beauty
born of intense order: the glistening plastic-wrapped blocks of cheese,
the shelves of cereal boxes lined up perfectly, and brightly colored produce misted and neatly stacked. Despite the dreamlike abundance,
there is nary a whiff of food in the place. You can't smell the strawberries or the fresh bread. You can't even smell the garlic, which wafts just
outside the store's doors. It's like shopping in an idealized still life.

Sparrow hardly turns into the extra-wide produce aisle when her
voice breaks into a girly trill. She has run into freckled-faced Margee
Berry, one of the eight cookoff contestants and a "chick," as they've
come to call themselves. The two women cooked next to each other at
National Chicken in April. They abandon their carts to hug. Berry's
eyes widen when she notices the crew. She steps back from Sparrow to
get out of the camera's view.

Sparrow moves on down the produce aisle. Wilner hustles ahead of
her, her sandals slapping loudly on the tile floor. She shoots a look at

Sparrow as she methodically picks over several baskets of chili peppers, looking for red ones for a garnish. Sparrow gives up and moves down the aisle to the scallions, which she will use as a garnish. She holds up an organic bunch. Too big. She rolls her cart down to the nonorganic and digs through the basket, plucking out bunches for closer inspection. Several carts back up behind her. None of the shoppers, eyes glazed in a grocery store trance, seem to notice Wilner and her camera or that they could easily maneuver around Sparrow. Instead they wait, too deep in their stupor to even ask Sparrow, intent on the scallions, to move her cart. She finally settles on a bunch and continues on, the logjam loosening behind her.

Sparrow trawls up and down the aisles while Wilner dashes ahead of her this way and that. Sparrow doesn't know the store, so she keeps doubling back, her bevy of followers trooping along behind her. The store manager joins us, a young, handsome Hispanic man who grew up in Gilroy when it was still a farm town and he walked through tomato fields on his way to school. He calls out directions from off-camera to Sparrow, who barrels along as Wilner tries to keep up. Sparrow nabs a jar of honey before Wilner arrives with her camera. Wilner directs Sparrow to put it back on the shelf. Sparrow picks it up again, reexamines it, and drops it in her cart. Then she repeats the series of motions, her bangles jingling and her eyes scanning the label each time. "That's it, Diane," Wilner coaches.

When Sparrow has found everything she needs—scallions, Japanese cucumbers, three packages of potstickers, honey, mayonnaise, butter, limes, and watercress—she stops and poses with her cart. Wilner drapes herself over a display of vanilla wafers back in the produce section.

"Say your name and what you're making," Wilner instructs.

"My name is Diane Sparrow. I'm making Asian Chicken Stacks with Wasabi Cream."

Jon stands in front of a swath of shiny Granny Smiths, proudly watching his poised wife. He holds her purse like a typical guy, with one hand out in front of him as if it's a dead animal in a sack. "Diane has lost forty pounds in the past year," he says to me. "Before that she wouldn't have been comfortable doing this shoot."

"How did you get involved in cookoffs?" Wilner prompts Sparrow.

"It started as a hobby and turned into an obsession. There is a network of contests, and some are really coveted. I sometimes riff off a product," Sparrow says.

A baby wails from a far corner of the store. A voice over the intercom drones. Dazed shoppers roll their carts by. Sparrow carries on like a pro, undistracted by the ordinary life around her.

〰 〰 〰 〰

Cookoffs are one of the few forms of competition where you are expected to make nice with your competitors at social events, usually voluminous meals, prior to the contest. Imagine two NBA teams having a potluck together the night before a game, or chess champs meeting for cocktails before a match.

From what I've seen this is easier for newcomers, such as Sanchez, most of whom feel they have won something closer to a raffle and so are on a good-luck high. Contesters are typically friendly at these events, with a few notable exceptions, but they don't typically join in with the abandon of the newcomers. They hold back just a little bit by not discussing their recipes or strategies. The fact is they are eating dinner across from someone they will do battle with the next morning, often for thousands of dollars. However, those kinds of tensions are eased here because of the relatively small prizes.

At Gilroy the contestants are invited to a dinner of freshly caught tuna and Caesar salad held by the outdoor pool at the cookoff chairman's well-appointed house. Everyone is here, most with spouses. Half of the contestants are from California. In addition to Chan and Sanchez there is a Braille translator from outside Sacramento and an engineer from southern California. He manages the Keck Interferometer, which links the world's two largest telescopes high atop a volcanic peak in Hawaii. This is his fourth trip to Gilroy. He won first place in 1994. A kind of forlorn widow from New Jersey with dark bags under her eyes came the farthest. It is one of the first contests she felt up to entering since her husband died. She came by herself. There is another Iowan, a former contester and teacher, Kim Landhuis. Now a law student, Landhuis only had time to enter this contest this year. She is a Garlic Cook-Off alum. She took the crown in 1998.

Sanchez is still clueless about the contesters he's up against. He's all salesman braggadocio. As he sips wine, he goes on about how he sent in only one recipe, that he did it on a dare, that he just threw his potstickers together. Sanchez begins to sense that this cavalier attitude isn't going over too well with other contestants, several of whom worked very hard to get here. He tones it down.

Everyone sits down to dinner as the sun sets, turning the treeless, buff foothills of the Diablo Range a subtle mossy green before fading to black. The wind picks up and ripples the pool. Sparrow pulls her silk wrap around her. She is in high spirits, drinking white wine, chatting about contesting, talking trash about a local contest she believes has shut her out, and extolling her recent Pillsbury submission. "It's truly inspired." She won't give any details other than to say, "It's a dessert."

The only dark cloud on her horizon, a red garnish still eludes her. After her stint with the Food Network this afternoon, she had Jon drive her to every market they could find in Gilroy, looking for small red peppers. No go. "Now I won't have any red on the plate," she worries, "and I haven't gotten to practice with my plate."

The evening winds down. Most of the guests have an early morning ahead, and the evening chill grows quickly. As Sparrow gets up to leave, she walks past where Chan is sitting with her husband and son. The threesome all wear thick glasses and have dark hair. Sparrow pauses.

"Who do you have picked to win, Roxanne?" Sparrow asks. Chan, still sitting, looks slightly stricken. She smiles, laughs a little, and looks away from Sparrow.

"I don't know, Diane," Chan answers.

In response, Sparrow doesn't offer whom she's picked but moves on to other small talk. The two wish each other luck and say good night.

~ ~ ~ ~

Most cookoffs are created to push a product, whether it be foil oven bags or chicken thighs. Gilroy's garlic cookoff is meant to publicize a place. The cookoff and the festival have inarguably put little old ho-hum Gilroy on the map by inextricably linking it with what has become almost everyone's favorite seasoning, garlic. Don Christopher says that before the festival Gilroy wasn't known beyond the Bay Area, and then it was known only as a town quick to hand out speeding tickets.

Since the festival, Christopher finds that everywhere he goes people have heard of Gilroy, even in France. Once he was at the craps table in Reno and a passerby noticed his jacket with "Gilroy" emblazoned on it. They interrupted his game to ask, "Isn't that where the garlic festival is?"

That the small city is so well known is an amazing feat. Gilroy, named for a nineteenth-century Scottish barrel maker, is a decidedly unhip, sleepy burg at the southern tip of Silicon Valley. Even the residents say so. The Victorian storefronts downtown have been given over to antique stores. To the west of downtown there is a stretch of 1950s motels with vintage neon signs along a dusty commercial throughway. Gilroy's pulse can be found along the Hecker Pass Highway, a four-lane road lined with shopping plazas.

In the past ten years or so Gilroy has evolved into a small bedroom community to San Jose, less than an hour's drive north. Its relatively affordable housing prices—$410,000 for an average home in 2001—have drawn tech workers to this southern outpost of Silicon Valley. Still, the town has yet to lose its rural character. A stray rooster, stepping lively on the parking lot behind the hotel, woke me up on Saturday morning. And, of course, there is the garlic smell.

Gilroy has always been defined by what it has grown. First it was a grain capital, then a tobacco capital, then dairy. By the 1920s it was prunes. This is where the Christophers come in. Don Christopher's grandfather, Ole Christopher, a Danish immigrant, worked his way up from baler to prune rancher in San Jose. His sons took it from there, transforming Ole's ranch into one of the largest prune growers in the region.

The third generation veered slightly off course. Don Christopher, then a twenty-year-old eager to strike out on his own, bought 10 acres in Gilroy in 1956. He wanted nothing to do with prunes, which he considered exceptionally boring to grow. He planted more stimulating produce: bell peppers, sugar beets, and garlic. He pretty quickly gave up on sugar beets; he still grows bell peppers, but it is garlic that has made him a fortune. His company has five hundred year-round employees and a seasonal harvesting crew of two thousand. Christopher Ranch's 4,500 acres of garlic account for 10 percent of the United States' total acreage. He is the region's largest shipper of fresh garlic.

In 1979, Christopher had his doubts about a garlic festival, but he still joined forces with Rudy Melone, then president of Gavilan College, to put on the first one. Melone had read about Arleux, France, a town of about 3,500 garlic growers in northern France, near the Belgian border. The village, which grows more than enough garlic for France, holds a December festival that draws sixty thousand people according to the festival website and culminates in a garlic ball in the town hall. Melone read that Arleux had the nerve to call itself the Garlic Capital of the World. He wouldn't stand for it. Melone would prove that the title rightly belonged to Gilroy with its $30 million-plus industry at the time.

This seemed to require a festival. Both Melone and Christopher thought that, if nothing else, a festival would boost the sagging community pride. Teenagers regularly repainted the town's highway sign to read Kilroy. Garlic was just another crop to a city low on self-esteem. When they told the mayor about their idea, he thought it was a joke. Undaunted, they scraped together $19,000 to put on what they considered a huge party for the State of California.

The first festival was held in recently harvested fields where festival-goers were welcome to gather up the small bulbs left behind in the unsettled earth. Fifteen thousand people showed up, three times more than expected. They had to send to Monterey for more seafood. They had only five thousand tickets, so the minute they collected them, they resold them. An emergency call was made to Budweiser: Don't send more kegs, send a truck of beer.

Now a horde of people three times the size of Gilroy's population descends on the hamlet during the last weekend of July. This army of sunblock-slicked festival-goers clogs the streets, tramples the grass, and generally takes over Gilroy. It may be a huge bother to the locals, many of whom get the heck out of town, but the festival raises $250,00 for a long list of local charities. Moreover, the festival has long since achieved Melone's original goal. Devoted garlic aficionados may prefer the Garlic Is Life Festival in Tulsa, Oklahoma—saying Gilroy's fete is too crowded and features only one of six hundred subvarieties of garlic. Regardless, Gilroy continues to be known as the Garlic Capital of the World. Even after the garlic crops headed south to San Joaquin, Gilroy's claim lives on.

This is, at least in part, thanks to the cookoff, which has been part of the festival from the start. The Great Garlic Cook-Off is a money loser for the festival, but that doesn't count the value of all the publicity it generates. Reporters love competitions, especially wacky ones. The cookoff draws press from around the country and even the world. Reporters file stories from "Gilroy, the Garlic Capital," repeating the phrase far and wide, reinforcing the title. This year *CBS Sunday* is here, as is the aforementioned Food Network, CNN, ABC, the BBC, and television crews from Germany and Korea. For that matter, I am here.

~~~~

Early summer mornings can be perplexing to newcomers in Gilroy. A fine gray mist blankets the woolly terrain, cooling the air. It is the kind of damp chill that makes you reach for jeans and polar fleece and ditch the straw hat. If you do, you'll be one panting dog in a few hours when the sun soaks up the fog and comes banging down on your head.

That is why Sparrow sports a sleeveless blouse despite the foggy nip. She and Jon are loading what is essentially a kitchen's worth of equipment into the trunk of their rental car in the motel parking lot. Jon runs upstairs to their room to retrieve another roller suitcase stuffed with gear. A bearded cameraman from the Food Network hovers nearby, his camera trained on Sparrow. She was laughing it up last night, but now her eyes are dark, intense, and fidgety. She wants to get going. She recounts that she woke up in the middle of the night terrified that her arugula had frozen in the motel mini-fridge. It hadn't.

By 7:45 A.M. Jon has loaded the trunk. The cameraman and I squeeze into the backseat, and off we go. We head west on the wide-open Hecker Pass, passing the shopping plazas, their great expanses of parking lots as empty and forlorn as fallow fields. We turn into one big lot. Sparrow hasn't given up on finding a red garnish for her plate.

After briefly wandering aimlessly around the expanse of tar, Jon finds the Nob Hill store, and Sparrow heads in with the cameraman in tow. Sitting in the car and watching his wife charge into the store, Jon says, "Sometimes it gets to be a little too much." Sparrow quickly emerges with a carton of cherry tomatoes and a few orangish chilies that she found buried in a pile of green.

We zip south to the Christmas Hill Park, which is deliciously quiet at this early hour, and pull up to the cookoff area just a little after 8 A.M. Eight cooking stations, each with a stove, a sink with running water, and a three-foot stretch of countertop, have been set up on a stage surrounded on two sides by bleachers. A thin gray canopy hangs overhead to fend off the day's expected heat.

"Cooking is my stress reliever," Sanchez tells me as I notice his meaty hands shaking. He is already jamming like a restaurant prep cook. He is roasting garlic. His mandoline perches on his counter, ready to go. He has set three pans on the stovetop. A photo of his wife and daughter is tucked into the plastic frame that holds his recipe. He is dressed as if for a family cook-out in a big shirt with a bold Asian-like design in black and red.

Sanchez is running on less than three hours of sleep. He was up until 3:15 A.M. pacing and then woke just before 6 A.M. when a horrifying thought cut through his slumber: What if he forgot to thaw the duck breast? He rushed to the refrigerator. All was well. "I'm too wired up to be tired," he says.

In contrast to Sanchez, almost rubbing it in, Sue Vogelsanger, the Braille translator at the stove next door, is yucking it up with her volunteer assistant as if there is something hysterically funny about rinsing a glistening pink log of pork tenderloin. A self-described "chronologically advanced" cook, she is making the peppily named Garlito-Porkito, an oven-roasted pork tenderloin in a bath of canned pumpkin, amaretto, forty cloves of garlic, and two tablespoons of coffee. The coffee is something she picked up in the Midwest, she explains. "You're not looking at a worried lady" she calls, and then laughs. Sanchez lets out a short, tight-chested "heh-heh" without looking up from his countertop. Chan hasn't even arrived. She is due to turn in her dish second, after Sanchez.

At 8:10 A.M. the contestants get the go-ahead to start cooking. Sanchez hits the gas. In short order he loads scallions, celery, carrot, cilantro, and ginger into his food processor, pulses away, and then tosses the mirepoix into a sauté pan. Although his fingers tremble, he moves assuredly. Meanwhile, the other contestants look up with confused expressions. Each cook is not to start cooking until two hours before their turn-in time, beginning at ten-minute intervals, but for some reason all the contestants have been given the go-ahead. That means Sanchez will be the only cook held to the two-hour time allotment. He notices but doesn't say anything.

Ten minutes into Sanchez's speed cooking, Chan pulls up with husband and son. She is the image of composure, with her lean frame dressed in a kind of chef's whites: white linen pants and turtleneck. Chan calmly unpacks her dishes and ingredients, turns on the oven, and begins rapping the eight eggs for her frittata against a mixing bowl one at a time. The oven is working this time, she reports, "so we're ahead of the game."

By 9 A.M. everyone is cooking in earnest. Sparrow has trimmed the hairy roots off her scallions and stuffed them in a clear pitcher of water so they stay crisp. Everyone has a volunteer helper, but Sparrow is one of the few who has really put hers to work, washing and chopping a produce shelf of vegetables. Landhuis, the law student in big black sunglasses that make her look like Imelda Marcos, whacks away at small pieces of beef with a twelve-inch blade. Her volunteer, an older man with linebacker shoulders and a pot belly, has draped himself across her stove as he talks to her. Landhuis's husband, a pasty pediatrician, tries to stay out of her way. He takes a quick step forward and tucks her apron band under her collar. Family members on stage are verboten, but nobody seems to notice the doctor or Jon Sparrow, who is wandering around with his video camera.

There is only a handful of people in the bleachers, and most are contestants' relatives. The fog has begun to thin. Backstage, the six judges, mostly chefs, stand in a semicircle listening to an explanation of the scoring system, rating each dish from one to ten in taste, presentation, creativity, use of garlic, texture, and, surprisingly, ease of preparation. The scores do not specifically determine the winners but are to be used by the judges as a guide to pick their three top recipes.

Back on the cookoff stage, things are beginning to run a bit amok. Sparrow has nicked a finger through rubber gloves. Chan's oven has gone on the fritz, just as in '99. She has cranked it up to 500 degrees, but her frittata is still a yolky pool. Likewise for Vogelsanger, who has quit laughing now that her oven won't come up to temperature. The lady is now "worried" as her pork tenderloin bobs in a tepid bath. As a legion of male volunteers swarm onstage to attend to the stoves, Sanchez struggles with an ornery gas burner. It's too hot, but if he turns it down, the burner goes out. Add to that, "I'm way ahead of schedule. It's making me nervous. I might have forgotten something."

On the other hand, things are going so swimmingly for Landhuis that, after dramatically transforming rice noodles into great poofy white pillows in a saucepan of hot oil, she covers her creation with paper towels, neatens her already neat station, and dashes from stove to stove collecting contestants' autographs in her cookoff cookbook. A psyche move? Maybe. Sanchez takes a break from his problematic sautéing to sign her program with his quaking hand.

Chan tosses a cupful of garlic over her salad, sending the scent into the air as the stage fills with people. Mr. Garlic, a fiftyish man dressed in Birkenstocks and what looks like a huge diaper, prowls the stage throwing his bare, hairy arms around any woman within reach. There are two camera crews hovering around the stoves, the Food Network and CBS's *Sunday Morning*. An army of volunteers in T-shirts sets the table for the judges, filling the glasses with water and wine as if readying for a dinner party. California food personality Narsai David, a short, smiley man who cultivates a kind of old-fashioned look with his graying Vandyke and bow tie, begins jabbering at the crowd about purple garlic: "There is no such thing."

Meanwhile, a klatch of judges goes from stove to stove, asking the contestants polite questions. This is a peculiarity in the cookoff world. Contestants are typically kept away from judges, and vice versa, so that personality doesn't influence the score. The judges are moving in an unfortunate reverse order, starting with Sparrow, who will turn her dish in last, and working their way toward the contestants who are feeling the pressure of the clock ticking.

So after making aimless conversation about California with Chan, one of the judges, a chef from Boca Raton, Florida, arrives at Sanchez's station near 10 A.M. Sanchez has ten minutes to go. As Sanchez tremulously pulls the potstickers out of a sauté pan and carefully places them on small, square white dishes, the chef quizzes him on the portable tool case he used to tote his kitchen equipment.

"Even a Cuisinart fits in there," the chef says in wonder.

"Keep that in mind when you're judging," Sanchez jokes.

Sanchez nestles small bowls of soy sauce on each of the six plates of potstickers. His meaty paws still quivering, he delicately sets sail a sliver of garlic on top of each pool of soy sauce, then balances a pair of chopsticks across the bowls. "Good," he says softly. He takes a step back, out of range of the plates, turns to his volunteer helper, and high-fives him. Then, since he has a few more minutes, he decides to add a touch of water to each bowl of soy, risking wrecking his carefully laid out display. The volunteer and I watch nervously.

The judges have taken their seats. The bleachers are suddenly packed. As the volunteers swoop down on Sanchez's station and snatch the potstickers, David holds forth on botulism over the mike.

A contestant's dish is delivered every ten minutes, supposedly arranged so that the spiciest dish, Sparrow's, comes last. A volunteer first slowly walks it across the stage to show the crowd, who appreciatively oohs and ahhs, then whisks it to the back of the stage where a gaggle of women armed with knives and spatulas falls upon it, divvying it up for the judges. The judges then take a few small bites and, poker-faced, begin marking their scorecards. Several of the judges unwittingly hold their cards so it is easy to see them.

Presentation is up and down. The Salmon Wellington, a twist on the traditional beef dish, looks stunning; it is neatly wrapped in golden phyllo encircled by orange slices. Chan's is nice but ultimately is just a big salad in a bowl. The New Jersey widow with the circles under her eyes has set lemon slices and hearts cut from aluminum foil around her entry, a flaccid, oozing block of lasagna smeared with red pepper sauce. Vogelsanger's tenderloin floats in a viscous pumpkin gruel.

When the volunteers descend on Berry's station, she is missing. She's behind the stage at a troublesome grill. Add to that, a spectator asks for her autograph in the final minutes of cooking her shrimp. She hurriedly lays out the shrimp along the edge of a plate and turns over a soufflé dish of couscous in the middle. As she sauces the couscous, its neat drum shape slumps on one side. The volunteers scoop up the dish and run, leaving Berry holding a handful of capers in midair. "I forgot my garnish," she says.

Landhuis's dish goes in, a stunning yet inexplicable display. All the puffed rice noodles look like packing material. Then, just shy of high noon, Sparrow's dish is picked up. In the end she eschewed the hint of red she had looked so long and hard for and made a kind of bouquet with purple chopsticks and curly scallions. The judges struggle to eat her stacks. They topple over when the judges cut into them. A few judges set aside their silverware and eat them with their fingers.

The judges do not tarry. They wipe their mouths with their napkins and quickly finish their scoring. The contestants are called to the front of the stage to stand behind their dishes. The sun washes down on them, and the now sizable crowd, which seems dominated by Sanchez's relatives and friends, cheers enthusiastically. The contestants smile broadly. Chan leans over and says something to Sanchez.

Third place and $250 go to Berry. Second place and $500 go to Sparrow. First place, the garlic crown, and $1,000 go to *Adam Sanchez*. The crowd explodes and rushes the stage. Sanchez's elderly mother jumps from her seat and bursts into tears. His baby daughter accidentally gets knocked over and wails. His friends yell, *"Party."* David places the garlic crown atop Sanchez's head. It will stay in Gilroy this year.

〰〰〰

This is Adam Sanchez's grand prize winner from Gilroy's 2001 Great Garlic Cook-Off.

GARLIC MARNIER DUCK POT STICKERS

MARINATED DUCK BREAST

7 ounces skinless, boneless duck breast (one whole breast)
1/3 cup Grand Marnier
1 cup orange juice
1/2 teaspoon cornstarch
1/4 teaspoon granulated garlic
Pinch of salt

Lightly score both sides of the duck breast with a sharp knife. Place in a shallow dish or plastic bag. In a small bowl, whisk together the Grand Marnier, orange juice, cornstarch, garlic, and salt. Pour over the duck breast and marinate for 1 hour.

ROASTED GARLIC

1 whole head garlic
Extra-virgin olive oil
1/2 teaspoon dried oregano
Salt and pepper to taste

Preheat oven to 375°F.

Slice the top off the garlic head. Place in a small baking dish or garlic roaster. Drizzle lightly with olive oil and sprinkle with the oregano. Season with salt and pepper. Cover tightly with foil and roast until the garlic is golden brown, about 45 minutes. Allow to cool and then squeeze the softened cloves into a small bowl and set aside.

DUCK POT STICKERS

15 to 20 roasted garlic cloves
4 scallions, white part and 2 inches of green part

1 stalk celery
1 medium carrot, cleaned and cut into 1-inch pieces
1/2 cup cilantro
1 (2-inch) piece fresh ginger, peeled and cut into 2 pieces
1 1/2 teaspoons Chinese hot oil
5 tablespoons plum sauce
1 teaspoon soy sauce
Pinch of salt
3 teaspoons toasted sesame seeds

1 tablespoon olive oil
Pinch of salt
1/2 teaspoon Grand Marnier
1 small orange, zested

1 package pot sticker wrappers
1 cup olive oil

1/2 cup soy sauce
1/4 cup white vinegar

Place the garlic, scallions, celery, carrot, cilantro, and ginger in a food processor and pulse until finely chopped. Place in a medium mixing bowl. Add the Chinese hot oil, plum sauce, soy sauce, salt, and sesame seeds and set aside.

Coat the bottom of a medium skillet with the 1 tablespoon olive oil. Place over medium heat until very hot. Remove the duck breast from the marinade and add it to the hot skillet with 1 or 2 tablespoons of the marinade. Lower the heat to medium, cover, and cook for approximately 20 minutes, turning often until cooked through and well glazed. Transfer to a cutting board and allow to cool slightly. Mince the cooked duck breast and return it to the skillet, adding a pinch of salt and the 1/2 teaspoon Grand Marnier. Cook over high heat until browned. Remove from the heat and add to the reserved vegetable mixture. Add the orange zest and stir until well mixed.

Separate 24 pot sticker wrappers. Place 1 heaping teaspoon of filling on each wrapper. Avoid getting any filling on the edges or the wrapper will not seal properly. Wet the edges with water and fold the wrapper in half to form a half-moon shape. Seal the top center of the wrapper by pressing between the fingers. Make 2 pleats, working toward the bottom left corner. Repeat, working toward the bottom right corner. Set aside.

Heat the 1 cup olive oil in a deep frying pan. Add half of the pot stickers to the hot oil and cook until browned and crisp. Remove to a platter and keep hot until ready to serve. Repeat with the remaining pot stickers.

Mix together the soy sauce and white vinegar to use as a dip for the warm pot stickers.

YIELD: 6 SERVINGS

∿∿∿

Diane Sparrow won second place at the 2001 Great Garlic Cook-Off with this architectonic dish.

ASIAN CHICKEN STACKS WITH WASABI CREAM

2 tablespoons butter
1 1/2 pounds skinless chicken thighs
1 small red chili, halved and seeded
4 cloves garlic, peeled
1 dried star anise
1/4 cup freshly squeezed lime juice
18 gyoza wrappers
3 tablespoons sesame oil

SAUCE

1/2 cup soy sauce
3 tablespoons sesame oil
1 tablespoon honey

2 tablespoons rice vinegar
4 cloves garlic, minced

WASABI CREAM

1/3 cup sour cream
3 tablespoons mayonnaise
2 teaspoons wasabi powder
1 tablespoon fresh lime juice

8 scallions, cut into thin strips
1 medium cucumber, peeled, seeded, and cut into matchsticks
1 cup fresh snow peas, cut into small julienne pieces
1 bunch fresh watercress

Heat the butter in a medium skillet. Brown the chicken thighs on the skin side in butter for a couple of minutes. Flip over and place the chili, garlic cloves, star anise, and lime juice in the skillet. Cover the pan and cook over medium-low heat for 30 to 35 minutes, or until the chicken is very tender.

While the chicken cooks, prepare the gyoza wrappers by heating a skillet over medium-high heat. Brush both sides of the wrappers with sesame oil. Place the wrappers in the hot pan a few at a time until just beginning to brown and form bubbles on the surface. Flip over and do the other side. Place on a rack to cool and continue with the remaining wrappers. Set aside.

Combine the sauce ingredients and set aside. Combine the wasabi cream ingredients and refrigerate until ready to serve.

Remove the chicken from the cooking liquid. Using two forks, shred the chicken. Place the chicken back in the pan with just enough cooking liquid to keep it moist. Place over very low heat to keep warm.

Stir together the scallions, cucumber, and snow peas. Toss with a little of the prepared sauce.

To serve, drizzle some of the sauce on each serving plate. Place 1 gyoza wrapper on a serving plate. Top with some of the watercress. Layer on some of the shredded chicken. Add another wrapper to the stack. Top with some of the vegetables. Add the last wrapper to each stack. Top with the wasabi cream and additional fresh scallions if desired.

YIELD: 6 SERVINGS

CHAPTER 4

ROXANNE

There are sixty steps leading to Roxanne Chan's front door. They start at the side of an old garage stuffed with building materials on a curving residential street in the Bay Area. They quickly ascend the steep slope, almost like a ladder. My lungs immediately strain. I go into hiking mode, my eyes to the ground, ready to power up the hill just to get the climb over with. Then out of the corner of my eye I notice the bright silhouette of flowers and lift my face. I have left the standard suburban world behind and entered a secret garden of sorts. Chan and her husband have remade this narrow slice of hillside that is their front yard into a lush private park. As the path winds uphill, I pass mallow and monkey flower in bloom on the right. On the left I pass berry bushes caged in chicken wire and terraced beds crowded with weighty squash, cucumbers, and tomatoes. I pause by a swing tucked in a crook in the path, then push on to find a multitiered fountain. The water spills into progressively bigger ponds, one with shiny, plump, white and gold koi lolling, another with water lilies lazily adrift on top. Pots of bowed, top-heavy orchids line a patio.

I knock on a heavy wooden door, and Chan, in stocking feet, appears. She has pale skin and a crown of fine, tightly curled dark hair, almost like an Afro. She looks the least little bit Asian at a glance, but she's not. Chan is her married name. Her maiden name is Parmelee, an old French Huguenot family that made its way to Connecticut in the 1700s.

I've stopped by Chan's house in Albany, the next town up Interstate 80 from Berkeley, on a late September afternoon en route to Napa Valley for the Sutter Home's Build a Better Burger Contest. Chan had planned to go to the cookoff as a spectator with Barbara Morgan, but the attack on the World Trade Center made the outing seem too frivolous. She beckons me in, and we embark on a tour of her quiet home, starting with what I have specifically come to see: her kitchen. I want to see the room that has given birth to hundreds of winning recipes.

I step onto the darkly lit landing, a midpoint between two floors. I follow Chan, whose tall, lean form is outlined in light as we head to the sunny upstairs. The kitchen is immediately to our left. It is not especially big, nor does it have that faux restaurant feel with all the stainless steel fixtures, such as a brawny Viking stove, that have become de rigueur in contemporary designer kitchens. She doesn't even have that much working space on her worn wooden counters, and there is no island. She does have something I've rarely seen in a kitchen: a view.

Through a large, sunny square picture window over the sink I look east across the flats of Albany, the orange roofs tucked among the evergreens, to the soft outline of the Berkeley Hills. The view is that of a lookout tower, a peaceful vantage point from which to consider the world below and beyond. The panorama simultaneously calms and invigorates. It is the kind that gets the brain waves flowing. Here, Chan riffs and experiments, connecting the dots from, say, soy sauce to coffee to ribs, or pumpkin to fresh ginger to chunky peanut butter. As the cars zip along the city grid, the sun sets the terra-cotta-tiled roofs aglow, and the wind toys with the spiked cypress trees, she chops and mixes her way to the further reaches of American cuisine.

It is only fitting that Chan should create on high, given her lofty status in the world of contesting and her long list of prizes: 450 to date, including 15 grand prizes and 36 first prizes. The evidence is before me. There are three spiral-ring notebooks on a counter shelf. They are held together with tape and bulge with mementos—photos, ribbons, and clippings—of Chan's winnings. One wall of her kitchen is covered with framed awards, including her stove plaques from the '96 Bake-Off® contest and the '97 National Chicken and all of her 22 *Better Homes and Gardens* awards. This contest doesn't offer a lot of cash—$400 for first place—but has huge bragging rights among contesters.

"I used to win a couple of times a year," she says in her tight, slightly hoarse voice. "People were complaining that the same people were winning all the time. So now you're lucky to win once a year." She won this April with Spring Asparagus Slaw (slaw is one of her strong points), so she doesn't expect to win anything else from *Better Homes and Gardens* in 2001. That hasn't stopped her from trying, though.

≈≈≈≈

Contesters like Chan are a mixed blessing to cookoffs and recipe contests. Contest organizers agree that they produce some of the best recipes. They work like so many test kitchen cooks, putting in long hours developing recipes, carefully considering what the sponsor wants, and crafting innovative, trendy dishes with mass appeal. They don't screw up the entry forms like the newbies. At cookoffs they are accustomed to the pressure and so aren't nearly as inclined to snafus as the first-timers. "Those are good people to have in your cookoff," says Diane Kirkbride of the National Beef Cook-Off.

Richard Lobb at National Chicken also likes how they police the contests, not wasting a second to point out a copycat recipe or any breach of the rules. The problem is that contesters are too good. They do dominate contests. Contesters often account for one-quarter to a one-half of the finalists at some cookoffs. At Better Burger they have won seven of the ten grand prizes to date. "It has been a concern to us because we really want this [contest] to be accessible to anyone with a grill and a good idea," says Stan Hock of Sutter Home's Build a Better

Burger Contest. Patsy Wright, an organizer of a grill-off for Jacob's Creek Vineyard, says of contesters, "Their attitude is very different from regular folks who are so excited and tickled." The contesters at the grill-off, she says, "were taking it more seriously, way more seriously" than the first-timers, which took some of the fun out of the event. One contester complained to Wright that the winner was picked because she was attractive. On the flip side, one of the newcomers bragged that he never drank wine, just Coke. You'd never catch a contester making a PR faux pas like that.

Kirkbride says there's a concern at National Beef, which she doesn't share, that the contesters coming back year after year can make the cookoff a little stale. A cookoff, unlike a recipe contest, is essentially a media event. If the same people are at every Beef Cook-Off, the thinking goes, the press might lose interest, Kirkbride says. "This contest for a long time had no limit, but then you were seeing the same faces." Unseasoned contestants can also resent going up against what they see as professionals. I was at a cookoff with three finalists, two of them serious contesters. When the first-timer figured out who her competition was, I could see her kind of just give up.

In response, a number of cookoffs now limit how many times you can participate. Almost everybody who wins a grand prize cannot re-enter. That goes for nearly all recipe contests as well. The National Beef Cook-Off now has a three-times-and-you're-out rule. The same goes for the Pillsbury Bake-Off® contest. National Chicken excludes only the grand prize winner, which explains why the same man from the District of Columbia has gone to five contests in a row. Gilroy's Great Garlic Cook-Off is comparatively lenient by not banning their winners. Anyone who places can't enter for three years. Still, no one has won the Great Garlic Cook-Off more than once.

In the barbecue and chili worlds, where everyone is essentially cooking the same dish, there are no limitations on how many times you can win. The same people return to compete year after year, but defending champions regularly fall. For example, only two people have won the International Chili Championship cookoff, the bigger of the two national chili cookoffs held in Terlingua, Texas, each year, twice in its long history. No one has ever won it three times. Mike Mills and his team were the only three-time champions at the Memphis in May World Championship Barbecue Cooking Contest. There are likewise few if any restrictions on past winners entering cooking contests at state fairs, where reigning champions are celebrated.

The rules excluding past winners and finalists have inadvertently encouraged a long-standing but ethically questionable practice among contesters: using a front. Accomplished contesters clandestinely supply recipes to friends and family members to enter in a contest. Sometimes they do it to get around a contest that limits the number of entries. Mostly, though, they do it to compete in contests that they have "won out of." That way they can keep their hand in the competition, albeit secretly, and have a shot at attending the cookoff as their front's guest. "I can't do it, but I have friends who do it," Chan says. "Everyone has to live with their conscience."

Consequently, when the relatives of a top contester show up at cookoffs, there is often the suspicion that the recipes are not their own. This makes for grumbling about some contesting couples and families, such as the Bradley and DeSantis clans, both of which have had multi-generations compete. Barbara Morgan says that when her daughter got into the 2000 Bake-Off® contest, people thought she had supplied the winning recipe. Morgan says she couldn't give her daughter a recipe if she wanted to. "They don't know my kids," Morgan says. "Julie would be so insulted."

Suspicions are especially high when male relatives or the children and grandchildren of contesters make it to a national cookoff or score in a recipe contest. With the men this may be reverse sexism at work. People more readily accept that a daughter or a sister of a contester can cook well enough to make the grade than a husband or a son, especially if it is a baking contest.

Shirley DeSantis says her kids learned young that no recipe was set in stone. Though they might be dubious about the contest entries she served for dinner, they eagerly critiqued them and offered suggestions. All three grew up to be contesters. DeSantis has helped them with filling out the entry forms, primarily by putting their recipe into standard format and translating things like five packets of soy sauce into a measurable amount.

DeSantis was at a cookoff when she overheard two women comparing notes on what they had entered in their grandkids' names. She thinks they are the minority, but "how do you really know?"

The contests are well aware of fronts. At Sutter Home, head judge James McNair is wary of making a finalist out of a spouse or relative of a contester. Pillsbury excludes after three visits not only the contestant but the contestant's children, siblings, spouse, parents, and even roommates. In response, many contesters take a break from entering the Bake-Off® contest after they have gone twice to give their families a shot, either with their own recipes or with ones supplied by the contester.

There is some gray area here. The process of creating a recipe can be a very collaborative one, so much so that several people can claim authorship of a dish. Some contesters brainstorm with family members for ideas and then develop the recipes and hand them back. If the relative formulated the central concept, can't she lay claim to it even though she didn't don a kitchen apron?

If you enter a finished recipe in someone else's name, there is no gray area. You have broken the rules and perhaps even committed a criminal offense. Many contests require finalists to sign an affidavit saying that the recipe is original and their own. If it is not, the contestant perjures himself when he signs on the dotted line.

Chan does work on contests with her thirteen-year-old son, a computer whiz who already has his own repair business that he runs out of the family's small guest house. However, contests specifically for kids require parental involvement. Food companies don't want to be accused of encouraging kids to reach for the chef's knives solo. Chan has also worked with him on Pillsbury entries, which verges into the gray area. As one would expect, given his mentor, Tai-Tien has done well in the kid contest world even though school and his business don't allow for a lot of time tinkering in the kitchen with his mom. In 1999 he was one of ten finalists in the Southern Living/Piggly Wiggly Cook-Off for kids, which won him a $100 savings bond and a turn on the *Tonight Show* with Jay Leno.

~~~~

When I tell people about contesters, they assume they are all middle-aged midwestern house fraus in aprons churning out endless renditions of casseroles. When I mention that professional women and men, even a retired general, enter these contests, the response is a disbelieving "really?" There is some truth to the stereotype. Most of the contesters are in their forties or older. They are mostly white. They are mostly women. Many are homemakers, like Norita Solt who says, "Women's lib gave us a choice. I chose to stay home." I've found they are also confident if not outright type-A's. They have a penchant for using honey in savory dishes. They also often have mothers who were either bad cooks or absent from the kitchen. For example, Liz Barclay's father died when she was eight. Her mother went back to work, leaving the cooking to Barclay and her two sisters, five and three. "She'd fall asleep after work, and we'd wake her up and say, 'Pork chops on the table,'" Barclay says.

From there the stereotype begins to fall apart. There are house cleaners and gallery owners. There are Ph.D's and high school graduates. There are convenience cooks and gourmet cooks. Contesters can be found far and wide. If any state dominates, it is California, specifically the Bay Area, home to Kurt Wait, the first million-dollar winner in the Pillsbury Bake-Off® contest, and Priscilla Yee, a formidable contester with a long list of wins. Barbara Morgan and her daughter also call the Bay Area home. And there is, of course, Chan.

Chan is a transplant, but after more than thirty years on the West Coast, she thinks of herself as thoroughly Californian. She never looked back after leaving tiny Phelps in the Finger Lakes area of New York. She found small-town life smothering, and the Anglo-Saxon homogeneity of the region boring. When she decided to marry Bock, her family was aghast that he was Chinese. That only intensified her urge to get out, which the couple did.

Chan and I stand side by side in her living room, which feels like a roomy crow's nest. We look west to the endless sweep of the Pacific. A distant arc of red against the field of blue marks the Golden Gate Bridge. Then we bring our focus in closer, first to the deep forest, a state park that bumps up against their property, and then to her muse: her garden. Chan's garden, which surrounds the house and then sprawls down the hillside, is an endless source of inspiration for her cooking, providing bushels of produce to experiment with, such as the white raspberries she used in a torte and the kumquats, golden beets, and carrots she turned into a slaw.

We gaze down at the patch behind the house where she grows herbs and more unusual plants, such as Jerusalem artichoke, white Chinese chives, amaranth, and flowering quince. "I think I lost my saffron," Chan says, scanning the garden. There are scrubby winter pear trees. Chan poaches the fruit. She also has a pomegranate tree. She uses the rosy juice in marinades. There is a hedge of silvery pineapple guava, the perfumey egg-shaped fruit Chan mixes into fruit salads.

We continue the tour of her unusual house, which curls around the crest of the hill, the rooms spinning off a central axis like the chambers of a shell. She and her husband, an agricultural biochemist, designed the house and then built it with the help of architecture students from U.C. Berkeley in 1976. There are eight octagonal windows and a solarium festooned with Spanish moss and bromeliads. We arrive back at the chunky red wood dining room table that her husband made, and I grab a seat under an oversized Chinese fan unfurled against the wall.

She plucks a worn, stuffed manila envelope from her kitchen bookshelves, reaches inside, and pulls out a handful of white paper. She spreads the sheets on the table. Chan works on contests almost every day, serving her creations for dinner that night. This is her to-do file: copies of the rules of all the contests she is currently working on. There are six in all, from the Old Farmer's Almanac Recipe Contest ($100 grand prize) to Campbell's 20-Minute Recipe Challenge ($20,000 grand prize and your photo on a can of soup). She also pulls out a sheet for a brand-new cookoff sponsored by *Southern Living* that has caught her eye; it has a $100,000 prize, which makes it the second highest paying cookoff. She points out a couple of contests that she just finished. Chan likes to send her entries in long before the deadline to beat out anyone with similar ideas.

"I had a lot of good ideas for Rice-A-Roni," she says. "I had a harder time with Kikkoman. I thought about that for a week."

The unusual Kikkoman contest (grand prize of a trip for two to Japan) required that you come up with a recipe with a "signature sauce" that could then be used three additional ways. She had stewed on it as she walked down her sixty steps to the grocery store or when she was bent over in the garden tugging on leafy weeds. In the end she came up with a number of entries, which she sent in well before the August 31 deadline. One entry was Black Magic Ribs. Everything in the rib sauce was black: black coffee, molasses, black bean garlic sauce, soy, black pepper. She did add a hint of color: orange peel. This Black Magic Sauce could also be used in chili, to marinade Cornish hens and grill them, or tossed with soba noodles.

This is the level of creativity that has distinguished Chan, who has long been considered one of the most innovative contesters. *Sunset* magazine, which has published more than fifty of her recipes, has described Chan as "an artist in the kitchen." She has walked pasta carbonara through the garden, adding watercress and asparagus. She New England-ified a strata with dried cranberries, horseradish, and walnuts. She meditated on paella to come up with burgers of pork sausage, shrimp, and ground chicken flavored with saffron.

This gourmet edge, however, can work against Chan, because her dishes can strike judges as a touch too exotic. This may explain why she has made it to the Bake-Off® contest only once in her long career. Cookoffs have always stressed using readily available ingredients. In the '80s, when Chan began contesting, that was a much shorter list, one that her recipes often veered from. Now that American supermarkets bulge with the likes of chayote, hoisin sauce, and feta, contests are much more open-minded about ingredients. When couscous won the '98 Bake-Off® contest, that signaled open season on the ethnic food aisle.

The irony is now that American cooks have this cornucopia down at the corner A&P or Piggly Wiggly, many contests have become obsessed with time, pushing contestants to become efficiency experts. So Chan is once again at a disadvantage since "quick and easy" has become the mantra for many competitions. This has made for an emphasis on prepared foods, truncated ingredient lists, and little prep time, all of which run contrary to Chan's style of cooking. "Cooking takes time. If you do creative cooking, it takes more time."

The quintessential example is the National Beef Cook-Off, which now limits ingredients to six and cooking time to a slim half hour. Chan believes harsh restrictions such as these produce bad dishes. She points to the '99 National Beef winner, which used a can of tropical fruit cocktail, as a case in point. "Yuck," says Chan. "Fruit and beef. I don't know." Of the finalists' recipes for this year's Beef Cook-Off, Chan likes only two, including Janice Elder's Oriental Express Beef Lettuce Wraps, but of the eighteen others she says dismissively, "I'm sorry." When Gadsby won National Chicken last spring with his chicken cakes, Chan thought, "Oh, no. Chicken is going to go the way of Beef."

However, Chan is hardly disillusioned enough to quit contesting and even enters National Beef religiously. She'd throw in her kitchen towel only if she stopped winning, and there doesn't appear to be any threat of that in the near future. Besides, it's not just the cooking that has her hooked but the intellectual challenge of figuring out what sponsors want. She just wants to give them something that actually tastes good.

For the "Family Favorite in 30 Minutes" Roni Recipe Contest, it was obvious that Rice-A-Roni wanted a dish for the whole clan that would be—the dreaded phrase—quick and easy. Her answer was to crossbreed two kid favorites that adults find agreeable, pasta and pizza—thus, Pizza Style Pasta. She chose her qualifying product, a box of Pasta Roni Angel Hair Pasta with Parmesan Cheese. Then she made a sauce from a can of pizza sauce, sliced pepperoni, a jar of sliced mushrooms, a green pepper, sliced black olives, and shredded mozzarella. The entire prep and cook time was fifteen minutes. This may seem a tremendous waste of Chan's cooking talents, almost an affront, but the contest has hardly proved an insult to her intelligence. So far she has read this contest nearly perfectly. In the past two years Chan nailed a first place of $1,000 and then a grand prize of $5,000.

Having polished her entries for Rice-A-Roni, she's begun mulling Nestlé's Best Dressed Meals, with a grand prize of a trip for two to La Varenne cooking school in Burgundy, France. She walks to a kitchen counter and grabs a box. It's a Buitoni packaged focaccia mix, one of the qualifying ingredients. She's thinking of experimenting with it and serving the results for dinner, but it's already midafternoon. "I'm not sure I can pull it together."

She considers the box, turning it around in her hands while she thinks out loud about the contest. It requires a photo of the dish, a growing trend in recipe contests. "Ease of preparation is 35 percent," she says. "They say nothing about taste, so what it looks like in the picture and ease of preparation are the most important." She's thinking of some kind of layered torta. "It has to have color, maybe olives and roasted red peppers." She could make it on a cookie sheet or on a pizza stone, and then I hear her voice change slightly. The aha! moment arrives. "I could mold it into a muffin cup." She looks at me, and we both smile.

〰 〰 〰

Roxanne Chan's proudest win was second place and $5,000 at the 1999 National Chicken Cooking Contest with this unusual dish.

TEA-SMOKED CHICKEN WITH SESAME VEGETABLE RELISH

4 boneless, skinless chicken breast halves
1/4 cup raw rice
1/4 cup molasses
1/4 cup brown sugar
1/4 cup black tea leaves
1 stick cinnamon
1 tablespoon whole allspice
Vegetable Relish (recipe follows)
Sesame seeds

Line a wok or stockpot with foil. On top of the foil place the rice, molasses, brown sugar, tea leaves, cinnamon stick, and allspice. Stir gently.

Place a small rack over the mixture and arrange the chicken breasts on the rack. Cover and cook over medium heat for 10 minutes. Remove from the heat and let stand for 10 minutes. Slice the chicken. Place Vegetable Relish on a serving dish and arrange the chicken on top. Garnish with sesame seeds.

MAKES 4 SERVINGS

SESAME VEGETABLE RELISH

In medium bowl, mix together 2 tablespoons sesame oil, 2 tablespoons seasoned rice wine vinegar, 2 cloves crushed garlic, 2 teaspoons soy sauce, 1/2 teaspoon crushed red pepper, 1/2 teaspoon grated orange peel, 4 tablespoons finely diced water chestnuts, 4 tablespoons finely diced red bell pepper, 4 tablespoons finely diced carrot, 4 tablespoons finely diced celery, 2 tablespoons chopped cilantro, and 2 small green onions, minced.

CHAPTER 5

FEAR OF GRILLING

Women have a long, long history of cooking over fires. In fact, until last century that's the only way they had ever cooked since the first cavewoman roasted a sinewy chunk of woolly mammoth over a prehistoric blaze. But you wouldn't know it by the storm of fretting that even a pint-sized Weber Smoky Joe can set off in accomplished home cooks. A charcoal grill can bring out the titmouse in the most ardent of feminists, who are only too happy to revert to a traditional gender role and hand the rumbling, dusty bag of briquettes to their husband, father, son, boyfriend, or even the guy next door. This demureness is not entirely their fault. Since the invention of the backyard barbecue, women have been propagandized into believing that they aren't up to outdoor grilling. Take, for example, James Beard and Helen Evans writing in their 1955 book *The Complete Book of Outdoor Cookery:* "We believe that charcoal cookery is primarily a man's job and that a woman, if she's smart, will keep it that way." Still, our grandmothers and great-grandmothers, masters of dampers and keepers of daylong flames in the wood stove, would be aghast at our girliness over a charcoal grill.

The Sutter Home's Build a Better Burger Contest is a case in point. A woman didn't even take the grand prize until 1996, the sixth contest.

That is a total anomaly in the world of female-dominated cookoffs. In the 2001 contest there are eight contestants, only one of whom is a man, Richard Rizzio. He is one of the few contestants who did not feel compelled to practice building and keeping a fire going in a grill. Unlike most of the other contestants, he does not pinch his face tight, bite his lip, or wring his hands when discussing the g-word. But then, nothing much rankles Rizzio since he fought in the Battle of the Bulge. The two female contestants who are unfazed by the grill are both culinary-school-diploma-carrying personal chefs.

Everyone else has thought long and hard about grilling. Joyce Bowman, wanting to avoid a repeat performance of her '96 Better Burger when she couldn't get the fire to light, purchased a chimney and went to work on the grill in her backyard. After the World Trade Center attack, she drove to the Raleigh airport to ask if she'd be able to carry on her chimney. The answer was, luckily, yes.

Freewheeling Kristine Snyder in Kihei, Hawaii, was going to blow off practicing even though she hardly ever grilled over charcoal. In fact, she didn't even own a charcoal grill. Her husband, Dan, insisted she practice. He made her call around and find one to borrow, a tall order in Hawaii where they grill so much that they all use gas.

After many phone calls all Snyder turned up was a blackened hibachi that someone at church had. She practiced once with Dan coaching. He yelled at her the whole time, and the coals took forever to burn down, maybe because of the island's constant humidity. Without Dan she practiced a second time the night before she left. The coals burned down but never got hot enough, so the burgers languished.

Grilling brings out all Diane Sparrow's insecurities. The fact that Sutter Home is her third cookoff in just over six months does nothing to boost her confidence with charcoal. A few years ago she bought a Weber charcoal grill, what the Better Burger contest traditionally used, specifically to test recipes for the cookoff. Still, she has far from mastered it. She tapped her pal Ruth Kendrick, Dutch oven champ and female fire expert, for advice. Kendrick told Sparrow what she told Julie DeMateo the previous year: Try keeping a fire going all day. Sparrow took the advice to heart because DeMateo won the 2000 Better Burger.

Sparrow bought three hip-high bags of charcoal and went to work on her Osage patio. She lit the fire at around 9 A.M. and kept it going all day, adding charcoal as she went, keeping an eagle eye on two thermometers, and making sure the needles twittered around 400 degrees. Around 6 P.M., she declared the trial run a success.

Whatever self-confidence she built up that day was quickly undermined when she learned that Better Burger would not be using Weber grills. Sparrow emailed the contest organizer to ask what exactly it was using. The answer was Aussie Grills' Monaro, a hefty patio-worthy contraption that resembles a gas grill with nifty attached side tables. Sparrow pulled up photos of the stately Monaro on the Web and studied them. She searched in nearby stores for the real deal so she could study it in person, but no luck.

Sparrow arrived at the contestants' orientation late Friday afternoon to find an altogether different grill. Waiting for her was the Walkabout, a portable boxy number with an ashtray that adjusted up and down and a shallow fire pit. Then she drew the last position in the cookoff, a very bad spot by her estimation. She would turn in her burgers behind Bowman's chipotle-packed buffalo burgers, which Sparrow was sure would sear the judges' taste buds. Her heart sank.

No wonder she was thrilled to find herself sitting across from Allan Reitzer, president of Aussie Grills and Company, at the Friday night pre-cookoff dinner. Reitzer, a tall man with a tan and thinning blond hair, had been a popular man during cocktail hour as contestant after contestant cornered him and tried to work him for some insider information. He resisted, thinking it wasn't fair unless he gave tips to everyone.

However, he couldn't resist doling out some advice to Sparrow when she told him that she planned to cook her burgers five minutes per side. Reitzer countered that was way too long. Three to four minutes per side would be plenty, he announced. For Sparrow this was like manna from the gods—grilling advice from a man, and from the owner of the company, no less. She promptly abandoned her game plan, one based on weeks of careful practice.

What Reitzer didn't know and Sparrow forgot to mention is this—her burgers are unusually thick.

～～～

In the scheme of the national cookoff world, Better Burger is a relative baby. Yet from the get-go in 1990, with its sizable purse, $10,000, Better Burger made the contesters' short list of cookoffs to enter. In addition to the grand prize, the ten cookoff finalists win a weekend for two to Napa Valley at the height of the grape harvest. The vineyard wines and dines them at their private Victorian B&B Friday night and then gives them a wad of cash to go out on the town Saturday night. When the winery doubled the purse to $20,000 in 2000, the contest came within a hair of knocking National Chicken, with its $25,000 prize, out of the triple crown lineup.

Better Burger was started for the same reason that other cookoffs are created: to push a product. Only Sutter Home added a twist to the standard logic of promoting one product to sell another. They would push hamburger to sell wine. In fact, wine is not even a required ingredient.

In the early '90s wine still had a snooty reputation, a beverage for the well fed and well-heeled. Ads routinely showed fancy-schmancy people sipping chardonnay and the like in fancy-schmancy restaurants as they celebrated newly purchased vintage yachts and ate chateau this and that. The snob appeal wasn't helping a vineyard like Sutter Home, which mostly has produced easy-on-the-wallet wines sold in grocery store aisles, aisles that middle-class and blue-collar schmoes typically rolled their carts right past en route to the beer case.

Stan Hock, the winery's PR director, wanted to demystify wine, to show that you could drink it with the most ordinary of foods, to make it as humble and American as apple pie. Wine doesn't go with apple pie—well, moscato, maybe—but it does go with the all-American burger. They considered pizza, but it is not typically a summer food nor does it have the patriotic heft. "No matter how humble, the hamburger seems like an all-American symbol," says Hock.

Burgers had other advantages. First, burgers would tap into the summer grilling season, giving the vineyard an ad campaign for the warm weather months when sales typically droop. Second, teaming up with hamburgers would free Sutter Home store advertisements from the ghetto of the rarely traversed wine aisle. Advertisements for the contest could be put in the well-trod meat section. A burger cookoff it would be.

"It worked well from the outset," Hock says. "We went to grocery managers, offered a $10,000 prize, told them that if people see this, they are going to want to buy more ground beef, buns, and other stuff to experiment with. Managers said, 'Yeah.'"

Hock considers the cookoff "the number one retail wine promotion." Other vineyards, such as Turning Leaf and Jacob's Creek, have followed suit by holding their own occasional cookoffs, bolstering Hock's claim. As with most advertising campaigns, he has no hard numbers to prove it, but he points out that retailers love it. The vineyard has tried to back off the contest and even made it into a sweepstakes one year, but store owners begged them to leave well enough alone. "We think it's getting tired or old, but when our account people go in, store managers ask about it. In many ways we may be tired of it, but they aren't."

To Hock's thinking, he also helped revolutionize wine marketing with Better Burger. "Now wine is for every day," he says. "It's funny to see these ads, see people lounging around their house. Ten years ago you had to know the secret handshake to enjoy wine. It's all changed."

The only hitch the contest has run into has been in its home state. In California, essentially the nation's vineyard, residents are banned from entering the cookoff. No Californian can currently enter the cookoff in her backyard. That is why you will not see the likes of Roxanne Chan or Barbara Morgan or Priscilla Yee at Better Burger. You can blame it on beer.

In the late '90s, Anheuser-Busch ran a promotion, Buy the Beer, Get the Gear, which ran afoul of California's Department of Alcoholic Beverage Control. Every bottle of beer purchased earned you points, which, like Green Stamps of yesteryear, could be used to buy items such as glasses with Busch logos. The ABC calculated that one person would have to buy 270 beers a day during the promotion to get the ultimate piece of gear, a pool table. The department learned that fraternities were holding huge parties where enough beer would be consumed to earn the brothers a pool table.

The ABC, using a rarely enforced state law, took Busch to court. The law prohibits breweries from giving consumers anything worth more than 25 cents. For wineries, the limit is $1, distilleries $5. California won. Starting in 2000, Better Burger was closed to Californians, who had until then supplied half of the contest's entries.

There has been some effort to scrub the law, but it was undermined by—as Hock puts it delicately—"a certain large winery." That would be the E. J. Gallo Winery, the Goliath of wine producers worldwide. Gallo sells in excess of $1.4 billion worth of wine annually, according to the vineyard's website. "They don't want the regulation overturned," Hock says, "because they can do TV advertising. Smaller wineries with smaller ad budgets cannot afford national television campaigns. They rely on these kinds of promotions." The state legislature won't consider a change in the law until the wine companies are lined up neatly on one side or the other, Hock says.

≈≈≈≈

The other irony of the BBB is that in dumbing down wine, it ultimately transformed the burger into gourmet grub. There are few restraints. The time limit is three hours, a relative light-year for the fast-food sandwich. Patties can be made from ingredients other than beef. In fact, an all-beef burger hasn't won the grand prize since 1994 when Kurt Wait won the $10,000 for his Portobello Burgers.

These are not your father's burgers. Contestants empty the spice cabinet into the patties and top them with everything from jicama to watercress. Reading over the winning recipes you may find yourself reaching for your food dictionary to look up, say, ciliegines, which one grand prize winner tucked into ground veal and beef. Another stirred ginger juice into ground chicken. One of this year's recipes calls for tamarind paste.

James McNair, a prolific San Francisco author who pioneered the single-subject, one-word-title cookbooks, such as *Chicken* or *Pizza*, was recruited as a judge the first year. He had just published his 1990 *Grill*. He is also a shameless burger-phile, eating at least one a week. For the second contest he was made head judge and has remained such ever since. Better Burger has been a good gig for McNair. During his twelve-year reign he has published one cookbook on burgers, which included recipes from the contest, and produced *The Sutter Home Napa Valley Cookbook*, which included two contestants' recipes. He has also become the winery's food consultant, developing recipes, pairing food and wine, and talking to the press. On the personal front, McNair spent so much time in the sunny clime of Napa Valley that he opted to leave damp, windy San Francisco behind. He bought a bungalow in the quaint downtown of St. Helena. It has a swimming pool and a single floor, which makes life less painful for his arthritic German shepherd.

Most cookoffs use teams of people to weed through entries. In contrast, Better Burger's entire screening has become a two-man show in recent years. McNair and his longtime partner in business and life, the stylist and photographer Andrew Moore, screen some 1,500 submissions between them. Also, unlike other contests, people's names are not removed from entries, and each year McNair recognizes many of them.

The entries trickle in all summer, and then an avalanche arrives Labor Day weekend, the deadline. That leaves the two-man team just a few days to choose the finalists. They hole up at home and live on takeout while they weed. Knee-deep in recipes, McNair usually gets an acute craving and has to make a run to the local burger joint for his favorite, a patty topped with a huge deep-fried onion ring and filled with blue cheese, bacon, pickles, and barbecue sauce.

As many as half of the entries are disqualified right off the bat, many "because we insist that ingredients be listed in order of use," McNair says. "That even gets professional chefs." Then there are the people who use the wrong size of paper, forget to put their names on the recipe, or leave out the number of servings. McNair finds that men, although kings of the backyard barbecue, tend to flub entry forms. McNair also often weeds out anyone who doesn't include salt in the recipe or doesn't heat the bun. "That turns me off immediately."

The remaining recipes are then checked for originality as best as

McNair can. He mostly relies on his memory, which covers the contest history and easily detects the surprisingly numerous submissions that are variations on or sometimes even exact copies of past Better Burger grand prize winners. Out they go.

McNair, like every American, has strong personal preferences concerning burgers. He is an unabashed fan of the western style—burgers heaped high with relishes, sauces, sautéed vegetables, and what have you—over the plainer but easier-to-get-in-your-mouth eastern style. He tries not to let his burger biases influence him, but, hey, burger experts are human, too.

He and Moore narrow it down to about fifty, and then choose the ten winners, two from each of five different regions. They look for originality and good flavor. They also want to get a variety of recipes in each contest. During this process not one burger is thrown on the grill. They don't test the recipes, a big difference between Better Burger and most major cookoffs.

Even without cooking the burgers, McNair goes into each cookoff with an idea of who the grand prize winner will be. This go-around he was thinking that Claudia Shepardson, the contestant from New York, might be it with her Green Mountain Burger. He also says Snyder's Soy-Glazed Salmon Burgers and Sparrow's Fruit of the Vine Burger are in the running. He is right about half the time. The wiggle factor is execution. Over the years he has eaten a lot of burger blunders served up by flustered contestants. One year a burger arrived at the judges' table essentially uncooked. "A judge asked me, 'Do I have to eat this? It's bloody raw,'" McNair remembers. "Some people can write a good recipe, but they have trouble cooking it."

The odds are good that a contester will take the burger trophy again this year. Only three of the ten are total contest newcomers: Norma Molitor, a slight, redheaded Californian recently transplanted to Austin, Texas; Patty Honda Blezard, a culinary student from Honolulu; and L. Monique Porche-Smith, the young personal chef from Georgia and one of the very few black people I've seen at a cookoff. They are all amazed to learn that there is such a thing as a contester.

What they don't know is that the contesters are equally amazed by them. At the grip-and-greet Friday night in the parlor of the vineyard's Victorian inn, as the giddy contestants swap life details over glasses of merlot and chardonnay, the contesters learn of the newbies' professional cooking credentials. This is a shock, and I notice some of the contesters' faces freezing in pleasant smiles at the news. Most cookoffs and recipe contests exclude professional cooks, and the contesters assumed the same at Better Burger. Not so. This, as it turns out, will be a pro-am cookoff.

Given the cookoff's record, the contesters have nothing to worry about, though worry they do. Out of the last eleven contests, at least seven have been won by contesters. Looking over the lineup, I think chances are good for a repeat. Three of the five contesters, Sparrow, Bowman, and Rizzio, have had major wins and are all serious contenders for the $20,000. I don't think the fourth contester, Norma Fried, an elderly woman from Denver with ginger hair and transparent skin, has a prayer with her Pastrami Bagelburger. The fifth, Snyder, has a great-looking recipe, Soy-Glazed Salmon Burgers with Ginger-Lime Aioli.

Snyder is a wild card. She has the least experience of any of the contesters, having started entering national contests only two years ago. The tall blonde with the big personality has only one previous national win to her credit, a slot at the 2000 Bake-Off® contest where she won $2,000 for her Fiesta Shrimp Tacos with Cucumber Salsa. She cut herself six times with the brand-new knives, four of the cuts requiring bandages. Her stove was next to the youngest contestant, an eleven-year-old media magnet with floured cheeks and a messy ponytail. Snyder had to throw elbows to keep the press horde from crowding her out of her station.

There is kind of a classic American fairy tale quality to Snyder's recent life, a story in which two people move west, from Seattle nonetheless, and remake themselves. The couple married, and not long afterward Dan retired, selling his printing and graphics business. Snyder, who is seventeen years his junior, eventually left her job as a production manager in the sports garment industry and began studying the harp. She had played the instrument on and off her whole life but never could afford to buy one until marrying Dan. They went to Maui for what was supposed to be a year, to manage some apartments and windsurf. After a mere four months they decided to call Maui home and bought a fixer-upper.

Dan worked on the house and became a devoted windsurfer, hitting the blue waves every afternoon in Kihei despite knees that bow out from years of downhill skiing and running. Snyder began her new career as a harpist, a smart move when you live in the wedding capital of the world, host to twenty thousand nuptials annually. Before long Snyder was lugging her harp to the beach to play Pachelbel's *Canon* at wedding after wedding. Then she landed a regular gig plucking Beatles tunes and other pop standards at the Ritz Carlton's swank restaurant. She couldn't surf and play the harp on the same day because the water sport was murder on her hands, so the more she played the harp, the less she windsurfed. She didn't miss the bruises, cuts, and Portuguese man-of-war stings.

Snyder did miss her Seattle cooking club. Her nostalgia prompted her to enter her first cooking contest, the Maui Onion Contest. Her Maui Onion Wheels won the 1998 contest and the $100 grand prize. She won again the next year, the next year, and the year after that. She has won so often that she's not allowed to enter anymore.

For Sutter Home she created a kind of salmon cake on a bun with an Asian twist. Snyder seasoned the salmon burger with fresh mint, Asian hot chili sauce, lime juice, green onions, sour cream, and a garlic-ginger–flavored aioli. In her recipe she directs the cook to "sip a glass of Sutter Home Sauvignon Blanc" while making the soy glaze.

As flip as she is, Snyder admits the prize money would come in handy just now. The aftershock of the terrorist attacks in New York and Washington has shaken Maui's tourist industry. The Ritz Carlton has closed its restaurant. Snyder lost her regular gig, not to mention that twenty weddings were canceled. Besides, the cookoff is on her forty-first birthday.

〜〜〜

Joyce Bowman has been at contesting the longest, since the mid-'80s when she won a cake contest at the local shopping center. She has come on really strong in the past five years. She is no Edwina Gadsby or Janice Elder, but Bowman's record is more than respectable. In addition to her '96 showing at Better Burger, she has been once to National Chicken and twice to Pillsbury. She is due at her third National Beef next weekend. Like many contesters she downplays her wins and her prospects even though she came within a hair of winning a million dollars with her cooking prowess.

At the '96 Bake-Off® contest, the first time the contest prize ballooned to $1,000,000, Bowman won her category, bread, coffee cakes, and sweet rolls. That meant she was immediately $10,000 richer. Then she stood onstage with three other contestants as a cart with a shiny silver cover on top was rolled out. The cover was lifted, and all eyes fell on Kurt Wait's Macadamia Fudge Torte. Bowman didn't win enough to change her life, but the 10K bought her her first used '92 white Caddy. When she swapped that for another used Caddy, she kept the license plate. It reads PILSBURY.

Bowman is a veteran of 4-H competitions in her native Ohio. She studied home economics at Ohio State University, then taught until her two children were born. She has a head of thick brown hair and a beautiful smile. She has an easygoing, talkative manner—she tells funny stories about her husband's bad temper—unless, that is, she's in a cookoff. She hates having to talk to the press or spectators while competing because "they use up your time," she says. In fact, she has asked Sutter Home to keep the press, meaning me, away during the cookoff.

After researching five years' worth of finalist recipes, Bowman created Ranch Hand Grilled Buffalo Burgers with Chipotle 'n Honey Glazed and Corn 'n Avocado Salsa. Coming in at thirteen words, not counting the two countrified 'n's, the recipe has by far the longest title. Bowman got the idea for her buffalo burger when she noticed it in the meat case of her local grocery store. The butcher told her that buffalo has a much stronger flavor than beef and that she should use a fair amount of seasoning. She has thrown in two cloves of garlic, six tablespoons of fresh cilantro, two chipotle peppers, and one tablespoon of cumin. With all that, she reports happily, the buffalo tastes like hamburger.

Richard Rizzio has a very round bald head and moist eyes behind big glasses. At seventy-six his belly is big enough that his pants are belted dangerously low on his short frame. His voice is froggy. The $20,000 would make a big difference to him and his wife, Marie. They are, as Rizzio puts it, "not from an upper-income bracket."

The couple lived for twenty years in the tiny dell of Frankenmuth on Michigan's Upper Peninsula. Rizzio was a clothing salesman working on commission and selling to the mom-and-pop general stores. He crisscrossed the deeply wooded peninsula with a trunk full of sweatshirts, flannel shirts, and underwear. He didn't sell too many tank tops, as Marie says. She eventually joined him on the road after their kids grew up. "We were the only couple to have a coffee break in a different town every day," Marie says.

They tired of the long winters and heaps of snow. When Rizzio retired, they migrated south to relatively balmy Traverse City, Michigan. There he teamed up with his wife. Marie had been contesting and winning big for some time, and Rizzio decided "she shouldn't have all the fun." Rizzio quickly became a formidable presence on the cookoff scene. He went to National Beef. He won first place in the hors d'oeuvres category at the National Oyster Cook-off in Maryland. The way it works, they openly admit, is that Marie develops all the recipes. He is her tester and helps with suggestions, but the entries are primarily her creations. Some they enter in her name. Others they enter in his.

For Better Burger Marie created the veggie burger, based on eggplant sandwiches she ate after school as a kid. She practiced by cooking the patties on a skillet, and then when the entry form was sent in, it had Richard's name on it. "I was elected because she has never grilled," Rizzio says.

This is technically breaking the rules, but the Rizzios don't even try to hide it. "She went all through his ingredients at the orientation to make sure they were all there," Sparrow tells me.

Nothing gets past Sparrow, especially here at Better Burger. It took her five years to crack this contest. It had become her Holy Grail. "When I didn't get in the third year, I thought, 'What is wrong with these people?'" she says. For her fourth attempt Sparrow adopted a totally new approach. Rather than crafting recipes at the computer and sending them in without ever setting a foot in the kitchen, she thoroughly tested all her recipes. By the August 31 deadline she had sent in twelve recipes.

On the Saturday afternoon of Labor Day weekend, Sparrow found a message from the contest director on her answering machine. She didn't say why she was calling Sparrow, only that she'd call back. Sparrow stuck to the phone, refusing to leave the house for the rest of the weekend, which was blessed with sunny blue skies. She waited all day Sunday for the phone to ring and then again on Monday. Finally, Tuesday morning, the call came. Sparrow was a contestant. Her winning recipe was the Fruit of the Vine Burger, a combo beef-pork burger with feta, chopped grape leaves, and black grapes thrown in. Sparrow considered it her best. Sparrow, dumbstruck by her good luck, sat down and cried. Not only was she going, but she had a shot at winning.

Then Sutter Home posted the finalists' recipes on its website, and Sparrow started her customary precontest teeth-gnashing and self-doubt. The more she read over the recipes, the better they looked and the worse hers did. "I am very intimidated. They are all very creative recipes," she emailed me. "Jon is laughing at me. He is wondering what I thought—that mine would be good and all the other nine would be really bad? Well, I guess I could hope!"

When Sparrow gets nervous, she gets busy. She began testing ingredients. She tasted four kinds of sun-dried tomatoes and three kinds of tomato preserves. In the two weeks before the cookoff she made her Fruit of the Vine burgers at least ten times. "It was the charcoal that was worrying me. What if I seared them and moved them to the side, how would that work? It was timing, timing, timing."

On September 11, as the World Trade Center buildings came down in a fiery shower, all of Sparrow's practicing seemed for naught. The fate of Better Burger, scheduled for September 22, was uncertain. The following week there was no word about the contest's fate.

In the meantime, both Terry Ann Moore and Claudia Shepardson, accomplished contesters in the New York City area and friends of Sparrow, bowed out. Sparrow worried that the two were pressuring Sutter

Home to delay or, worse, cancel the cookoff, "which was appalling to me after trying to get in for four years," Sparrow says. Her suspicions were right on the money. "It was unclear whether we would continue," says McNair. "The two withdrew immediately and urged us not to have the contest."

Both Moore and Shepardson posted their decisions on the chat room of Cooking Contest Central. That set off a chain reaction. The standard cheerleadery "You go, girl" responses to Moore's and Shepardson's withdrawals became so enthusiastic that the next thing Sparrow knew, people were calling for the contest to be canceled and for Sutter Home to donate the money to the relief effort. Someone suggested that if enough contestants decided not to go, Sutter Home would have to bag the cookoff.

Sparrow felt that all eyes were on her. Nobody named her by name, but she felt the postings were directed at her, the only other Better Burger contestant who regularly participated in the chat room. Sparrow waited for someone to come to her defense. Nobody countered the suggestions to cancel the cookoff. The Web discussion brought home how high-schooly and how cliquey the group could be. Sparrow felt that she was choosing whether to be in or out.

Late that afternoon Sparrow rose to her own defense, posting an eloquent, even patriotic, explanation of her decision. It read in part, "We must support those who need more time to heal, but we also must not let any more victory go to our attackers." That same day Sutter Home echoed Sparrow's thoughts and declared that the cookoff would go on. Bin Laden or no, the grills would be lit. "We thought we were celebrating an American original, and it was our patriotic duty to do it," McNair says.

〜〜〜〜

The morning of the cookoff, Sparrow beat everyone to breakfast by a good half hour. I find her at 7:30 A.M. parked by a window in the Sutter Home Victorian's solarium with a plateful of fresh fruit and a few slices of the inn's freshly baked English muffin bread. "You have to try this," she says, waving a piece of the toasted, buttered bread, the morning

slants of sun glinting off her onyx ring. The hardwood floors glow
honey. White linen lies crisply on the tables. As I head into the dining
room, where I find a voluminous breakfast spread, I can hear the bub-
bling voices of the cooks in the kitchen. Everything is so beautiful and
peaceful, I'm having trouble waking up.

This 1884 Victorian, surrounded by stately palms, gardens that recall
Provence, and a formidable fence that is locked at night, is a big part of
the prize for the contestants. A bottle of wine can be had any time of
the day for the asking. The guest rooms are ample and filled with turn-
of-the-century antiques. An ungodly line of cars drones by just outside
the gate, but whatever window you look out, there are pattering foun-
tains, roses in full bloom, vine-covered pergolas, and the gentle profile
of the Sierra foothills.

This little paradise is lost on Sparrow just now. She did not come to
Napa Valley for a vacation but to pull down the $20,000 and Better
Burger bragging rights. She is not smiling very much. She doesn't exactly look nervous but more edgy. "I've been thinking of the advantages
[of going last], and I've worked it out in my mind," Sparrow says as she
stabs a piece of melon. "As Norma Fried pointed out, they remember
the last one."

When the Rizzios, who seem to always move through the world side
by side like Siamese twins, tentatively wander into the quiet solarium
from an outside door, Sparrow manages a smile and calls, "Good
morning." There is something about the Rizzios' age and frailty that
makes everyone half-yell at them and overenunciate, although neither
has seemed hard of hearing. "Why don't you come start my charcoal?"
Sparrow jokes to Richard.

"I don't think they'll allow that," says Rizzio, who quickly backs out
of the room, Marie by his side, toward the breakfast buffet.

"I'm kidding," Sparrow calls after him and shakes her head.

After a few minutes the Rizzios, plates in hands, quietly settle at a
table at the other end of the room from Sparrow. Bowman breezes into
the room, smiling, easygoing, offering a round of hellos, and trailed by
her aunt and cousin, two bespectacled women with amused smiles al-

ways on their faces. Rizzio asks Bowman about National Beef, where she'll compete next week. She loudly ticks off a list of contesters who will be there, ending with Bob Gadsby.

"Gadsby?" Richard croaks.

"He won National Chicken," Bowman says, raising her voice a notch. "You know, he used a roasted chicken."

"Oh, he used the roasted chicken," Rizzio says with just a hint of derision, and he and Marie nod their heads together knowingly.

Bowman and her relatives settle at a table between Rizzio and Sparrow. Just as she is about to sit down, she overhears me mention my visit with Roxanne Chan to Sparrow. Bowman freezes. "Roxanne Chan," she interrupts, her voice racing and panic rushing over her face. "Is she going to National Beef?"

I assure her no, and Bowman, obviously relieved, settles in for breakfast. We all eat and chat quietly at our individual tables. The rest of the contestants slowly filter in, the two from Hawaii showing up last. Patti Honda Blezard, her thick, dark hair ruffled, her laugh low and throaty, seems as if she's suffering from the excesses of last night's rich meal and free-flowing wine. She and Snyder complain loudly about the time change from Hawaii. "My husband woke me up, and I said I just fell asleep," Blezard says.

"In the middle of the night I remembered we need to recalculate the recipes," Snyder says. "Why didn't I examine the grill better? I don't know how the top comes off."

"I was thinking that, too," Blezard says.

While the Hawaiians sip coffee, they grow more animated, cracking each other up, voices rising in girly trills. The older contestants quietly clear their breakfast plates and head to their respective rooms for their last preparations for the cookoff. Sparrow, the first to leave the breakfast room, has to organize a roller suitcase filled with kitchen gadgets and ingredients she brought from home, including her own tomato preserves.

Accordingly, this older group shows up first in front of the inn where a white van is due at 8:45 A.M. to take them to the vineyard. Eventually, all the contestants are in the van but one, Snyder, who has vanished. While everyone chats politely, they keep eyeing their wristwatches and looking at the inn's front door. Just as they are about to leave without Snyder, the blonde comes galloping down the front walk. She had lost track of time, she explains.

At the ranch, the plush lawn is set up as if for a fancy outdoor wedding. Eight white canopies that rise in a fanciful peak have been set in a neat rectangle. There's a cook station under each tent, each complete with white-tableclothed work table, a bench-sized cooler, and the dreaded grill. At one end of the rectangle is a much wider canopy and a long table. This is where the judges are due at noon, when Rizzio will turn in the first burger. Near this table sits a large clock on an easel. Just now everyone feels as if they have all the time in the world, but the second hand already sweeps around the clock at a maddening pace.

The contestants scatter to their various tents and examine the tools laid out as if for surgery. There is a shiny chafing dish, a kitchen knife, cutting boards, and pitcher of water. "Are you kidding? What do we do with these?" Snyder says, picking up a large pair of tongs and working them like a lobster claw. Molitor looks blankly at her reflection in a mammoth stainless steel bowl. "I've never used a bowl this big," she says.

The younger contestants are clumped together at the far end of the rectangle where they hoot, cackle, and generally make a lot of noise. The three older women, Sparrow, Bowman, and Fried, make up the silent side of the rectangle. Off to a corner, Rizzio, who seems to have no natural allies in this group, is a tented island unto himself.

Cardboard boxes of ingredients are delivered to each station. Sparrow gets her box and some bad news. There are no black grapes, which her recipe calls for, in the local markets. Instead they've gotten her champagne grapes and bigger red grapes. Sparrow tastes a champagne grape and considers it closely. The flavor is good, but the size is a problem. They are too big to go in as is. "I'll try to cut them," she says.

Everyone ties on a white Sutter Home apron and gets to work prepping, and pretty soon the thonk, thonk, thonk of bad knife technique fills the air. A three-man crew from the Food Network wanders from tent to tent. As per Bowman's request, I can't talk to the contestants while they are working. I plop down in a chair next to Marie Rizzio, who sits in the sun, feet propped up on a chair, reading a fat novel. She has a scarf around her neck, jauntily knotted to one side. Her thin, frizzy black hair sticks out from underneath her white ball cap. The only spouse on the scene just yet, she has sat within earshot of Richard so she can get him a coffee if he wants one.

At seventy-six, Marie is an anomaly of her generation, a talented cook who always worked from scratch. She chalks it up to her Italian-American parents. Like a lot of immigrant children, she grew up in a parallel food universe. While other mothers stirred up Jell-O salads, her mother made her own pasta and bread. Her father bought fresh fish every Friday at Navy Pier in Chicago. They'd put the blue crabs in the bathtub where Marie could play with them until they were due in the kitchen. "When you grow up in this environment, you can expect to cook this way," Marie says.

Like many women of her time, Marie was a housewife. She was a touch ambivalent about her domestic role except in the kitchen. "You shouldn't say you are *just* a homemaker but that's how you feel sometimes," she says. "You need something extra. This was my way of getting approval. Being a good cook is a good portion of my personality."

She began entering contests in the early '90s. Since then she has won eight trips, including one to Sicily, home to both Richard's and Marie's grandparents. They've also been to France, England, and Mexico. They bought new furniture and carpeting with her prize money. When she hit the jackpot with the grand prize at National Chicken in 1999, she used the $25,000 to buy a beige Buick Century. Most, if not all, of this would have been otherwise impossible for the two retirees.

"Did she tell you what happened this summer?" Richard calls from his tent. "Scared me to death."

This past March, Marie was laid flat by a severe muscle inflammation that left her limp with fatigue. At one point she couldn't even pick up her head. Rizzio feared the worst. She was put on a whopping dose of the new cure-all, prednisone. All her hair fell out. She improved slowly during the summer. Sutter Home was the first contest she worked on since getting ill. This trip marks the fact that life is getting back to normal for the Rizzios.

After September 11 they never considered not coming to the cookoff, not even after the two other contestants dropped out. In fact, it occurred to her husband, Marie says, that that only improved his odds of winning. "I hate to say it, but he was delighted," Marie says.

I look over at Rizzio, who is the first to start his fire. His thick glasses sliding down his nose, he cuts his eggplant into thick slabs and brushes them with olive oil. He'll grill them, then chop them up to make up the veggie burgers. Everyone else is still prepping. Sparrow splays little champagne grapes with a huge kitchen knife. Bowman goes at a neat pile of scallions.

Snyder trims fat from a slab of rosy salmon as about two dozen sweat bees buzz her. "These bees," she says, shaking her head and ponytail to shoo them off. "Garnish done," Norma Molitor announces to herself.

Porsche-Smith, the personal chef from the Atlanta area, has morphed into a kind of a friendly motor-mouth, chopping and calling out to different contestants: "How you doin'?" If this was a poker game, you'd think Porsche-Smith was bluffing. She has even dressed in chef's whites, as has Blezard. She magnanimously calls out to see if anyone needs help, as if she has already tied up the grand prize. Bowman, now quiet and intense, unlike her breakfast self, is the current focus of her gregariousness. "I spent every summer in North Carolina growing up," Porsche-Smith bellows. Bowman doesn't answer.

Rizzio lays his eggplant on his grill, at last something actually cooking that the Food Network can shoot. The three-man crew moves in. They've put a mike on his belt, and the weight almost pulls Rizzio's pants off. As I watch the crew interview Rizzio, I notice Snyder wildly swinging a cutting board at the bees. Then Rizzio explodes, "Oh, my God." He turns on his heel and rushes to the grill. His eggplant is burning. The crew retreats sheepishly, and Rizzio rescues the charred vegetables.

"Almost ready to roll," Molitor calls. "Sorry, I talk to myself," she says, turning to Rizzio.

"Just as long as you don't answer yourself," he says.

"Whooooop," Snyder yells from the other end as a large cucumber flies out of her hand and skitters across the lawn. She scoops it up and rubs it off on her apron.

I run into Snyder's husband, Dan, who has been staying out of harm's way, roaming the grounds or lounging at a table. He is a lean man with a short, blunt bowl cut and a crooked leg. He talks about his wife as if she is an overgrown teenager. He does this with great affection. "Every time she leaves the house . . ." he says and crosses himself.

By 11 A.M. everyone except Bowman and Sparrow has gotten a chimney of charcoal going without a hitch despite all the earlier worrying. Sparrow is in such good shape prepwise that she takes a break and goes from tent to tent snapping everyone's picture. When Sparrow stops at Snyder's station, Snyder looks up from her cutting board, bees hovering near her face and her mouth open incredulously. "Are you done?"

This is the first year the cookoff is a public event, with a burger buffet and a funk band up from San Francisco. A few attendees in sundresses and khaki shorts have begun to trickle in. The band begins its sound check, and a black man in a beret says over the mike loudly, "I want some collard greens, some eggs and bacon, a hamburger, and sweet potato pie."

"Yeah," calls out Porche-Smith.

In the last hour of the contest almost all the contestants start to fall behind. Everyone stops talking. The bees are now in every station, dogging the contestants as they bend over their workstations. The man doing the sound check repeats "hey, hey, hey, hey, hey" over the microphone, then starts making popping noises. One of Rizzio's burgers falls through the grill, and as he tries to rescue it, he comes close to burning the others. He's so undone that his spatula hand shakes.

"Thump, thump, thump, thump"—the sound check guy is now at the drums.

"Do they have to do that to us?" Bowman says, looking up for one split second as she molds patties.

Spectators toting glasses of blond Chablis amble into the cooking area, pausing by cooking stations to ask questions. This is not the way it's supposed to work, and contestants, faces drawn, force smiles and polite responses as they rush from grill to work table to cooler. Finally, a Sutter Home worker shoos the spectators away. The Food Network crew prays for the unending sound check to end. They can't shoot while the guy continues to babble into the mike. "Hello, hello, hello," he repeats while the threesome grimaces.

I can't take the sound check myself, so I go in hunt of the judges. McNair, a hamburger hat worn beret-style on his head, has convened them in a nearby building. With the exception of McNair, they are all area restaurant chefs and owners, all men except for Cindy Pawclyn, the star chef of Mustards Grill down the road in Napa. McNair steps over to me and whispers that he has one judge who can't eat the Bayou Burger because he is allergic to shellfish, and another who can't eat the salmon burger because he can't eat fin fish. "I've never heard of that," McNair says.

McNair has them start to judge the recipes for originality by reading them. No discussion is allowed at this point. They slouch in chairs, pens in hand, and read away. It's as quiet as a college exam. Outside, the sound check has devolved into drum pounding. "It's the count-down," McNair cracks.

Just shy of noon the judges head out to the lawn, to a long table where three big bowls of watermelon chunks await them. They sit down Last Supper–style, with everyone facing the contestants. Every five minutes a contestant will turn in five burgers cut in half so the judges can bite from the middle. "Hey, hey, hey, yeah, yeah, hello, hello," the sound check guy persists as Rizzio hands in his eggplant burgers and the discriminating munching begins.

I walk from station to station as the clock ticks off each contestant's final five minutes. Molitor, next up, already has her burgers assembled and in the chafing dish. She is right on time and coolly delivers her burgers to the judges. As she walks away, though, she notices them struggling to pull the halves apart. "Did I cut them? Should I cut them?" she calls out, rushing back to the judges' table.

Blezard, next up, struggles with a cranky squirt bottle as the funk band takes the stage and blasts into "You didn't have to love me like you did, but you did, and I thank you." It clogs on every other squirt, so she has to keep clearing it with a toothpick. When 12:10 comes, she is still squirting and toothpicking, squirting and toothpicking. Her burgers arrive a few minutes late.

"Do I get extra time? She was late?" Snyder, next in line, calls out. No one answers her.

At most cookoffs the judging goes on behind closed doors, and just now that seems like a pretty good idea if only because it is not a pretty sight. As the judges chew, toppings squirt out of their burgers. They have to open wide, exposing crooked teeth and pink tongues, to get the thick burgers into their mouths. They have sunflower seeds on their lips. Viscous toppings catch in the corner of their mouths. And they are grimly unexpressive and untalkative, like the taciturn Danes at the table in *Babette's Feast*.

Snyder race-walks her burgers to the judges at 12:15, followed by the likewise prompt Porche-Smith at 12:20. Then 12:30 comes and goes as Norma Fried hacks at her Pastrami Bagelburgers. Fried leans all her weight onto her quivering knife arm while trying to hold a burger and bagel together with one hand. I look away expecting imminent carnage. At last she splits all five, and then makes her way to the judges' table at 12:35. Pawclyn takes one bite of the Pastrami Bagelburger, snickers, sets it down, and begins scoring as Fried walks back to her station.

Bowman, who was easily ready to go at 12:30, cools her heels until given the high sign, then heads to the judges' table. That leaves Sparrow, who I'm surprised to find red-faced and tight-lipped, hovering over her grill. Gone is the relaxed picture-snapping demeanor of just a little over an hour ago. *Why* is apparent. Her fire is white and ashy. The two-inch-thick burgers are a flaccid brown. They aren't cooking the way Reitzer said they would. Sparrow lowers the grill to get the burgers to sear.

The band cranks up "Uptight (Everything's Alright)," as Sparrow hovers over her grill. She stabs a meat thermometer into one plump burger, removes it, reads the numbers, and shakes her head. She flips one, and it starts to come apart, springing a leak of bloody juice. She soldiers on, turning each burger delicately. The patties hardly have grill marks.

The judges are finished with Bowman's burgers and now wait for Sparrow. They stare at her. She sighs and spatulas a burger off. One by one she carries them to the table and lays them on slightly burned slices of crusty bread. Her hands fly. She spoons relish onto each burger and tops them with a slice of bread. A digital timer bleats by the grill. She doesn't pause to turn it off. A burger tumbles as she slices it. She hastily sets it aright. She scoops up the plate and strides to the stage. She musters a broad grin when she reaches the judges' table and then quickly beats a retreat to her tent, where she wordlessly dives into cleaning up.

Sparrow's burger halves are divvied up among the judges. They pause to examine them. A judge with small glasses screws up his face. The judges nibble delicately at the end of their burgers, jot a few notes, stand in unison, and leave the cookoff grounds to add up their scoring.

In her station Sparrow fumes: "Drawing last place is the kiss of death. I thought I was in control being last with nobody right behind me. This is not my excuse, but Allan of Aussie Grills told me to cook them three minutes per side."

There is little time for post-cookoff analysis yet. The contestants have to make their burgers again, this time for the People's Choice Awards. They're due to start turning burgers in to a panel of spectators at 1 P.M. This round is far less eventful because no one seems nearly as worked up—some of the contestants even crack a bottle of wine and start sipping. Maybe it's because the People's Choice goes for a mere $5,000, as opposed to the $20,000 grand prize. Sparrow puts her burgers on much earlier and doesn't have a doubt they are done when she turns them in. The only hitch is the large clock falling off the easel and breaking not long after the contestants start to deliver their burgers, but no one seems to notice.

The winners will be announced in two hours. Most of the contestants melt into the crowd. I find Sparrow at her cooking station, drinking wine and cackling with Snyder. They complain about the professional chefs in the contest. Sparrow is sure Porsche-Smith and her Bayou Burger have tied it up. I notice Rizzio wandering by, holding Marie's purse and looking lost and forlorn by himself. Whenever Sparrow beats herself up because of her performance today, her smile fades. Snyder counters with a torrent of praise. "I worship you," she says at one point. "I want to learn from you."

Meandering through the crowd, I come upon McNair. He won't say who won but hints at a few who didn't. Rizzio's burger had great flavor, but McNair declared the texture "mush." Bowman's buffalo burger had far too much cumin in it. Likewise, the Pastrami Bagelburger was way overspiced with its tablespoon of pastrami seasoning. It tasted like too much salt, McNair says. The burger was also overcooked. It never had much of a chance, though, because none of the chefs thought a bagel would work as a bun. And there was one burger that was "uncooked." I guess Sparrow's, and McNair nods. That narrows it down considerably.

It doesn't take much more meandering and chatting before another judge leaks to me who won. I had guessed right. It's Snyder. When McNair sings out her name, Snyder's eyes go as wide as a little girl's and her mouth slackens. Sparrow gives her a hearty victory hug. Her husband turns to me and says with a big smile, "Now she's going to be impossible."

A few days later on the phone, Sparrow reports that she was totally shocked by Snyder's win. "It was not the most gourmet," she says, then theorizes that it's the second year in a row the contest has gone for a fish burger. "It was refreshing, probably like a palette cleanser," Sparrow says. "Being in the middle helped, too."

Sparrow tells me that her son is convinced the grill was put together wrong, which caused the ash to build up and cool her fire. "That guy with the Aussie Grills company has never grilled before, and if he has, it was on the finest gas grill," she says. "I should never have listened to him. If I ever got to go back, I'd make a much thinner burger," she adds. "If it's really thin, they can throw anything at you."

〜〜〜〜

Kristine Snyder took the $20,000 grand prize at the 2001 Sutter Home's Build a Better Burger Contest with her Asian-inspired fish burgers.

SOY-GLAZED SALMON BURGERS WITH GINGER-LIME AIOLI

AIOLI

1/2 cup reduced-calorie or regular mayonnaise

2 tablespoons sour cream

2 cloves garlic, minced

2 teaspoons minced fresh ginger

1 tablespoon fresh lime juice

1/4 teaspoon salt

SOY GLAZE

1/3 cup low-sodium soy sauce

3 tablespoons honey

1 tablespoon rice vinegar

1 tablespoon cornstarch

1 tablespoon plus 1 glass chilled Sutter Home Sauvignon Blanc

BURGERS

1 egg

2 tablespoons aioli

2 tablespoons sour cream

1 tablespoon fresh lime juice

1 teaspoon Asian hot chili sauce or bottled hot sauce

1 1/4 pounds skinless salmon fillets, finely chopped

2 green onions, thinly sliced

2 tablespoons chopped fresh mint leaves

2/3 cup bread crumbs

1 teaspoon salt

Vegetable oil

4 sesame buns, split

1/2 cucumber, peeled, seeded, and julienned

Radish or soybean sprouts for garnish (optional)

Prepare a grill with a medium fire for direct-heat cooking.

In a small bowl, combine the aioli ingredients. Reserve 2 tablespoons for the burgers and chill the remainder until serving time.

To make the soy glaze: Combine the soy sauce, honey, and rice vinegar in a small, heavy saucepan. Mix the cornstarch and 1 tablespoon wine in a small bowl until smooth and add to the soy mixture. Place on the grill and stir the mixture until the glaze boils and thickens slightly, about 3 minutes. Meanwhile, sip a glass of Sutter Home Sauvignon Blanc, saving the remainder for sipping while you grill. Set the glaze aside.

To make the burgers: In a large bowl, whisk together the egg, aioli, sour cream, lime juice, and chili sauce. Stir in the salmon, onions, mint leaves, bread crumbs, and salt, and combine. Coat your hands with vegetable oil and form 4 patties. Brush the grill with vegetable oil and grill the patties until browned on the bottom, about 3 minutes. Recommence sipping Sutter Home Sauvignon Blanc. Turn the patties and brush the cooked side with soy glaze. Cook for 3 minutes, turn, and brush the other side with glaze. Grill just until done, about 4–6 minutes, turning and brushing with glaze frequently.

During the last few minutes of cooking, toast the buns, cut side down, on the outside of the grill. Place the cucumber strips on the bottom half of each bun, top with a burger, aioli, and a bun top. Garnish with sprouts if desired.

SERVES 4

Head judge James McNair had picked this entry by Diane Sparrow to win the 2001 Sutter Home's Build a Better Burger Contest. That was before she had all kinds of trouble keeping her grill hot enough.

FRUIT OF THE VINE BURGERS
WITH CALIFORNIA RELISH

CALIFORNIA RELISH

1/2 cup California Golden Raisins (approximately 2 ounces)

2 tablespoons Sutter Home California Zinfandel wine

2 tablespoons grapeseed oil

1/4 cup sun-dried tomatoes packed in oil (approximately 1 ounce)

1/2 small red onion, cut in chunks

1 teaspoon kosher salt

2 small chipotle peppers in adobo sauce

3 tablespoons tomato preserves

BURGERS

12 ounces lean ground beef

12 ounces lean ground pork

8 grape leaves packed in vinegar brine (approximately 1 ounce)

2/3 cup chopped black grapes (approximately 4 ounces)

1/4 cup Sutter Home California Zinfandel wine

1 teaspoon kosher salt

1 teaspoon crushed dry green peppercorns

2 ounces feta cheese, crumbled

1 (1-pound) loaf country-style bread, preferably roasted garlic or herb
    flavor

1 small bunch crisp lettuce leaves

4–8 grape leaves packed in vinegar brine

Additional grape leaves and black grapes for garnish (optional)

Prepare a grill for moderate direct-heat cooking.

Place the California Relish ingredients in a small food processor and pulse until the relish is coarsely chopped. Remove and place in the refrigerator until ready to serve.

To make the burgers: Place the beef and pork in a mixing bowl. Remove the tough stems from the grape leaves, roll up, and cut into julienned strips. Add to the bowl. Add the grapes, wine, salt, crushed pepper, and cheese. Mix lightly and form into 4 oval patties.

Lightly oil the grill grates. Place the prepared meat patties on the grill over the hot coals. Grill for approximately 5 minutes per side, or until desired doneness is reached. While the burgers are cooking, cut the bread into 1/2-inch slices. When the burgers are almost finished, place the bread on the grill to lightly toast both sides. Place a piece of grilled bread on each plate and top with some of the lettuce. Place a burger on the lettuce and top the burger with 1 or 2 grape leaves. Spoon on a generous amount of California Relish. Top with a second piece of grilled bread. Place on grape-leaf-lined plates and garnish with bunches of black grapes if desired.

SERVES 4

CHAPTER 6

NATIONAL BEEF

Going into the 2001 National Beef Cook-Off, most bets were on big Bob Gadsby to pull down the $50,000 grand prize. The Rooster had ruled at National Chicken, and the hens feared the same at Beef. And he was back at the prepared foods, using both precooked beef and ready-to-eat mashed potatoes in his Steakhouse Beef Wraps. Even if his recipe smacked of a midnight refrigerator raid of leftovers—mashed potatoes rolled in a tortilla—Gadsby had the aura of a winner. Contesters believe in lucky streaks. Sure, you have to research the trends and analyze the contest, but when the dish goes to the judges, it's still a roll of the dice. You are either on or off, and Gadbsy was on, or so it seemed. The day of the cookoff, September 29, was even on his fiftieth birthday. When word spread that he might not make it to the Beef cookoff in Tucson, a collective sigh of relief was exhaled in kitchens across the country as everyone's chances temporarily improved.

Gadsby did ask the organizers of the cookoff to cancel it, thinking the event was inappropriate so close to the terrorist attack. In addition, his request for leave to attend the contest in late September had been denied by U.S. Customs honchos in the wake of the World Trade Center and Pentagon attacks. Border stations were put on high alert, and that meant not a person could be spared, including Gadsby.

Gadsby oversees Montana's twelve small airports, where planes now had to be meticulously searched just in case an Arab terrorist had tucked some plastic explosives among the cargo. Gadsby was working twelve-hour days, seven days a week. It was a "knee-jerk federal reaction to make the public feel safe," according to Gadsby. A few days before the contest Gadsby got the go-ahead from his higher-ups to take a four-day weekend and compete for the fifty grand. Even though he still thought the cookoff should be canceled, Gadsby booked a 6:20 A.M. flight. On such short notice and with such long workdays, he had no time to practice making his wraps. This, Edwina told me a few days before the contest, was making "Mr. Calm" nervous.

National Beef is a big deal. With a grand prize of $50,000 and a half-dozen $10,000 awards, it is the second-highest-paying biennial contest after Pillsbury's. It has also evolved into the toughest cookoff. It is the 100-meter dash of cookoffs. Contestants have exactly thirty minutes to make their dish, and they are closely timed. They get to make their dish only once. If they burn it or drop it, tough luck.

At the comparatively leisurely Bake-Off® competition, contestants have five hours to make their dish three times, leaving plenty of time to visit with each other, pose for the television cameras, and deliberate which of their three attempts to send to the judges. At Beef there is not even time to go to the bathroom. Contestants rush back and forth between a stove, microwave, and prep table like rookie short-order cooks. Stories are legion of flustered contestants giving up and tearfully chucking whole roasts into the trash can.

Beef is also one of the oldest contests. It was begun in 1974 by what was then called the American National Cowbelles, a group of ranchers' wives. The first cookoff was held in a Denver high school and had a grand prize of $800, chump change compared to Pillsbury's then prize of $25,000 but enough money to catch the interest of some cooks. Thirteen cooks from twelve states competed in the school's auditorium. The first winner was a man, Howard Camden of Michigan, who made Roast-Style Brisket of Beef.

By the late '70s beef sales were beginning to take a licking. Consumption had risen steadily after World War II, thanks in part to the backyard barbecue and the fast-food industry. Beef sales peaked in 1976. Then Americans began to lose their ravenous appetite for beef as health advocates blamed T-bones and burgers for clogging arteries with slippery globs of fat. Enviromentalists turned on the cow, once thought a docile and lovely creature, and recast it as a ravager of the land with its high-methane manure and wanton grazing.

Beef needed some good PR. In 1979 the Beef Industry Council joined forces with the cowbelles, injecting enough cash to increase the number of contestants to fifty and raise the grand prize to a respectable $1,500. What was mostly a western and midwestern event became a truly national cookoff. The food media took notice. Each state held its own qualifying round, and the winner went on to the national contest in Omaha. At the national, contestants had four hours to prepare their dishes, which had to use two to four pounds of beef.

That year Julia Child was recruited as one of six judges. It was her first turn as a judge for a national contest. She scribbled on her comment sheet of one entry "dismal look with coagulated sauce,"of another "slightly boxy taste but quite good." The team of judges selected Fiesta Crepes en Casserole, a Tex-Mex version of the French standard. Lavelle Breland of Mississippi made cornmeal crepes and then stuffed them with ground beef, cream-style corn, tomato sauce, and an envelope of taco seasoning. Child declared the dish quite pretty and wrote, "The cornmeal crepes were a new idea to me, and I also liked the pleasant Mexican flavoring in the meat." Child judged again the next year, 1980, when another brisket took first place.

Then James Beard took over the celebrity judge role for '81, when the contest tapped Sweet Meat Bars, a kind of ground beef variation on mince meat pie; it had a can of whole cranberry sauce, a gob of orange marmalade, and a heap of brown sugar. The whole apparatus was topped with a sickly sweet glaze of confectioners' sugar, milk, and rum.

The contest continued to favor elaborate dishes through the 1980s. Sauces were served in bowls carved out of vegetables. Meat loaves were served *encroûté*. Briskets were slow-cooked in the oven. Contestants even had to decorate their cooking stations.

Those days are long gone. During the '90s, National Beef succumbed to the siren song of convenience cooking. The ingredients were restricted to eight and the cooking time to an hour. Ingredients were further whittled down to six, with beef counting as one. Even garnishes counted as an ingredient. The time was whacked to thirty minutes.

Cookoff organizers also dramatically decreased the number of contestants, from fifty to twenty. With the larger number, some so-so recipes were making it to the national cookoff because one had to be selected from every state. Cutting the number to twenty also saved money, which left more cash for the prizes—thus the boost to $50,000. Both moves were controversial in the beef industry. The complaint was that twenty contestants didn't make for a critical mass, and the constraints on prep time and ingredients made for uninspiring recipes. The cookoff wasn't much fun anymore, they complained. Diane Kirkbride, chair of the cookoff, disagrees. "We went through a stage where we had the most beautiful, elegant recipes," she says. "But did people really make them?"

The bigger purses have kept the contesters interested. They may grouse about the growing restrictions, that it impedes their creativity, but they still enter in droves. The evidence is before me here in Tucson where the contesters, fifteen strong, totally dominate. They queue up at a towering silver coffee server in a spacious lobby of the Loews Ventana Canyon resort. It is 8:30 A.M. and people are making small talk in the hushed tones of a library. Although everyone arrived in Tucson yesterday, this breakfast orientation is the first gathering of the contestants for the twenty-fourth annual cookoff.

There are several major leaguers. Janice Elder is here with her husband of thirty-two years, Larry, a businessman on the verge of opening his own art gallery. The good-looking, urbane couple has reigned over the cookoff world since the mid '80s even though it's an off-and-on kind of hobby and they both have demanding careers. They both have been to National Beef before. He went to Pillsbury three times, knocking the couple out of that contest. Janice might have left National Chicken last spring empty-handed, but this summer she won a recipe contest sponsored by Sandeman's Port and *Chocolatier* magazine. The prize was an all-expenses-paid trip to Lisbon, Portugal. And now here she is at Beef. As with most male contesters, Larry followed Janice into contesting. However, no one suspects that Janice feeds Larry recipes. As with Bob Gadsby, Larry is considered a contester in his own right.

The couple does brainstorm together, just like the Gadsbys. Whoever has the basic idea for the recipe sends it in, Janice says. In the case of Beef, it was her idea to spoon ground beef flavored with hoisin sauce and Asian peanut sauce into cup-shaped leaves of Boston lettuce.

Like the Elders, Priscilla Yee, a small, preternaturally young-looking retired financial analyst from the San Francisco area, has also won-out of Pillsbury. She was a finalist at the 1999 National Beef Cook-Off, where she earned a reputation for being standoffish. She won the $10,000 grand prize in this year's Quaker Oats "Bake It Better with Oats" contest with her hybrid cinnamon bun scones.

Having gotten into Chicken and now Beef, Pat Harmon, the retired town clerk from Pennsylvania, has a shot at the triple crown this year. She just has to get into Pillsbury. Practically as soon as she is done competing at National Beef, she is due at the Bellagio in Las Vegas to compete in the finals of the Great Australian Barbeque Cookoff.

Joyce Bowman is here, fresh from competing at Better Burger last weekend. This is her third time competing at National Beef. Susan Runkle, a Brit who lives in Kentucky, started contesting only two years ago when she retired from her pressure-cooker job managing personnel at an overnight delivery service. She won $25 in a horseradish contest, $400 in a monthly *Better Homes and Gardens* contest, and then "I got this bomb from Campbell's," as she put it. Her Polynesian Pork Chops beat out eight thousand entries to take the $20,000 in the Campbell's 20-Minute Recipe Challenge last spring. As part of the prize for her winning recipe, Runkle's photo was emblazoned on one million cans of Golden Mushroom soup.

Then there's a gaggle of contesters who have never quite hit it big but who hang on the edges of the winner's circle, such as Janet Barton, a

Mormon mother of four from Utah. She competed at the 2000 Bake-Off® contest, won $1,000 as a runner-up in the Campbell's contest, and won the Utah State Fair Spam contest. Julie Stutzman, Barbara Morgan's daughter, has won her share of second and third prizes. There's Marjorie Farr, a short, blunt-looking woman with a no-nonsense haircut, who at seventy-five looks as if she could outrun, if not outcook, her opponents. She and her husband have come to the National Beef Cook-Off seven times but have never won, as her bio notes, much to Farr's chagrin. "It makes us sound like idiots."

And, of course, there's Gadsby and his wife, Edwina. As one contester put it, Gadsby looks well fed. Edwina is on the plump side as well but not nearly so imposing. She hardly comes up to her husband's shoulder. She has beautiful shoulder-length raven hair, big eyes, and full lips. Compared to her husband, she comes across as reserved, which really isn't the case. It is just that Gadsby is so extroverted and so at ease in a crowd. Dressed in knee-length shorts, a T-shirt, gym shoes, and tube socks pulled up tight, he looks ready for a friendly game of softball. There is no sign of the nervousness that Edwina mentioned. Maybe the long flight calmed him. Ruddy-faced and smiling so that his eyes squint, he shakes hands and beams amiably down at contestants who introduce themselves to him. When Debbie Finley, a blond, birdlike first-time contestant from Texas, nervously asks him if she should wait for her hostess before heading in for the orientation, he just shrugs his shoulders and smiles. Hostess or no hostess, why should he care? He's the Rooster.

Moving through the gabbing, coffee-sipping contestants is a small army of broad women in red polo shirts and bulky white gym shoes. Their huge shirts, drooping off their shoulders and with short sleeves hanging past their elbows, are worn tunic-style, draped over widening middle-aged hips and haunches. The utilitarian shirts are set off by chunky turquoise rings, heavy southwestern silver necklaces, and bracelets. As they go, they quickly scan name tags, sometimes moving their lips as they read or tipping their heads back to use their bifocals.

These women are the Arizona Cowbelles, the heart and soul of the cookoff. Actually, these women now call themselves cattlewomen, a less colorful but more modern and, of course, inclusive term. Only a few state chapters still use cowbelles, including Arizona, the sponsors of this cookoff. These cattlewomen come from all over the country, but mostly from the sweeping ranches found west of the Mississippi that are so big the term "acre" doesn't apply. Rather, the ranches are measured by sections or square miles of earth. These women are mostly government-bashing, pro-NRA Republicans. My National Beef tote bag is stuffed with literature with headlines like "Endangered Species Act Train Wreck!" and "Betrayed by the Feds."A cattlewomen in her mid-seventies proudly pulled her wallet out of her purse to show me her concealed weapons permit, which was prominently displayed in a plastic window.

These women have spent a goodly chunk of their lives at home in the kitchen, cooking and baking, keeping the cookie jar filled for their endlessly hungry rancher husbands, some of the few Americans who still need a diet high in calories and fat. They also work on the ranch and raise children. It is an incredibly consuming but in many ways lonely life, especially on the sprawling ranches of the desert states. These rancher wives don't see a whole lot of their peers.

This is where the cookoff comes in: It doubles as a de facto every-other-year-cattlewomen-off-the-ranch blowout. That is why they have paid up to $1,000 out of their own pockets to stay at this fancy resort on the northern border of Tucson. Being cattlewomen, though, they like to stay busy, and so they are here looking after the contestants, running the cookoff, glad-handing industry reps, and giving speeches. They are cooking, phoning, washing pots, checking IDs, giving directions, and grocery shopping. In between they are laughing loudly, making fun of each other, catching up, and generally having a good time.

The cattlewomen moving through the crowd in the lobby are the hostesses searching for their respective contestants. From what I've seen, this buddy system is unique to National Beef. Over the next two days these hostesses will basically be the contestants' valets, escorting them to each event on time, carrying their purses when needed, advising, calming, coaching, and generally tending to their needs. They are also ambassadors of a sort because their intent is to show the contestants that cattle ranchers are people, too.

The hostesses and contestants pair up, and everyone lines up at the breakfast buffet, a cornucopia of hefty American breakfast foods—shiny Danishes, slick home fries, moist sausage patties—all gussied up with silver and linen. This spread is fit for a posse of cowboys but not so fit for a group of middle-aged women likely to spend most of the day on their behinds. Regardless, the contestants load their plates, balancing strips of bacon and planks of butter-laden toast atop foamy piles of scrambled eggs. This food is, after all, free. Model-thin Finley, who had found her hostess, the ruddy-faced, turquoise-bejeweled Fita Witte, gets in line and scans the plentitude worriedly. Relief suddenly spreads across her face. "Look, they have Egg Beaters."

The contestants, along with their respective hostesses, take a seat at oversized round tables in a windowless conference room. As the munching begins, Kirkbride, a short, lively blonde, a take-charge type, pulls the microphone down so she can reach it. She starts the orientation by explaining why they went ahead with the cookoff despite the terrorist attacks. "We decided to follow the lead of the president and continue on," she says. "One contestant didn't come because her family did not want her to fly. We looked into getting her here by train, but she was coming from Vermont, it would have taken four days, and we could get her only one night in a sleeper car." The contestants nod knowingly.

Next up is what to do if there are any protesters. My ears prick. This is the first I've heard of protesters at a cookoff. The contesters look blankly at Kirkbride, who explains that animal rights protesters are known to show up at beef events. The hotel is on private property, so if protesters do make an appearance, the hotel staff will stop them at the front gate, she assures them. If the protesters manage to sneak in, well, "Your hostess will know what to do." No one asks a question. There are more pressing issues, as quickly becomes clear.

Kirkbride begins reading the contest rules out loud but doesn't get through the first one before hands fly up around the room. The questions are fielded by Kirkbride or the slight culinary center director who roams the floor with a microphone like a talk show host. What is the altitude? Not high, about 2,000 feet, but Kirkbride sends someone to check. If you finish your dish in advance, can you reheat it? No, Kirkbride says. Will the potatoes be washed? Yes, Kirkbride says. Where will the knives be? On your tray, Kirkbride says, then adds, "Keep in mind that these are brand-new, sharp knives. We don't want contestants to cut themselves." This prompts a contestant to ask if there will be any paper towels. Yes. Lastly, who are the judges? A trim, bespectacled woman next to Kirkbride rises and answers solemnly, "That is confidential information at this time."

"We can tell you they are food people versus cowboys," Kirkbride quips. "And the exact altitude is twenty-eight hundred feet."

The crowd breaks camp, and we walk outside into the heat, across the frying-pan-hot tar parking lot, past the health club with the treadmill-gerbils huffing and puffing in the windows, along the empty tennis courts, and into a large, single-story building. This is where the cookoff will be held tomorrow morning. The contestants are here now to check what is called the tray viewing, during which they examine their recipe ingredients, set neatly on a plastic tray covered with a white cloth napkin. This is essentially when the competition begins because the tray viewing could make or break a contestant tomorrow.

If the produce is fresh enough, the quantities are correct, all the ingredients are there, and the contestants are happy, they sign off on the tray. Once they pen their signature, there is no going back. If they didn't notice an ingredient missing, tough. If they decide later that the lettuce is a little too wilted, tough. And so the contestants, especially the contesters, typically stare at their tray for long, silent minutes. They know from experience that you can read a recipe fifteen times and still space out putting in the salt. Cooking is plagued by forgetfulness. If the ingredients are not up to snuff, the contestant does not sign off on his or her tray, and the cattlewomen head to the local grocery stores. Those contestants will return later in the evening for a second tray viewing.

The trays are brought out several at a time and placed on a long table at the back of the hall. Looking over her tray, Yee learns that the oranges for her recipe have been refrigerated. She asks for new, unrefrigerated ones. On his tray Gadsby finds smaller tortillas than his recipe calls for. He asks for the bigger ones.

As the tray viewing proceeds, the rest of the contestants crowd into a cookoff station to watch a demonstration of the newfangled Maytag Gemini Range, an electric stove with a slick porcelain top. The stations are plenty roomy and have a lot of tabletop space. However, the work surface is several steps away from the stove, not an ideal setup. The stovetop seems a little tricky, too. If a pan is more than an inch wider than the burner, designated by a neat black circle, or if it isn't flat, the heating element will turn itself off. Susan Miller, a stylish, slim grandmother from Phoenix, scrunches up her face in worry. Her pan, a favorite she brought from her kitchen, may be too big. She hurries back to her room to retrieve it.

Meanwhile, at the tray viewing Debbie Finley's eyes dart around her tray as her hostess, Fita Witte, stands by her side. They make a striking pair. Finley is a tall, wispy blonde with a reedy, girlish voice. She is a computer wonk totally out of her element. Witte is a broad, short woman with a dark-haired, salt-of-the-earth beauty. Before them is a gravy-logged piece of mud-brown pot roast in a plastic sack, a shiny tube of refrigerator crescent rolls, a package of Cheddar cheese shredded like confetti, a small tub of sour cream, and an onion the size of a baseball, fixings for her Roast Beef Cheddar Pockets. "The onion is a good size for cutting," Finley says.

While Finley deliberates, Bowman rushes back, breathless, to the tray viewing. "My daughter sent me back to ask about the basil because it was black," she explains. Finley wonders out loud how she will serve her Roast Beef Cheddar Pockets on the contest's large white plates. She used much smaller plates when practicing at home. One pocket per plate is going to look pretty lonely, and a blob of shiny white sour cream on a shiny white plate isn't going to help matters. Could she at least have small glass bowls to serve the sour cream in? Finley asks. The culinary center director is called over to mediate.

"We'll try to get eight small ones, but I can't guarantee it because it's not official," she says.

As the two women turn from the tray viewing, Finley looks nervous and a little discouraged. Witte has been to seven cookoffs. At one she was the hostess for a prize winner, a psychologist from Nashville, she says proudly. "If the contestants get nervous—which you will," she says, looking at Finley, "they cut themselves and spill stuff. It happens to everyone. So you just suck it up and go on." Finley listens intently to Witte, then looks at me and says, "I thought of this as a lottery thing, like winning a free trip."

I see Miller walk briskly back into the hall, gripping her pan in one hand. She heads straight for a stove, turns on a burner, and puts the pan down. Off goes the burner. Miller sighs. Across the room Gadsby inspects a cooking station. The work table comes up to about mid-thigh on him. He asks if the tables can be raised to the height of the stove like a kitchen counter. "Maybe" is the answer. "At National Chicken I ended up sitting because the table was so low," he says with a laugh.

I notice a red-shirted cattlewoman posted by the front doors scanning the room. She has wide cheeks, thin brown hair parted smack in the middle, and a matter-of-fact manner. She is head of security. Unbeknownst to the contestants, she's there on the lookout for animal rights protesters, who have a habit of showing up at any pro-beef event, the cookoff included. They showed up at the '99 contest, she says.

"In Omaha they piled out of a van in bathing suits with some banner," she says. "I can't remember what it said, but they came when they knew the TV cameras would be there. Wherever we go, there are a few protesters. They've never been disruptive. They've even shown up at 4-H fairs in Texas," she adds.

Another cattlewoman, listening in, says, "You have to be brave to do that in Texas." The cattlewoman in charge of security nods.

What has the cattlewomen on edge is that in recent weeks the Animal Liberation Front and the Earth Liberation Front have struck twice in Tucson. On September 8 the two organizations claimed to have set fire to a McDonald's restaurant. Then this week the life-size statue of Ronald McDonald at the Ronald McDonald House was covered with swastikas, anti-fast-food graffiti, and ALF and ELF. "We don't want someone in their last five minutes of cooking to have a balloon full of paint lobbed at them," the security cattlewoman says. That is why only people with official cookoff name tags will be allowed in the contest room.

The contestants drift out of the room and back into the heat. They have a couple of hours to themselves. Two aquamarine pools, rows of tennis courts, and a thirty-six-hole golf course, garishly lush and green against the rosy taupe of the Arizonan desert, beckon. Truth be told, it's really too hot to do anything except doze off in the chill of an air-conditioned room or lazily sip ice tea in the shade of the hotel's out-door café, which is about as ambitious as anybody's plans are, except Miller.

Poor Miller has a big problem on her hands. She needs to buy a new pan, one big enough to hold a one-and-one-quarter-pound chunk of boneless beef chuck but not so big that it turns the burner off. A new pan, any cook knows, has a mind of its own. You have to get to know your pans and break them in, even the nonstick kind. Susan Miller will have to do this while vying for $50,000. The prospect makes her scowl. While Miller races back to her room for her purse, bracing herself for an afternoon of traffic and grocery stores under the bleaching Arizona sun, the rest of the contestants contemplate naps and the paperback thrillers they've brought along with them.

They disappear into the sprawling resort. The horseshoe-shaped, desert mission-style hybrid, Loews Ventana Canyon, wedges into the base of the mountains. From the front of the resort you can look past the surreal golf course, over an incongruent man-made waterfall, and down into the near treeless valley that is Tucson, a low-slung city of one-story stucco houses and boulevards wide enough to land a jet on. Out the back of the resort you immediately raise your eyes to the rosy-colored rubble of the mountains and their strange inhabitants, the towering saguaro cactuses. Ramrod straight, their few branches like arms akimbo, these cactuses eerily resemble soldiers on lookout, espe-cially as the sun falls and their lean, dark silhouettes seem to grow twofold against the gloaming, and their deep stillness is so filled with anticipation that your eye can trick you into thinking a branch has stirred.

There is a sign on this side of the resort, just a few steps away from the rooms, that warns guests to stay clear of any wild animal. I've heard that a boy was bitten by a rattlesnake on the hotel's grounds this summer. Just now, though, there is hardly a reptile-obsessed eight-year-old boy to be found. In fact, this posh resort is almost empty. Essentially late summer, this would normally be a slow time of year, but the nosedive in tourism since the terrorist attacks has made the resort quieter than a hospital.

You hear only the soft thud of your own footsteps down the sprawling carpeted halls that lead to the rooms. You mostly have the elevator to yourself. You can show up at the resort's waterside restaurant at the height of the dinner hour and get a table without a reservation. There are always spaces at the front of the parking lot. The effect should be calming, but instead an inertia has settled over the resort, which is only made worse by the unbearable heat.

〰 〰 〰

The spell is broken the moment the National Beef folks gather together around 3 P.M. in front of the hotel where sizable buses purring in the the sun await to ferry them to Old Tucson Studios, a hybrid movie set and theme park in the Sonoran Desert just west of the city. No one seems to know what to expect, maybe a fake shoot-out. There is nothing like being treated as visiting dignitaries to raise people's spirits, and the contestants and their companions are plainly in a good mood. The cattlewomen are bubbly as well. They wear big sunglasses and cackle.

The bus fills up quickly and lumbers out of the resort. It heads south into the valley toward Tucson, then turns west and follows the northernmost cross-town road, the bald Catalina Mountains rising to the right, the city to the left. Less than a mile from the resort some sad-sack rancher rises from his seat and plugs in a video that begins to undulate across all the miniscreens. Bobbing and weaving with the motion of the racing bus, the rancher fiddles with the knobs on the deck. He looks surprised when the image actually straightens itself out. It's a Japanese cartoon in which the characters have eyes the size of dinner plates. "Oh, my grandchildren watch this," a cattlewoman sitting next to me says. "I hate it." No one can resist looking at the screens. There is no sense trying to watch the desert landscape roll by because the shades have been pulled on the bus. "I'm going to show you some propaganda and then we'll hopefully have some fun," the rancher says over the mike.

The cartoon flips to the image of beef cows, and a program on the cattle industry proceeds. It is full of upbeat statistics, pro-beef sermonizing, and mooing. The moment it's done the big-eyed animated characters flip back on. The rancher turns down the sound but leaves the cartoon running. Holding the microphone so close to his mouth that you can hear his ragged breathing, he asks the crowd in a rough baritone, "What do you look for when you buy beef?"

"Price per pound," a voice up front chirps.

The rancher pauses, then lets out a deep sigh worthy of Job over the mike. His shoulders slump. His eyes darken.

"That's what is wrong with this business," he says and then launches into an indecipherable description of how meat is graded. His consonants make thumping noises as he nearly lips the mike. The contestants nearer the front of the bus listen politely, but in the back a steady stream of chatter builds. The rancher is preaching to the choir as far as the cattlewomen are concerned. The contestants, like most Americans who buy their burger wrapped neatly in plastic from a carefully arranged grocery store's refrigerated shelf, don't really care to know how it got there. The rancher's earnestness and passion are totally lost on this giddy bunch.

The bus has now hit the rounded hills of the Sonoran Desert, and it begins to roll like a cruise ship in rough water as the cartoon continues to flicker. Back-of-the-bus conversation trickles out. The riders' faces begin to pale, to tighten. "Where's the throw-up bag?" the cattlewoman next to me says.

The rancher is undeterred, energetically describing how raw beef is aged and the microbiotic breakdown of a cow carcass. Like a preacher his voice gets stronger and stronger as he drives home his sermon. "Beef has taken a bad rap. Too fat. Too this. The consumption of beef is up," he booms. "Chicken had its run, and people got tired of it."

The rancher finishes as if he has just given up, snaps off the video, and drops heavily into his seat. The blinds are raised, and everyone breathes a little easier. The bus lurches into Old Tucson under a blue sky. We queasily pile off the bus, only to step into the bright heat of the late afternoon. Arizonans are always explaining away the heat by saying, "It's a dry heat," but the truth is it is still uncomfortably hot, like a sauna. The sun hits you with a knockout punch while the desert sucks every drop of water, not to mention lotion, out of your pores. The red shirts are busy handing out bottled water and shepherding us, half-blinded by the sun's mean glare even with sunglasses on, through Old Tucson's entry gate. On the other side, everyone dashes for what little shade there is, rips the top off the water bottles, and drinks deeply.

Looking around we find we have time-traveled back to 1860s Tucson, when the city was a frontier town with nothing but dirt roads, hastily built buildings, and its fair share of outlaws. This antiquated version of Tucson is the creation of Columbia Pictures. In 1939 the studio built the set for the movie *Arizona*, starring William Holden and Jean Arthur. The movie set a high bar for realism, prompting the movie industry to move away from studio backdrops to shooting outdoors.

The movie set has been used off and on ever since. Pretend cowboys John Wayne, Gene Autry, Jimmy Stewart, and Burt Lancaster have walked its dusty streets. The set was used steadily through the '90s, but not often enough to keep a steady cash flow. So it has been transformed into a kind of historic village, but one less interested in historical accuracy à la Williamsburg and more interested in family fun. There are pony rides, something called "Critterville," a candy store, and, of course, a gift shop.

A cattlewoman announces that we have forty-five minutes to look around, and then we are due at the High Chaparral Ranch for a live show. Rather than poke around in the hot sun, we amble up the street, kicking up a low cloud of dust on our way to the ranch. A few women, purses clasped like weapons, duck into the gift shop. Most of the group, still a little squeamish, keeps moseying toward the ranch, dodging the sun as they move from patch of shade to patch of shade.

At the ranch we find two sets of bleachers next to a corral, on the other side of which is an outdoor stage. Mountains rise all around. Everyone heads for the bleachers in the shade and takes a seat. Baxter Black, the cowboy poet and large animal vet of National Public Radio fame, takes the stage, a dot in blue jeans and a cowboy hat across the corral. The show starts with the "Star-Spangled Banner," which is played as four young women in enormous skirts and sombreros, each holding a flag that ruffles in the wind, gallop sidesaddle around the corral. From the first note the crowd stands, and everyone wells up. I see Finley on a bleacher below me look tearily at her husband.

The show is a hodgepodge of mariachi music and traditional Mexican dancing on the distant stage, intermixed with animal demonstrations in the corral. A horse named Mousy prances to a bouncy tune for what seems an eternity. A half-dozen or so expressionless cowhands on horseback face off against a small herd of befuddled cattle. The whole idea is for a cowboy and his horse, called a cutting horse, to separate one cow from the group, a task that looks a whole lot simpler and uneventful than it is and is pretty much lost on this nonranching, nonhorseback-riding, overheated, slightly bored crowd. The dust kicked up by the horses blows over us as we clap politely when cued.

"It's really hard to stay on a cutting horse," a cattlewoman behind me says to no one in particular.

When the Rim Fire Stock Dogs appear in the ring, flat on their bellies, eyeing the still befuddled cattle, everyone in the bleachers perks up. Dogs are something we can relate to, and as the Border collies dash and nip at the cattle, we smile and applaud. Then the girls riding sidesaddle in their beautiful crinolined skirts that cascade over the horses' haunches close the show, riding in hypnotizing circles as a perfectly round white moon rolls out from behind the mountains.

The show over, we tramp around the corral to a large barn. Inside, fans whir, pumping in the cool evening air. Wagon wheel chandeliers hang from the ceiling. A field of round tables is set for dinner. Upon stepping through the door, I'm handed a plate and sent through a chow line worthy of a cattle drive. Biscuits, baked potatoes, and good-sized steaks are forked from large chafing dishes and plunked down unceremoniously on my plate.

I grab a seat in between Janice Elder and another contester, Lori Welander. Witte and Finley sit across from me. I dig into what proves to be one of the best steaks of my life. I ask Elder what she thinks her chances are for tomorrow. She says, "I'm going first, which isn't good strategically." Welander recounts one of her cookoffs, a state beef cookoff in Vermont where she had to grill outside in minus 10 degrees. Someone accidentally set off the fire alarm, and when the firemen rushed into the building, they knocked over Welander's grill. She had to start over. She got home at 1 A.M.

"My husband said, 'This is supposed to be an honor?'" Welander says.

I reach for more sour cream for my baked potato, and the bowl that was brimming with neat little white packages is mysteriously empty. Just then another rancher, a lean white-haired man in jeans with a large oval silver buckle, takes the stage. Hands in his pockets, he launches into a slide show about the beef industry, his voice rough and angry. He rails against the enviros, the federal government. The cattlewomen cheer here and there. Again the contestants listen politely, like guests in a foreign country. "This isn't typical of cookoffs," Welander leans over and whispers to me.

By 8 P.M., after coffee and chocolate cake, it's time to get the contestants back to the resort for the second tray viewing. We are loaded back on a bus, and just as we all settle into our seats, a person in a skeleton costume suddenly pops up on the bus's front steps and waves. The gesture is friendly, as are the eyes looking through the skull sockets, but the image is so incongruent that I start. A protester, I think. Nobody else seems to notice, and the specter disappears as quickly as he appeared, his white bones vanishing into the desert night.

The ride back is peaceful and quiet, as if it's much later than it actually is. I suspect the contestants are mulling over their strategy for the next morning. Back at the resort my suspicion proves true as I walk with Finley and Witte through the dark to the second tray viewing. For a first-timer, Finley has gotten in the groove quickly. She ticks off her game plan for her Roast Beef Cheddar Pockets. "At 12:16 I'll put them in the oven, and I'll take them out at 12:29. Do you think that's enough time?"

Witte nods. She tells Finley not to worry about how to serve the sour cream, and she holds up her purse, which is filled with mini plastic containers of sour cream. Witte cleaned out the bowl on our dinner table at Old Tucson, thus the missing sour cream mystery is solved.

The cattlewomen are waiting for the contestants with the trays at the end of the cookoff room. Each contestant gives his or her tray a quick once-over and signs off, even Gadsby, who learns that the cattlewomen did not find the twelve-inch tortillas his recipe calls for. Everyone signs off, that is, except Yee. She carefully examines each orange that the cattlewomen have set out for her on the far end of the table. Head bowed, her dark hair covering her face, she holds each in her hand, weighing them one by one. She asks to see the bag of oranges she rejected that morning and begins to methodically go through them. There are now about three dozen out on the table. Yee's recipe, Cumin-Crusted Beef Steaks with Relish, calls for two or three.

Yee's hostess, a large, round woman with a canvas bag hooked on her arm, waits quietly behind her. All the other contestants have left. Yee, silent, her face expressionless in concentration, continues to pass the oranges from one hand to the other, gently squeezing them, tossing them ever so softly to better feel their heft, trying to decipher just how much juice might be locked inside these inscrutable fleshy spheres, for one bone-dry piece of citrus might just cost her $50,000.

◊◊◊◊

When I mention the world of cookoffs, I'm always asked if there are cat fights. To most people's disappointment, the answer is "not really." Sure, there are high emotions and tears sometimes, especially at the Bake-Off® contest. And while many contestants hit it off, some don't. There is some backbiting, some jealousy, and a fair amount of gossip, but less than you would expect given the money that is at stake. Women still put such a high premium on being nice that most of them help each other at cookoffs, lending ingredients and advice, cheering one another on. That is why, even though each contestant is competing individually, a team spirit often dominates.

Women, especially the pre–Title IX generation, have such conflicted feelings about competition that they are even reluctant to let on that that is what they are actually doing. Among most of the contesters competition is a dirty word—even for the women with full-time careers. Everyone is at pains not to be too serious, hiding their competitive streaks behind good manners and self-deprecatory comments. When I ask about the c-word, it constantly prompts the b-word, backstabbing, as in there is no backstabbing. I constantly point out that competition can be positive and healthy, that it doesn't imply bad sportsmanship. I mostly get blank stares in response. A few, such as Pat Harmon and Barbara Morgan, will admit they contest because they like competing, but almost everyone else talks about all the friends they've made and the places they've gone.

Consequently, male contestants, who are at ease competing, often ruffle the feathers of these female contesters. The competition style of men includes a lot of boasting. They want to appear confident. This is often translated as rudeness by women contestants, whose style is to display a total lack of confidence. When Diane Sparrow saw a video of the Great Garlic Cook-Off, she was appalled by how Adam Sanchez predicted on camera that he would win.

This is why in the nicey-nice world of contesters, Yee is one of the few controversial figures. She behaves as if she is competing. The native Californian often keeps to herself at cookoffs, not joining in the party atmosphere. Contesters know her by name and wins, but few know her personally. Here at this National Beef, Yee, who came alone, does not socialize with the other contestants but spends most of her free time with her hostess, Jeanene Wehrbein, a gregarious small-town newspaper editor from Nebraska. Wehrbein follows her around like a bodyguard. At the last National Beef Cook-Off in Omaha, where Wehrbein was chair, Yee got a reputation for being difficult and particular. Wehrbein tells me that when word got out that she was Yee's hostess, other cattlewomen told her, "Oh, golly, you have Priscilla," and basically wished her good luck. Wehrbein was unfazed. She is quick to point out that Yee sent the '99 cookoff organizers an effusive thank-you note.

When I first come upon Yee, all I know about her is that she has won a lot. I notice that she is intense and that her natural expression is a bit of a scowl. At the second tray viewing I stay on after the other contestants have left and watch her meticulously sort the oranges. When I ask a question, she either ignores me or answers with one word. I back off and let her concentrate. Then after she has selected her fruit, I attempt to walk out into the night with her, chatting as we go. She'll have none of it. She charges ahead of me, with Wehrbein huffing and puffing to keep up. Over her shoulder she says, "I'm sure you can find someone more interesting to talk to," and leaves me standing in the dark.

Yee also has a bit of a reputation as a bad sport. Roxanne Chan, who has met up with her at several cookoffs in California, describes her as a "fierce competitor, not a friend." "She's fine if she wins; if she doesn't win, watch out," Chan says. Morgan says Yee will not congratulate the winner. "She gets angry. She leaves suddenly. She gripes about it. Unfortunately, that's her personality."

The other knock against Yee is that she's good, very good. Morgan met Yee at a newspaper cooking contest in California. Morgan was a contestant, and Yee was a judge. The two women became friends, and for years, Morgan says, they talked nearly every day by phone. For years they lived only six blocks away from each other in Concord. You'd never catch Yee sending in a recipe she hadn't tested, a comon practice among contesters, Morgan says. "She does what none of the other contesters do," Morgan says. "She perfects it, makes it ten times. When she thinks she can't get it any better, than she sends it in."

This dogged, methodical approach has produced many prize-winning recipes since Yee started contesting in the 1980s. She made national news in 1991 when she won the $7,500 grand prize in Campbell's Soup "How to Get President Bush to Eat Broccoli" recipe contest with a lemon sauce created with a can of cream of broccoli soup. In 1997 she won $20,000 at a Cooking Light cookoff with Brownie Cheesecake Torte. This year she won $10,000 from Quaker Oats for another crossbred baked good, Cinnamon Bun Scones. Edwina Gadsby thinks this is why other contesters are critical of her. Edwina competed with her at a Cooking Light cookoff in Birmingham last spring. There, another contestant told Edwina that she didn't care who won as long as it wasn't Yee. "I think the only thing they have against her is that she is talented."

Maybe too talented. Yee grew up in a family of cooks in California. "You learn how to brush your teeth. You learn how to tie your shoes. You learn how to cook. That's how I was brought up," she says. While working at Pacific Bell, Yee cooked after hours to relax. "I would be cooking anyway. I guess I figured I might as well do something constructive with it," she says. She liked how contesting pushed her to try new foods and techniques. Pretty quickly Yee began to win. Yee went to the Bake-Off® contest three times in the '80s, knocking herself out of the contest. She never won a prize.

Then Yee's friends and family members began showing up at other contests. Everyone assumed Yee was feeding them recipes. Morgan says Yee accompanied a coworker, Linda Rahman, to the 1990 Bake-Off® contest, where Rahman won the $50,000 grand prize with Blueberry Poppy Seed Brunch Cake. Kurt Wait, another of Yee's coworkers at Pacific Bell, and her boyfriend, according to Morgan and others, began winning contests. In 1993 he came in second at the Great Garlic Cook-Off with Tomato Shortcake with Garlic-Crusted Scones. In 1994 he won Better Burger with Portobello Burgers. Then he became a Pillsbury finalist with a recipe many contesters assumed was Yee's. That recipe, Macadamia Fudge Torte, won the first-ever million-dollar-prize. It also made Wait the first man to ever win the contest.

Morgan had her doubts about the scones being Wait's recipe. "It wasn't the kind of recipe that a man would put together. I somehow couldn't see him making scones," she says. Then the night before the Bake-Off® contest prizes were announced, Morgan spoke on the phone with Yee, who had not accompanied Wait. Morgan says that Yee couldn't stop talking about it, she was so excited. "I said, 'You're not even in this one.'" Before Morgan hung up, Yee said, "I'll call you tomorrow."

The next day when Wait became a millionaire, "She didn't call me, and I didn't call her because I didn't feel this was right. All conversation ceased between us," Morgan says. Morgan also noticed that in news stories Wait changed his story. After his Better Burger win in '94, he told a reporter that he'd begun cooking only a few years before, after he had gotten a divorce. After he won Pillsbury, he told reporters that he'd taught himself how to cook in college, honed his craft reworking recipes from *Bon Appétit,* cooked for a houseful of roommates while in his twenties, and then cooked the family meals when he was married.

A Bake-Off® contest worker told me off the record that Wait did a beautiful presentation at the contest and came across as a bona fide foodie. The worker had no doubts that his recipe was his own and had never heard any accusations that it wasn't. Yee denies any connection with Wait, and says, "Ninety percent of what's on the rumor mill is not totally true. A lot of people gossip as a hobby." Wait never responded to any of my calls.

Morgan says she and Yee didn't speak for five years, until the spring of 2001 when they met up at the Farmer John "Go Hog Wild" Cook-Off in Santa Monica. They both competed for the grand prize of a Harley-Davidson—Yee with Warm Pork Salad Cubano, Morgan with Golden State Warm Artichoke and Bacon Crostinis. Neither won the bike, but both went home with leather motorcycle jackets. Yee was there with her sister and niece, who were finalists, Morgan says. Morgan was there with Chan. "We started talking like nothing had ever happened," Morgan says, but the renewed friendship didn't change her mind about Wait's torte.

"I felt in my heart that was Priscilla's recipe because I recognize Priscilla's recipes," Morgan says.

〜〜〜〜

Around 7:30 A.M. on Saturday the cookoff gets off to an inauspicious start. The judges are missing. They should be at a copious buffet breakfast orientation, but aren't. Sherry Hill, the cookoff director, who sits waiting at an empty table for them, is flummoxed. She can't telephone the judges because the hotel's front desk has been ordered not to put

through any calls to their rooms, a safeguard against overeager contestants. The desk will only put through calls from the cookoff worker in
charge of the judges.

While Hill madly dials her cell phone trying to find the judges' liai-
son, at the other end of the resort on a large, sun-baked terrace, the contestants, decked out in tomato red National Beef shirts, crisp white
aprons, and toques, pose for their official group photo. Gadsby, a head
taller than everyone, is back and center, making him look like a chef
with his legion of underlings. Diminutive Yee is off to one end, poker-
faced, the only one not in a National Beef red shirt. Elder, in the middle of the front row, flashes a big photogenic smile. The photographer,
a mustached man in tight jeans, calls for the cattlewomen hostesses to
join the contestants.

"Do you have a wide lens?" someone cracks.

A weathered, turn-of-the-century chuck wagon serves as the back-
drop. The cook, who has a waxed handlebar mustache and a kind of af-
fected, laconic, Old West style of talking, kneads dough. He prefers to
work actual cattle drives, but today he has "prostituted himself." He
has thrown dirt on the concrete and then built a campfire, over which
he bakes biscuits in a cast iron Dutch oven hung on a tripod. The contestants gobble them up with honey like hungry cowpunchers.

It is time for the grand entrance. All the contestants, toques pulled
up high or squashed like berets, line up in alphabetical order at the
door to the cookoff building. An announcer, the elderly cattlewoman
with the concealed weapons permit, groans their names and slowly
reads each bio over a microphone inside as the contestants step into
the room, past a small, applauding group of spectators, including the
security cattlewoman, who scan everyone's shirt for name tags.

With half of the contestants in the room, it becomes clear that the
grand entrance is taking too long. The first contestant, Elder, is due to
start cooking in ten minutes. So the last four or five names are read in
quick succession, which causes a traffic jam at the front door. Welander
starts into the room and then, confused because she didn't hear her
name called, steps back on top of Yee, who heard her name and tries to
pass her. "Let the contest begin," the cattlewoman intones.

This will be the voice of time for the next five hours, as it announces when contestants can pick up their ingredients, when they can enter their cooking stations, and when they must deliver their dish. The contestants will rotate in and out of cooking stations in fifteen-minute intervals so that only three cooks will be working at once. The hostesses accompany the contestants into the cook station, but essentially they are not allowed to do anything but sit there and smile. There are secret monitors on the floor to make sure this rule and all others are followed. They are instructed to be so subtle that if anyone is disqualified, nobody, not even the contestant, will know.

At 8:15 A.M. sharp, Janice Elder steps into her station and calmly goes to work. All eyes are on her as a large group of cattlewomen and contestants huddle around her workstation. Elder looks up occasionally to flash a smile at the crowd, but otherwise she goes about her business unfazed by the attention. She has a temporary National Beef tattoo on the back of one hand.

"She's very neat," says Finley, who, with her husband, also a computer wonk, intently studies Elder for tips. Elder's husband, Larry, also watches, but off to the side and behind his wife so she can't see him peering at her every move. Even though Elder has her beef browning on the stove, two heads of Boston lettuce neatly pulled apart, and ends trimmed off the cucumber, all within ten minutes, Larry is bug-eyed with anxiety. A first-timer from Ohio enters his station at 8:30 A.M., so not all eyes are on Elder anymore. Still, Larry moves to the other end of the hall. "I just ruined myself," he says. "I got the hell out of there. I was making myself too nervous."

The Ohioan, looking flushed, his toque pulled taut, immediately slops some balsamic vinaigrette on the table. He is all flapping arms and beady eyes, rushing back and forth from the table to the stove as he makes his dish, a salad served atop a prebaked pizza crust. His wife stands nearby, issuing instructions in a low, insistent voice as she videotapes him. This is against contest rules, but nobody seems to notice. He yanks a panful of pizza crusts out of the oven, and one doughy disk spins off onto the floor. He scoops it up, flustered. He knocks his glass of water over, then grabs it quickly, sending water in a neat arc onto the table.

Meanwhile, Elder spoons her browned, seasoned meat into the Boston lettuce leaves she has arranged on a plate. It is now 8:40 A.M., five minutes before Yee can enter her cooking station. She paces in front of the pantry table. The announcer hardly gets out "Priscilla Yee, you can now enter your cooking station," and Yee is in her station next to the Ohioan.

Yee, suddenly animated, runs back and forth from her worktable to the stove, bouncing on the balls of her feet. She throws the four chuck eye steaks into the pan, and as they begin to cook, the rich smell of beef finally begins to fill the room.

"Janice Elder, you have five minutes to present your dish to the judges," the announcer drones.

Elder loads her four plates on the top of the regulation two-tiered cart, straightens her toque, and awaits the final call to roll her dish to the judges. When she does, she pushes her cart through the crowd, which parts and applauds. Near the doorway to the judging room, Elder poses for a photo with her dish. It is the last she sees of her Oriental Express Beef Lettuce Wraps. Two cattlewomen wheel Elder's dish over to the judging room and hand it over to two more cattlewomen, who whisk the steaming lettuce wraps into the judges' secret sanctum.

The cookoff builds up a head of steam as contestants rotate in and out of the cook stations. The hiss of sizzling meat and the rhythmic thump of chopping fill the room. Gadsby and his wife have disappeared, but all the other contestants are either cooking or watching.

Marjorie Farr sits at a table across from her husband, who is in a wheelchair, busily scribbling a game plan for her Sonoran Beef Steak. "I'm writing it out because I get nervous. I don't like this thirty-minute limit," she says. She's hoping that this time will be the charm, that she'll at least win a $10,000 category prize. She has hung her hopes on what is essentially a breaded cube steak topped with ranch dressing. Farr ducks into her station at 9:30 A.M. and with shaking hands begins concocting her sauce. Thirty minutes later, when the announcer drones that it's time for her to go the judges, she throws her hands up in victory. Just then Miller steps into her station, towing a suitcase filled with gear. Although her new pan appears to work fine, she barely keeps up with the clock. At the two-minute warning, Miller has just begun to plate her Seared Chuck Steak on Pesto Potato Pancakes, a decidedly unappetizing mud brown, made worse by the bright white plates. Regardless, off it goes. Miller barely has time to straighten her chef's hat.

At 10:15 there is an hourlong break so the judges can digest. Only a few people drift outside to the terrace where the chuck wagon still sits. "Come warm yourself by the fire," the chuck wagon cook calls to me and just about any woman who walks near the wagon. He and three other men in cowboy hats sit near the fire, shooting the breeze in low voices and drinking beer out of tole coffee cups. Most of the talk is about water, the lack of it. The cook tells of a waterless urinal, to which the others murmur amazement. "Now the guy who thought of that is driving a Cadillac," he says.

One of the main points of the cookoff is to let nonranchers, such as myself, meet ranchers, "to get to know us as people," as Kirkbride said. So I strike up a conversation with one of the men, who is puffed and scared like a retired boxer. The problem is that every time I speak with a rancher, male or female, I end up listening to a diatribe about environmentalists. These tough-minded people can get to seeming a bit thin-skinned. This guy is no different even though he no longer has a ranch. He sold it and now makes his living as a locomotive engineer. He still talks all rancher, easily going off on the "communist enviros," who, he says, "get one or two Ph.D.'s and get whacked out. They probably take acid." He is dressed in standard rancher attire—cowboy boots, jeans, and the requisite long-sleeved shirt—even though it's well over 90 degrees. He bought his first short-sleeved shirt ever to go to Barbados in August. Some ranchers wear short-sleeved shirts, he concedes, "but it don't look good."

I duck back inside the cookoff. Just inside the door is the security cattlewoman and a plainclothes police officer. They've spent the morning scanning people's chests, looking for name tags. The family of one contestant forgot theirs and was sent back to their rooms to get them. Otherwise, the morning has been completely uneventful—no raging, antibeef protestors have attempted to breach the resort.

The cookoff gets under way again as Joyce Bowman enters her station. She throws together her Mediterranean Beefy Basil Roll-Ups in fifteen minutes, including standing them on end and arranging them so sculpturally that spectators clap. Then she stands by her cart, plumping her hat, straightening her apron, and chatting with her hostess as the clock ticks down the remaining time. Across the room at a table, Finley, her chef's hat pulled over her long blond hair, huddles with Witte. "Do you have my bag?" Finley asks her, meaning the canvas one filled with her cooking utensils. Witte answers no.

"Okay," Finley says calmly.

The two women stare at each other, then Witte, like a superhero, disappears and reappears within seconds, the bag clenched in one hand. As Finley walks off, with Witte tailing her, her husband calls, "I'll try not to nag," then turns to me and says, "She's about as nervous as when she got married."

Smiley, boisterous Harmon tours the cookoff floor before going out to lunch with her daughter, who has driven down from Scottsdale. She is ridiculously composed, especially considering that she has the last slot of the day, 1:30 P.M., a bad position. Harmon is one of the few people not cowed by Gadsby at all. "Everybody can't win all the time," she says as she leaves the room.

Meanwhile, Susan Runkle, jaw clenched, steps into her cooking station and begins churning out Tuscan Beef and Pesto Pasta, which calls for precooked pot roast with gravy. As straight-faced Runkle stirs the ingredients in a big bowl, a film crew zeros in on her. Standing close by, her husband, a bald, retired Navy pilot, bares his teeth in a wide, exaggerated grin. Runkle looks at him blankly, bewildered, and then catches on and smiles for the camera. "She doesn't show anything," he says to me. "She's a total Brit, stiff upper lip, but she's all screwed up inside. I've had some experience with that."

Gadsby reappears not long before he's due to cook, the first he's been seen on the contest floor since the grand entrance four hours before. "I went to my room and did some Montana Zen," he reports. He took a nap, and Edwina ironed clothes. His chef's hat is squeezed onto his head. His apron barely reaches his hips and is stretched across his stomach. The ties aren't long enough in back to make a bow, only a truncated knot. "I'm starting to get a little worked up. I've been through it several times in my head," he says.

His worktable will not be raised, but if it bothers Gadsby, he doesn't show it. Edwina is the one who looks tense as her wide eyes go back and forth across the room. The couple watches as Welander, convinced she doesn't have a chance, merrily goes to work on her recipe, BBQ Beef Brisket with Smoky Cheddar-Chili Potatoes, which requires mostly stirring and heating. She makes comments to the crowd ("Nothing worse than cold potatoes") as if she is giving a cooking demonstration.

Gadsby, carrying his tray, follows soon after, smiling broadly, and the crowd, including most of the contestants, shifts to his station. He nonchalantly pops the cooked roast in the microwave. A fuse blows. His hostess starts waving her arms, calling for help. A young man in a tie bolts from the crowd into Gadsby's station. While he tinkers with the microwave, Gadsby gets to work. He heats oil in a pan on the stove. He sits down at the worktable as if it were a desk, to slice two red onions. The microwave comes back on. Gadsby leaves the onion chopping to put the beef back in. His smile is gone. He is sweating lightly. Edwina, standing by herself in the audience, watches him quietly, unsmiling.

Everything starts going according to plan; the onions are sautéing in his pan, and his ingredients are carefully laid out on the table. The microwave buzzes. Gadsby pulls the beef out, sets it aside to rest, and puts the ready-to-eat garlic-flavored mashed potatoes in the little oven. It goes dark again. The young man in the tie rushes back into Gadsby's booth and revives the microwave again. A cattlewoman asks Gadsby if he needs extra time. He says no. He settles back into his chair and begins sawing away at the hunk of beef like a patriarch at a family meal. He doesn't look up at the crowd.

Back from lunch with her daughter, Harmon cooks up a storm in the station next to Gadsby. Harmon smiles and jokes, looking as comfortable as if she's in her own kitchen. Hardly anyone notices her because all eyes are on Gadsby. He has grown visibly flustered as he tries to roll the steak, mashed potatoes, and onions into the small tortillas. It is like trying to pack too many clothes into a suitcase. There are more ingredients than tortilla. Although Gadsby does his best to roll them up delicately, they unfurl and mashers ooze out of either end. Onions pop out. Beads of sweat run down his face. In the audience Edwina sighs and looks away for a moment.

"Bob Gadsby, you have five minutes," the voice of doom says.

Gadsby begins fumbling with the tortillas. Now in a rush, he rolls them up sloppily. There are leftover ingredients scattered around the table. He just can't fit everything in. He arranges the wraps gently, leaning them against one another. "It's a pretty presentation," says Elder among the onlookers. "Like Stonehenge," Yee offers. He sets the plate on the cart as the call to go to the judges comes. He has just made it. "Who says it isn't hot in the kitchen?" he says, breaking into a smile as the onlookers clap. As soon as his photo is taken, Gadsby walks to his wife. Edwina kisses him and takes his hand. "You were about to see a grown man cry," he says.

〜〜〜〜

Cattlewomen don't get much opportunity to dress up out on their ranches, so the cookoff awards dinner is a kind of prom night. Freed of their baggy red shirts, the cattlewomen have morphed into fashion plates. They have slipped into long velvet evening numbers, squeezed into short black dresses, or draped themselves in caftanesque gowns. They have dug deep into their jewelry boxes. Long strands of faux pearls droop from their necks. Big, sparkly earrings pinch their ears. Family heirlooms jingle on their wrists. This is, after all, a girls' weekend, so what better way to top it off than by dressing to the nines and then sizing up one another. They have even persuaded their husbands to wear suits, but a number of men register their protest by retaining their cowboy hats and boots.

After drinks in a huge lobby, the decked-out gathering is herded into a hotel conference room with a sea of tables elaborately set for dinner. The lights are turned down low. A svelte woman in a clingy beaded number belts out pop tunes on a stage up front. On either side of her, slides flash. A photo of the American flag rippling majestically in the wind alternates with the National Beef Council's logo, a blazing red checkmark over the word "Beef" in big black letters. There are also photos of steers and an image of an American eagle, a tear in the corner of its eye, in front of the World Trade Center.

Once the guests have found their place cards, the contestants are brought into the room one by one. As each name is announced, a spotlight hits the contestant who is standing in the doorway on the crooked arm of a tuxedoed guy, who then escorts the contestant into the room. When the light hits Gadsby, who has stars and stripes hanging from his neck over his Buddha belly, a young cattlewoman at my table exclaims, "Whoa, look at that tie."

A cattlewoman offers a benediction as the formally attired crowd bows their heads: "You own the cattle on a thousand hills, and we are your caretakers. Send forth springs from the valley and cause the grass to grow. Close the mouth of the bear and the mountain lion and keep your cattle safe." Amen said, dinner gets under way. Hotel servers in white shirts run in circles around the floor, filling wineglasses and delivering a whopping plateful of salad followed by a frighteningly overcooked wad of filet mignon. No one says anything, but we chew hard and at length. Photos from the morning's cookoff are flashed on the screens at the front of the room. The mood is already almost nostalgic about the twenty-four hours that have just passed, like the last night of a vacation.

Head judge Jan Hazard, still chewing her dessert, is called to the podium to announce the winners. There will be nine in all: four first places ($10,000), four runners-ups ($5,000), and a grand prize winner ($50,000). So nearly half of the contestants will walk away with some cash.

The first name is Janice Elder, a runner-up for her Oriental Express Beef Lettuce Wraps. Elder pops up and gracefully strolls to the stage, a spotlight trailing her. Next, Finley, blinking, mouth agape, is called to the stage, a $10,000 first prize for her Roast Beef Cheddar Pockets. Harmon bounds up merrily to claim $10,000 for her Tex-Mex Smoky Chili Hash. Welander, dressed in a shirt with a pilgrim-like collar, looks vaguely stricken when her name is called for a runner-up. As she passes me, she mutters out of the side of her mouth, "I don't deserve this."

Eight names have been called. Gadsby is still in the audience. So are Yee, Bowman, and Miller. Anyone still seated could be the grand prize winner. Marjorie Farr still has hope that this will be her year. Hazard reads the final name: *"Pricilla Yee."*

Necks craning, everyone looks around the room for Yee, who, stunned, has yet to stand up, so the spotlight flits around the room looking for her. Her hostess finally pulls her up out of her seat and wraps her in a bear hug. Yee cuts such a small figure that not everyone sees her until she is near the front of the room. She takes the stage, smiling broadly, her face lit up unlike it has been all weekend. Once she is handed the award, Yee wells up.

The 2001 National Beef Cook-Off is suddenly over. The winners exit the stage. Yee is whisked out of the room for media interviews. Gadsby, empty-handed, begins making the rounds of the tables, glad-handing each winner like a statesman. The cattlewomen stampede from the room as if they have had it with their panty hose.

Yee is in a small room with the cookoff marketing team and the film crew. They interview her for the press release and the cookoff video, asking her what she'll do with the money. She is unsure; maybe she'll put down new kitchen flooring or pay off her car. She is animated, laughing and even joking. The only frown that crosses her face is when her hostess suggests she come up with recipes for prepared beef.

The plan is for Yee to spend most of the next day learning the "beef message." Then she will do a series of satellite interviews with TV morning shows around the country, starting at the ungodly hour of 3 A.M. Monday to catch the East Coast.

"Sounds okay to me," Yee says.

"You just got to get her to talk a little bit more," Yee's hostess adds, then turns to me. "She's never been married, so she's within herself."

Someone asks Yee if she wouldn't like to call someone. She pauses, then says, "I guess so."

〜〜〜〜

On the plane ride back I spot one of the cookoff contestants and her husband. When we reach elevation, she comes down the aisle to my seat, and we chew over the cookoff. She was surprised Welander's dish won a prize. "It was the simplest," she says. Yee's dish, she points out, was similar to the last winner because it used oranges. She wonders out loud if that's what the contest is looking for, fruit and meat. She says the cattlewomen were glad to say good-bye to Yee, who having won can't enter the contest again. Of the second tray viewing when Yee pawed through the oranges, she says, "Any of those oranges were fine."

I'm not so sure. I'm beginning to think it's the small details that make or break contestants at cookoffs, that perfectionism rules the day. A week or so later when I call a couple of the judges to ask them about their experience, I find my proof. I ask one judge about individual dishes. Yee's struck her as the winner immediately.

I ask about Gadsby's. I still can't believe mashed potatoes would work in a wrap. She tells me the potatoes actually worked. They helped hold the wrap together. Why didn't it get a prize? I ask. Because it was disqualified.

The Rooster was disqualified.

It turns out Gadsby didn't use all his ingredients, which the rules say he must. When he left out some of his meat to accommodate the small tortillas, he punted, $5,000, $10,000, who knows, maybe $50,000. In my mind I see him signing off at the second tray viewing, accepting the smaller tortillas, whereas Yee slowly weighed each orange in her hand as the night grew darker.

〜〜〜〜

Priscilla Yee, a longtime contester from Concord, California, won $50,000 for her streamlined recipe for a little-used cut of beef at the 2001 National Beef Cook-Off.

CUMIN-CRUSTED BEEF STEAKS WITH ORANGE-OLIVE RELISH

4 boneless beef chuck eye or chuck top blade steaks, cut 3/4 inch thick (about 1 1/2 pounds)
2 to 3 medium oranges
1 1/2 teaspoons ground cumin
1 teaspoon salt
1/2 teaspoon pepper
1 jar (7ounces) roasted red peppers, diced
1/3 cup coarsely chopped Kalamata olives
1/3 cup diced red onion
Orange slices and Kalamata olives

1. Grate 2 teaspoons of orange peel from the oranges; reserve the oranges. Combine the orange peel, cumin, and salt in a small bowl; remove and reserve 2 teaspoons of seasoning for the relish.

2. Heat a ridged grill pan or large nonstick skillet over medium heat until hot. Add pepper to the remaining seasoning and press evenly into the beef steaks. Place the steaks on the grill pan. Cook chuck eye steaks for 9 to 11 minutes (top blade steaks for 10 to 12 minutes) for medium-rare to medium doneness, turning once.

3. Meanwhile, peel and dice enough reserved oranges to measure 1 1/2 cups. Combine the diced oranges, red peppers, olives, onion, and the reserved 2 teaspoons of seasoning in a medium bowl. Mix well. Serve the steaks with relish. Garnish with orange slices and olives.

MAKES 4 SERVINGS

CHAPTER 7

CREATION STORIES

Robert Pavey had a high fever, 102, high enough that the hard-charging, forty-three-year-old real estate broker stayed home from the office. He had the chills, the works. While the nanny took care of his young son and his wife went off to work, he stayed in bed. Looking for something to read, he grabbed what was on the nightstand, his wife's cooking contest newsletter. He had entered a few contests, inspired by his wife who had won $1,300 with a salmon recipe. The announcement for the new Post Selects Cereal cookoff caught his eye.

This contest was more complicated than most. You had to come up with a recipe using one and a half cups or more of one of four cereals: Blueberry Morning, Cranberry Almond Crunch, Banana Nut Crunch, and Great Grains. Then you had to write 250 words about the perfect brunch you would throw for family and friends featuring your recipe. Eight finalists would compete in New York City for $10,000 and the title of America's Most Amazing Brunch Host.

Pavey dozed off, his fever pulling him down into a dream-filled sleep. He dreamt that he was at the contest in New York. It was one of those crystal-clear, hyper-real sleepscapes, the kind that fills your every cell with an overwhelming sense of omnipotence. The theme of his brunch was Halloween. He was dressed as a ghost, his wife as a witch, and their son as Eddie Munster. He had heaped their many Halloween tchotchkes, including plastic jack-o'-lanterns and fake cobwebs, on the table. He had made French toast. He stood on a stage in front of an audience making an acceptance speech. He was the winner. He was America's Most Amazing Brunch Host.

He awoke. The dream was so real that he called his wife and asked when was the last time they were in New York. For Grandpa Sam's birthday, she said. He hung up and wrote down everything that had happened in the dream, scribbling on the newsletter and the envelope it had come in. When his wife returned home, he showed her what he had written. She checked his temperature again to see if it had spiked. It hadn't.

Pavey refined the recipe. He tried making French toast using croissants and stuffed them with blueberry preserves and Great Grains cereal. He sent in his entry: Thriller Filler Berry French Toast. His wife thought the whole incident was a hoot. They both forgot about it in the rush of their lives. She is a social worker in Miami-Dade County. Pavey sells a house about every five days, on average, for a total of $15 to $20 million in sales a year. He runs three miles or lifts weights every morning. They have one adopted son and a foster daughter.

In September, Pavey received a call at his office from Post. He was one of the eight finalists who would be flown to New York. Pavey tells me on the phone from Florida, "I was so stunned, I asked her, when will you announce the finalists, and she said, 'I just did.' I called my wife, and she didn't believe it."

He'll be the only man in the brunch-off, which slightly intimidates him even with his mile-wide competitive streak. If he wins, he'll use the $10,000 toward the adoption fee of their foster daughter, he tells me. Between that and the crazy way he came up with his recipe, I can't help rooting for Pavey.

∿∿∿∿

Contestants are constantly asked to recount the creation story of their recipes. Most have to do with getting by in a pinch, being out of an ingredient and reaching for another, necessity-is-the-mother-of-invention tales. Few are as mysterious as Pavey's, but he unwittingly used one of the techniques favored by some serious contesters: dreaming up recipes. Pavey was the only one who told me about such an elaborate dream, but a number of contesters keep notebooks by their bed. They find recipe ideas come to them as they are falling asleep or waking up, when brain waves smooth out to nice, gentle arcs. The trick is to rouse yourself and write down the directions for the three-layer cake that materialized in your slumbering imagination. Otherwise, like a dream, it will vanish into the deadening demands of everyday life.

Contesters differ from the average cooking contestant because they do not wait for inspiration to strike. They cultivate it. Thus the ever-present notebooks. Claudia Shepardson keeps notebooks in her kitchen and in her purse, in addition to the one on her nightstand. She never cracks a cooking magazine or cookbook without a notebook by her side. Shirley DeSantis, a longtime contester and steady winner, thought of most of her recipes when she was in the car taxiing her high school kids to orthodontist appointments, soccer practice, and play rehearsals. She carried a tote bag filled with three-by-five cards, envelopes, a notebook, and contest information. While she waited for her kids, she brainstormed her entries.

Some contesters work best at the computer, pounding out on their keyboard a neo chicken potpie or putting a new slant on tuna casserole and shipping it off via the electronic ethers untried. This is typically how Diane Sparrow works. The contesters who actually invent in the kitchen—like chemists, adding a little of this and a little of that to hit the right formula—make a point of writing down every tiny tweak to a dish, even an extra quarter teaspoon of salt. Don't ever think you'll just remember what you did, warns Pat Harmon, "because you won't."

If the creative juices are trickling rather than gushing, contesters have other means to spark their culinary imagination. They improvise on old standards such as pot roast or tuna salad, changing the spicing, the cooking style, or the central ingredient. They rework past entries. They cross-pollinate dishes or ethnic cuisines. In fact, contesters were cooking fusion long before toque-topped chefs discovered the style in the '80s.

Jean Sanderson did all of the above when she rode a wave of chicken Kiev creations to five cookoffs in four years, as she describes in her book *The Million Dollar Contest Cookbook*. The central concept of chicken Kiev is brilliantly simple: butter on the inside, butter on the outside, white meat in between. A chicken breast is rolled around a wad of herbed butter, sealed, and then fried. Sanderson first free-associated on the stuffed aspect of the dish. She filled crescent dinner rolls with chopped mushrooms, cream cheese with chives, butter, cubed chicken, and seasoning. She dipped the pastry Kievs in melted butter, coated them with crushed seasoned croutons, and baked them. Chicken à la Crescents won her a trip to the twenty-second Bake-Off® contest in Hawaii.

Next she replaced the traditional filling with cheese and green chili, and deep-fried the roll of poultry to come up with Mexican Chicken Kiev, which got her to the 1972 National Chicken. She returned to the Bake-Off contest® with Fiesta Chicken, reusing the cheese stuffing idea but taking it one step further. She rolled the stuffed breasts in crushed cheese crackers and taco seasoning, then microwaved them. She won $5,000 and a new microwave. The comminglings became more complex. She pulled ideas from her Mexican Chicken Kiev and her Fiesta Chicken, then traded bird for cow. Beef Kiev Ole won her a slot at the 1975 National Beef Cook-Off. Lastly, she reworked the cream cheese filling of her first Kiev creation and rolled catfish fillets around it. Voilà! Farm-Raised Catfish Kiev Style. She won first place at the National Catfish Cooking Contest.

What worked then for Sanderson works now. Most of the Post finalists have used the same techniques. The formidable Camilla Saulsbury applied Caribbean flavors to an American standard to come up with Calypso Crab Cakes with Fresh Mango-Papaya Relish. Instead of using bread crumbs, she ground up Great Grains cereal.

Liz Barclay, the school administrator who was at National Chicken the previous spring, reworked a dish that she recalls eating long ago, a chicken salad served on a carrot cake. She used the idea for a Gold Kist recipe contest, then reworked it again for Post, giving it a German twist.

This version is Tarragon Chicken Salad on Cranberry Almond Crunch Kuchen. She uses Cranberry Almond Crunch in the kuchen. Norita Solt, a mega blue-ribbon winner from Iowa, crossed her favorite dish, bread pudding, with Bananas Foster to create Creole Banana Nut Crunch Bread Pudding with Creamy Brown Sugar Sauce. Most of the bread in this bread pudding is two cups of Banana Nut Crunch Cereal. From Creole food her brunch theme, Mardi Gras, naturally followed.

Solt's story gives me second thoughts on backing Pavey. Cooking contests, no matter how silly they may seem at times, are incredible mental lifts. Even winning a small contest with a tiny purse improves the spirits. Solt could use a lift just now. For the past month she has been driving one hundred miles each way from her home in the Quad-Cities to spend the day with her ninety-nine-year-old Aunt Gy, who has had colon surgery. Solt doesn't expect her beloved Aunt Gy to make it. A few weeks back Solt competed in a qualifying round for The Great Australian Barbeque Cookoff in Chicago. She was given a broken thermometer, which made her overcook her pork tenderloin and knocked her out of the finals in Sydney, Australia. Her husband, an accountant, recently lost his job. The small contracting company he worked for went bankrupt. "We may have to move," she says, sighing. "We aren't going to starve. I'd love to bring home that $10,000. If not, I'll go back to work."

Solt has put her considerable energy into Post in the time she has between hospital runs. In addition to the bread pudding, she has planned a menu worthy of Brennan's: Cajun Sausage Eggs Benedict, Cheesy Corn Grits, Spicy Boiled Shrimp with Roumalade Sauce (Solt's spelling), and Pecan Biscuits. Solt will drape Mardi Gras beads across the table and scatter a few feathered masks. She has practiced tucking packing boxes under the tablecloth on her dining room table to make platforms for her dishes. "I like elevation," she says. She's even going to mix up Bourbon Punch because what would a Mardi Gras brunch be without booze? She is confident except for Saulsbury. "I know she's very thin, which makes me very uncomfortable," Solt says. "I've been there. I used to be skinny. Just knowing how meticulous Camilla is, I can't get too cocky."

Saulsbury is the last person most people would expect to find at a cookoff. She is relatively young for a contester, thirty-one. She has straight blond hair that falls below her shoulder, a fine-featured face with a gently pointed chin, and dark eyes. She is single but has a serious boyfriend. No one mentions her without mentioning how beautiful she is. She modeled in high school. She, however, is not just a pretty face. Saulsbury is a twenty-first-century Renaissance woman with a long list of accomplishments that would make her hateful if she wasn't so gracious. She plays the viola and violin. She is a long-distance runner. She teaches kickboxing, spinning, aerobics, and Pilates among other ways of working up a sweat. Teaching exercise has underwritten her graduate studies at the University of Indiana, where she is working on a doctorate in sociology. Her doctoral thesis subject, home cooking, was inspired by her experience on the contesting circuit. "I find it fascinating the way people think of food," she says.

She can be highbrow about food: M.F.K. Fisher was the greatest influence on her cooking. Or lowbrow: the Crock-Pot is her favorite kitchen tool. Saulsbury comes from a family of cooks in Albany, California. She cracked her first cookbook when she was seven or eight, when most girls are just pretending that their Barbie dolls are making dinner for Ken. After she had two recipes published in *Sunset* magazine, her mother suggested she check out contests. Saulsbury knew of Roxanne Chan, also in Albany, and of Kurt Wait in nearby Redwood City. In January 1997 she settled down in front of her computer in her Bloomington apartment and typed in "cooking contests." Cooking Contest Central, with its extensive list of contests, magically appeared. In short order she got an honorable mention in the former Paul Newman contest, a slot at Sutter Home's Better Burger, and a $400 monthly award at *Better Homes and Gardens.* In two years she has won a total of twelve contests. She arrives at Post having won $20,000 in August in the "What Do You Do with Your Pace" recipe contest for Jambalaya Shortcakes with Cayenne Cream and the annual grand prize from *Better Homes and Gardens* of $5,000.

The morning of the Post cookoff, which begins at an ungodly

5:30 A.M., Saulsbury tackles her table decorations like Martha Stewart on speed. As I sip coffee and Solt wanders around a kitchen island, saying, "I just feel so totally disoriented," I watch Saulsbury, her long hair pulled back in a ponytail, wrestle her table onto its side and go at it with a staple gun. In short order she has attached a grass skirt to the edge and covered the top with sand, creating a mini table-top beach. I hear a whoosh. She has popped open a beach umbrella. Solt and the other contestants are still unpacking their ingredients.

Meanwhile, Pavey, who resembles Teddy Roosevelt with his full mustache, row of straight white teeth, and close-cropped dark hair, tests his fog machine, filling the room with a thin white smoke and the smell of burning plastic. He climbs a ladder with a dangling rubber shinbone in hand. He seems all fired up, unlike his wife, Zita, who sits nearby with dark circles under her eyes. Their four-year-old son snoozes deeply in a stroller. They are surrounded by brown paper bags filled with Pavey's supplies. From the ladder Pavey asks his wife to move a bag. She can't, she whispers. The rules are she's not supposed to touch anything. There's nothing in that bag for the cookoff, Pavey says, exasperated.

"Well, they don't know that," she hisses.

It's really too early for cordial spousal relations, not to mention competing for $10,000. This cookoff is unusual on several counts in addition to the predawn start. It is being held in a cooking school, the Institute of Culinary Education, on West Twenty-third Street in New York City, formerly Peter Kumpf's cooking school, so the contestants are working in top-notch kitchens instead of the usual jerry-built setups. They have chef assistants supplied by the school. They will need them. In three hours they have to decorate their tables, cook an entire meal, although the judges will taste only one dish, and give a presentation. It's half cookoff, half talent contest.

This is also the first company cookoff where I've seen a belly button ring. A first-time contestant from California sports chunky loafers, bell-bottoms, and a top so tight it seems to bow her shoulders. She has been given a delayed starting time because she spent a half hour last night on the crust of her Blueberry Morning Cheesecake. The Post people are worried that she's jumping the gun. "There's a lot of arranging going on," a Post worker says sarcastically.

Over the next few hours, as the sun rises and New York's tall buildings materialize in the morning light, the contestants work away. Barclay, in the earrings she made from a Post cereal box, is the coolest, talking up a storm with Solt and another contestant, a redheaded artist from Michigan. Solt struggles. The fruit for her salad is frozen. Her eggs aren't fresh enough. When she pulls her bread pudding out of the oven, she despairs. "It didn't puff up like I wanted."

"It looks okay to me," offers Solt's husband, Ron, who has mostly kept his distance, giving his wife a wide berth as he wanders around, Styrofoam coffee cup in hand. The redhead's husband, a first-time cooking contestant spouse, isn't so smart. He hovers, offers suggestions. She keeps telling him to go away, and he keeps drifting back. "Stop it," she finally snaps.

"I'm just trying to help," he says.

"No, you're not, you're interfering. Please leave," she orders. She stops cooking and glares at him over her halvies as he slowly ambles out of the room. Once he's gone, two ponytailed chef attendants snicker.

In another kitchen Saulsbury quietly keeps to herself as she cooks. Pavey works at the stove while his son—in his Eddie Munster getup and with a black widow's peak drawn on his small, square forehead—clings to his leg. When a cooking student tries to carry him out, the kid screeches, causing everyone to freeze. Pavey's wife, now in a black witch's outfit, stands nearby like a lady-in-waiting, holding a sheet with a big hole. This is Pavey's ghost outfit. He finally pauses to pull the sheet over his head. It is so voluminous that he has to hold it toga style with one arm and looks more like a Roman senator than Casper.

By 9 A.M., all the tables are set. A contester from Ohio in large red glasses, Lori Shamszadeh, has set goldfish in a bowl on her table. A Minnesota contester has set her table with mittens for napkins. The Californian has draped champagne grapes here and there. Pavey's is by far the hokiest. He has even made a ghost from a slightly pilled blanket and set it in one of the chairs.

Pavey is the first to present to the four judges, including B. Smith, the restaurateur and home arts goddess. She looks like a movie star in her red suit and shoulder-length dreadlocks. Pavey's son insists on sitting down, so two judges have to eat standing up. As Pavey reads his poem, his wife at his side with an embarrassed smile on her face, fog shoots out and ghouls cackle. A rubber hand keeps rising from a bowl of candy corn, demanding in a menacing warble, "I want a penny."

Saulsbury is up next. Her presentation is, by comparison, warm and polished, like a seasoned hostess. Barclay, with the well-practiced projection of a classroom teacher, reads the poem she penned for the contest, which ends, "Select me, dear judges, I know you will toast, a hostess like me, for my feast à la *Post*!"

This being a first-time cookoff, it's a little disorganized. The judges have little time at each table, and no one thinks to offer them water until Smith asks for it. Solt is brought into the room and launches into her presentation, not realizing that the judges are still at another table. Pavey's son keeps turning on the jack-o'-lanterns, which interrupt other contestants' presentations with ghoulish laughs. When the redhead gives her presentation, a sound man knocks his big fuzzy mike into Saulsbury's beach umbrella, which tumbles over onto the head of the redhead's husband. Despite her warnings, he hasn't stopped hovering.

As the judges deliberate, Pavey bemoans that he forgot to make his Bloody Marys, Solt bemoans the old eggs, and Barclay wishes she had said more. They all ask me who I think won because I saw all the presentations. I answer that I'm not sure, but the grand prize winner is a no-brainer to me. As much as I want Pavey or Solt to win, I'd wager it all on Saulsbury.

To my relief, Pavey wins second place ($1,000) and Solt finishes first ($2,500). Saulsbury, on being declared America's Most Amazing Brunch Host, says, "Wow," and wells up. "I want to thank all my graduate student friends for tasting, and my dad, who's sick, and he was supposed to be here."

Most of the contestants circle around Saulsbury to hug her and congratulate her. Shamszadeh, the Ohio contestant, abruptly begins to break down her table and pack up, as if she can't get out of here fast enough. She looks crestfallen, as though she might even cry. She tells me that she has fibromyalgia, probably brought on by three whip-lashes in three different car accidents over the years. She can't sleep and has given up her work as a graphic designer. Cooking is fine, but the stress of cookoffs brings on the muscle aches. "I don't know how long I can keep doing this," she says and empties the goldfish bowl into a plastic bag. Shamszadeh could have used a lift.

〜〜〜〜

Camilla Saulsbury won $10,000 and the title America's Most Amazing Brunch Host with this recipe at a cookoff held by Post Selects Cereal.

CALYPSO CRAB CAKES WITH FRESH MANGO-PAPAYA RELISH

3 tablespoons mayonnaise
1/4 cup chopped fresh cilantro, divided
1 tablespoon grated lime peel, divided
4 teaspoons fresh lime juice, divided
1 1/2 teaspoons ground ginger
1/2 teaspoon salt
1/4 teaspoon pepper
1/8 teaspoon cayenne pepper
12 ounces crabmeat
1/3 cup chopped roasted red pepper
2 cups crushed Post Selects Great Grains Crunchy Pecan cereal
2 eggs, separated
1/2 cup flour
1 1/2 cups fresh bread crumbs
1/2 cup diced mango
1/2 cup diced papaya
3/4 cup chunky salsa
4 tablespoons (1/2 stick) butter or margarine

In a large bowl, mix together the mayonnaise, half of the cilantro, half of the lime peel, half of the lime juice, the ginger, salt, pepper, and cayenne. Add the crabmeat and red pepper, and stir until combined.

Stir in the cereal. Stir in the egg yolks (the mixture will be soft) until well blended.

Form the crab mixture into eight 3/4-inch-thick cakes, using a generous 1/4 cup for each. Coat the cakes with flour on both sides, shaking off the excess. Beat the egg whites until foamy and brush on both sides of the cakes. Coat with the bread crumbs. Cover and refrigerate until ready to cook.

Meanwhile, in a medium bowl, mix together the mango, papaya, salsa, remaining cilantro, remaining lime peel, and remaining lime juice. Set aside.

Melt the butter in a large, heavy skillet over medium-high heat. Working in batches, cook the cakes about 4 minutes per side, or until golden brown and heated through. Serve hot with the mango-papaya relish.

Great Substitute: Make the relish with only mango or papaya, or try adding another tropical fruit such as chopped pineapple.

MAKES 4 SERVINGS

∿ ∿ ∿ ∿

Robert Pavey won third place in the Post Selects Cereal 2001 Brunch Contest with this recipe he dreamt up.

THRILLER FILLER BERRY FRENCH TOAST

1 cup half-and-half
2 eggs
1/4 cup plus 2 teaspoons sugar
1/4 cup brandy
1 teaspoon cinnamon
1/4 teaspoon salt
Pinch of ground nutmeg
4 large croissants

8 tablespoons blueberry preserves
2 cups Post Selects Great Grains Crunchy Pecan cereal
2 cups sliced strawberries
3 tablespoons water
1/2 cup (1 stick) butter or margarine
Cool Whip Whipped Topping (optional)

In a small bowl, mix together the half-and-half, eggs, 1/4 cup sugar, brandy, cinnamon, salt, and nutmeg until well blended. Pour into a 13 x 9-inch baking dish and set aside.

Cut the croissants in half lengthwise. Spread the blueberry preserves on the bottom half of each croissant. Sprinkle 1 cup of cereal over the preserves. Top each croissant with its top half, pushing down gently to adhere.

Place the prepared croissants into the egg mixture. Let stand for 10 minutes, turning once. Meanwhile, combine the strawberries, water, and the remaining 2 teaspoons sugar in a medium bowl. Set aside.

Melt the butter in a large skillet over medium heat. Cook the croissants in the butter until slightly golden. Turn gently and cook the other side. Place on a serving platter. Add the strawberry mixture to the skillet and cook about 3 to 4 minutes. Pour the strawberries over the croissants. Sprinkle with the remaining cereal and serve with thawed Cool Whip Whipped Topping if desired.

SERVES 4

CHAPTER 8

COPYCATS

One morning a few weeks after Saulsbury returned from New York, she turned on the television to *Good Morning America*. This was not her usual morning routine, but she was curious to see who had won the Apple Pie of Emeril's Eye contest. A woman in a red cardigan stood next to Emeril Lagasse in his chef's whites. She was Marsha Brooks of Carmel, Indiana. She had won with her Crunchy Caramel Apple Pie. The pie, she explained, was a big hit with her small town's potluck dinner crowd. She liked to make it in the fall. Brooks said her special ingredient was TLC, tender loving care.

Huh? thought Saulsbury. The recipe name sounded very familiar. Saulsbury hardly ever made apple pie, but she had made one once from *Better Homes and Gardens* because it used a jar of caramel topping. Saulsbury sat at her computer, went on the Web, and typed in the recipe name. There it was, word for word, on the *BHG* website. It was published in the October '97 issue in a story entitled "To Grandmother's House We Go." The pie was attributed to Betty Hessler, a grandmother and former apple grower in Belding, Michigan. Hessler had concocted the recipe in '92 for the Michigan Apple Promoters, a group of fruit grower wives. She added oatmeal for a dose of healthful fiber and the caramel because "you always eat caramel apples in the fall." She entered it in some local contests. Then it ran in the *Chicago Sun-Times,* and *Better Homes and Gardens* picked it up.

Hessler, the copy read, liked to use moderately tart apples, such as Idareds, Jonathans, or Northern Spys. Brooks did break with the *BHG* recipe on this issue. She suggested bland Golden Delicious apples or sugary Fujis.

The contest rules read that the recipe must be original. If Brooks had adapted the recipe, Saulsbury would have kept mum. This was an exact replica. Brooks hadn't even changed the title. Saulsbury decided to turn the Carmel copycat in. She emailed *Good Morning America* to inform them of the recipe's true origins, directing them to the *BHG* website. Days and then weeks went by. Saulsbury never received a reply. She told other contesters of her discovery, and they, too, emailed *Good Morning America;* like Saulsbury, they never heard back.

In the meantime, the pie's television debut buzzed around Belding, a small town nestled in the crook of the Flat River outside of Grand Rapids. Friends and neighbors who spotted Hessler's recipe called her with the news. When Hessler went to the grocery store, people stopped their carts to tell her, "I saw your pie on television."

Hessler's niece called *Good Morning America* to report that Brooks's pie belonged to her Aunt Betty. A television show rep called Hessler and eventually sent her a box of *Good Morning America* coffee cups, T-shirts, and hats. That was good enough for Hessler, who sent back a thank-you note.

"We had a good time about it, a good laugh," Hessler says. The funny thing is, she says, her son suggested two years before that she enter her recipe in the *Good Morning America* contest, but Hessler never got around to it. "The next thing we know there was the Crunchy Caramel Pie on the television."

"Gosh, it's a good promotion for apples, to get that recipe out. That's why I did it to begin with."

Meanwhile, Brooks was given an Outstanding Citizen Award in early December by the Carmel City Council for winning the pie contest with Hessler's recipe.

〰〰〰

Was Brooks a cheat? Yes, but giving her the benefit of the doubt, possibly not intentionally. She might not have read the rules. She might have naively misunderstood the concept of "original." Any cook who repeatedly uses a recipe unwittingly begins to feel it belongs to her. Who hasn't referred to a dish cribbed from a cookbook as "my soufflé," "my chowder," "my chocolate cake." Brooks may have copied the recipe down on a three-by-five card and filed it in her recipe box, forgetting that it ever had origins outside of her own kitchen.

This is why unoriginal recipes pop up with some frequency in cookoffs and recipe contests. In 1995, Edwina Gadsby won one of ten slots at the now-defunct Great Salad Toss, a cookoff sponsored by Fetzer wines in California. A woman from Michigan, who Gadsby said proved to be a sore loser, had a recipe, Layered Salad with Cumin-Honey Vinaigrette, that rang a bell with her. Back home in Montana she found it verbatim in an issue of *Bon Appétit*. "It is my impression that there are a lot of people out there who don't grasp the concept of original."

"Original" is a big, squishy word in the world of recipes. Recipes are like paper money, constantly passing from hand to hand, dispersed far and wide, each set of fingers leaving its own marks, each person thinking the bill belongs to him alone. By the time the bill is worn and soft, who had first held it as crisp and new is many hands ago and long forgotten.

Likewise, family recipes passed down over generations—Grandma's this or that—turn out to have come from Fannie Farmer, who may have lifted it herself. Among the recipes I inherited from my grandmother, handwritten on envelopes and notepaper in her tiny, loopy scrawl, are instructions for such midcentury standards as Jell-O salad, Brown Betty icing, and Swedish cookies. One recipe is entitled Joan's Coffee Cake, promising a personal imprint. Joan is my mother, and her recipe turns out to be a basic crumb cake. There is no Joan in Joan's Coffee Cake.

This is why recipes written in standard format are not copyrightable. The Copyright Act lays it out plain and clear. Protection does not extend "to any idea, procedure, process, system, method of operation, concept. . . ." Cookbooks are copyrightable as a collection, but even then the individual recipes within are not protected. Only recipes with substantial literary expression are protected. For example, Smokey Hale's recipe for a grilled steak from *The Great American Barbecue and Grilling Manual* would qualify. He writes: "When a ready steak meets the heated grill, they seize each other with the intensity of newlyweds. At the proper time, they will turn loose. Flip them over with a spatula, not a fork. They will grab again. When they turn loose the second time, the honeymoon is over and it's time to get on with business."

Standard directions—grill for five minutes on medium-high, turn with a spatula, grill another five minutes until desired doneness—are not copyrightable. Without the colorful adlibbing, copyright law does not consider a recipe an "original work of authorship."

The truth may hurt, but it can also free you. The lack of copyright protection assures the free flow of recipes, which any cook who has stood dumbstruck before her open fridge wondering what to cook for dinner knows is essential. Imagine if every time someone wanted to publish a recipe for roasted chicken, he had to track down the cook who first roasted a chicken and ask for permission. It's just not possible. Ethics dictate, however, that a cook not claim a recipe as her own creation when it is not. Ethical food editors and cookbook writers who lift a recipe note its origins when possible.

The elusiveness of originality in recipes hasn't stopped many contests from requiring it. Originality is not necessary in contests based solely on execution, such as chili and barbecue, but it's of central importance to company- and industry-sponsored events. They want new, creative ways to use their product, not recycled recipes taken from magazines and cookbooks. They are putting up the big bucks to put American home cooks in a creative mood, not a copying mood.

Most originality rules bar recipes that have won other contests or that have been published. That does not mean a contestant can't adapt these recipes. Contests generally use the same rules for originality that cookbook authors and cooking magazines use. When adapting recipes, three major ingredients must be changed. What constitutes a "major" ingredient is a judgment call, but suffice it to say that adding more salt or changing the variety of potato doesn't do the job.

To ensure that these rules are followed, nearly all contests require finalists to sign an affidavit stating the recipe is "original." This legal document, the thinking goes, should be intimidating enough to separate the cheaters from the straight shooters. "We put some of the onus back on them," says Marlene Johnson of the Bake-Off® contest. It also serves as a wake-up call. Johnson says some finalists, when faced with the affidavit, disqualify themselves, realizing they had overlooked or misunderstood the originality requirement.

Many contests also keep an eye out for copies. At one magazine, a food editor told me, red flags go up if a contest entry comes out perfectly on its first testing. If it is a Jell-O recipe, the staff will send it to Jell-O to check, and a turkey recipe goes to Butterball. Head judge James McNair at Sutter Home's Better Burger relies on his own extensive memory of past contest entries. Each year he weeds out entries that are exact copies of past Better Burger winners.

Some contests hire agencies for the sleuthing. Since its beginning in 1975, the International Food Institute, an independent test kitchen in Chicago, has worked on a long list of national contests for products such as Bay's English Muffins, Butterball Turkeys, and Kraft Marshmallow Cream. Their home economists, cum private eyes, check recipes in a library of five hundred cookbooks, old and new. Then they go on the Internet. "Over the years we've found a number of copies. Many times they are in the smaller cookbooks, in Junior League or PTA cookbooks, or in food company cookbooks," says Angela Kaye, a home economist and the institute's director.

The Web has made it easier to screen recipes, but it has also made it more difficult to create original ones. Since the mid '90s, recipes have proliferated on the Web at a stunning rate, with such sites as epicurious.com, which boasts more than fourteen thousand recipes. Food companies post their own voluminous banks of recipes. Even home cooks proudly put their own concoctions up on the Web. What these home cooks don't realize is that once their recipe is on the Web, it is considered published, meaning that it is no longer national contest material. "In the near future originality will be nearly impossible," says Kaye. "The world is getting smaller and smaller."

Pillsbury puts recipes through the most rigorous screening. Recipes travel a long road to become finalists, and on the way they are eyed by seasoned home economists who can practically recite chapters out of the *Joy of Cooking* and will yank any recipe that is familiar. After two passes the surviving entries are whipped up in Pillsbury's test kitchen and tasted by a panel. If a recipe gets the go-ahead, it is specifically vetted for originality. A team of three to four home economists will bear down on the recipe, flipping through Pillsbury's sizable library, even cracking foreign cookbooks. Having seen and eaten the recipe in the test kitchen, they know exactly what they are looking for.

"They don't want to find things, but when they do, they are pleased," says Maggie Gilbert, who oversees the Bake-Off® contest's screening and judging.

Of the major contests, National Chicken takes the most lackadaisical approach. Until the early '90s the contest didn't even require entries to be original, believing such a rule was unenforceable. They changed their minds after the April 1991 contest in Little Rock, Arkansas. Judith Markiewicz, a thirty-three-year-old food science major from Canton, Ohio, won the $25,000 grand prize with Southwestern Fried Chicken. Head judge Jan Hazard dubbed it "southwestern shake and bake." Another judge, Jonathan Susskind of the *Seattle Post-Intelligencer*, wrote of Markiewicz's dish, "The chicken was so crisp and juicy that at first I didn't realize it was skinless." He dubbed Markiewicz "a pleasantly promotable person, almost a Cinderella tale. . . . And, bless her heart, she wants to be a food editor." He added that a few magazine editors told her to send them her resume once she graduated.

It became clear to some of the reporters at the press conference following the awards ceremony that the Cinderella tale might unravel. When asked about the genesis of her recipe, Markiewicz volunteered that the dish came from a magazine and that she "had played with it."

"What magazine?" a reporter asked.

"*Bon Appétit*," Markiewicz answered.

The April 1990 issue, to be exact, in which freelance food writer

Abby Mandel penned Spicy Southwestern Oven-Fried Chicken. Markiewicz, it turned out, had played around with the recipe very little. Other
than drop a word from the title, Markiewicz had changed a pinch of
ground cloves to an eighth of a teaspoon, slightly decreased the amount
of salt, and added 1/4 teaspoon of pepper. Mandel complained in the
Chicago Tribune: "She changed a little something, but it's nothing compared to the rest of the recipe." Mandel estimated that she had received
$250 from *Bon Appétit* for the recipe, or 1 percent of Markiewicz's take.
Mandel said the legal issues were "muddy" and that she had no plans
to file a suit. "Then you go to the ethical issue, and it isn't muddy. It's
totally unethical."

The National Broiler Council stood behind their winner. Markiewicz
hadn't broken any contest rule, and most assumed she'd naively copied
the recipe. Still, she had given the contest a black eye. Contest losers
mailed the two recipes to food editors across the country, and newspaper stories appeared with such headlines as "Amazing What a Little
Pepper Can Do for Leftovers" and "The NBC Turkey."

By July the contest had announced a major rule change: "Entries
must be original. Original is defined as not previously published in the
same or substantially the same form. Contestant finalists will be required to certify that the recipe entry is original."

However, the contest did not institute any kind of screening. It relies
on contestants' honesty as expressed in their affidavit, says Richard
Lobb, a spokesperson for the National Chicken Council, formerly the
National Broiler Council. Lobb also looks to contesters for enforce-
ment. "We can rely on them to self-police. They take the contest very seriously."

By '97 the contesters were on the job policing one of their own,
Teresa Hannan Smith, a contester from Santa Rosa, California. Smith
had a good list of wins to her name, including $2,000 in the '92 Pills-
bury Bake-Off® contest with a cross between a club sandwich and a
pizza. Her husband, Gary, had won a vacation to Scotland and London
for two in Bay's English Muffin contest in 1996. When Smith was
named a finalist for National Chicken, a number of contesters recog-
nized her recipe right away. Yucatan Chicken with Peach-Avocado Salsa

was a reworking of her Yucatan Pork Tenderloin with Peach-Avocado Salsa, which had won her the grand prize, a weeklong trip for two to Tuscany, in the 1994 Specialty Brands (Spice Islands) "Cook Up a Trip" recipe contest.

Smith had recycled her winner, swapping pork for chicken, doubling the olive oil from one to two tablespoons, and using oregano instead of cilantro. Contesters generally rework recipes that bomb in a contest, but they typically retire winners. Smith was flaunting this convention; moreover, to many people's eyes, the revamped recipe did not include three major changes. The chicken was a change, the oregano, maybe, but doubling the olive oil from one to two tablespoons was very iffy.

Several weeks before the contest someone anonymously sent a copy to the National Broiler Council of the pork recipe as published in a contesting newsletter. Smith still arrived at the cookoff in Hilton Head in April along with the other fifty finalists for the Forty-second National Chicken. That night someone slipped a copy of Smith's winning pork recipe under contest director Nancy Tringali's hotel room door. Copies were also somehow sneaked on to two judges' scoring clipboards, although the meaning was lost on them.

The day of the cookoff, Tringali kept the information about Smith's recipe to herself until it emerged as a front runner after two rounds of blind tasting. Then she told the judges about the pork recipe and left it to them to decide if the two recipes were different enough. Jo Mancuso, then editor of the *San Francisco Examiner*'s food section and a neophyte cooking contest judge, says the judges ruled that Smith had made enough changes. They weren't happy about Smith's Yucatan Chicken being adapted from her previous winner, Mancuso says, but it was by far the best dish.

At the press conference following the awards ceremony, Smith was asked, of course, where her recipe came from. She talked about the inspiration she found in her own backyard in Santa Rosa, where peaches, limes, oranges, and tomatoes grew. She never mentioned her winning pork recipe. She didn't know that the judges already knew. The contesters were really stewed. Cheryl Lynn McAtee, a first-time contestant and third place winner from Washington, didn't know about the controversy until she swung through the reception room that night and overheard people grumbling about Smith. Back home McAtee received an anonymous envelope postmarked in Alabama containing the contest newsletter that reported Smith's pork win.

A few days after the contest the National Broiler Council issued a statement acknowledging the chicken dish's pork roots. No one seemed especially bothered at first. Most of the judges went home and wrote experiential stories for their papers, either mentioning the controversy in passing or not at all or as the sour grapes of bitter contesters. Mancuso, an award-winning journalist, broke rank and decided the controversy over Smith's win deserved a story of its own.

Mancuso tracked down the contestant who had slipped the recipe under Tringali's door. It was Sandra Collins, the contestant from Colorado. "This threatens the integrity of cooking contests in general," Collins told Mancuso, "because if you can have one recipe and win the grand prize and basically turn around and reissue it with very few changes, then what's the competitive fun? Most of us are creating new recipes for each contest."

After the National Chicken controversy, Smith dropped out of the contesting circuit. I tried to reach her, but my messages and a fax got no response. For her *Examiner* story, Mancuso, who was not invited to judge National Chicken again, managed to interview Smith only by email. Mancuso asked Smith if she would do anything differently in future contests. Smith responded, "Why change a winning recipe?"

〜〜〜〜

Former orchard owner Betty Hessler of Belding, Michigan, created this recipe, which was published in the October 1997 issue of Better Homes and Gardens. *On November 8, 2001, Marsha Brooks of Carmel, Indiana, won the* Apple Pie of Emeril's Eye Contest *on* Good Morning America *with the same pie.*

CRUNCHY CARAMEL APPLE PIE

1 pastry crust for a 9-inch deep-dish pie (homemade or store-bought)
1/2 cup sugar
3 tablespoons all-purpose flour
1 teaspoon ground cinnamon
1/8 teaspoon salt
6 cups peeled, thinly sliced apples
1/2 cup chopped pecans
1/4 cup caramel ice cream topping
1 ounce TLC (tender loving care)

CRUMB TOPPING

1 cup packed brown sugar
1/2 cup all-purpose flour
1/2 cup quick-cooking rolled oats
1/2 cup (1 stick) butter

To make the crumb topping: Stir together the brown sugar, flour, and rolled oats. Cut in the butter until the topping is like coarse crumbs. Set aside.

1. In a large mixing bowl, stir together the sugar, flour, cinnamon, and salt.

2. Add the apple slices and toss gently until coated.

3. Transfer the apple mixture to the pie shell.

4. Sprinkle the crumb topping over the apple mixture.

5. Place the pie on a cookie sheet so the drippings don't drop into your oven.

6. Cover the edges of the pie with aluminum foil.

7. Bake in a preheated 375° oven for 25 minutes, then remove the foil and bake for another 25 to 30 minutes without the foil.

8. Remove the pie from the oven, sprinkle with the pecans, and drizzle with caramel topping.

9. Cool on a wire rack and enjoy warm or at room temperature.

CHAPTER 9

PARTY PEOPLE

When I was at Sutter Home for the Better Burger contest, the vineyard's chef warned me about going to the chili cookoffs in Terlingua. He said it gets pretty rough and there is a lot of nudity and carrying-on—like spring break only in the high desert. At National Beef in Tucson I mentioned to a taciturn, white-haired rancher that I was headed to Terlingua. "They have a beer-drinking goat there," he said with a glint in his eye that seemed to hint at other similar wonders in store. In preparation for my trip I read up on Terlingua and nearby Big Bend National Park. The pamphlets didn't mention the guzzling goat, but they did go on and on about flash floods, dehydration, poisonous snakes, and mountain lions and bears, and said that if I was drowning, had been bitten, or was dying of thirst, the likelihood was slim that anyone would come to my aid. The week before I left I called around about Rio Grande raft trips. When I mentioned that I was coming for the chili cookoffs, the rafting provisioner, a woman, told me, "If you see little old ladies there, don't drink with them. They do it for a living. They look like your grandmother, but they aren't. They drink Jägermeister, and they have drunk many a man into his grave." Given all the warnings, I thought I should bring my husband with me. It was not a hard sell because a beer-drinking, party-hearty, chili-cooking mob in a for-gotten corner of Texas wilderness appeals to men in a way it doesn't to most women.

We flew into Midland, Texas, last night. In the squeaky clean new airport we had learned that our luggage was waylaid. It is now Friday morning, the day before the cookoff. The suitcases are still on standby on the East Coast. We can't wait. We load our pathetically few belong-ings, a jug of water, a camera bag, and a satchel stuffed with reporter de-tritus into a cavernous SUV. Still dressed in my pantsuit, I climb behind the wheel, and we head off for the no-man's-land of Big Bend.

Big Bend is where Texas bumps into Mexico as the Rio Grande pulls a 350-mile-long U-turn and the Rocky Mountains bottom out before crossing the border. The elevation dips to 1,800 feet along the milky green river and tops out at Emory Peak's 7,825 feet. In a thirty-minute span you can go from the shade of a lush bamboo grove along the banks of the Rio Grande, through the sun-blasted shrub desert of prickly pears, creosote bush, and ocotillo, to the crisp Alpine-like air of the Chisos Basin at 5,200 feet. There are plants and critters here that don't live anywhere else in the United States, such as the forlorn-looking Mexican drooping juniper and the Big Bend mosquito fish, a shiny little guy that has been around since the mastodons. It's all breathtakingly weird.

Once upon a time Big Bend was a leafy woodland, but then the gla-ciers melted. A hot wind blew up from Mexico and kissed most of the deciduous trees good-bye. Ever since Big Bend turned into a desert, it hasn't been a hot spot for human habitation. When the gold-crazed Spanish passed through in the mid-sixteenth century, they named it El Despoblado, Uninhabited. Today a mere eight thousand souls call Brewster County home, a region bigger than Connecticut with its 3.5 million residents. Terlingua is no longer a true ghost town, but this is where people come to disappear. It is rumored that the Unabomber's brother, the one who turned him in, is hiding out here.

We drive west along a treeless, endlessly flat horizon punctuated only by the perpetually bobbing oil field pumpjacks, which set a rhythm going in your head that you can't shake. As soon as we turn south at Pecos, the spooky black outline of the first of several mountain ranges rises before us. Between them and us the land rolls and pitches like ocean swells. We hardly talk as our eyes try to adjust to the scale. I follow the line of a barbed wire fence in the far southern distance. The sun breaks loose from a cloud and throws its rays down on top of a distant caramel-colored butte. About the only other cars on the road are pickups driven by cowboy-hatted ranchers. They lift a finger or two from the steering wheel of their trucks in an understated howdy. Of the scattered ranches and houses we pass, a good number are gutted and charred, the wind and sun the only inhabitants.

Pulling into Alpine, we revel in the joys of city life in the relative megalopolis after a morning passing through this virtually empty vista. We slide the rental SUV into a drive-in and consider the cheery, shiny menu. We order BLTs on buttery slabs of Texas toast, lick our fingers clean, and then say good-bye to civilization as we zoom down the open road through the shadows of the mighty Christmas Mountains.

Four hours after leaving Midland, we pull into a dusty camper- and RV-infested lot along a two-lane highway between the intersection that is Study Butte and the nowheresville of Terlingua. This is the grounds of one of two championship chili cookoffs taking place this weekend. We've arrived late, and I am anxious to find the cookoff director. I step down from the SUV with no hat, no sunscreen. I take off my suit jacket and earrings in an attempt to dress down. Then I make my first tactical error: I ask my husband to wait in the car. I hardly walk twenty feet away, around a whale-sized RV, and find myself surrounded by a half-dozen middle-aged, sunburnt men lounging in folding chairs, gripping dewy cans of beer. It is like waking bears. They spring from their chairs and circle me. They thrust cans of Coors at me and chant, "Have a beer, have a beer." They are good-natured but persistent. I say I can't. I have to find the director. They'll take me to her as soon as I toss back a brew, they respond. Thanks but no thanks, I try; my husband is waiting in the car. "Forget about him," one jowly guy says, taking my arm gently. "You're with us now."

〰〰〰

In Terlingua, as I expect, I find a refreshing parallel cookoff universe to the company-sponsored, well-mannered events I've become accustomed to. These are cookoffs to cut loose; ribald, boozy carnivals where chili is the excuse to carry on no matter what your age. You'll find fewer avid cooks and many more aging partyers. A chili cook explains to me how he's having a bad "pee year" because the full moon is so bright that he can't relieve himself in the wide open. Cooks name their stew Road Kill Chili or paint on their Coleman stove the image of a man running from an outhouse with flames shooting out of his behind. Tomorrow's festivities include a wet T-shirt contest as well as—with a nod to gender equity—Mr. Buns-off. A chili cook tells me that one year he had to pull a woman off the stage four times during the wet T-shirt contest because "she kept pulling her pants down."

The Bake-Off® contest this is not.

Regardless, many of the same impulses are in effect as at other cookoffs: the competitive streak, the desire for recognition, the camaraderie. What is different about the Terlingua chili cookoffs is that everything is multiplied by ten—the fun, the competitiveness, the cooking. They are extreme cookoffs. You have to get yourself to the middle of nowhere at your own expense; set yourself up a kitchen of sorts on a gravelly patch of earth under a beastly sun; party for a day or two until your insides are as puckered as your desert-scorched outside; and then rise early one morning to stir up a gallon of chili in three hours while fending off bugs, dust, and drunks calling themselves "hug therapists." All this just for bragging rights.

Those rights are substantial, especially in Texas where chili is the official state dish and there's an honorary chili advisor to the governor. Even to non-Texans, a pitiable people in these parts, chili inspires religious-like devotion. People say things like, "He doesn't care about chili" or "He doesn't understand chili," as if this simple frontier stew was an inscrutable philosophy privy only to true believers. People carry on about barbecue like this as well, but at least in the barbecue world there are more variables—cuts of meat and types of sauces—that demand more of the cook. In competitive chili there is only one bowl of red—meaning cubed meat and absolutely no beans—and you'd better

not screw with it. Everyone has chili-making secrets, but if you're looking for a creative outlet, the church of chili is not really the place. You
show your devotion by making not a new chili but the ultimate chili.
That is why people talk about eating chili and competition chili, the
latter being the one that reaches for the stars. "If you want to know
whether someone is a chilihead," says chili champ Allegani Jani Schofield, "you start talking about how good yours is, and he'll say, 'I cook
the best chili in the world.'"

This pursuit and the deep desire to party while doing so is what
binds this otherwise disparate tribe of chiliheads together. Competitive
chili cooking is not a hobby but a way of life. To be a chilihead is to be
a kind of foodie Deadhead. Chiliheads drive far and wide, spending
most weekends in a car crammed with chili fixings, speeding down the
highway to a distant cookoff where they will brew up another pot, suck
down a load of beer, and pack up a campground site's worth of gear.
That's why very few chiliheads cross over into the world of major company cooking contests. They don't have the time. I came across only
two who did it: Jim and Gloria Pleasants of Williamsburg, Virginia. Between the two of them, they had gone to Pillsbury and Better Burger,
among other national contests, as well as qualified twelve times for the
World Championship Chili Cook-off in Reno. At the height of their
chili days, when they lived in San Antonio, they entered about forty
chili cookoffs a year, which doesn't leave much time for thinking up
Bake-Off® contest entries.

Chili champion Dixie Johnson from Lamar, Missouri, says she and
her husband, Junior, a disabled factory worker, have gone to chili
cookoffs every weekend except for four in the past ten months. "We
don't play cards or boat or golf or any of that," Johnson says. They became chiliheads about fifteen years ago to escape the drone of everyday
life, Johnson explains. Junior was a volunteer fireman, and chili freed
them from the tyranny of his twenty-four-hour pager. They left their
teenagers at home to care for, as she puts it, the four-legged members
of the family. "It got so the kids would say, 'What weekend are you going to be home so we can plan something?'" Johnson says. Even after
Junior developed fibromyalgia and had to leave his job overseeing all

the screws and bolts that put TV stands together, the Johnsons did not retire their pots. That would mean giving up their considerable social life.

"We probably have more friends in the chili world than anywhere else," Johnson says. "Chili people are everyday people. Some live paycheck to paycheck, and some are wealthy and have big fancy RVs. But when you get down there, everybody is the same."

I hear this from chiliheads over and over, that the meat stew is a great leveler of class and education. Before a chili pot, all cooks are created equal, and so on. That's the kind of culinary democracy Americans just lap up. For a country built on individual rights, we sure love blending into a homogeneous group. We're happiest when we are stirring the melting pot together. And so chili makes for one big tribe, but as with most tribes, chili has had its rifts—deep ones. This explains why tomorrow I will drive back and forth along a five-mile stretch of winding two-lane highway between two championship cookoffs, the smaller but longer titled 35th Annual Original Terlingua International Frank X. Tolbert–Wick Fowler "Behind the Store" Championship Chili Cook-off and the four times as big and more succinctly named Terlingua International Chili Championship. Every year they are held on the same day, the first Saturday in November, at nearly the same time, forcing chiliheads to choose one or the other. These two cookoffs—as well as a third, the one in Reno—were once one, but that was a lot of cubed meat ago, long before the Balkanization of the chiliheads.

There are various stories as to how the first cookoff was born in 1967. They all start out the same, with a small group of men sitting around eating chili, drinking and dreaming. One version goes that one of the men, Frank Tolbert, a cantankerous columnist for the *Dallas Morning Sun*, wanted to promote his book *A Bowl of Red*. That's a bit suspect because his book came out in 1954. There was, however, a reprinting in 1966. Another story goes that another of the men, Carroll Shelby, the famed race car driver, and a friend had a ranch, 150,000 acres of rocks and rattlesnakes, that they wanted to sell in Terlingua. To do that they needed to put the former ghost town on the map.

Whichever version you choose, the first Terlingua chili cookoff was, like most cookoffs, a publicity stunt. Wick Fowler, a journalist and renowned chili cook, at least among his friends, was drafted to defend Texas's chili honor against H. Allen Smith, an easterner who had the audacity to write an article entitled "Nobody Cares More About Chili Than I Do" for *Holiday* magazine. The first cookoff ended in a draw, with one of the three judges declaring his tongue "ruint" and refusing to vote. This required another cookoff. Besides, the stunt had worked. Spectators were estimated at a thousand, including reporters from AP, UPI, *The Wall Street Journal*, *Sports Illustrated*, and the *London Daily Mirror*.

The cookoff joined forces with the Chili Appreciation Society. The society had begun as a group of Texan men devoted to the preservation of chili, good chili. They would commune around steaming bowls of chili, break soda crackers in unison, and chant, "I pledge allegiance to CASI and to the camaraderie for which it stands, one comestible indigestible, with heartburn and gas pains for all. So help me, Chiligula." This silly male bonding belied the seriousness of their mission: to protect their beloved bowl of red from unseemly renditions. They papered the world with definitive chili recipes and fought the intrusion of beans wherever they could. Chapters sprang up far and wide. These chapters then held cookoffs where you could earn your way to compete in Terlingua, and the competitive chili world quickly began to heat up.

All was well in the land of chiliheads until 1975. Blind judging had been instituted. A point system had been established. The cookoff had become a legit cooking contest. Tolbert was the director. Then some of the chili alpha dogs turned on each other. Again, there is more than one version. The year before, C. V. Woods, the Texas-born California engineer and businessman who brought the London Bridge to Arizona and the 1969 world chili champ, announced from the stage to a record crowd of ten thousand that the winner was "a goddamned woman." That was Allegani Jani Schofield, who Tolbert describes in *A Bowl of Red* as "an extremely decorative Houston woman." She was the first woman to win the cookoff, and it landed her a contract with the Eileen Ford model agency. Tolbert was none too pleased with Woods for cussing out Schofield in her moment of triumph, Schofield says. On his website Carroll Shelby, also a Californian, says Tolbert was steamed because he and Woods had flown in a CBS crew that year, and it had snubbed Tolbert.

Either way, Tolbert got royally pissed off and told Woods and Shelby they could take their cookoff to California, Schofield says. The two men did. They took the name, World's Championship Chili Cookoff, too. It turned out that Shelby had secretly trademarked it. That cookoff, run by the International Chili Society (ICS), has since moved to Nevada, and it's the only one of the three with a cash purse, $25,000.

The next split also had to do with Tolbert, who is described generously as a curmudgeon or less generously as an asshole. Even friends such as Schofield admit he had a temper. As one story goes, Tolbert showed up at the '82 cookoff with two foreign chiliheads. When they were turned away because they hadn't earned any points to qualify, Tolbert had a fit. Other cookoff organizers resented what they saw as Tolbert's despotic ways, bringing whomever he wanted to the cookoff and not following the point system. They organized a bloodless coup. When Tolbert went to sign the lease for the land for the '83 cookoff, the dissenters had already rented it. They informed Tolbert that they were now in charge, and he could join their board if he wanted to. Tolbert told them where they could put their bowl of red, stormed down the road, and set up a rival cookoff behind a hilltop general store, thus the "Behind the Store" part of the title.

Feelings were hard, real hard, at first. Kathleen Tolbert Ryan, who runs the Tolbert cookoff now, says her dad even received death threats. He oversaw only one breakaway cookoff. In 1984, Tolbert died in his sleep at seventy. Grief did not unite the chiliheads, who only became more entrenched in their own cookoffs. "They were probably happy he died," Ryan says. "They were so malicious." The two cookoffs ended up in court in little old Pecos in 1988 over the CASI name. The Tolbert faction lost. "The CASI name belonged to us," says Ryan ruefully. "We even had a dachshund named CASI."

Both sides say the controversy has died down over the years, and there are occasional mumblings about reunification. But sore feelings still rise easily to the surface. The Tolbert chili cooks wag their heads at all the CASI rules, which are lengthy and include such gems as cooks can neither shoot firearms nor set off fireworks. They also point to the mob of rowdy spectators that descends on CASI. The CASI cookoff typically draws some three hundred competitors, but the hangers-on can number five thousand or more. The Tolbert cookoff draws one hundred cooks or fewer, and the whole gathering totals about one thousand. "This is like a family picnic. That's like a company picnic," says Bud Rozell, a Dallas chilihead and member of the Tolbert cookoff board. "Here you can camp by a cook and even get some chili on you, especially the way my wife cooks."

The CASI people talk of the Tolbert loyalists like spoiled crybabies who aren't tough enough for serious competition. In their defense they point out that CASI chili cookoffs, which number more than 500, raise over a million dollars annually for charity. They say "they are there for the fun of it," says Doris Coates, a longtime CASI cook and champ. "That doesn't excite me." Each takes exception with the other's raunchiness. Johnson tells me that CASI cooks look down on the Tolbert cookoff's wet T-shirt contest. In the same conversation she explains that this year at the CASI cookoff no motor vehicles will be allowed to drive around the competition area during the cookoff. "They drive dune buggies and old jalopies, and they have girls who lift their shirts up. That's fine, but the area is dusty. It stirs the dust up, and it gets in the chili."

~~~~

After extracting myself from the Coors drinkers on Friday, I make a quick tour of the Behind the Store cookoff as the sun sets. Texas and American flags flap in a rising wind. The smell of propane and strains of country music drift over the makeshift campground that fans out over a bald, scrabbly hill. On a stage at the bottom of the hill, a dozen or so judges, most with leathery tans and bloodshot eyes, gather to solemnly evaluate milky green margaritas. I stop to talk to a smirking cook whose thinning hair is pulled into a ponytail—the one having the bad pee year. He's a housing inspector in Dallas or, as he puts it, "I prevent trailer trash." He extols the Tolbert cookoff at length to me, ending by waving a hand like a tour guide at the tight ring of crests to the east. "This is our view. This is the fucking Chisos Mountains," he says. "You can quote me."

We head down the road in the dark to the CASI cookoff, which by comparison is like driving into a vast refugee resettlement. There are roads winding around every which way, all lined with every kind of tent, camper, and RV. We actually get lost in what is called Crazy Flats. This is where the cookoff spectators are allowed to set up camp, far away from the competition area. In our car's headlights we catch glimpses of partying around campfires and poses of shirtless, souped-up young men marching through the dark barking, "Show us your tits," at any passing female. Finally we make our way to the stage where a band has just started playing a kind of Texas swing. There are a lot of men standing around watching the partner dancing because there are about ten of them to every lone woman. The cooks break down to a natural fifty-fifty split of men to women, but the gender scale tips heavily to men among the spectators. A skinny college-age fellow pushes his friend into me and orders, "Ask her." I move close to my husband. Regardless, a tall man nearer my age steps close to me, crashing my personal space, and says, "You wanna dance?" I shout over the music that I don't know how to two-step, which is like saying I have a third leg. This scares him off. My husband asks me, "What did that guy say to you?" while nearby a lanky, pale-skinned blonde pulls apart her glow-in-the-dark choker and flings the shiny green liquid over her friends and innocent bystanders as she laughs uncontrollably. When the singer on stage asks rhetorically over the mike, "You know when you have a relationship that is going really well?" a tight huddle of bikers shout in unison, "No-oh." Revelers wander away from the concert, with red devil horns atop their heads, flashing in the deep desert night.

We hightail it out of the CASI cookoff with a good idea of where the night is headed there. We have to drive the one hundred miles back to Alpine, which is where we found the closest available hotel room. The limited rooms in the Terlingua area are usually booked a year in advance. Driving back on the winding road toward Study Butte, we notice small flickering lights on a nearby hill. We pull off and drive up to the

Terlingua ghost town, which looks like a leftover prop from a Wild West movie. There's a short row of beaten nineteenth-century buildings with a broad porch and an old adobe theater that has been transformed into a restaurant and club. There is also a small graveyard filled with the long-dead miners who dug the mercury that put Terlingua on the map. In honor of the Mexican Day of the Dead, some chiliheads have placed a votive candle on each grave. Their small flames flickering in the dark are what caught our eyes from the road.

About thirty people amble around the graveyard, talking in hushed voices and occasionally kneeling down to make out the names on the wind-beaten wooden gravestones. It's so quiet. I'm suddenly struck by how the desert feels like the sea at night and how incongruent this gentle act, this remembering the dead, is amid the craziness of the cookoffs. I try to add up the jumble of the day, the lunar, savage beauty of the landscape, the oases of man-made insanity that have temporarily sprung up in this wilderness, and now this. But it just doesn't add up, and that is what I'm beginning to find so appealing about the chili cookoffs in Terlingua.

〰〰〰〰

Saturday morning breaks cool across the bare earth. When I arrive at the Tolbert cookoff, the mood is much more subdued than the night before. The chiliheads, coffee mugs in hand, have lined up quietly at the stage to get their oversized Styrofoam cups. In three hours' time they will fill this cup with chili and hand it back in. I find Bob Plager, bearded, bespectacled, and beer-bellied, near the front of the line. Plager is wearing a T-shirt emblazoned with a large red chili pepper and the words "Suck on This." His watchband is coated with turquoise. The requisite cowboy hat covers his head. He is one of only two people who have won the championship more than once. He won in '96 and '98. His girlfriend, Kathy LaGear, won the ICS cookoff in Reno in '98 and the grand prize of $25,000.

"We're kind of the king and queen of chili," Plager says.

Plager is semiretired, often leaving his pool cleaning and repair business in the hands of his manager so he can crisscross the country in his RV, going from chili cookoff to chili cookoff. He has been a chili-head since 1980 but didn't start winning until he divorced his first wife, painting her out of the scene on his chili-cooking stand, and hooked up with LaGear. She insisted that he quit socializing so much during cookoffs and tend to his chili, which he calls Pools Brew. The couple often fights at cookoffs, Plager says, because LaGear is so serious, and though he now keeps watch over his chili pot, he still likes to cut up and have a good time. "She's cooking on a virgin pot, which I've been teasing her about a lot."

I follow Plager up a makeshift dirt road to his cooking spot, a few minutes' walk from the central stage and on a crest overlooking the cookoff. Here Plager, LaGear, and about a dozen of their friends have set up their Coleman stoves in a row under a series of pop-up tents. LaGear is seated near her stove, expressionless behind a pair of big black sunglasses. "That looks pretty," Plager says, handling her new Farberware pot. She ignores him and focuses on making her 24-Karat Chili.

Among the group there is a realtor, a pilot, a retired doctor, a prison cook, and a man who won't exactly say what he does or where he lives. "I just have a lot of addresses," he explains. They all appear to be early to late middle age. They all still like to party. They are the kind of friends that can yell, "Goddamn it, shut up," at each other without anyone's getting too sore. They are also crossover cooks, a rare breed in the hot-tempered chili world. They regularly compete in ICS cookoffs, including the championship in Reno. One cook even plans to go over to the CASI cookoff this afternoon. Plager got the group hooked on the Tolbert cookoff by making it easy on them: He brings all the equipment.

In short order, everyone has a pot of chili cooking except Plager, who cooks a "two-hour" chili and is in no rush. "I boil the crap out of it," he says. While the tinny melody of "California Dreamin'" plays on the box, the crossover chiliheads tip their plastic bags of carefully cubed chuck to drain off the watery blood. They set out boxes of Sazón Goya, a seasoning mix heavy on MSG, and grind their own spices. Then they make their "dumps," the tipsy chili cook's crutch. Dumps are little packages of premixed spices that are numbered in the order they should be added to the pot. Usually a chili cook has between three and five dumps. When the kitchen timer rings, he adds the dumps in order. This only works, of course, if you can still read the numbers.

"You get out here and get drinked up, and you don't know what you're doing," one of the cooks tells me.

"Aw, shut up," someone yells from the other end of the tent.

When Plager finally gets cooking, he quickly busts out his secret ingredient: prunes. Chili cooks are generous with recipes, and you can easily find prizewinners in a number of cookbooks. Secret ingredients are another thing. Plager, however, does not hold back with his crossover comrades. Like a magnanimous papa, Plager hands two prunes to any cook who wants them. The prunes are for floating on top of the simmering chili for fifteen to twenty minutes. It's a technique Plager picked up at a chili cookoff in Memphis. That cook had picked it up from a Food Network program. The prunes, Plager tells me, deepen the chili's color and give it a smoother, richer taste. They are not fail-safe, however. If the chili cooks too hard or the prunes are in too long, the dried fruit can blow, shooting prune particles every which way and ruining a perfectly good bowl of red. No chili judge is going to appreciate plucking a sticky bit of prune shrapnel off his tongue.

I leave Plager and his crew floating prunes, and I head down the road to the CASI cookoff. The makeshift campground appears like a surreal mirage in the rounded cactus-studded hills. I drive in past a sign that reads "What Don't You Understand About 5 Frikkën Miles per Hour." Even one mile an hour kicks up a fine blond dust that hangs in the air. We park and make our way to the cookoff area where 325 cooks are spread across a flat stretch of parched earth the size of a football field. These chiliheads stir away under bright white peaked tents that shine under the full-bore sun. Given the size, the group is very civilized, almost quiet. The bikers and college kids are nowhere in sight. The only sign of the rowdiness to come are the oversized bottles of booze plucked from coolers here and there, and the Mardi Gras beads piled around some cooks' necks.

I find Dixie Johnson near the front of the cookoff, close to the stage where they'll announce the winners. Johnson came out of nowhere last year to cinch the championship, the first non-Texan woman to win, which she says earned her some cold shoulders. Whatever the Texans thought, Johnson has proved a model champion, a kind of chili missionary. She cooked chili wherever and whenever she was asked over the past year, whether it be for a 4-H dinner for hundreds or going up against the ICS champ at a cookoff in Illinois, lugging along her bronze chili pepper trophy for people to see. She didn't have to compete because all past champions automatically qualify for this cookoff. She did it "to promote chili" and win new, young converts. She's worried about the graying of chiliheads. For this cookoff Johnson pulled her supplies in a child's red wagon, which she plans to leave, stuffed with school supplies, at the local grade school.

"She's the most gracious person, so giving," says a friend of Johnson who's here in Terlingua for her first cookoff. Johnson wells up.

Johnson has a youthful hairdo, long, dyed-blond locks that fan back from her face. She's wearing red lipstick, which matches her oversized red polo shirt. Her husband, Junior, wears the same shirt and white shorts. Junior is a wan man with a crew cut and fleshy bags under his eyes. The painful tinglings of his fibromyalgia keep him awake at night. The two are cooking their own pots, using the same exact recipe as they did last year when Dixie won. Junior's didn't even make it through the first round of judging.

This is an emotional day for Johnson, who hates to give up her championship title, which is a foregone conclusion. There's been only one back-to-back winner in the history of the contest, so Johnson is just aiming to make the top ten. She reaches in her bra and plucks out a small plastic dinosaur to show me. She found it at another cookoff. It's for good luck.

I meander around in the heat, kicking up dust and inhaling the hot, dry air. The sun bleaches the desert taupes almost to white. Almost everyone keeps to the shade of the tents, and I decide to do likewise. At the back of the cookoff area I step under the tent of the Bottom of the Barrel Gang, where I find Bob and Doris Coates. Sitting on the table in front of their stove are two bronze chili pepper trophies, each emblazoned with a map of the world. Doris won in '91 and Bob in '99. Bob tells me proudly that Doris, a tall redhead, tastes "in colors." She has a reputation of being a chili sage. When a new competitor, a man from Pennsylvania, stops by to ask her opinion of his chili, she advises, "Right on heat. Right on salt. A little light on chili powder flavor. Your meat—" She pauses, takes another bite, and swishes it around in her mouth like a wine connoisseur. "The spices aren't driven into the meat." Her advice: Hard-boil the meat and then let it sit.

Doris has been coming to Terlingua since 1979, back when she was a single mom and came with friends to be on the safe side. "It could get a little adult," she says. "The rest of the chili cookoffs are family affairs, but not this one."

Bob was her prom date in high school. They rediscovered their high school crush at their twentieth reunion. Bob, a fleshy man with a fading tattoo on his arm, is in the moving business, "the only fellow a woman will let in the house and look under the bed and in the closets." Doris got Bob to cook chili, the only dish he cooks. "It was to make Monday through Friday go away," she says. "It beat paying a therapist."

While their two pots of chili cook, Doris regales me with stories of how wild they once were. In New Orleans they got thrown out of Pat O'Brien's, line-danced down Bourbon Street, and made a corsage out of hundred-dollar bills for a waitress. "We were a hard crowd to run with." No more, she says with a wistful smile.

At noon the cooks turn in their Styrofoam cups filled three-quarters full. Cooks are given a numbered ticket that corresponds to their cup of chili. The chili, though, goes in to the judges anonymously, with the number covered up. Only after the winners are selected are the numbers revealed. The chilies go through various rounds of judging until twenty remain, and those are sent to the finals table. This system is designed to foil "marked meat," tipping off friendly judges as to which chili is yours by, say, putting a layer of cumin at the bottom of the cup. If your cup has been altered in any way—even with a small mark such as the crescent imprint of a fingernail—you'll be disqualified. This explains why the cooks hold their precious cups so gingerly.

As the chili turn-in proceeds, the show competition starts. There is no easy way to describe the show competition except to say it's typically inane, a kind of hallucinatory talent contest. It was invented to pass the time while the judges scored the many cups of chili. There is a group of men dressed like women, of course. They smoke cigars, dance, and grab passing young women. A revivalist minister sings the glories of chili. The crowd favorite by far is the Spice Boyz, seven guys in white T-shirts, khaki pants, and chef's hats playing air guitar on top of a long RV.

The hijinks are fun to watch but I'm due at the judging tent. So many judges are needed for this system that spectators can sign up for any of the first four rounds. My husband and I signed up even though we have grave doubts about our chili know-how. I grew up eating Cincinnati chili, a cinnamon-spiced version using ground meat that is served over spaghetti. I never mention this chili offense within the Texas border. My husband grew up in Minneapolis where spicy means too much salt in the hot dish. Neither of us has ever had chili without beans. I'm also worried that all the chilis will taste the same. How much variety can there be in a simple meat stew flavored with dried chilies?

A lot, as it turns out. My husband emerges from the first round of judging, during which 330 chilies were reduced to 165, and I head in with the next group to halve that number, which are divided among tables of eight as cases of the ubiquitous Miller Lite and Coors are wheeled in. Celery, cheese, and bread are placed on the table to clean our palates. We are a mostly sober group, but I notice a few judges weaving to their tables, especially one in a hat with a ram's horns. We are instructed not to talk about the chilies, only to score them quickly from one to ten on aroma, consistency, red color, taste, and aftertaste. Only one spoonful per chili is allowed, and there's no retasting. The chili cups will move around the table, assembly-line style. We pass the cups quickly, tasting each one with a clean plastic spoon, which we then decisively toss with a flip of the wrist into a cardboard box in the middle of the table. I have no problem dividing the good from the bad. The lower-grade chilies are one-note wonders, all heat up front with nothing behind. They taste scorched or the meat is gummy. The better ones grab you with their complexity. Like good wine they light up parts of your tongue that you didn't even know you had. One is fiery at first, and then the mellow warmth of cumin spreads across my tongue followed by a velvety chocolate-like finish. This chili is a revelation to me, and in that moment I swear off beans and ground meat. It will be only Texas chili for me from here on out.

We race back to the Tolbert cookoff to hear the winners announced. Of the top ten, six are from Plager's tent. "It's the prunes, I tell you, the prunes," Plager says. When the winner, Alan Greiner from Round Rock, Texas, makes his way to the stage, he says into the mike, "I can't believe it."

"We don't believe it, either," someone yells from the crowd.

"Oh, shit," Greiner says as he's handed his championship Coleman stove.

Greiner's team also came in second in show, so he tearfully calls his team up on the stage. They launch into lip-synching "God Bless America." I notice a woman in the front in a cut-off T-shirt jiggling around while she sings. The mostly male crowd, the testosterone running high, pushes up around the stage. The wet T-shirt contest is next. Many of them remove their cowboy hats and sing along. At first all I can think of is how cheesy the moment is, standing in the waning desert sun with a group of drunken wannabe cowboys listening to the national anthem karaoke style. Only in America, I think. Then a heartfelt cheer swells from the crowd, then another. To my surprise I start to well up. Maybe the long day in the sun or just the breathtaking raw beauty is getting to me, but I'm suddenly overwhelmed with love for my countrymen. Where else would anyone think to clash chili pots in the untamed landscape of the Wild West, to turn a no-man's-land into party central? Where else would anyone raise a plebeian dish to such exalted status? Where else would adults cling so to the fun-loving daftness of their youth? Only in America, I think as the crowd hoots and hollers again. I bow my head so that the brim of my hat covers my face and no one will see me dab a sentimental tear away.

We are in the SUV, racing back to CASI to catch the announcement of their winners, where it turns out that Johnson didn't even make it through the first round of judging. As we drive I recount my soggy epiphany to my husband. He bursts out laughing. He was standing much closer to the stage and saw exactly why the crowd was cheering.

One of the singers, the one in the cut-off T-shirt, was playing peekaboo, lifting her arms so that her nipples gave the crowd a good Texas howdy. Every time she gave the crowd a boob-shot, they roared. Only in America, I think.

~ ~ ~ ~

Bob Plager won the 1996 and 1998 Original Terlingua International Frank X. Tolbert–Wick Fowler "Behind the Store" Championship Chili Cook-off.

BOB PLAGER'S POOLS BREW CHILI

2 pounds chuck tender roast, trimmed of fat and gristle and cut into small cubes
Vegetable shortening, such as Crisco, for browning the meat
1 (14-ounce) can beef broth
1 (14-ounce) can chicken broth
1 (8-ounce) can tomato sauce
2 pitted dry-pack prunes
Water if required

SPICE MIXTURE #1

1 tablespoon paprika
1 teaspoon onion powder
1 teaspoon garlic powder
2 teaspoons beef granules
1 teaspoon chicken granules
1/2 teaspoon salt
1 tablespoon chili powder

SPICE MIXTURE #2

2 teaspoons cumin
1/2 teaspoon garlic powder
1/2 teaspoon onion powder
1/2 teaspoon black pepper
1/2 teaspoon salt
4 tablespoons chili powder

SPICE MIXTURE #3

1 tablespoon chili powder
1 teaspoon cumin

Salt to taste

In a heavy medium-size pot, brown the meat in a small amount of vegetable shortening over high heat. Drain off the excess shortening. Add the beef broth, chicken broth, tomato sauce, prunes, and spice mixture #1. Bring to a boil, lower the heat, cover the pot, and cook approximately 2 hours. Remove the prunes and add water if necessary. Cook the chili longer if the meat is not yet tender. Thirty minutes before turn-in (or before serving), add spice mixture #2 and cook over low heat. Fifteen minutes before turn-in (or before serving), add spice mixture #3 and continue cooking over low heat. Salt the chili to taste and serve hot.

YIELD: 4 TEXAS-SIZE SERVINGS

〰〰〰

Dixie Johnson of Lamar, Missouri, won the 2000 Terlingua International Chili Championship. She named her chili for first lady Bess Truman.

BESS'S BEST CHILI

Gray 3 pounds cubed beef chuck tender (or chili grind) in 1 tablespoon Crisco shortening.

Add:
1 (8-ounce) can Hunt's tomato sauce
1/2 (14 1/2-ounce) can Swanson chicken broth
1/2 teaspoon cayenne pepper
2 teaspoons Wyler's instant chicken bouillon
1 tablespoon Pendery's Fort Worth light chili powder
2 serrano peppers, seeded
1 (14 1/2-ounce) can Swanson beef broth

1 1/2 tablespoons onion powder
2 teaspoons Wyler's instant beef bouillon
1 teaspoon Pendery's cumin

Bring to a boil and cook about 1 hour (depending on whether you are using cubed or ground meat). Remove the peppers and add the following:

3/4 teaspoon Pendery's white pepper
1 packet Sazón Goya
1/4 teaspoon salt
3 tablespoons Gunpowder Foods Texas red chili powder
1 teaspoon garlic powder
1 tablespoon Pendery's cumin
2 tablespoons Pendery's Fort Worth light chili powder

Adjust the liquid with the remaining chicken broth or water. Cover and cook for 30 minutes. Add the following:

1/4 teaspoon brown sugar
1 tablespoon Pendery's Fort Worth light chili powder
1/4 teaspoon Gunpowder Foods Hot Stuff
1 teaspoon Pendery's cumin

Reduce heat and simmer/cook for 10 to 15 minutes. Adjust the chili's final taste for salt and for front and back heat.

CHAPTER 10

WAITING FOR PILLSBURY

Driving south on two-lane 218 from cutified, antiquey St. Ansgar, Iowa, the road bends like a wide sleepy river and then shoots straight for Osage. It's the Saturday after Thanksgiving, and the farms have long stood idle. The fields are laid bare. Blanched, chewed-up cornstalks, the refuse of the harvest, speckle the coffee-bean-colored earth. Just north, a heavy rain drums the land. Here the sky only glowers. A solid band of sullen gray stretches taut across the flat horizon. The barn doors of the neatly kept farms are closed. The houses are silent. The cows in a pasture stand motionless. If time is passing, as it certainly must be, the material world gives no clue.

A few miles outside of Osage, a single ray of sunshine cuts diagonally through the iron-colored band of clouds and like a searchlight lands on a mushroom-shaped water tower and illuminates the bold letters across its girth: OSAGE. The effect is hopeful. Suddenly all bets are on this upstart ray of light, that it will break the spell of stillness, the day will surge ahead, and a happy future will unfurl for all.

Four or five blocks from the illuminated water tower, in a turn-of-the-century house that needs a coat of paint, Diane Sparrow waits for a call that could change her life. It came once before, two years ago. She didn't expect it then, but now she does, so she is holed up this afternoon, her ear listening for the phone and her eye on the computer, waiting for Pillsbury.

Sparrow, flashing a broad, toothy grin, greets me on her front porch. She wears a blue chambray shirt with an embroidered Doughboy just above the breast pocket. The white gremlin, arms spread, mitten-shaped hands flung open, appears to leap joyfully out of Sparrow's pocket and let loose with its maniacal giggle. "It's for luck," she explains. She leads me inside and gives me a quick tour of her house. In the kitchen I notice that a magnetized white notepad on the fridge has one item scribbled on it: *Get notified by Pillsbury.*

Every other year Pillsbury traditionally calls the one hundred Bake-Off® contest finalists on Thanksgiving weekend. Most aspiring finalists don't know this. The contesters do, and so they wait by their phones in their homes all around the country. Forget Christmas shopping. Forget going with the family to a matinee performance of the local, half-baked production of the *Nutcracker Suite.* The clock will tick away their holiday weekend while they listen for the ring. The phone becomes their constant companion and worst enemy in its imposing silence. Whenever it does bleat, the contesters jump as if they were goosed or just remembered a forgotten cake in the oven. They answer with a breathless "Hello." If it's a friend's voice on the other end, they'll sigh, or, worse, if it's a telemarketer, they may unleash their pent-up fury. "You wait and wait, and then the phone rings and it's someone wanting to know whether you want MCI or Sprint," Sparrow says. "It's really aggravating."

Sparrow has been pretty much a shut-in since Wednesday night. She didn't really expect Pillsbury to call Thursday, on Thanksgiving, but she was home all day anyway cooking the holiday meal. Two years ago when Pillsbury called to say she'd made the cut for the 2000 contest, the phone rang on Friday. So this year she spent all day Friday inside, waiting for lightning to strike twice. It didn't. Today, while she dashed downtown for an errand or two, her husband, Jon, pulled the morning shift by the phone.

Now she is hunkered down in the hush of her roomy Victorian house while Jon has gone off to shoot a family portrait. The house is cluttered and dark. The period colors of her house—forest green walls and maroon velvet upholstery—gobble up what little natural light meekly seeps through the windows. The only lights Sparrow has turned on are those on her tall, skinny Christmas tree squished in a corner of the parlor. Candles flicker here and there. The computer shines as bright as a fluorescent bulb in her denlike first-floor office.

For the umpteenth time today Sparrow plops down in front of her computer and opens her email to see if Pillsbury has called any of her contester friends. I look over her shoulder. Nothing. Then she scans the chat room on Cooking Contest Central for new postings about Pillsbury. There's one from earlier this morning. Claudia Shepardson's new daughter-in-law received a call from Pillsbury. "That's no coincidence," Sparrow says as she scrolls past the message. The chat room is unusually quiet. The only new posting is from someone querying how Pillsbury's call will show up on caller ID. "Oh, for God's sakes," Sparrow says and closes the page. "Why isn't Pillsbury calling anyone?"

A glorious, many-layered cake oozing chocolate materializes on her computer screen. This is the recipe she has pinned all her hopes on: a towering stack of pale tortillas alternating with layers of Pillsbury chocolate icing. For luck she is using a photo of her creation as a screensaver. This is the cake she alluded to at Gilroy but wouldn't give me any specifics. Now it doesn't matter, and she spills. One morning this past summer she had just woken up and was lying in bed when the recipe appeared to her like a heavenly vision. "It was brilliant, totally brilliant." Her brain on fire, she got up, dressed, and raced to the grocery store and back with the ingredients. "It worked right away," she says. "I couldn't have imagined it would work that well. The kids loved it so much they requested it a couple of times."

Then Sparrow made a bold decision.

Most people who enter Pillsbury send in as many recipes as they can, thus upping the chance that one makes the cut. These folks are just trying to get in the Bake-Off® contest. Sparrow wants more than that this time. She wants a solid shot at the $1 million. Like a serious bettor at the track, she has developed a strategy based on the contest's past grand prize winners.

Baked goods have historically taken the majority of the grand prizes; chocolate desserts alone account for more than 25 percent. Entrees have won a measly seven out of thirty-nine Bake-Off® contests. Neither a snack nor a vegetable dish has ever won the grand prize. That explains why Sparrow was sure she would not win the grand prize at the 2000 competition with her sweet-savory Picadillo Pies in the Casual Snacks and Appetizers category. The most she hoped for was a $10,000 category prize. She went home empty-handed. That's why this time she has placed all her bets on the dessert category.

Sweet it would be. Sparrow took it a step further. Rather than enter as many recipes as possible in the dessert category, she decided to enter the one recipe she considered a serious contender for the big dough: her tortilla cake. In the end her husband talked her into submitting several versions of the cake. One was made with the same ingredients but was rolled like enchiladas. Sitting at her kitchen table, she shuffles through the computer printouts of the recipes and sighs. She hands me a few to inspect. Single-spaced typed instructions nearly fill the page, a big no-no in contest land. "That is why it won't make it," she says. "It was a long shot to pick one recipe."

Her heavy oak front door swings open, and her eldest son, Jason, his wife, and Millie, their wiggly chocolate Labrador puppy, step into the parlor. Jason, a wide-faced, wide-set man with a ball cap riding up on his forehead, lives in a nearby town. Three out of Diane's four sons live in the area. Twenty-something Nick and Eric live together in Mason City. The youngest son, Adam, lived at home until this summer when to everyone's surprise he enlisted in the Air Force.

"Have you heard?" Jason asks as he puts eight-week-old Millie on the floor, who, like a wind-up toy, springs into action.

"No, not yet," Sparrow answers. She looks nervously down at Millie. She's agreed to puppy-sit overnight. She's going to be home the whole time anyhow, and when Millie was at the house for Thanksgiving, all she did was snooze under the dining room table. Care instructions for Millie are minimal. Jason assures his mother that the puppy is house-broken. Sparrow looks a little dubious. Millie grabs a mouthful of her khaki pants. Jason pries the pup loose. The daughter-in-law runs out to the car for Millie's toy, a small beanbag bird. "She'll be fine here at Grandma's," Jason says.

"I'm not her grandma," Sparrow says quickly.

The couple has hardly left when Millie wobbles into the living room and drops two oval-shaped turds on the carpet. "They weren't even to the corner," Sparrow says, dashing for a roll of paper towels. She dispenses with the puppy poops, washes her hands, and returns to her office. Another scan of her computer turns up nothing new. "Where's Millie?" Sparrow asks suddenly, whirling around in her chair. We track her little brown body down in the kitchen, where she is noisily munching food from her bowl on the floor.

Sparrow's kitchen is essentially a trophy room. It is stashed with goodies she has won over the past four years, from the almond double-door, ice-making Whirlpool fridge, one of her first wins, to a weighty set of Le Creuset cookware, her most recent coup. Three full sets of knives, two Henckels and one Wusthof, sit on her kitchen counter. The flattop stove and G.E. Advantium oven were both prizes, as are the KitchenAid food processor and mixer. A dozen or so cookoff aprons are clumped together on a hook. A tumble of Pillsbury Doughboys and little stuffed chickens in striped stockings from National Chicken fill a shelf. Charcoal-colored pieces of Calphalon crowd a pot rack. She has stashed the Calphalon roasters and pasta pots in her cupboards.

"I even have the water pitcher," she says, pulling it down from a shelf.

The kitchen, though, tells only half the story. Altogether she has won four food processors and five KitchenAid mixers. There is a fourth set of Wusthof knives in the attic. Sparrow opens the door to her closed-in back porch, and the smell of a wood fire wafts in. Millie lifts her nose from her bowl and wobbles out on the porch to investigate. Here is where Sparrow keeps one of the three smokers she has won in Cook-shack contests. She smoked the Thanksgiving turkey in this stainless steel, thigh-high boxy number, which she won with Smoked Peach Napoleon with Tortillas. Another prize, a Green Egg barbecue grill, which resembles a jade green mini-spaceship, sits on her patio. The only thing she lacks is "a big gas grill." She does not plan to buy one. She'll win it.

She has even equipped her sons' kitchens. Eric, Nick, and Jason have a KitchenAid mixer and food processor in their kitchens. The three brothers share a small Cookshack smoker. Sparrow still has leftover prizes. She has begun selling them on eBay. She recently sold one of the Cookshack smokers on eBay for $355. "It's almost like contesting, the thrill of it," she says.

The door opens, and in comes lanky, good-natured Nick, his recent girlfriend in tow. They hardly say hello before kneeling down to cuddle Millie. The new girlfriend has long, dark, straight hair and a calm smile.

"Do you have your cell phone?" Sparrow asks Nick.

"Yes," he answers, eyes glued on the puppy.

"Make sure it's turned on," Sparrow says.

Nick is part of the Pillsbury backup plan, one that may still get her to the Bake-Off® contest, albeit as a spectator. Sparrow brainstormed ideas with Nick, a twenty-five-year-old computer techie. She did the same with her husband, talking over recipes during their morning five-mile walks. The three of them have sent in more than forty entries.

Diane slips back into her office. The glowing image of cake softly lights her face in the growing dark. There is an email from Liz Barclay, a contesting friend. She's off to see a movie, the second *Harry Potter*. "How can she go out?" Sparrow says. There's also a new posting on the website chat room. The wait has proved too much for one woman who has posted a long, whiny paragraph.

"This was my first baking contest, and I think it will be my last, at least for Pillsbury," Diane reads out loud. "With all of the hard work, excitement about the possibility of winning, the expense of making the recipes, and then it all ends with disappointment. What a bummer. I should have bought stock in Pillsbury as I'm sure my purchases alone increased their stock value."

"Oh, boy," Diane says and sighs. "It is weird that nobody is getting called."

Nightfall creeps through the windows, the first noticeable shift in the day's constant light. Sparrow turns on only one lamp in the dark house. It is just past 5 P.M. She has nearly given up on the day but holds out a little hope that Pillsbury will call. The front door swings open again. This time it is son Eric, also lanky but dark-haired and wound tight, with his steady girlfriend.

"Have you heard?" Eric calls to his mother.

"No," Diane says flatly.

Eric wanders toward the kitchen, rubbing his stomach. "I'm fearsome starving."

"Here." Sparrow plops an ample basket of homemade kettle corn on the table, then sets out a bowl of orangish smoked salmon spread. Sparrow squats to rummage in a cupboard and emerges with a set of short knives topped with plump, ceramic Doughboys. "It's for good luck."

Suddenly the house comes alive. Everyone, Millie included, circles the kitchen table ready to munch. "Here's big, bad Jon," Eric calls as Diane's red-faced husband comes through the kitchen door, chilly raw air trailing off him.

"Anything?" Jon asks Diane.

"No," she answers and pops a cracker into her mouth. "I'll check the computer."

Jon drops wearily into an armchair near the kitchen table. The blackness of a starless night has descended outside. The Christmas tree glows in the corner of the parlor like a low fire. Millie jumps on one of Jon's feet, and his tired face breaks into a smile. She grabs hold of a shoelace on his work boot and starts gnawing. "She's cute," he says.

Jon is ambivalent about Pillsbury this go-around. He wants his wife to go very much, but he does not want a call himself. Getting *the call* would mean giving media interviews, lots of them, and Jon has a deep dread of public speaking. He once passed on a university teaching job because it required talking in front of people. He attributes this phobia to losing his father when he was four years old. The first time he got a haircut after his father's death, when he climbed into the big chair, the barber asked him, "What does your daddy do?" Young Jon was speechless. "I was just frozen."

What he would like to do is accompany his wife, as he did in 2000 when he had a high time. There, he recounts, Sally Pillsbury, the dowager of the Bake-Off® contest, essentially mooned him. George and Sally Pillsbury always lead the Grand March, the parade of the one hundred contestants two by two into the contest room. Jon was milling around near the front of the line, near the Pillsburys, as the contestants found their place behind the couple. Suddenly Mrs. Pillsbury turned around so that she was facing the contestants and had her back to Jon. She hitched her skirt up and pulled down her slip.

"She just bared her whole hind end to me," Jon says.

"It wasn't bare," Sparrow calls from the kitchen.

After a lengthy back-and-forth, Eric and his girlfriend depart for a Chinese restaurant. Nick announces he and his girlfriend are going to a movie, only to sink comfortably into an armchair.

"Do you have your cell phone turned on?" Sparrow asks.

"It's only a daytime number, so I'm going to leave it in the car," Nick says.

"What are you going to say if they call?" Sparrow asks.

Nick doesn't answer, just smiles.

"What did you say when the teacher asked you if your mom helped with your homework?" He smiles again. After some more chitchat, Nick hoists himself out of the chair, and the young twosome depart. Millie escorts them to the door, then wanders under a chair where she falls into a deep puppy sleep. Sparrow looks at her watch. It's past 7 P.M. She's officially off the clock. The wait is over for today. She goes to the kitchen and, amid all her Calphalon, Le Creuset, KitchenAid, Wusthof, and Whirlpool, starts dinner: French onion soup, quiche, fruit salad, and a green salad. It's been a discouraging day, not just because she wasn't called, but because none of the contesters were called. She points at the Post-it on the fridge.

"I had only one thing on my to-do list."

〜〜〜〜

Even though Sunday turns out to be another somber, raw day, Sparrow has recovered her optimism. "I woke up this morning and thought that one of the three of us will be called," she says. "I had a lot of good recipes." However, the mood on the website has completely deteriorated. When Sparrow checked it around 7:30 A.M., she found more brokenhearted, near-hysterical messages.

She tries to quiet the growing panic with some reason. She and Jon count how many contesters have been finalists in recent cookoffs. They crunch some numbers and figure out that historically about 20 percent of the contestants at cookoffs are contesters. Jon drafts a posting for the website. "What do you think?" he asks as she reads over his shoulder.

"That's not how I would write it. It doesn't sound like me," she says. While Jon tweaks the copy, Millie chews on a houseplant, and Sparrow gathers up her shoulder bag, black car coat, and shopping list. She couldn't wait around today even if she wanted to. She has signed on to cook this year's annual Christmas Advent lunch at her church next Saturday: chicken thighs with honey mustard sauce on rice pilaf, an Asian-style coleslaw, cream cheese gingerbread muffins, and tiramisù for 160 elderly women.

"If you've had a good contesting year, you should give something back," she says.

We're off to Rochester, about an hour's drive northeast across the state line in Minnesota. Here she finds good produce and plenty of ethnic foods, thanks to the Mayo Clinic, she thinks, which fills the small city with doctors and their big salaries and upscale tastes. As we drive across the checkerboard of farmland that lies between Osage and Rochester, she claims she is relieved to be away from the phone. "A watched pot doesn't boil," she says. Does she really believe that? I ask. "No. I'd rather sit by the phone."

Out of the house, a shopping list in hand, Sparrow finds that the afternoon flies. After wandering through the wilds of Sam's Club where everything is Gulliver-sized, we end the trip in the Asian section of a large grocery store. This pocket of fermented black bean sauce, cans of Thai coconut milk, and burlap sacks of jasmine rice tucked into a far corner of the store is one of Sparrow's muses. She wanders the few aisles, plucking cans off the shelf, reading their ingredients lists, and weighing their heft in her hand. She is taken with a squirt bottle of orange red Chinese chili sauce. She tosses it into her basket.

I drop Sparrow at a mall where Jon is waiting in a noisy food court. He has no Pillsbury news. The couple grabs a fast-food taco and are home in Osage by 6:30 P.M. As soon as she is through the front door, Sparrow goes straight for the computer. There's an email from a contester friend, Shirley DeSantis; her granddaughter was called. It appears a flurry of calls was made between 2 and 6 P.M. There are six postings on the website by contesters who were called by Pillsbury during the afternoon. Sparrow's hopes rise.

Over the next few days Sparrow cooks and waits, cooks and waits. A friend from the church comes over to help make the Advent lunch. She offers to take Sparrow out for lunch, but nothing doing. Sparrow won't leave the house for fear the phone will ring. She won't even help deliver the finished tiramisùs to the church freezer. There are a few more postings on the website, but this Bake-Off® contest is looking like a relative shutout for the contesters. Contesters Pat Harmon and Susan Runkle, who were both at National Beef, have been tapped. Some contester relatives have been called. By Thursday when I call, Sparrow is ready to blow.

"There are some really upset people, and I'm one of them," she says on the phone. "I'm going to have to quit contesting because I said if I ever got to be this bad of a sport, I'd quit. There are four kids going. Julie Stutzman, her eleven-year-old daughter is going. They called her husband to say he was a finalist. He submitted one recipe. We did so much research and put so much work into this. This woman that doesn't even have a stove. Carolyn, she's going. There's a bunch of us that are just livid. If it's a lottery, they should tell us."

She mentions in passing that she did get a call on Monday from Reynolds' Hot Bags. She's won a trip for two to New York City where she will compete for a trip to Jamaica. Sparrow is so upset over Pillsbury that the Reynolds' news just feels like a bitter consolation prize. The conspiracy theories are flying, she tells me, that Pillsbury weeded the contesters. How else to explain that so many top contesters, like the

Gadsbys, didn't make the cut? The last Sparrow heard, the Montana couple was still waiting by their phone. "There isn't any contest you end up with this few contesters," Sparrow says. "I think they are trying to avoid the appearance of favoring contesters, and it's going to come up and bite them in the butt."

CHAPTER 11

COOKING WITH FOIL

The contesters are bereft, especially, surprisingly, Liz Barclay in Annapolis. Never mind that Barclay has a full life: a fulfilling career as a director of admissions at a private school, a master's degree from Harvard University, an attorney husband of twenty-five years, two sons, one a professional soccer player, and a beloved flat-coated retriever named Ajax. Barclay's natural high energy and optimism totally fail her. All she can think about is that she will not be one of the Bake-Off® contest's one hundred. She is plagued with second-guessing. Did she make spelling errors or other mistakes in any of her twenty-five entries? she wonders. Maybe she focused on the wrong category by entering so many in Luscious and Lighter. Maybe she overanalyzed the deceptively simple contest.

"When the door to Pillsbury closed, I became depressed," she tells me on the phone. "My husband says get over it." She can't. She stews on all the wasted time. She devoted the summer to creating Pillsbury recipes, racing from school to the grocery store most afternoons, putting her experiments on the dinner table each night as she announced, "This is a winner." In the end she came up with twenty-five, most of them her specialty: low-fat vegetarian concoctions. She burned through blocks of tofu and cartons of Egg Beaters. She crafted Healthy Hot and Sour Soup using a package of Green Giant Create a Meal!, coleslaw mix, a can of green chilies, tofu, and chow mein noodles. She rolled up Low-Fat Breakfast Burritos filled with sausage substitute and El Paso salsa. She invented Health Harvest Quiche from Pillsbury's refrigerated piecrust, Green Giant frozen carrots, broccoli, and cauliflower, and reduced-fat mozzarella. She would print a copy of each recipe, proof it, then let the copy sit for twenty-four hours before proofing the recipe one last time. This diligence has gone totally unrewarded.

Having gone to the 2000 Bake-Off® contest in San Francisco, Barclay knows exactly what she will miss. Her Pillsbury blues are only lightened by the fact that so few contesters were tapped for the Orlando event. This mystifies her, as it does Sparrow. Barclay knows she shouldn't, but she can't help feeling, as a contester, that she is entitled to Pillsbury. "If we can do something good with obscure food, we ought to be able to put together a dish with convenience foods that is a winner." She sighs and admits all is not for naught. She can recycle some of the Pillsbury entries into recipes for the first *Southern Living* Cook-Off, but not quite yet. "I don't want to look at them now. I need some distance."

That makes Barclay one of the few, if the only, contesters not jamming on *Southern Living*. Most contesters are healing their sizable wounds by obsessing over the new cookoff. The new contest, which promises a $100,000 grand prize, turns out to be perfectly timed for the Pillsbury rejects. In years past there hasn't been nearly as good a distraction, only National Chicken in the far distance of fall.

Southern Living has also turned out to be a very consuming contest. It is absolutely inscrutable. When the magazine announced the contest this past fall, there were about twelve sponsoring products, one of which you had to use in an entry. Since then the list of products has grown and grown, now topping thirty. This is making it impossible for the contesters to get a bead on the contest. Just when they think they have it figured out, six more disparate products pop up on the list. "We talk about the contest like it's an amoeba," says Roxanne Chan, who has sent in thirty-four entries so far.

Sparrow distracts herself from her Pillsbury disappointment by preparing for the Reynolds' Hot Bags Foil Bags "In the Bag" recipe contest. The cookoff is in New York City in mid-January. When Sparrow received the call that she was one of three finalists, she had to admit to the woman on the phone that she hadn't kept a copy of her recipe, Chicken and Apricot Couscous. Would she please email her one, she asked. She had written the recipe—for skinless chicken breasts doused with a sauce of primarily apricot nectar, mustard, and dried cranberries—off the top of her head and entered it via the Internet just as the deadline closed. Then in the rush to polish off her Pillsbury entries, she forgot about it.

Sparrow's sweet savory chicken, her kind of signature dish, was one of four hundred entries that the brand-new contest received. That's just a fraction of what established contests draw, but the Reynolds folks are still happy. They know the Hot Bag, as convenience products go, is a little cranky. The Hot Bag is essentially based on the old technique of roasting *en papillote*, of wrapping food in greased parchment and cooking it with its own steam. The difference is that the Hot Bag is aluminum foil, which is far more airtight than greased parchment, sometimes to a fault. The contest rules warn that meat and pork recipes require a tablespoon of flour. Without the starch, the bag might blow. In that case the cook would end up scraping pot roast bits off the oven walls while someone got on the horn to order a pizza. That's not the only challenge the bag poses. The steam bath it produces wrings the flavors out of most foods. Add to that, foods cook at different speeds in the bag, which is a problem because the pouch was designed, like a Crock-Pot, to cook an entire meal at once. As the label reads, "Great for Complete No Fuss Meals."

The bag went on store shelves in 1998 without any advertising. It sold well enough during the grilling season, but as the brand manager put it, "There's still room for growth." That's where the mini-cookoff comes in. Barker Campbell Farley & Mansfield (BCF&M), an ad agency in Richmond, Virginia, pitched the idea to Reynolds, and the company bit. The thinking was that the contest would promote the product, teach consumers how to use the bag, and solicit recipes. The contest would also generate some publicity, although Reynolds isn't working that angle as hard as, say, the *Southern Living* Cook-Off, with its big purse, fifteen finalists, and televised cookoff.

A contest seems like a quaint, old-fashioned marketing ploy in the age of focus groups and cool hunters, but the Hot Bags cookoff is just one of many new competitions that are continually popping up. Most will be only onetime events, but here and there a new competition will evolve into an annual contest. What marketing types like about them is what they produce: a motherlode of recipes. These are used in two ways, first as R & D. The hundreds to thousands of recipes that come out of these contests provide the company with new ways to use their static food product. Home cooks have both the creative distance and, given the prizes, the financial drive to see these foods anew. No one at Post had thought to stuff croissants with Great Grains cereal to make French toast or to grind up the cereal to make crab cakes. At National Beef, Priscilla Yee demonstrated that a little-known cut of beef could make a tasty panfried steak.

These contests also make good sense for magazines such as *Southern Living* and *Better Homes and Gardens,* both of which have an insatiable appetite for recipes. *Southern Living* can publish as many as one thousand recipes in a year. The new cookoff was devised to generate simple, everyday recipes, a file that often runs lean at the magazine's offices in Birmingham, Alabama. Given how the contest is designed, these recipes will also use the products of the magazine's regular advertisers.

Contest-generated recipes also double as de facto market research on both macro and micro levels. In a broad sense, companies look to these recipes to see what everyday American cooks are up to. For example, in the past ten years cooking contests have offered a case study on trickle-down cuisine, how once-exotic ingredients—such as chutney, salsa, dried cranberries, and curry—are being used in home kitchens, mostly to ethnically tweak such American standards as meat loaf and tuna noodle casserole. When a contest gets a wave of Mexican-

American entries or, say, a ton of recipes using pesto, companies take note. They may also use these recipes to gauge how home cooks are *actually* using their products. It's better than a focus group, says Ashley Foster, an account executive at BCF&M. "We get to hear from the horse's mouth, essentially. You can see what's working. We may think they do one thing [with a product], but they may do something differently."

As even market research goes, contest entries are pretty dubious data. That's because many of these recipes do not spontaneously combust out of America's kitchens. Rather, most contestants, especially the contesters, specifically craft them to win a prize. They cull food magazines, restaurants, and television shows for standout ingredients or unusual trends. They research the company and past prize winners so they can discern what the contest wants. Then they give it to them. Consequently, the recipes are not a barometer of how Americans cook at home but how Americans cook competitively.

For example, a judge at the recent National Beef Cook-Off told me she found it interesting to see so many dishes with chili adobos, the smoked, dried jalapeños in a dark red sauce of ground chilies, herbs, and vinegar. However, this was no sign that the average cook was popping a chipotle or two into her chicken pot pie. Contesters began using them in entries in the mid-'90s as a new twist on trendy spicy foods. They found them especially helpful in contests that limit the number of ingredients because the chipotle in adobo sauce packs a big flavor punch, adding both heat and smokiness. The distinct flavor also helps a dish stand out from the crowd, although sometimes to a fault since too much chipotle makes for a harsh, overpowering heat, as judges know too well. When Pat Harmon first heard about them from other contesters four years ago, she had to order them off the Internet. Her diligence paid off. Her Tex-Mex Smoky Chili Hash, which used a mere teaspoon of the chili, won $10,000.

Moreover, many contest rules greatly influence the resulting recipes, especially if the number of ingredients and preparation time are limited. It is the height of irony for, say, Bake-Off® contest judges to declare that winning recipes indicate cooks want simpler recipes when the contest calls for "quick and easy" recipes and requires that one of their processed foods be used.

The folks at Reynolds took a rather level-headed approach to the four hundred recipes they received and did not read any huge trends into how the Hot Bag was being used. All the chicken entries proved that Americans still can't get enough of the white meat, but you didn't need a contest to figure that out. If anything, they were a little underwhelmed. Fifty of the top recipes were passed on to Pat Schweitzer and Betty Thompson Morton, the lab-coated home economist duo whom the company has made into celebrity spokeswomen. "You get the canned soups and sour creams that enter," Morton says. "The ones that are really good rise right to the top. If I seem disappointed, it's because my expectations were really high."

The majority of the recipes were too bland. They found that cooks who were overly health conscious didn't add enough fat or salt. Even the more creative recipes turned out to be surprisingly tasteless, including a recipe that used Asian fish sauce, soy sauce, garlic, and onion. Many entries stretched the idea of fusion too far. "Sometimes they work well," said Schweitzer. "Other times they are fighting in your mouth."

In the end Pat and Betty had a few ideas to develop, five recipes to post on the company's website, and three solid finalists. In addition to Sparrow's chicken they selected Priscilla Yee's Savory Salmon Provençal, a two-pound fillet layered with artichoke hearts from a jar, herbes de Provence, canned plum tomatoes, red onion, and kalamata olives. They also selected Jamaican Jerk Beach Party, a recipe by Rebecca Wanovich, who owns her own insurance agency in Pittsburgh. As Sparrow points out, this recipe looks strikingly like the dish on the Hot Bags package. Not long before the contest, Reynolds notifies the three finalists that they will have to give a brief presentation at the cookoff. Sparrow writes hers, hitting hard on the family theme of the contest. She is worried about going up against Yee for the first time.

The three arrived in New York on Saturday, January 12. Sparrow brought her longtime girlfriend from Osage. Wanovich brought her husband. Yee brought "friends" but will not tell me more than that. After having a reasonably friendly phone conversation after National Beef, I'm back to square one with Yee. She won't even tell me their plans. "I'm not the social chairman," she says.

The finalists have all their time to themselves until Monday morning, the fourteenth, when they meet in the lobby of their bright midtown hotel and are driven to a grocery store. On the creeping crosstown drive, Yee sits silently in the front seat, dressed in a black coat, black pants, black shoes, and black sunglasses, while Sparrow makes friendly small talk about contesting with Wanovich in the backseat. Like most newbies, Wanovich is totally surprised to find out how seasoned her competition is. Sparrow, trying to draw Yee into the conversation, asks her how many contests she has won. Yee harrumphs in the front seat and then snarls, "When's the last time you saw me at a cookoff, Diane?" National Beef this fall, I think to myself.

At a store with a big sign that reads "10 Reasons to Buy Organic," the three finalists struggle to find more ordinary ingredients. The only salt they can find is pellet-size sea salt. Sparrow paces the aisles searching for apricots canned in apricot nectar. She can only find the fruit in pear juice. Yee squeezes tomato after pale tomato looking for one that resembles the plump red numbers she buys back home in California. She allows me to follow her but mostly ignores me and answers my questions succinctly and without smiling.

After their ingredients have been purchased, to the tune of $180, the threesome is chauffeured back across town to Macy's, where they stroll through the women's coats department lugging their plastic grocery bags with them. The cookoff will be held in a private cooking school on the store's ninth floor. The walls are lined with poster-size photos of famous chefs, including the omnipresent Emeril Lagasse. "Look at how young he looks," Wanovich says.

The trio will work in the school's demonstration kitchen, which has a long length of counter and a tilted mirror suspended overhead. The school's staff is there to assist them. As with many first-time cookoffs, a number of the details have not been worked out. This becomes clear when Sparrow begins firing questions, such as "Who plates the recipe, me or an assistant?" No one seems to know. Sparrow has brought her own dishes, chunky white crackleware, but Wanovich hadn't even thought about how to present her dish. "This is a lot harder than I thought it would be," she says, her expression tensing.

For about two hours the three cooks work away. Wanovich can't find a crinkle cutter for her potatoes. She didn't bring her own because she didn't think airport security would allow it. Sparrow is prepped in no time but opens her can of apricots to find they are ancient and disintegrate at a mere touch. The cooking school director grabs her purse and dashes out for the items. Using tweezers, Yee silently, meticulously pulls out bones from her plank of ruddy salmon. A contest organizer, a young woman in a slitted short skirt who resembles Jennifer Lopez, begins to fret that Yee is taking too long.

A small audience files in, including Sparrow's friends Pat and Betty in their white lab coats and Wanovich's husband. Yee's "friends" are no-shows. Sparrow stands nervously, one hand on her hip, waiting for apricots and watching the clock. Moments before Sparrow has to put her Hot Bag in the oven, the cooking school director returns breathless, and lugging cans of apricots in nectar. She found them at a Korean market, she tells Sparrow, and made the owner open them to make sure they were good. A crinkle cutter, she reports, could not be found. Wanovich smiles, thanks her for trying, and soldiers on.

Sparrow goes first, talking as she puts together her Chicken and Apricot Couscous. She shows a photo of her grandchildren, describing how she cooks with them, and rather than having a sinkful of dishes at the end of the session, she says, "I can just crumple up the bag." Sparrow does a yeoman's job. Wanovich is no slouch, either. Then Yee, expressionless, gives a brief, matter-of-fact explanation of her dish and begins wordlessly to construct it. The only noise is the rustling sound of the bag as she stuffs it with the salmon. Going on presentation alone, Sparrow has clinched it. The presentation, though, doesn't count at all in the judging.

I have to admit that after the mayhem of chili, I'm a little bored with another company cookoff. I had kind of hoped a bag would explode. Now I'm secretly rooting for Sparrow and hoping Yee will lose so I might get a firsthand view of her poor sportsmanship that I've been told about. When I taste the three dishes, I realize it is not to be. Sparrow's dish turns out to be surprisingly flat; the sweet flavors of the fruit just don't stand up to the bag's rain forest–like interior. The potatoes in Wanovich's dish are nearly raw. Yee's dish, which is simple, straightforward, and tasting mostly of good-quality salmon and briny olives, is clearly the winner.

The judges withdraw and in about twenty minutes make their choice, which is, as I guessed, Yee. She breaks into a wide smile, the first of the day, and her face softens and her whole posture relaxes. She has won the trip to Jamaica plus a beach bag filled with goodies. At the prodding of a photographer, she rifles through the bag like a little girl on Christmas morning, pulling out a beach towel, a snorkel mask, and a large box of candy. "What are these?" she says giddily, holding them up for me to see. "Gob busters?"

~ ~ ~ ~

Priscilla Yee won the Reynolds' Hot Bags Foil Bags "In the Bag" recipe contest in January 2001 with this recipe.

SAVORY SALMON PROVENÇAL

1 Reynolds' Hot Bags Foil Bag, large size
1 red onion, sliced
6 salmon fillets (4 to 6 ounces each)
2 cloves garlic, minced
1/2 teaspoon salt
1/4 teaspoon black pepper
1 1/2 teaspoons Herbes de Provence or dried salad herbs, divided
2 cups plum tomatoes, cut into 1-inch chunks
1 jar (6 ounces) marinated artichoke hearts
1/3 cup pitted and halved kalamata olives

Preheat the grill to medium-high or an oven to 450°F. Place the bag in a 1-inch-deep pan.

Place the onion slices in the bottom of the bag. Arrange the salmon fillets, skin side down, on top of the onion. Sprinkle with garlic, salt, pepper, and 3/4 teaspoon Herbes de Provence. Layer the tomatoes, artichoke hearts, and olives over the salmon. Sprinkle with the remaining Herbes de Provence.

To seal, double-fold the open end of the bag.

To cook, slide the bag onto the grill or leave in the pan and place in the oven. Grill for 14 to 16 minutes in a covered grill or bake for 25 to 30 minutes in the oven.

Use oven mitts and a knife to cut the bag open. Fold back the top to allow the steam to escape.

SERVES 6

CHAPTER 12

DO YOU WANT TO BE
A MILLIONAIRE?

Every four years the Winter Olympics fall near the Pillsbury Bake-Off contest®. That was the case in 2002. This naturally leads to all kinds of comparisons between the two competitions. For example, on the Forum, the chat room on the Cooking Contest Central website, competition-bound participants were dubbed "Team Forum," and postings wished them good luck with a patriotic fervor. The analogies between the global sporting competition and the American cooking contest are a stretch, as a G.E. exec's comments to a crowd of contestants makes clear. "We don't have the snow. We don't have the mountains. We don't have the athletes from around the world. But we have you, one hundred of the best bakers in the world." Still, it's as close to an Olympic competition as the cookoff world has. The Bake-Off® contest is the best known and has long been considered the most prestigious. There is a press corps of one hundred-plus reporters to publicize the event. The freebies flow voluminously for the contestants, starting with the spanking new G.E. Advantium stove given to every contestant. Moreover, this is the contest that proclaims you "cook extraordinaire" across the land, the kitchen equivalent of Miss America, and it does so on national television, no less.

Fifty-three years after the first Bake-Off® contest, the shine has yet to wear off. Today's contestants may not wear kid gloves or use their husbands' names the way early contestants did, such as the very first grand prize winner, Mrs. Ralph E. Smafield, yet these liberated fillies covet the crown just as much. Just how many people enter is top secret, as are many things about the contest. Pillsbury won't even say why they won't give the numbers. All the company representatives parrot the same line: "in the tens of thousands." That vague estimate seems conservative, especially in the age of online entries, which has boosted interest in the contest.

The $1 million prize doesn't hurt. It is a steep slide to the next highest cash prize, which is now *Southern Living*'s $100,000. As recently as 1994, Pillsbury's grand prize totaled a mere $50,000, still above the majority of contests at the time. Pillsbury got to worrying that the pile of greenbacks didn't mean much in light of multimillion-dollar lottery jackpots. Fearing the media might lose interest, Pillsbury, then owned by the London-based Diageo Corporation, jacked up the sum to a whopping $1 million in 1996 to ensure the contest's top spot. "The British are gutsy," says George Pillsbury. Since Pillsbury merged this fall with its longtime rival General Mills, the fate of the contest and the grand prize has worried devotees. General Mills execs are cagey whenever they are asked about the next contest, explaining in neutral terms that they are evaluating it. But who would want to be known as the company that killed the Bake-Off® contest?

Although the bulging pot of gold is the main draw, contestants often have trouble wrapping their brains around the king's ransom. They come up with surprisingly modest and decidedly middle-class ideas for how they would spend the mountain-high heap of cash. Almost everybody says they would: (a) pay for their children's college education and (b) renovate their kitchen. There's next to no talk of exotic trips, career changes, or even expensive cars. Maybe they have trouble thinking big because they get here by thinking small. It's a big leap to go from tinkering in your kitchen to being in the running for $1 million. Who would ever guess that a mini inspired moment in the kitchen, such as tossing curry into a corn salad or dumping a jar of salsa into meat loaf, might win you a free trip to Orlando, a chance to become a millionaire, and instant, if fleeting, celebritydom.

Contestants in the 2002 event had to invent a recipe using at least one of twenty-eight qualifying Pillsbury products. For example, they could choose Pillsbury Creamy Supreme Frosting, Progresso Bread Crumbs, or Green Giant frozen corn. The latter accounted for kernels of corn atop pasta, tucked in enchiladas, and peeking out of couscous. Corn even turned up in coleslaw along with a can of mandarin oranges.

It wasn't until the 1960s that convenience products became staples of the contest. Now Pillsbury Flour is not even on the list of qualifying ingredients for 2002. Not one baked good was made from scratch. Instead, biscotti are made from muffin mix and tortes are made with tubes of cookie dough. If you wanted to bake one of the desserts from this contest, you can't just take a flour tin from the cupboard and go to work. You'd need to jump in the car, zip to the grocery store, fight your way down an aisle, and buy something like Thick'n Fudgy Double Chocolate Deluxe Brownie Mix or, in the case of Piña Colada Fudge, a can of Pillsbury Creamy Supreme Vanilla Frosting—that is, if you could find these *convenience* items. In fact, only a dozen of the one hundred recipes could be considered "from scratch," and that's using the term to include taco-seasoning packets. It is the great irony of this contest that it is less about cooking than it is about assembling. You don't need to be a gourmet cook or even an especially good one to make the grade. What you need to be is a crack problem solver, someone who can rework ready-made biscuit dough into piecrust or refrigerated breadsticks into mini-pizzas.

Keeping up with the fast-paced, out-of-breath, everyone-stressed-out times, the contest calls for recipes that are "quick and easy," words repeated over and over like a mantra. Most of the recipes take fifteen minutes, except in the Luscious and Light category, a new division with no limit on time or ingredients. In this category recipes could take a relative light-year to prepare, such as the Spicy Asian Lettuce Wraps. This dish takes fifty whole minutes and calls for a shocking fourteen ingredients.

On paper the contestants come across as varied as a group of mostly white, middle-class, middle-aged women can. There are ten men to ninety women. The ages range from two eleven-year-olds, both the granddaughters of seasoned contesters, to a seventy-six-year-old Arizonan with a new hip who described the genesis of her recipe as "an idea in my head." This is an educated crowd. The U.S. Census found that 26 percent of American adults over twenty-five have earned a bachelor's degree or more. Sixty-eight percent of the Pillsbury contestants can make that claim.

There are more than twice as many full-time working women, thirty-two, as homemakers, fifteen. Among the contestants are a forensic scientist, a stay-at-home father of eleven-month-old twins, a sitcom writer, a retired colonel, a critical-care nurse, a country-and-western singer, a marathoner, a hospital administrator, and a bank teller. Although the contest is considered a kind of midwestern affair, California contributed the largest number of contestants, eleven, trailed by Florida's eight. The contestants include natives of Kenya, Burma, and England.

〜〜〜〜

The rest of the country knows only of the Bake-Off® contest itself, the scene of manic stirring, chopping, and sautéing. In fact, it actually begins two days prior to the contest, the very moment the contestants arrive at the airport and the total immersion experience of the contest begins.

And so on a bright February Sunday morning a young woman with a neat blond ponytail stands at the bottom of the escalator that cascades into the nearly empty baggage claim area of the Orlando International Airport. She holds a small, handwritten, cardboard sign that reads: "Pillsbury Bake-Off® Contest."

The blonde smiles tentatively, self-consciously at the few travelers gliding down the escalator. She is met by blank stares until a woman with a smooth, round face in a windbreaker and jeans descends into view. Her big eyes zero in on the sign and immediately widen. She smiles back at the young woman, who responds with a relieved, full-teeth grin.

Cindy Schmuelling makes a beeline for the blonde with the sign, drops her purse, and darts to the baggage carousel just as a mob loaded with what appears to be their life's belongings—kids carrying bulging backpacks that sag below their bottoms and parents with car seats hitched over a shoulder and a stroller tucked under an arm—spills into the baggage claim area. The crowd of capri-panted, polo-shirted vacationers pushes up against the carousel and all heads crane to the left, looking for bags. Schmuelling is unfazed, and like a seasoned business traveler, she parks herself, along with two wiggly grade-schoolers in purple stretch pants, at the front of the pack. A bell rings, and the carousel heaves into action. Everyone leans forward as if on cue, and the parade of dusty, rumpled black bags begins.

Schmuelling peers at the chute where the bags are ejected, ready to pounce. Overhead a TV monitor intercuts news flashes ("Israel will keep Arafat confined" scrolls across the screen in big black letters) with the magical images of a woman on a trapeze. Schmuelling doesn't notice the TV screen, nor does she realize she's inching her way closer to the chute. In fact, she's well beyond the stanchions that mark where passengers can stand. An enormous black airport worker inhales as he slowly tucks in his shirt, sighs, and strides over. With an easy authority he shoos her back just as she nabs her first suitcase.

"I'm in a cooking contest," she says in her defense.

"Well, I'll expect some samples," he responds to the non sequitur.

"I'm trying to win a million dollars and get my husband off my back," she says.

"Should I touch that?" he says, looking at me.

Schmuelling laughs, grabs her bags, and dashes back to the blonde with the sign. A middle-aged man with a frayed mullet haircut takes Schmuelling's luggage and leads her through the airport's open-sesame doors into the soft embrace of Florida's tropical air. Schmuelling, who half-runs to keep up, turns her head right and left as she quickly looks around. She climbs on the bus he motions to and plops down in a seat. I follow right behind.

The bus lumbers out of its parking spot and circles the airport, picking up stray contestants here and there from various terminals as it goes. It is relatively early in the day, so the bus fills up only a third. The contestants from the West Coast aren't expected until the end of the afternoon. Schmuelling is all eyes, sitting upright, trying to soak up everything, even the airport with its neatly landscaped grounds. The bus hits the highway and heads northwest across a flat, swampy terrain dotted with low-rise buildings, a Super 8 Motel here, a long-term-storage unit there. Mostly, though, it's surprisingly undeveloped, just a scrubby, tropical terrain of leaning palms and swamp grasses. As we zoom by, a heron on a bald branch lazily stretches its wings.

"I'm in Florida," Schmuelling says to herself.

I'm trailing Schmuelling because she is a quintessential Pillsbury first-timer. She has just taken her first plane ride in nearly twenty years, which made her palms sweat and stomach groan. At forty-one she is taking her first trip by herself. Her husband, a retired Air Force officer, stayed home in northern Kentucky because of the expense. There's a $400 fee for guests plus airfare, and as Schmuelling says, "He doesn't really get" what a huge deal the Bake-Off® contest is. This is the first ever cooking contest that Schmuelling has entered, which she did on the advice of her astrologer. Lastly, this is as close as Schmuelling has ever come to a million dollars.

"Look at those billboards," Schmuelling calls out, still perched on the edge of her seat. Outside the window a hairless rubber ET drapes his extenuated fingers over a sign and makes puppy eyes. Will Smith in black Ray-Ban sunglasses smiles cockily from another. They are all ads for Universal Studio Theme Park, reminders that we are in the eastern epicenter of American celluloid fantasies. This is where people come not to make movies but to step inside them.

The bus veers down an off-ramp, zooms along a kind of lush boulevard, and then makes a wide left-hand turn into a drive with a sign for the Portofino Bay Resort, which remains unseen behind a wall of trees and shrubbery. We pass espaliered grapevines—these make everyone's head turn—and then bound over a small bridge that allows a fleeting view of what appears to be a mirage: a sun-soaked Mediterranean seaside village smack in the middle of Florida's boggy interior. Everyone gasps. Someone at the back of the bus calls out, "There it is." Schmuelling's lips curve into a neat smile. Around another bend and faux paradise is found. We pull into what appears to be an Italian piazza, with a fountain, topiary, and cobblestones.

"Oh, it's good to be here. Thank you, God," Schmuelling says, then bursts out laughing.

The Portofino Bay Hotel is on the grounds of the Universal Theme Park and is in keeping—in a high-end-resort kind of way—with the film-set theme of the amusement park. On the flatlands of Florida, Loews Hotel re-creates the Ligurian village of Portofino, a much-photographed seaport on Italy's rocky northwestern coast. The fishing village has been duplicated in the smallest of details, such as the fishing dories moored in the man-made lake that doubles for the sapphire blue Mediterranean, the thousands of native Italian plants, and the elaborate trompe l'oeil details on the building exteriors. Hundreds of years ago Portofino residents could not afford the architectural niceties of Rome and Venice, so they hired artists to paint the moldings, columns, and pilasters. The builders of the Portofino Bay Resort could certainly afford the real thing, but they didn't want the real thing. They wanted an accurate reproduction of an illusion.

There's plenty to remind you that you are not in an Italian village, beginning with the life-sized cartoon characters parading around the place and the Italian opera that is piped everywhere, even outside. After checking in, we pass an oversized Woody Woodpecker with a menacingly bright red beak as we walk down a darkly lit corridor made to look like a street of small Italian village shops, complete with strings of lights strung overhead. The clash between real and fake, fake and faker, leaves you giddily off-kilter, as if you are wandering the terrain of a very happy dream where anything could happen, where you could even become a millionaire.

"There's shopping, that's good," Schmuelling says as we walk through the arcade. I break off to get my press tag. Schmuelling heads downstairs to the wing that Pillsbury has taken over for the next four days. The Bake-Off® contest is so big—nearly five hundred attended the 2002 event, and a huge room is needed for the actual cookoff—that few hotels can accommodate it. At the Portofino, the contest, like an invading army, has requisitioned the lion's share of the hotel's banquet and meeting rooms, including the sprawling, sunny Venetian Ballroom for meals and the windowless Tuscan Ballroom for the competition and the awards program. They have also claimed the Ligurian room for the judges, the adjoining Michelangelo and DaVinci rooms upstairs for the press, and the anteroom to the Tuscan Ballroom for the contestant hospitality center, which is kept stocked with coffee and bottled water. Just outside is the manicured Citrus Piazza, where contestants can get a deep cleansing breath of fresh air.

I catch up with Schmuelling outside the Venetian Ballroom at a long buffet table laden with silver serving dishes. We load our plates with salmon fillets, fingerling potatoes, salad, and fresh fruit. Schmuelling lugs a bulging blue tote bag that she was handed when she registered. The room is nearly empty. Silverware clanks against china. We grab some chairs at one of the ample round tables with white tablecloths. A small woman in oversized red glasses joins us. She is the guest of a contestant, a man due in later from California. The couple met at a previous Bake-Off® contest when they were both contestants. A waiter in white descends upon us, and Schmuelling orders a Coke.

"They have Coke products," Schmuelling says. "I knew I'd like this place. I can't wait to see my room. I'm going to jump on both beds."

Schmuelling plows through her plate of food—good luck has made her hungry—while the small woman describes her job working the graveyard shift at the post office. "What about you?" she asks Schmuelling.

"What about me?" Schmuelling says. "That's a good question."

She was a veterinarian assistant, she explains. In that job she cleaned cats' and dogs' teeth, which isn't easy. That got her thinking: If she could scrub animals' teeth, why couldn't she do it for humans, which pays better? She became a dental assistant. However, she left that job in December, she says without elaborating. Schmuelling pushes her plate aside, leans over, and digs into the tote. She comes up holding a Doughboy key chain in one hand and pens and pencils in the other.

"Look at that," she says, then digs back into the bag. She proceeds to pull out crayons, a transistor radio, a refrigerator magnet, a coffee cup, a knife set, and a ceramic trivet. She piles the goodies in front of her.

"Looky, looky," she calls as she holds up a bear-cub-sized stuffed white Doughboy like a trophy. "Isn't he beautiful." She cradles him in her arms briefly, then leans over the tote again, scanning for anything unopened.

"Here's one I didn't open," she says. She cracks the box and pulls out the knife set for the second time. "Oh."

After lunch I leave Schmuelling and go looking for contesters. In the hospitality room I quickly come upon Pat Harmon. She is standing in the middle of the room, looking as if she owns the joint, and is dressed in a shiny black workout suit with 2000 and a star emblazoned across the back in gold. She has got on sparkly gold gym shoes. Harmon, sixty-one, has a slightly crooked smile and a jokey, offhand way of talking. "Meet my shadow," she says, motioning to a very small woman hidden behind a mane of dark blond hair and big wire-rimmed glasses. The *Orlando Sentinel* has sent a reporter to follow Harmon during the entire cookoff. As one of the five three-timers—she went in '96 (Toffee Apple Coffee Time Bars) and '98 (Taco Taters)—Harmon is a major media magnet. She plans on relishing it. This is her last turn with the Doughboy. By getting in a third time Harmon has barred herself and her immediate family from future Bake-Off® contests.

She has brought photos of her cookoff room to show the Orlando reporter. It's a small room off her kitchen that she has stuffed with the memorabilia of all her wins: the silver bowl from National Chicken, the plaque from National Beef, and the kerjillion Pillsbury trinkets that she has won and bought. The wallpaper has a Doughboy border. A bookshelf holds a complete collection of Pillsbury cookbooks. She even knitted the Doughboy into an afghan. She was ready to throw it all out when she didn't make the cut for 2000. "I told Paul, me and the Doughboy broke up."

Late in life Harmon has found a national stage for her considerable competitive drive. She has always thought of herself as a high achiever but had limited opportunities to demonstrate her aplomb in the steel mill valley of Beaver County, Pennsylvania. which flanks the Ohio River north of Pittsburgh. Her dad, a steelworker, died when she was fifteen. There was no money for Harmon, an honor roll student, to attend college. No one really went to college in Beaver County in the '60s anyway, she says. They went to work for the steel mills. She became a secretary, married a steelworker, had two children, got divorced, and married another steelworker, a crane operator at Armco. Her creative outlet was that of most women of her generation: crafts. She made dolls and did needlework, winning contests at local women's clubs. She liked cooking but relied on cookbooks.

Harmon began entering local cooking contests in her early fifties, but didn't truly become a hard-core contester until she retired at fifty-six from her clerical job in the county treasurer's office. Since then she has entered at least one contest a week, even ones with a kitchen apron as a prize. In 1997 she riffed on the humble Italian meatball sandwich, transforming it into a trendy wrap for a contest put on by a Pittsburgh radio station. She won a weeklong trip to Rome. The couple took their first trip to Europe, visiting cultural hallmarks of the Western world such as the Sistine Chapel and the Roman Colosseum, all thanks to Harmon's inspired sandwich.

The first time Harmon went to the Bake-Off® contest she was so nervous about breaking any rules that she wouldn't even tell her mother the name of her recipe. Now she is such a seasoned veteran that not only is she not nervous, but she's a touch jaded. She is annoyed that Pillsbury keeps her waiting for her video interview. It is now forty-five minutes past when the interview was scheduled, and Harmon notices that they are taking contestants scheduled for later ahead of her. She is also not entirely over the flu that laid her flat the previous week and kept her from practicing her salad.

Harmon thinks she has a real chance to win this year, unlike '98 when she knew roasted wedges of potatoes coated with taco seasoning wouldn't add up to a million. Not only does she think her dish is a contender, but there has been a portentous sign as well. Over the years Harmon has noticed that a lot of winners have full-page photos in the cookbook. "I thought, What's up with that? Then I put two and two together. It's the consumer research score."

Ahh, the consumer research scores. Pillsbury inaugurated this score in '96 when the Bake-Off® contest jackpot ballooned to $1 million. The score is derived from showing anonymous consumers in unnamed grocery stores photos of the dishes and the recipes. Pillsbury won't say how many shoppers they ask. These mystery shoppers then rate the likelihood of their actually making the dish. They never swallow a morsel of any of the one hundred dishes. The score is a guarantee of sorts that Pillsbury gets what it pays for: a winner with mass appeal.

According to Harmon's theory the consumer scores point to the possible winners, thus identifying dishes to be predominantly displayed in the cookbook. If her theory is correct, all bodes well for Harmon. After getting a tiny picture in '96 and a half-page photo in '98, she has graduated to a full-page photo for 2002. Her Baja Chicken Salad with Taco Vinaigrette, a plump mound of sour cream in the middle and dusted with grated orange and white cheese, covers every inch of page 52.

Harmon is finally called for her interview, and she walks off, with the young reporter in tow. I scan the room and see Susan Runkle, who has just arrived from the airport, embracing her daughter. Runkle was at National Beef but didn't win any cash. Linda Miranda, a dark-haired contester from Providence, Rhode Island, stands alone. She sent in forty-five recipes, forty of which were desserts. She was selected for Arborio Rice Cakes with Mushroom and Olive Ragout. Jim Pleasants, Bob Gadsby-esque in height and size, towers over the room as he marches through. Unlike Gadsby, Pleasants is not given to smiling, and when I introduce myself and then ask about his contesting, he growls, "I'm not a contester," and moves on.

I hear a rhythmic swish-swish, like a big-thighed woman walking in polyester pants. I turn and see the Pillsbury Doughboy ambling through the room. He is all poofed up with air and moves like an astronaut on the moon. When he stops, he teeters like a drunk, his fingerless hands thrown out as if to steady himself. Cameras click, flashes blink. I duck out onto the Citrus Piazza where I find Cindy Schmuelling gamboling about in the sun. Like Harmon, she's had to wait for her video interview. I tell her that Pillsbury will let me sit in on her interview. Her expression suddenly becomes serious. "I have to tell you something. This isn't my real hair," she says, grabbing a handful of her brown locks.

"I have cancer."

A couple of weeks after Pillsbury called, Schmuelling found out that the pain in her shoulder was not bursitis but the result of a tumor pressing hard on her liver. After hiding out for three years, the devious cells of ovarian cancer had returned. Her doctor wanted to operate immediately. Her prognosis was iffy at best. Schmuelling, knowing surgery would knock her out of the contest, said no. Plan B was devised. Schmuelling left her job. Her doctor gave her two industrial-strength chemo treatments, which blew her hair out. She packed syringes of Nupegin to boost her white blood cells. The operation was delayed until her return. Her husband of six years, Ray, was furious at first that she was putting off the surgery, but eventually he understood, she says.

She relates this quickly, as a way of explaining why she is wearing a wig rather than a description of how she has risked her life to be here. Right now the wig weighs more on Schmuelling's mind than death. "I can't wear it on the cookoff floor because the oven will frizzle it. It cost twelve hundred dollars, and it's the only one the insurance company will pay for." She has brought along a hat to wear on the contest floor, but she doesn't want to wear it for her official picture. She doesn't want to go down in history looking like a cancer patient. She has asked Pillsbury not to photograph her during the contest but hasn't gotten an answer yet.

When Schmuelling goes in for her video interview, she is led onto a wide stage set at one end of the competition room, which is filled with row after row of shiny white stoves. As she settles into a high director's chair, a young woman with curly hair brushes her cheeks with powder. Another assistant wires her with a mike. A bright light behind her head shines like a halo.

As it turns out, Schmuelling does not mention the wig or the cancer during the interview. The questions are not probing enough to prompt her to reveal such sad, dramatic news. Besides, it would be like announcing your divorce at a wedding. The interviewer wants to know how she came up with her recipe, what she will do with the million dollars, and if she has ever had a cooking disaster. She can't think of one.

"All I did was open a package of cookies, and look where I am," she says.

"Do you think there's some luck behind it?" the interviewer asks.

"I think there's some God behind it," she says.

After the interview Schmuelling and I go back to the lobby to see if her room is ready. The lobby teems with contestants pouring in. The Stutzman clan collapses on a couch, looking dazed and a bit bedraggled. The family has two contestants: eleven-year-old Melanie and her father, Ken. Julie, Melanie's mom and Ken's wife, competed at the 2000 contest. She is also Barbara Morgan's daughter. The foursome flew in on the red-eye, arrived this morning, and went straight to the Universal Theme Park. George and Sally Pillsbury, looking rather frail, wander through. Bolder contestants introduce themselves, but most just turn and whisper, "Look, it's George and Sally." Somehow the Doughboy has made it up here. A small, dark-haired boy announces loudly that he wants a hug, backs up, and runs full-steam at the Doughboy. The boy plows deep into the Doughboy's white girth, his arms spread wide in an embrace. Just then I feel a furry paw on my shoulder and turn to find Scooby-Doo's enormous black nose inches from my face. "Ha," Schmuelling laughs. He/she/it hugs me hard, hooking my waist with a paw while Schmuelling takes our picture. I free myself from the cartoon character's grasp and then watch out of the corner of my eye as the shaggy dog sidles up to an attractive teenage girl. She smiles uneasily as Scooby scoots up tight to her.

I go with Schmuelling to see her room, which has two queen-sized beds, a towering armoire, and a bathroom riddled with marble. Schmuelling quietly takes it in. While she naps and prepares for the gala dinner, I go off to explore the Portofino. I wander along cobblestone streets, past long rows of pointy cedars, through arched doorways, and over footbridges. I feel myself being lulled into thinking I'm in Europe, a delusion I don't resist. I think I smell fresh bread baking. I imagine I hear people speaking Italian. The moment I come across the pool, with its man-made beach and squawky rock music, I snap out of the waking dream. I also start to notice all the faux architectural details—even the shadows are painted on. I know this is based on the real Portofino, but suddenly I can't help doubting everything my eyes see in this artificial Mediterranean landscape. As I walk along the quay, I see that a full moon has risen early and hangs in the blue sky exactly over the domed bell tower. It clearly has a face tonight, right out of a Goya painting: eyes like sooty lumps of coal, a mouth shaped in an "oh" of surprise. I wonder if it, too, could be fake. I look harder, and the face transforms, the mouth curling into a smile and the eyes brightening. The face is strangely familiar, and I find myself gazing up at the Pillsbury Doughboy.

〰〰〰〰

On Monday morning Pillsbury indulges the press corps by sending us breakfast in bed. However, I feel like a vampire confronting a silver cross when I look down at the hearty slice of quiche, a bulging basket of sweet breads, and a bowl of granola in yogurt—basically enough food for three teenage boys. I'm still digesting courses four and five from last night's press dinner, not to mention that some of the wine I drank seems to have settled in pouches under my eyes. A good portion of the experience for contestants, company execs, and reporters alike is gorging as if it were Christmas. So I have at it.

Stuffed and dressed, I walk quickly to the contest epicenter, the Tuscan Ballroom, following a bowlegged man who holds on hard to his wife's hand on the escalator. Amid the sea of tables I find Schmuelling unhappily picking at a plateful of French toast. "It's too sweet," she says. Last night's dinner, however, was a fabulous "surf and turf kind of deal, potatoes mashed with their skins, and a crab cake appetizer," she says. "I even had a glass of wine. I'm more of a beer drinker. I treated myself."

After dinner she called her older brother. The siblings are especially close, bound by a Dickensian childhood. Their parents divorced. Their father drank and womanized. He died at thirty-nine of heart disease when Schmuelling was seven. Their mother suffered from schizophrenia and couldn't care for her two children. Relatives brought up the children. When Schmuelling mentions them, her face hardens. Her youth left her with such little self-confidence that Schmuelling didn't think she was smart enough to drive a car. She didn't build up the nerve to get her license until she was thirty-four. On the phone last night Schmuelling recounted the entire day to her brother, from her plane flight to what she had for dessert. Then she gave herself a shot of Nupegin in the thigh and slept propped up to ease the throbbing in her shoulder. "I wish my brother was here. Isn't that terrible?" she says.

The room bustles, each linen-covered table nearly full. Waiters are on the move with silver pots of coffee and glass pitchers of orange juice. I see Harmon step into the doorway and look around the room, a kind of disapproving frown on her face. Schmuelling pops an oblong red pill and a round purple one with a swig of orange juice. There's about an hour until the contestant orientation, so I duck outside to get out of the air-conditioning and soak up some morning sun. I settle on a stone bench on the Villa Piazza. Here I come across Marie Giardina and her partner, two retired teachers from outside New Orleans. They are taking photos of each other in front of a fountain. Giardina walks heavily with a cane, but that seems to be her only nod to aging. She has that indefatigable optimism you often find in educators. After years extolling literature and poetry to high school students, Giardina set out on several different careers, including a graphic design business. The two women started it because "you have to have some stimulation of the brain."

Giardina's path to the Bake-Off® contest was a very direct one. She entered a local cooking contest, her first, and it required entrants to craft a four-course meal for under $20. Giardina came up with a meal that featured chicken wrapped in leeks. She took first place. "If it's this easy, let me get on the Web. I looked under 'cooking contest,' and Pillsbury came up. I sent in four recipes in each category and told all my friends I was going."

Thanks to her Berry Nutty Breakfast Muffles—a primo title, what with the word play and hybrid noun—the boasting was not for naught. "A muffle?" I ask. "You know, a muffin crossed with a waffle," she answers. "Oh," I say. A muffle is actually Pillsbury Nut Quick Bread and Muffin Mix souped up with dried cranberries, quick-cooking rolled oats, buttermilk, and two eggs poured onto a waffle iron. Each muffle is then topped with cream cheese and marmalade.

Like many of the contestants, especially the first-timers, Giardina is clearly carried away with the Bake-Off® contest. Even though she and her partner have traveled extensively, they have been wowed by their first twenty-four hours here, particularly the gala dinner. "I called my sister and asked her, 'Have you ever had a meal where they changed your napkin?' To me it was a special moment in my life," she says.

It's touches like that that win Pillsbury a legion of true believers. They leave, pampered and stroked to the hilt, ready to spread the Pillsbury gospel. Giardina sums it up when she says of meeting George Pillsbury, the contest's affable patron saint, "I was glad to shake his hand and look him in the eye. Their dreams are America's dreams. Their success is America's success. I'm glad to touch it."

I smile and nod stupidly. In my first twenty-four hours, the Pillsbury reverence is already getting a little thick for my blood. No other cookoff inspires this kind of carrying-on. I resist the urge to point out to Giardina that the contest is, after all, a huge publicity event designed to sell processed food and that the Pillsburys are not your average family striving for the American dream. But I've taken an instant liking to her and don't want to pop her bubble. It's high time I found down-to-earth Janet Barton. As I part, Giardina calls after me, "Come play bocce ball tomorrow at four."

I catch up with Barton at the contestant orientation. As usual she looks a good ten years younger than her forty-two years. She is quite pretty in a blond outdoorsy way. She has big eyes and a pointed chin. She is always dressed fashionably in an understated manner. She is a Mormon, but at least a hair irreverent. Her Molten Mocha Cakes call for Kahlúa—coffee and a liqueur—that's a two-for-one sin in her church. Barton explains it away by saying that Mormons aren't allowed to drink liquor or coffee, but they are allowed to eat it.

Barton is a second-timer. She is not a touch jaded like Harmon, nor is she gaga, either. When Barton went to the 2000 competition in San

Francisco, some contesters, including Sparrow, had her picked as a winner with her Cappuccino Crunch Muffins made with a boxed mix, toffee baking bits, chocolate chips, and instant espresso. Pillsbury sent a
film crew to her house in suburban Salt Lake City to shoot a segment
for the awards program. The media seemed especially interested in her,
as if Pillsbury were directing them to her. Barton was dubious about
her chances, thinking that muffins would never take the million. Sparrow told her that seating assignments at the awards ceremony indicate
winners. If you're far in the back or far off to the side, forget about it. If
you're near the front and near the aisle, you're looking good. So when
Barton saw that she was in the front row, just a few seats in from the
aisle, her heart fluttered. Then she thought, "Oh, come on." Barton's
instincts were right. A single-layer cake made with a brownie mix and
with a vein of cream cheese coursing through the middle took the cash.
However, there may be something to the seat assignments. The woman
sitting next to Barton won $2,000.

Barton married young, at nineteen. She dropped out of college and
quickly got pregnant at twenty with the first of her four kids. She has
encouraged her oldest daughter, who just got married at twenty-one, to
finish her college degree before starting a family. Barton regrets that she
herself didn't earn a degree, but she still has made her mark outside the
home with long-distance running (she has signed up to do a half-
marathon in Moab in two weeks), volunteer work with teenage girls at
her church, and, although she's ambivalent about it, cooking and contesting. "It's kind of sad when the only thing you are known for is
food," Barton says.

Barton has always been a good cook, even as a teenager. This past
Thanksgiving she received so many phone calls from friends and rela-
tives with cooking questions that her kids started answering the phone
with "Martha Stewart's." Barton won $250 as runner-up in the Quaker
Oats contest, $250 as a runner-up in Wheat Germ, and $1,000 for
Campbell's Soup. She took first place at a local lamb cookoff, scoring
$500, and wins every time she enters the state fair.

Still, Barton is always thinking of quitting contesting. She loves the
feeling of possibility that contesting gives her and the way the compe-

titions keep her eyes on the future, but she hates the letdowns. She refuses to make contesting a full-time hobby like her peers and will make
a recipe only once or twice—no belaboring a dish. She hit on Molten
Mocha Cakes on the first try. After eating a molten chocolate cake in a
restaurant, Barton, a chocolate freak, decided to try making one with
Pillsbury's brownie mix. She added three eggs, three yolks, two sticks of
butter, one cup of chocolate chips, and two tablespoons of coffee
liqueur to the dried mix. Sparrow and other contesters think Barton is in
the running again for the grand prize. There's one hitch: Jim Pleasants's
Banana Fudge Baby Cakes. Pleasants, the imposing retired colonel, created his version of molten cakes using another Pillsbury brownie mix,
with a squirt from the fudge packet creating the oozing middle.

As we settle into our seats in the second row at the orientation, Barton whispers to me out of the side of her mouth, "At the last one they
asked really stupid questions." Lola Whalen, the head of the test
kitchen, takes the stage. She has a halo of soft ash blond hair and a classic Minnesota accent—that tightness in the back of the throat that
shoots every vowel through her nose. For the first twenty minutes or
so Whalen reads from a prepared text, outlining the rules and what
the contestants can expect on the contest floor. Whalen opens the floor
to questions. Holding her hands behind her back like a soldier at ease,
Whalen patiently repeats the questions and then answers them. A
woman in back wants to know how she can drain meat during the contest. "We've provided you with a colander and a bowl." Can I bring my
cane in? Giardina asks. "Yes." Can I bring a book to read during the
cookoff? a young woman asks. "No." Can I garnish my dish with some
of my ingredients? someone asks. "No. You have to make your recipe
exactly as you wrote it."

I feel a slow panic building in the room as the jolly contestants begin to realize how many rules and potential pitfalls there are. Contestants start firing questions about every tiny detail they can think of.
Even eleven-year-old Melanie Stutzman is not immune. "If I make two
recipes and then decide which one to send the judges, will you reheat
it?" No, Whalen tells the grade-schooler. "We give it to the judges as
you deliver it."

"What about our hair?" Marilou Robinson, an elderly contester from Oregon, cries. "You don't want judges getting a mouthful of hair. Are we supposed to wear hair nets? I didn't bring a hair net."

Someone has the sense to ask how much the mysterious consumer research scores count for. Whalen answers quickly and emphatically, "We do not release that information." No one dares a follow-up.

Barton doesn't ask a question; she just cocks an eyebrow here and there. About an hour and a half later the crowd, a tad deflated, files back out of the room with instructions from Whalen not to wear their name tags at Universal Studio's amusement park this afternoon. "I don't want them flying around the park."

〰〰〰

About 1 P.M., Schmuelling, Sherrie Johnston, another finalist, and I step onto the ferry to Universal Studios. None of us knows exactly what the Universal Studios' theme park is, only that we have free tickets and a free afternoon. The boat cruises at a leisurely pace along a canal that leads through a wholly contrived landscape. The banks are planted in an orderly manner with all types of local flora. Great ferns spread their fronds like peacock tails. Slender trees with bark like snakeskin lean toward the boat. Yards of Spanish moss festoon their branches. We pass by the pink stucco façade of the Hard Rock Café Hotel, and strains of unidentifiable rock music slice through the boat's opera. We pass the Universal icon, a golden globe with the studio's name emblazoned diagonally like a sash, and then pull along a concrete quay. On either side of the river is City Walk, a lane of theme restaurants that looks like a Vegas strip. There's Emeril's Restaurant Orlando, Jimmy Buffett's Margaritaville, and a name I'm surprised to see chainified: Bob Marley—A Tribute to Freedom.

We go from the piped arias of the boat to the piped pop of City Walk. We're completely turned around, so we walk through the restaurant Wonderland toward the Universal Globe, which leads us to the amusement park gate. After our purses are searched, we push through turnstiles and are immediately overwhelmed by what lies ahead: an army of families on a forced march to have fun. We decide to bolster ourselves with lunch and turn into the first restaurant we see, the understaffed Café Beignet and Beverly Hills Boulangerie.

As we wait in line behind a woman who turns out to be ordering for a small tribe, Johnston describes her peripatetic life aboard a fifty-two-foot sailboat. Like Schmuelling, Johnston is on her own, her husband skipping the Bake-Off® contest. Neither woman has children. Both have small dogs. The general outlines of their lives diverge from there. Johnston and her husband threw over their high-powered jobs in Chicago (she was in pharmaceutical sales) for early retirement on the open seas. At one point they had two sailboats, one in Europe and one in the United States. As Schmuelling listens, she turns to me occasionally to flash her eyes in a "Can you believe it?" look. Johnston is so personable, though, that you can't hold the one or two yachts against her. She asks Schmuelling about herself. Schmuelling explains that she recently left her job as a dental hygienist.

"Good for you," Johnston says. "Are you doing something special?"

Looking down, smiling to herself, Schmuelling says with the smallest hint of sarcasm, "I'm doing something special."

We gnaw cheese and veggie sandwiches while two grade-school boys, their parents in a trance over tub-sized colas, wrestle on the ground next to our table. The hippie van from Scooby-Doo rides by with the Great Dane sticking out of the sunroof, waving like a campaigning political candidate. Lunch consumed, we wander off aimlessly. We pass a tribute to Lucille Ball and a stand selling rainbow-striped Afro wigs. We end up on a palm-lined Hollywood Boulevard circa 1930. There are movie-theme tchotchke shops everywhere you turn. A calypso band cranks up on the sidewalk. We come upon the first amusement ride, Twister, and launch into a series of "Do you want to go?" "I don't know. Do you want to go?" Johnston is being polite to Schmuelling, who actually looks scared. I'm supposed to be *following* them as a reporter, so I don't want to take the lead. We meander on.

By the time we get to Kongfrontation, my curiosity and my inner thirteen-year-old has gotten the better of me. I start toward the entrance, with Johnston right behind me. Schmuelling pauses to read the description in our guide: "Come face-to-face with movies' biggest star: King Kong." I point out a sign that rates it one of the park's easiest. Schmuelling nervously purses her lips and follows us.

We walk quickly through halls made to look like a graffiti-marred New York City subway station, pre-Giuliani. Fast-talking teenagers in headsets herd us onto a wide, suspended tramcar. A metal bar drops into our laps, and off we go into a Big Apple night. You can look in lit windows to see depressing SROs. Grime coats the brick buildings. The streetlights are dim. Suddenly the headset teenager at the front of the car screams, "There's Kong," and a dark, furry silhouette looms into sight. Everyone howls.

For the next ten minutes we screech and laugh as the gargantuan go-rilla bats our car, knocks over streetlights, and climbs up buildings. He even peers with one big black eye into our subway car. We arrive back where the ride started and are rushed out by the headsetted teenagers before we stop laughing.

Back outside, we amble along a reproduction of the San Francisco waterfront, where we find Earthquake—The Big One. Johnston and I turn in without a word. Schmuelling stops in front of a sandwich board. It spells out a long list of reasons you should not go on this ride, including if you have back or neck problems or are claustrophobic. She flashes those big eyes at me and says tentatively, "Okay."

Earthquake—The Big One turns out to have a long, boring lead-in with awkward audience participation, bad jokes, and film clips with creaky Charlton Heston describing how seismic events are re-created on screen. At last we are instructed to go out one door to get on the actual ride. Claustrophobic scaredy cats with bad backs are directed to the exit. Johnston and I break for the ride. Schmuelling hovers at the door. She is clearly petrified, but Johnston and I can't resist peer-pressuring her. "Come on," we call. A woman in her sixties or so with soft, fuzzy white hair and shamrock earrings breezes by Schmuelling. Suddenly she jumps in line behind us.

"If an elderly woman can do it, I can," she says.

We hurriedly load into a subway car, which slips down a tunnel and into a re-created station and stops. The smell of chlorinated water pricks my nose. Everything begins to shake and rumble. The station floor abruptly rises and cracks. A fire breaks out. I can feel the heat on my cheeks. Schmuelling and I look at each other and burst out laughing. The station roof caves, and a chunk of road with a car comes crashing down. The subway train lurches. Water gushes down a staircase. All this feigned destruction is hysterically funny.

Outside, Schmuelling, emboldened, yanks out her park map and says, "Let's do Jurassic Park," the scariest ride in the park. We can't find it on the park map, but I see that Jaws, "Go into the water with three tons of white fury," is close by. I lead the way. What follows is a solid hour of ride bingeing as we get drenched on Jaws, spun around on Men in Black, and shaken like martinis in Back to the Future. Schmuelling is now unstoppable, but Back to the Future riles my stomach, drills my hair barrette into my scalp, and rouses my inner claustrophobe. I make an excuse of needing to return to my hotel room to work. As I stumble toward the park's entrance trying to hold down burps, I watch as Johnston and Schmuelling—sunglasses on, maps in hand, purses on their shoulders—walk in step to their next ride.

The day ends for the contestants with a dinner at Mythos Restaurant, which is tucked into Islands of Adventure, another amusement park right next to Universal Studios. Islands is a hodgepodge of themes, Marvel comic book heroes, Looney Tunes characters, Jurassic Park, and Dr. Seuss. I come across Barton and her teenage son on the way there and follow them through Islands. They know it well after spending all afternoon there, riding The Hulk, a green curlicue across the sky, and Dueling Dragons, an insane dual roller coaster that does 360s. At first glance the riders seem to have their arms held high all the time. Then you realize the cars are suspended from the tracks, and those are the riders' feet dangling in the air, kicking around like so many centipede legs. Barton was no slouch. She went on The Hulk four times, she tells me.

"Three times," her son corrects her.

We pause in topsy-turvy Seuss Landing, with its curvy walkways the pink of cotton candy and streetlights that bend as if made from taffy. The park is nearly empty, the young Seussphiles probably already prepping for bed. Wide-eyed Whos, cowfish, and elephant birds look on as we consider which way to go. Just like the Portofino and Universal, there is no right axis to be found here. You have to navigate by instinct. We need to find the Lost Continent section of the park, where the Whos will be replaced by unicorns. At a fork in the pink path, Barton thinks we should go one way. Her son thinks the other. He's as polite as an American teenager can be, but being a teenage boy, he quickly grows tired of debating with his mom, turns on his heel, and goes. Barton and I follow. It turns out he's right, and we find Mythos, which looks like a volcano on the outside but morphs into a sea cavern inside. Underground streams run between booths. The high ceiling is puckered and dimpled like worn rock. Bowl-shaped lights like small fire pits cast a golden glow.

The restaurant is already packed and pumped. Everyone talks excitedly, juiced by a day risking life and limb on rides. The cave is fake, but it sounds like a cave, with all the diners' voices bouncing every which way. We three are directed outside where there are open tables on a dark patio overlooking a man-made lake—or, as the park brochure describes it, an inland sea. It's very Iron Age on the deck, with metal chairs so heavy you have to flex to move them. We can hear in the distance the roar of the roller coasters as they loop through the air and their human cargo shrieks like tropical birds in the night. Otherwise, it's much quieter outside.

Sharon Mutugi, a contestant from an Orlando suburb, joins us. She's one of the few black participants. She's also not staying at the hotel but instead drives over each day. Consequently, like a commuter university student, she is not in the thick of it and so is not nearly as slaphappy as the other contestants. I order a glass of wine from the waitress whose name tag reads "Aphrodite." Barton forgoes one. She is, despite the Kahlúa in her molten cake, a devout Mormon. Mutugi is hugely pregnant, so she also passes. A rising whoop from a coaster echoes through the dark. Unlike the buzzing party conversation of the dining room, the patio crowd is nearly mute. One contestant even sits by himself. The first course arrives, a bifurcated bowl of Maine lobster and corn bisque, a kind of soup version of the black and white cookie. The lobster side looks mysteriously brown in the dark of the patio. Barton takes a spoonful. "There's something wrong with this," she says.

Dinner improves with the main entrée, fusilli in a rich sherry and roasted garlic sauce with chicken and mushrooms. Barton talks about what it was like not to win in the last Bake-Off® contest. All the faux pas and dumb questions she suffered. On a Salt Lake City radio talk show, the ill-prepared interviewer asked her what it was like to win a million. "'I would have no idea,' I said. Then the guy got chocolate all over him. When I got home, my mother-in-law, who had been listening, called and said, 'You poor thing, that was horrible.'"

I ask about Mutugi's accent, which is vaguely British. She's from Nairobi. Her path from Nairobi to Michigan to Florida for school, jobs, and marriage turns out to be a standard middle-class one with just a Continental twist. Her arrival at the contest is a little more mysterious. She readily admits she's not a very good cook, nor does she like cooking, which her recipe makes clear. She seasoned two cups of green lentils with two cups of Old El Paso salsa and a packet of taco seasoning. Waiters arrive bearing Warm Banana Chocolate Gooey Cake accompanied by a melting dollop of Peanut Butter Ice Cream. We quit talking.

Word spreads that the buses are here to take everyone back to the hotel, and the meal ends hastily. Tomorrow's 6:30 A.M. breakfast call hangs over everyone's head. I catch up with Schmuelling and Johnston on the walk to the bus through the weird terrain of the park. As we pass what resembles a crumbling ancient ruin from Mesoamerica, they excitedly recount their afternoon, which included Schmuelling's personal challenge, Jurassic Park. The ride and its robotic dinosaurs turned out not to be very scary until the end, a breathtaking eighty-five-foot plunge down a water shoot that left Schmuelling soggy and exhilarated.

"I screamed all the way down and loved it the whole time." She pauses, smiles to herself, and adds as we pass a giant stone hand clasping a trident, "This will probably be the best thing that ever happened to me."

∿∿∿

After two days of making nice, eating vast quantities of lukewarm hotel food, screaming their heads off on roller coasters, and lapping up Pillsbury's constant attentions, the contestants are out of prep time by Tuesday morning. After a hasty buffet breakfast accompanied by a jaunty Dixieland band, pranks by celebrity host Marie Osmond, and then a group warbling of "God Bless America" that leaves some dabbing their eyes with their linen napkins, all one hundred contestants line up two by two behind the Bake-Off® contest king and queen, George and Sally Pillsbury, for the traditional entrance. With the bulbous Doughboy leading the way, the entourage strides through the crowd of media, company execs, and family members and into the room full of ranges to the bouncy "When the Saints Come Marching In." While the mob whoops and whistles, the kitchen warriors smile ear to ear, choke back tears, and blush.

The hooting and screaming swells as the contestants walk faster and faster. They storm into the contest room, a football-field-sized conference room with six rows of one hundred ovens, and lit as if for a night game. "When the Saints Come Marching In" morphs into a Ricky Martin number as the contestants stream down the center aisle of stoves and around the room, and then stop in front of their individual stations like a high school drill team routine. The music suddenly stops. It's time to face the stove.

While the crowd of family members, press, and company execs looks on, the 2002 contestants quickly mess the pristine gargantuan kitchen that Pillsbury spent the last week constructing. They slam cupboard and oven doors, and pile ingredients willy-nilly on the countertops. They dash to refrigerators and microwaves as if running a 100-meter sprint. Harmon, at the far corner of the room, grabs her chair, sits, and motors through her cupboard, yanking out serving pieces, mixing bowls, and utensils at a clip. Then she pauses. She has to go to the bathroom, and escorted by a runner, off she goes. Not everyone is so focused. Ten minutes into the contest there is still no contestant at range 67, the one across from Harmon. A small posse of yellow-shirted runners is sent in search.

Most of the contestants probably haven't cooked in such a small kitchen since their college days. Each has a shiny glass-topped G.E. stove and a Formica countertop measuring two by three feet. A cardboard plaque above the counter lists the range number, the contestant's name, and the dish. At one end of the room is a wall of shiny white refrigerators and a half-dozen microwaves. As with most cookoffs, there are no sinks. Contestants have to get by with a pitcher of water, a roll of paper towels, and a bottle of hand sanitizer. The room is chilly, but the bright lights that crowd the ceiling will soon change that.

Family members must stay on the other side of the rope that runs around the cookoff, but at 8:15 A.M. sharp, the stanchions are parted and a sea of press, cameras and notebooks in hand, spills out onto the floor. The media, too, acts as though a starting gun has been shot as they race-walk down the rows of stoves. There's more than enough adrenaline to go around.

Any cook knows how hard it is to concentrate with just one other person in the kitchen. All it takes is the momentary distraction of a husband asking if you've seen his wallet to wreak havoc on an entire meal. Suddenly you find yourself staring into a sifter of flour, frozen, wondering whether or not you have added the baking soda. There's something about cooking that lends itself to spacing out. That's why Martha Stewart beats the drum for *mise en place,* the idea being that if you set out all the ingredients before you start cooking, you're not nearly as likely to blank one out. But not even a well-laid-out *mise en place* can save you from a kitchen blunder when someone is blabbering at you. Cooking is such a nonverbal task that to converse while doing so can render even gourmet cooks momentarily incompetent.

So imagine cooking in a room with not only ninety-nine other cooks going at it but a few hundred reporters and company execs wandering by and peppering you with questions. This is what divides the contesters and the first-timers. The contesters, through experience, have learned to do TV interviews while checking the doneness of a cake. The rookies tend to get a little wild-eyed and blurt out "Oh, my God" in the middle of press questions as they lunge for the sheet of cookies they forgot about.

Pillsbury is well aware of this kitchen phenomenon. They tell the contestants not to be shy about politely brushing off the press. Runners will form a human wall around a beleaguered contestant, as they did with a ponytailed middle-schooler at the 2000 contest. That is also why they give the contestants 15 minutes to themselves before unleashing the media on them.

I catch up with Schmuelling at range 31, tucked between Sweet 'n Salty Crunch Bars, which call for shoestring potatoes, and Caramel Cashew Bars, which call for a jar of caramel apple dip. Schmuelling is wigless, her head covered by a blue poor boy cap that she ordered from the American Cancer Society catalog. She has stuffed it with cotton balls and secured it with double-sided surgical tape. The cap is smart looking, kind of cookoff bohemian, and doesn't scream cancer patient. She's bubbly but calm as she pats out the claylike refrigerated sugar cookie dough into pancake-sized rounds. "I'm baking. This is my element. Maybe the rides helped yesterday."

Bam, bam, bam. All of a sudden the contest floor sounds like a construction zone. I look around and see a woman two stoves down at range 29, a red, white, and blue kerchief smartly tied around her neck and going at a raw chicken breast with a mallet. Her plaque reads Denise Yennie, Chicken Florentine Panini. I page through my handbook and read that she's a working mom from Nashville, Tennessee. Yennie raises the mallet over her head repeatedly and slams it into the glistening pink slab of poultry. Bam, bam, bam. Paillards, I think; she's pounding out paillards. I didn't expect to see that here.

Schmuelling merrily reports that her official photo is all squared away. Before she takes her dish to be photographed, she will duck into the bathroom accompanied by a runner and tape on her wig. She pops in one sheet of cookies and starts mixing up number two, mashing brown sugar into dense refrigerated sugar cookie dough. "It's the way you hold your fork," she explains. "It's the way you push. You want the vanilla and brown sugar to be incorporated."

Barton is over at range 66, near where a tall, mustached runner stands to warn people about the electrical wires running across the floor and underfoot. "Watch your step," he yells at me. Barton, in black slides and a ruffled blue shirt, stands out among the Reeboks and baggy red blouses, which seem to be the Bake-Off® contest uniform. She also is one of the few contestants taking her time. That's part of her strategy. Her first batch, she has decided, will go to the display table. That will give her a chance to get used to the stove and see how her Mocha Molten Cakes fare at sea level.

Barton is oddly situated next to her stiffest competition, the intimidating Jim Pleasants, whom she has bravely taken to calling "Baby Cakes." They have both brought a squirt bottle to decorate their serving plates with squiggly lines of chocolate. They are both using ice cream scoopers to measure their batter into muffin pans. Their cookoff styles, though, are very different. Pleasants grimly and efficiently stirs away, while Barton makes small talk and cracks jokes as if she's at a cocktail party.

"Recipe coming through," a runner yells as a large blond woman heads to the sequestered judges with a glob of broccoli, couscous, and cheese just a hair past 8:30 A.M.

"You're coming to a big bump. Watch your step," yells the runner near us.

"Big bump. Watch your step," the other runner repeats.

This seems to set off a low-boil panic in the room, and I can hear the cooking speed crank up a notch. In fact, in just a few minutes, another runner yells, "Recipe coming through," and the whole "watch your step" call and response starts up again. It turns out this contestant jumped the gun. She doesn't have her checkout list and beats a retreat to her stove. Barton remains unflustered, so much so that when a company exec stops by her range and asks for a taste even though she hasn't set out her sample card, she quickly cuts him a slice.

"Recipe coming through" comes the call again.

"There goes Pat Harmon," Barton says.

Harmon walks in slow, careful steps, clutching either side of her Baja Chicken Salad with Taco Vinaigrette, which is piled dangerously high on an oval serving dish. Barton cuts a wedge of her molten cake and pops it into her mouth. "Watch your step," yells the runner.

I quickly tour the floor. Between the stoves and the overhead lights, the temperature in the room has lost its earlier chill. I don't spot any snafus, no stovetop oil fires or nicked arteries, but I hear that the top popped off someone's blender. As I pass by Giardina's oven, she calls over the stoves, "Don't forget, bocce ball this afternoon." The buzz is that the ovens are slow and no one can hear the timer beep. George and Sally Pillsbury parade down the rows of stoves like visiting royalty, signing recipe books and offering encouragement.

I stop by range 48 in the middle of the room where bespectacled, gracious Joyce Sproul bakes her first batch of Mexican Chocolate-Filled Cornmeal Cookies. As far as the Bake-Off® contest goes, Sproul's cookies strike me as a relatively sophisticated idea amid doughnuts concocted from brownie mix and Danish made from crescent roll dough. She mixes the cornmeal into refrigerated cookie dough and wraps it around miniature Dove chocolate bars. She glazes the cookies with melted cinnamon chips stoked with a dash of cayenne pepper.

Sproul drove with her husband and twenty-five-year-old son all the way from Bath, Maine, to Orlando. Her husband, a ponytailed former back-to-the-lander turned ship builder at Bath Iron Works, is afraid to fly. The trip took two days, which is nothing compared to the two weeks it took the couple to drive from Maine to Alaska once. They asked the rental car company for a Mercury but got a silvery white Caddy instead. "It was like being in a cocoon," Sproul says.

She is composed, like a second-timer would be, even though it has been a long time since she last donned the Bake-Off® contest apron, 1984. She won a designer scarf from a La Choy recipe contest with a quick-bread recipe made with canned bean sprouts. It wasn't too bad, she says. You couldn't even taste the sprouts. Soon after, Sproul broke into Pillsbury with Maple and Raisin Pull Apart, which she made with a can of biscuit dough. She spent the next eighteen years trying to return. "I'm more excited now because then I didn't know how difficult it was to get in." And she is in the much coveted dessert category. When asked who she thinks might win, she does not name herself but instead Barton's molten cakes and Milleniyum Chocolate Torte made by a marathon runner and a senior manager at Johns Hopkins Hospital.

"Why is this beeping?" Sproul says, turning to her softly bleating stove. "I'm afraid the stove has turned off." Finding it incredibly difficult not to offer advice, which could disqualify her, I flee the scene, hearing the beep-beep continue behind me. It turns out that Schmuelling, across the aisle, has hit a small glitch as well. Her huge cookies are running into each other, ruining their perfectly round shape. I don't need to bite my tongue. The new Schmuelling, who in the past forty-eight hours has morphed into an alpha lioness, has already figured it out. "What I'm going to do is make all three batches and then pick out the best-shaped nine and send those to the judges."

Back over at Barton's stove a small crowd of people, including the film crew from the Food Network, hovers, waiting for samples. Barton is working her mojo with the squirter bottle, carefully zigging and zagging. Then she carefully lays out a dozen molten cakes. Barton garnishes the plate with strawberries and chocolate drizzles, then hands over an extra cake to a Food Network crew member. He digs in as if he hasn't had breakfast while we, molten-cake-less, watch quietly, awaiting his judgment.

"It's to die for," he says with his mouth full.

Next door to Barton is Pleasants, who has been all work and no play at range 65. He is making final preparations to send his plateful of baby cakes to the judges. Squirter bottle in hand, he makes chocolate loops on his glass serving plate, delicately arranges the baby cakes, and then with his large, meaty hands sprinkles powdered sugar over them. He begins scooping ice cream and carefully places the frosty disks on the plate. Then disaster strikes.

Just as Pleasants holds a scoopful of ice cream over the plate, a runner, a woman plastered with pale foundation makeup, taps him hard on the shoulder from behind. The disk of ice cream tumbles onto the plate and splats, making a mess of a chocolate squiggle. "I'm sorry. I'm so sorry," the runner says, taking a step back with each apology. I feel the seismic rumble underfoot of a sizable man about to explode. If there were animals on the floor, they would flee. "I'm sorry, I'm sorry," the runner continues. He doesn't even turn to look at her. Barton and I step backward as well.

He picks up the offending scoop, throws it in a bowl, and wipes off the plate with a towel. "I had it right. There've been too many interruptions," he says out loud but to himself. I leave Barton to fend for herself. "Watch your step," the mustached runner calls after me as I beat my retreat.

Life is calmer up by Harmon, even with all the reporters following her. Not only is the *Orlando Sentinel* reporter trailing her, but a reporter from the *Pittsburgh Tribune-Review* has also been stuck to her side. And the Food Network was all over her when she nicked a finger and had to send a runner for a Band-Aid. While I watch, she breaks a manicured nail and laughs it off. "I'll live." She tells me that when she took her dish to the judges, she passed Osmond who called out, "Oh, that will feed Danny." She struggles to toss her salad, gingerly turning the leaves. She designed her dish for four servings, but Pillsbury revamped it to serve six. It just barely fits in the bowl, and glistening lettuce threatens to tumble out.

I swing by Ken Stutzman's range where he is nonchalantly constructing Savory Crescent Bites, a kind of Mediterranean updating of pigs-in-a-blanket. He and his daughter, eleven-year-old Melanie, also a contestant, have been besieged by reporters. This father-daughter face-off is just the kind of story reporters gobble up. They've been photographed in chef's hats, frowning at each other as they cross wooden kitchen spoons. Frizzy-haired Melanie loves all the attention, telling anyone who asks that she'll beat her dad and smiling so big that you can see every wire in her braces. Ken, who is also dogged by reporters for being one of the ten male contestants, is far less enthralled with the media mayhem. When Osmond showed up at his range and told him to stick an olive in her mouth, he was shocked. "I said, 'You want me to feed you an olive?'" Yes, she answered. And like a lover, Stutzman popped one in her mouth.

There are still three hours to go, but about a quarter of the contestants have already sent their dishes in to the judges and to the display table. All they have left to make are samples, and they aren't obliged to do that. I can't help thinking that the contest must have been much more exciting when it was truly a race against the clock, back when yeast could still be found on the floor. The quick and easy theme has taken most of the challenge out of the actual contest. Almost all the contestants have far more time than they need. They tell me their recipe is so easy "you'd have to be an idiot to screw it up." They say this with pride, but it utterly depresses me. For a million bucks it just seems that they should have to sweat a little, maybe whisk egg whites until stiff or at least mince an onion correctly. As usual the knife skills are appalling. Ka-thonk, ka-thonk rhythmically echoes through the room. The sound of a bread knife revving up catches my attention, and I look over at Denise Yennie again, kerchief still perfectly in place, as she carves her Chicken Florentine Panini into neat squares. I take heart again with the paillards, then duck out for some fresh air and coffee.

When I return to the contest floor, I find Schmuelling in her wig. She put it on to take her cookies to the judges and then wore it back on the floor so the photographer could get a picture of her by her stove. The photographer asked Schmuelling to pose with the oven door. Schmuelling complied, hoped for the best, and opened the door. Luckily, the front of the wig did not scorch, so she has kept it on. She also figured out how to stagger her cookies on the cookie sheets to get the shapes she wanted. In short, everything is going swimmingly, just as it has since she landed in Orlando. "I'm telling you, I am blessed."

The tension has evaporated from Barton's station. Pleasants has turned in his cakes to the judges. Now he's feeling quite chatty. He does most of the cooking since he retired in '89, and his wife still works as a pharmacist. He launches into a description of his kitchen. He redid it four years ago but tossed everything out this summer and started anew. "I have sinks at either end and a warming drawer," and so on. Barton nods as he itemizes. He'll even talk about contesting, although I don't dare use the term again. He had a big year in 1990 when he got into the Bake-Off® contest and then won the former Bay's English Muffin cookoff, which scored him and his wife a trip to France. Then he won the first Sutter Home's Build a Better Burger Contest. "When I enter, I usually go," he says.

"Recipe coming through."

"You're coming to a big bump," runners yell.

When Pleasants turns back to his already very orderly countertop to straighten it up, Barton whispers something to me. "What?" I mumble. She holds a hand up to her mouth and slowly enunciates "I beat him." She got her molten cakes in first. After the ice cream incident, Barton realized that she was ahead and decided, given how similar their desserts were, that she should get hers in first.

It's almost noon and the cooking has dramatically wound down. Some contestants have already left the floor, having taken their range plaques with them. Most contestants are just talking by their stoves. Marilou Robinson, who had fretted about hair nets in the orientation, sits in front of her station, her legs propped up on her cupboard unceremoniously and her pants hitched up, exposing her pale, loose calves. The few contestants who are still cooking are doing so quite intently. A runner has been stationed by Mary Capone and Steve Mandell, whose ranges are side by side, to shoo reporters away. Mandell, slim and bespectacled, is hunched over his Milleniyum Torte, intently icing it. The cake has to be cooled twice for a total of two hours. Capone is red-cheeked as she works on her Parmesan Chicken with Pasta Rags. The runner, a General Mills employee, fends off reporters in the politest way, offering a pained smile. "I feel bad," she says.

Most of these remaining contestants are here by design. Ashley Shepardson, contester Claudia Shepardson's daughter-in-law, holds off because she wants her citrus gazpacho to be as cold as possible. Sproul wants her cookies to be the last dish the dessert judges taste. Capone wants to reduce the chances that her dish will need to be reheated. Mandell's torte takes three hours and thirty minutes from beginning to end, which explains why he is still here and didn't make the cake a third time. He didn't have enough time.

Then there's Dean Phillips, the only contestant in shorts. Phillips just hasn't had a good morning, and it shows now. The young software developer, who recently finished up his post-doc studies, frantically plates his Smoked Turkey Quesadillas. He's visibly sweating and is having trouble answering questions from the Food Network crew, which has zeroed in on him. His eyes are blank as his hands fly over a counter filled with gaping cans and dirty silverware, searching for a package of cheese. At 12:43 Shepardson gracefully strolls behind him, not slopping a drop of her bowlful of fruity gazpacho. Two minutes later Phillips tosses a smattering of cheese over his quesadillas and leaves the floor for the judges. That makes Sproul the last contestant. At 12:49 she delivers her cookies to the judges, and almost immediately a crew begins taking the contest floor apart.

Just outside the contest room, all one hundred dishes are lined up on two long white-linen-covered tables surrounded by stanchions. This food is neither to be eaten nor touched. It is solely for looking, a kind of exhibit of American food. The desserts are holding up well, but, unfortunately, much of the rest of the food looks like a church supper gone bad, with cheese oil pooling atop casserole dishes and garnishes going limp. The avocados have turned a gray-brown on top of Harmon's salad. The sauce on Susan Runkel's Saucy Pork Medallions with Spiced Couscous has congealed. The Santa Fe Chicken Bread Bowls are downright scary looking, as if the small rounds of bread have erupted some viscous lava. And the sole fish dish, Fiesta Flounder Fillets, truly reeks.

~ ~ ~ ~

Wednesday morning breaks with grave news on the radio and television: a cold front has moved into central Florida. That means the mercury has dipped to an arctic 55 degrees. A brisk wind kicks up the fake harbor, which gently rocks the fake fishing boats. The real ducks paddle and preen happily in the sun. Hotel guests in short sleeves, caught off guard by the new chill, hotfoot it across the windswept piazza.

The turn in weather has had no effect on the contestants' spirits. I find them excitedly munching their last gratis buffet meal, this spread featuring eggs every which way—spilling out of brioche, wedged into gaping croissants, mixed into a kind of kugel. The dining room display is half the size of the other meals, a sign that the 2002 event is quickly winding down. In fact, the contestants have been told to have their bags packed and waiting by their hotel room door in case they are the million-dollar winner. The first bus to shepherd nonwinners to the airport leaves at 11:30 A.M., a mere half hour after the awards ceremony ends.

Given all the secrecy around the Pillsbury Bake-Off® contest, the company shows out-of-character and maybe unwise faith in us reporters to keep a secret. Around 9:30 A.M. on the morning of the awards ceremony, the thirty or so reporters are shepherded into a windowless room. A sign outside the door reads "Restricted Access." Before the awards ceremony, before anybody is even seated in the awards ceremony room and while the contestants are still munching from the egg-every-which-way buffet, we are about to be told who the winners are. The reporters are not supposed to tell the contestants that the press will be briefed in advance. Still, all the contestants seem to know. Anyway, it's fairly noticeable when the reporters get up from breakfast almost en masse and hurry from the room.

Pillsbury makes this leap of faith so that reporters can taste the winning recipes. Reporters can also give their editors a heads-up before the morning news meeting if they have a grand prize winner in their circulation. Of course, passing along this inside information carries a risk. One year contestants overheard reporters talking about the winners among themselves. There are about twice as many seats as needed, so the journalists spread out through the room and quietly scribble in their notebooks as the winners' names are read off. I know only one of the thirteen. Even though they have just had breakfast, the reporters rush the sample table and begin chewing. While they eat, they compare opinions. No one is overly impressed with any of the dishes except for one, the winner of the G.E. Innovation Award. Everyone seems to agree it is truly tasty. The million-dollar winner isn't bad. It's fine. It just doesn't seem worth a million. But then even *über* chef Thomas Keller's revolutionary butter-poached lobster recipe doesn't seem worth a million.

As the press files out of the room, we run smack into the contestants milling around the entrance to the awards ceremony room. I see Schmuelling and Johnston, and turn on my heel, not trusting my poker face. I walk straight into the awards ceremony room and grab a seat behind a $2,000 winner whom I recognize but who doesn't know me, Steve Mandell, the creator of the Milleniyum Torte. A curly-haired woman half-hops over me and plops down in the seat next to me. It's Mandell's wife, an attorney sporting a lot of rings and jingling bracelets. She ruffles Mandell's neatly combed hair. We get to talking, and it turns out the Mandells know Ernie Crow, a contestant I met at the 2000 competition. It was his third time, so he had knocked his whole family out. Still, Crow's wife has managed to come back, accompanying a friend, Mandell's wife tells me.

What had been the contest room yesterday with one hundred cranking stoves has been transformed into a television set. Chairs fill the floor where ovens once stood. The lights are turned low. Air-conditioned mist swirls in the spotlights. The seats for the contestants are numbered the same as their ranges, but they are not in sequential order, which causes a fair amount of confusion, hunting around, and seat-swapping. Contesters are reading the tea leaves of their seat assignment. As Julie Stutzman passes me, she tells me excitedly, "Ken is on the aisle. Melanie is in the front row. That's not bad, either."

Mandell is seated on the aisle. Janet Barton sits several chairs in from the aisle. Pat Harmon is in no-man's-land, tucked to the far right of the stage, the second seat in from the end. I can't find Jim Pleasants or Schmuelling. A cameraman walks slowly down the aisle, looking at a sheet of paper, and then, to my eye, looks directly at the winners. I can't believe that nobody notices, but then again, everyone is so giddy with anticipation, like Christmas morning times a hundred. For the past three months these people's lives have hung in the balance as a million dollars dangled over their heads. Within the hour that great possibility, that bright, shiny, golden question mark, will be snatched away from all but one. That contestant's life will be forever changed, thanks to good luck or God's will or talent and hard work. The rest will return to normalcy thanks to bad luck or God's will or their ineptitude.

Finally, everyone is seated and the doors are closed. No one will be allowed in or out during the broadcast. "The potty break is all over, so we hope you all went," a producer with a head mike says from the stage. He instructs the contestants who win to show a lot of excitement, and he makes the crowd demonstrate how loudly and enthusiastically they can clap. Perky Marie Osmond takes the stage, and the program gets under way.

In each category she reads off the four winners. They remain seated and, despite the producer's directions, tend to react with big smiles rather than the hysterical gushing that the producer hoped for—except for one who jumps as though she's been shocked. Mandell just smiles for the camera, but his attorney wife launches out of her chair and thumps him hard on the shoulders. These are the $2,000 winners. The $10,000 category winners are announced and invited on stage. In short order Osmond has invited a postman from Modesto who baked chicken wings in the oven, an artist who crossbred pad Thai with fettuccini Alfredo, and Denise Yennie, the woman who made chicken paillards. Yennie, decked out like a political candidate in a bright red blazer, appears composed except that she stands very rigidly and seems to be slightly hyperventilating.

"You look so calm," Marie said.

"Oh, my God," Yennie exhales, and then sucks in air.

Osmond works her way to the dessert category, the one that everyone expects to produce the grand prize winner. There is no mention of a molten cake or a baby cake. Neither Schmuelling's nor Sproul's cookies score. The $10,000 category prize goes to a muscular-looking California homemaker for her pies made of canned filling and refrigerated biscuit dough. An unspoken collective "Huh?" runs through the room. I try to see Barton's face, but her hair is covering it.

Now the ninety-six contestants in the audience, their lives crashing back to normal, pay attention only out of curiosity. They sink into their chairs. Some fight tears. Others shrug and smile. Osmond opens the envelope with the name of the million-dollar winner. The four contestants onstage either look at the floor or at the ceiling. Osmond yells: *Dennis Yennie.* A heap of confetti showers onstage. Yennie tenses up, holds her hands to her face, trembles, and seems to have trouble breathing again. Her tall husband rushes onstage. That's it. The 2002 Bake-Off® contest is over.

Much of the audience quickly rises to its feet and rushes the door. There is no lunch waiting for the contestants. No one has been allowed to check out late. The only remaining perk is the free bus ride to the airport. Harmon and her husband are at the head of the pack. She is no longer thinking about fame and fortune but about changing into her travel pants for the plane.

Yennie takes a seat in a chair on the edge of the stage for an impromptu press conference. Behind her, the contestants who have hung around line up one by one to have their picture taken with Osmond. While Yennie answers questions, she keeps mentioning that her win is "divine," that she is "blessed." None of the reporters touch this. Instead they ask why she used spinach ("We use a lot of spinach right now at home, so spinach was on my mind"), if her two teenagers like it, ("They were lukewarm at first, but now they like it"), and if the recipe doubles easily ("yes")—hard-hitting food-reportage kinds of questions.

While this line of questioning continues, Yennie somehow manages to sneak in some interesting details about her life, one that makes her seem a thoroughly modern Bake-Off® contest winner. She is a CPA and has an MBA. She asked to be laid off from her last job at a capital growth fund that was going down the tubes. She wanted a new challenge. She has spent the last year starting a consulting business, which applies the creativity of cooking to business. "[Cooking] is project management at its finest. So many women don't realize they are doing project management. How you create in a kitchen is no different from how you create in business."

Yennie says she packed as if she would be going to New York and told everyone she wouldn't be back until the end of the week because she'd win. "My goal was to make a million by the time I was forty, and now I've done it." How will she use the money? She'll "leverage it," she says. No one can think of a follow-up question to that.

～～～～

Now comes the post-Bake-Off® contest analysis. Over the next few days the contesters mull over the results on the phone and via email. The consensus is that many of the winners are too ordinary. No one can figure out the chicken wings win. The panini is okay, but quite complicated. As Sparrow points out, it's a lot of steps to make "a sandwich." She also scoffs at the panini being in the Light and Luscious category at 500 calories per serving. As for Yennie's sweet-and-sour glaze made from vinegar, chopped onion, and sugar that wowed the judges, Sparrow points out that a bottle of Italian salad dressing would have worked the same and been far simpler. As for the mini apple pies, Sparrow says, "People just about gagged on that."

Harmon is just relieved that a dessert didn't take first place again. "People are overly impressed with dessert." She's especially happy that Banana Fudge Baby Cakes didn't score a prize. "I was really glad he didn't win because I thought he was arrogant," she says on the phone. "He told somebody when he sent it in that he thought he would win. He'd hardly give you the time of day."

On the phone from Utah, Janet Barton admits that she really thought she had a chance at winning this time and that she was disappointed. Jim Pleasants's wife told Barton that the two similar desserts had canceled each other out. She, too, was a little shocked at the Grands! Little Pies win. "Canned apple pie filling! Makes you question what they are looking for."

Barton had trouble enjoying the family vacation in Florida after the contest. She's been second-guessing her recipe ever since. "Maybe it wasn't unusual enough, trendy enough. I used only one of the Pillsbury products. Maybe it was too plain." Barton is especially discouraged after reading a story on the Web by one of the judges, Carolyn Jung, of the *San Jose Mercury News*. Jung describes how she was overwhelmed with the sweetness of many of the desserts and that one of the judges used a spit cup. Barton worries it was her cake that was spat. It turns out that it was the Piña Colada Fudge and the Poppy Seed Swirl Loaf that got ejected mid-chew by a judge from *The Detroit News*.

They also look for some kind of pattern. Sparrow says the buzz is that there was no way a dessert using one of the brownie or cake mixes would win a big prize. The mixes had to be sold off as part of the Pillsbury and General Mills merger. Of the four dessert winners, only the Milleniyum Torte used a boxed mix.

What gives all the conspiracy theories an extra boost is that the judges in their newspaper stories have outed the consumer scores. The contestants now know they count for a shocking 50 percent of the score, enough—as in the case of Lemon Poppy Seed Puffs—to knock a dish out of the running. When the computer issued the five top score winners in the dessert category, the judges were shocked that the much-liked puffs weren't on the short list and that the so-so Raspberry Pecan Cream Cheese Bars were. Then they realized it was the work of the consumer research scores.

If the consumer scores didn't have the contesters talking, what Harmon finds on the Web does. Harmon learns that a contestant she had befriended is a caterer. According to Pillsbury rules, you cannot be a "food professional." Harmon calls Pillsbury and is told they knew she was a caterer and that was okay. The contest rules are open to interpretation by Pillsbury, and the company is the final arbiter. When Norita Solt finds out about the caterer, she's furious. At Pillsbury's behest she turned down royalties she won as part of a Gedney Pickles contest. The company sells jars of her recipes with her picture on the label, but she doesn't earn a cent. Pillsbury told her, she says, if she accepted royalty payments, that would make her a food professional and exclude her from future contests.

Then I hear that Marilou Robinson, the elderly contester at the Bake-Off® competition who had put her legs up on her counter, has died. The word is that her doctors told her not to go to Orlando but she ignored them, wanting one more turn with the Doughboy. That makes me think of calling Schmuelling. The news is not good. A CAT scan found a second tumor, this one smack in the middle of her chest. There's no point in operating, she's been told. She sounds resigned, tired. The Bake-Off® contest, she says, makes for a fitting conclusion to her difficult life.

"That was the best four days of my life," she says. "I'm so glad I got to go. I told the doctor that, and he said, 'You made the right decision. They would have opened you up and then closed you back up, and you wouldn't have been able to go.'

"Pillsbury was a way for me to say, 'Hey, I did something really great.' It was a lot more than the million."

~~~~

Denise Yennie won the $1 million grand prize at the 2002 Bake-Off® contest with this gussied-up sandwich.

CHICKEN FLORENTINE PANINI

1 (10-ounce) can Pillsbury refrigerated pizza crust
1 (9-ounce) package Green Giant frozen spinach
1/4 cup light mayonnaise
2 garlic cloves, minced and divided
1 tablespoon olive oil
1 cup chopped red onion
1 tablespoon sugar
1 tablespoon vinegar (cider, red wine, or balsamic)
2 boneless, skinless chicken breast halves
1/2 teaspoon dried Italian seasoning
4 (4-inch) slices provolone cheese

The preparation time is 35 minutes.

1. Heat the oven to 375°F. Unroll the dough and place it in an ungreased 15 x 10 x 1-inch baking pan. Starting at the center, press out the dough to the edges of the pan. Bake for 10 minutes. Cool 15 minutes or until completely cooled.

2. Meanwhile, cook the spinach as directed on package. Drain well and squeeze dry with paper towels.

3. In a small bowl, combine the mayonnaise and 1 of the garlic cloves, mixing well. Refrigerate.

4. Heat the oil in a small saucepan over medium-high heat until hot. Add the onion and cook, stirring, for 2–3 minutes or until crisp-tender. Add the sugar and vinegar. Reduce heat to low and simmer for 3–5 minutes or until most of liquid has evaporated, stirring occasionally.

5. To flatten each chicken breast half: Place, boned side up, between 2 pieces of plastic wrap or waxed paper. Working from the center, gently pound the chicken with the flat side of a meat mallet or rolling pin until about 1/4 inch thick. Remove the wrap. Sprinkle the chicken with Italian seasoning and minced garlic.

6. Coat a large skillet with nonstick cooking spray and heat over medium-high heat until hot. Add the chicken and cook for 8 minutes, or until browned, fork-tender, and the juices run clear, turning once.

7. Cut the cooled pizza crust into 4 rectangles and remove from the pan. Spread each rectangle with 1 tablespoon mayonnaise mixture. Top 2 rectangles with chicken, spinach, onion mixture, cheese, and the 2 remaining crust rectangles, mayonnaise side down.

8. Heat a large skillet or cast iron skillet over medium heat until hot. Place the sandwiches in the skillet and place a smaller skillet on the sandwiches to flatten slightly. Cook about 1–2 minutes, or until crisp and heated, turning once. Cut each warm sandwich into quarters.

YIELD: 8 SANDWICHES OR 4 SERVINGS

CHAPTER 13

NATIONAL CORNBREAD

Emotions run high after Orlando. Contesters who went are in postpartum depression. Some of those who didn't go are still pissed off. I don't know if it's all the raw nerves, but after months of congratulatory send-offs and best wishes on the Cooking Contest Central chat room, a bona fide cat fight breaks out. It starts out innocently enough when Pat Harmon notices the name of a professional chef, Florida's Wolfgang Hanau, on the winners list of Alaskan Seafood's "Wild About Flavor" contest. This sets off a heated exchange about contests that allow food professionals to enter. Some contesters are for it, welcoming the challenge, but others are not. It turns out that a fair number of contests, more than anyone thought, take all comers, even chefs. However, Alaskan Seafood isn't one of them. Harmon's point all along has been that contestants should play fair and follow the rules. She and some other contesters email Alaskan Seafood about Hanau. Soon after, the contest's winners list vanishes from the Web. This sets off a debate on whether you should turn in cheaters or not. Some worry that the fuss will discourage companies from holding contests. Harmon and others insist on a level playing field.

Then contesting doyenne Barbara Morgan posts a rather vague condemnation, not wanting to name names, of a major contester who was recently caught breaking the rules and was barred from competing at a national cookoff. The offending contester had won more in cash prizes in the past year than the contest allowed. Morgan's point is the same as Harmon's, that everyone should honor the rules. But Morgan's last paragraph, an afterthought, really, is what everyone zeros in on. Morgan writes that contesters who don't travel should not enter contests with trips as prizes. Again, Morgan doesn't name names, but everyone knows that she is talking about Claudia Shepardson. After the World Trade Center attack, Shepardson bowed out of Better Burger because she was afraid to fly. For the same reason, she turned down a trip to Costa Rica that she had won in another recipe contest. Still, she has continued to enter contests with trips as prizes, which really annoys Morgan. The chat room buzzes as contesters rush to Shepardson's defense. At home, Morgan's inbox fills with hate emails.

When I call Morgan, she is livid. She rants about how all the big prizes have made contesters greedy, that before the Bake-Off® contest's $1 million or prizes of fancy-schmancy excursions abroad, there was a real congeniality among the old-timers. No more. "This isn't so with this younger group," she says. "It's a me, me, me thing. It's self-centered. They only want to win and get notches on their belts. They don't care who they have to walk over to win."

Eventually equanimity returns to the chat room as the contesters get back to business, concocting recipes and scoring prizes. An April 30 deadline looms for three biggies: Gold Kist Farms chicken recipe contest, a perennial favorite, dangles a weeklong tour of Tuscany for two before the contesters' noses. Mrs. Fields's annual contest has added a new twist that will appeal to the extroverts: the grand prize of $1,000 includes a trip to California and a walk-on appearance on the soap *Days of Our Lives*. The second annual Pace recipe contest promises a shiny outdoor kitchen worth $20,000 to the cook who comes up with the best recipe using the company's jarred salsa, picante sauce, or salsa con queso. Consequently, contesters spend their days with salsa, chicken, and cookie recipes ricocheting around their brains—except for Diane Sparrow, that is.

Sparrow's second-oldest son has just gotten engaged. He has asked her to cook all the food for his summer wedding. There will be four hundred guests for a Friday evening outdoor reception on his woodsy spread of eight acres. They would like a cheesecake for the wedding cake, and would she stitch together the flower girl's dress, too? Most mothers would shriek, "Do what?" Not Sparrow. The wedding prep leaves her next to no time for contesting other than a stint at the National Cornbread Cook-off. She's one of this year's ten finalists, along with her pal Ruth Kendrick and contester Terry Ann Moore. There are a few lower-rung contesters as well, at least one a Bake-Off® contest alum.

Now in its fifth year, this is the most contesters the cookoff has ever drawn. Previously, Camilla Saulsbury and Susan Runkle had entered on a lark, but most contesters didn't bother because the prize was a relative pittance and you had to pay your own way. This year the cookoff will pay travel costs, and the grand prize has been increased to a respectable $3,000 plus a $2,500 stove. When Sparrow asks festival organizers the reason for the bigger prize, she is told, "So we could get people like y'all."

The little town of South Pittsburg, to the west of Chattanooga along the Tennessee River, has designs on giving its annual corn bread festival a national reputation. That's where the contesters come in. The first four cookoffs were dominated by southern cooks who didn't mind paying their own way to demonstrate their corn bread acumen. If the cookoff was to receive national attention, it needed to pull in contestants beyond the old Confederacy—thus the additional moolah. The contest also received many more entries, over one thousand, which translated into many more good ones but also a lot more bad ones. They got their usual crop of recipes that call for Martha Washington or Martha Stewart cornmeal instead of Martha White, a contest sponsor.

They ended up with ten recipes that stretch corn bread every which way: mixed with fontina cheese, doused with hot sauce, laced with Dijon mustard, and topped with sliced almonds. Sparrow cross-pollinated corn bread with buffalo wings, sautéing chicken tenders in hot sauce, topping them with the batter, and then serving a wedge with a blue cheese mayo sauce. Kendrick went for the obvious, southwestern food, with her Cowboy Cobbler, essentially a chicken chili topped with a slab of corn bread.

For the first time the contest has drawn a number of contestants from well beyond the boundaries of the old Confederacy. Kendrick came the farthest, all the way from Utah. Another is from Texas. Moore is from New Jersey, which the Tennesseans seem most impressed by.

South Pittsburg was optimistically named for its cousin to the north in Pennsylvania, but the local mines never fulfilled their promise. The largest employer is Lodge Cast Iron, with sixty-five employees. The town is mostly a bedroom community to Chattanooga. When a bypass was built around the river hamlet in 1996, South Pittsburg elders began to worry that their downtown businesses were doomed. It was a relief not to have the semis barreling through, belching diesel fumes and growling like cranky grizzlies at each of the six traffic lights. They feared, though, that everyone, not just trucks, would sail past the downtown on the bypass now. They got to thinking: What if they had a kind of annual party to invite people downtown? And so another American town hung its hopes for the future on an annual food festival. The first National Cornbread Festival and Cook-off, sponsored by Lodge and Martha White, was held in the spring of 1997. Corn bread was a natural choice. Locals hoard their grannies' recipes. They eat a crumbly wedge nearly every day.

There are strong opinions about corn bread in the South. The big no-no is sugar. To add sugar to your corn bread is the same as tattooing the word *Yankee* on your forehead. It marks you as more than a northerner, as a kind of food baby who isn't tough enough for the real McCoy. The corn bread cookoff, being an inclusive culinary event, did not ban sugar as an ingredient. This festival was not to be a preservationist ode to the traditional dish. Rather, the festival looked to the future of corn bread, a time when the golden round would regularly meet up with the likes of fresh basil, goat cheese, and Dijon mustard, when it might no longer be an accompaniment but the main course itself. The cookoff requires competitors to remake this southern standard into an entrée using at least one cup of cornmeal. There is one nod to the dish's roots: It must be cooked in a skillet, but not any skillet. The organizers were shocked the first year when competitors showed up with nonstick cake pans and the like. "We couldn't imagine someone not using cast iron," an organizer says. The next year they changed the rules to read: "All recipes must be cooked in a cast iron skillet."

The night before the cookoff I spend a good hour in Sparrow's no-nonsense motel room near the highway listening to her and Kendrick try to psyche each other out. Moore and her husband quietly look on, their eyes going back and forth as if they are watching a tennis tournament. "I match my dish," Sparrow says.

"I match my dish and my tablecloth," Kendrick counters.

Whenever the two try to pull Moore into the taunting, asking her strategy or something, Moore says, "I'm just happy to be here." Moore, who has neither Sparrow's style nor Kendrick's gregariousness, comes off as a cookoff wallflower with her long, thin hair and girlish voice. This belies Moore's long list of wins. She has been to the Bake-Off® contest three times in a row. She won $25,000 from a Blue Bonnet contest for an almond-flavored yellow cake filled with amaretto custard, pears, and fresh raspberries, and coated with white chocolate frosting. She also has a knack for the unusual contests, such as the White Castle Hamburger cookoff, which requires that ten of the square patties be used in a recipe. She was one of ten finalists for What a Surprise Onion Soup. She put a burger in a bowl, covered it with onion soup, and melted cheese over the mess.

Sparrow has laid out across the low motel dresser a pile of cheese, fruit, and crackers that she hauled from Iowa, but most of it goes untouched. Kendrick, short-haired, bright-eyed, and fair-skinned, is dieting to reduce her sizable frame. "I've lost eighty pounds," Kendrick announces, then drapes herself across one bed, her head held in the crook of her hand. A Mormon, she won't touch the wine. Kendrick tells Sparrow that she has "a little something" for her cookoff table. Sparrow starts quizzing her, but Kendrick trills, "One only knows," and snickers.

"What do you have?" Sparrow asks again.

"Just something fun to look at," Kendrick says.

Kendrick admits she hadn't tested her recipe before sending it in, and when she did, she discovered it was too spicy. Sparrow didn't test hers, either, "but I was smart enough to cool mine with blue cheese mayo sauce."

"I can get my dish in the oven in ten minutes. How about that?" Kendrick counters.

They're joking, but not. They'd love to beat each other, especially Kendrick who has come in behind Sparrow in a couple of contests. Sparrow had told me earlier that when she learned Kendrick had reseasoned her cast iron pan, she did hers as well. Sparrow pensively sips some white wine from a plastic cup and nibbles on a wedge of cheese. "I can't wait to see what's on your table," she says. "My mind is racing. Terry, should we go to Wal-Mart now?" Kendrick turns to me, holds a hand to her mouth, and whispers out one side, "I'm not doing anything. I'm just getting their minds going."

〜〜〜〜

Saturday morning I drive west from Chattanooga through the lush Tennessee River Valley under a pale gray sky. The highway dips into Alabama and then swoops back over the Tennessee state line. Everything is just green, green, green from the early spring rains. The only break in color are the occasional billboards advertising fireworks stores. The mountains are not awe-inspiring but considerable, especially as they crack wide open to the north and form the Sequatchie River Valley. Just before the road bolts north for Nashville, I pull off on an exit ramp that swings past another fireworks store, this one with a three-story-high rainbow-hued neon sign all lit up like a Vegas casino. I continue on to South Pittsburg, passing a gaggle of scarecrows dressed in gingham on the road median. Someone has also tied yellow bandanas in some young trees. Obviously, I'm on the path to the Cornbread Festival.

Chattanooga is on Eastern Standard Time, or what they call fast time. South Pittsburg, only thirty minutes or so away, is on Central Time, or slow time. I left at 9:30 A.M. to get there by 9 A.M. Regardless, when I arrive, the festival is already hopping with fleshy people munching bags of kettle corn, gnawing clumps of golden chicken on a stick, and slurping drinks out of coconut shells cradled in their palms. The festival runs most of the length of South Pittsburg's old-fashioned Main Street, a mostly broad, treeless stretch of humble Victorian storefronts mixed in with a few '50s-era blocky buildings, such as the stretch of glass that houses the Valley of Prayer School. There's a small department store, a music store, a pawn shop, a secondhand clothing store named Neat Repeat, and a store selling safes. They've all stocked up for the twenty to thirty thousand corn bread lovers expected this weekend.

The Cornbread Festival has many of the standard trappings of Any Festival, U.S.A.: the jostling, noisy amusement park rides; the crafts booths selling middling art, hokey birdhouses, and glow-in-the-dark chokers; the 5K race. A man with a thick black ponytail and a small round mike—jammed up so close to his nose that at first I think it's a huge mole—cranks on a Peruvian flute. There are homegrown touches such as the bluegrass jam tent, the bass fishing tournament, and a card table with a handwritten sign that reads: "Sign up here to win a free yard spraying." The bite of fresh manure also spices the air at one end of the festival, near a large, wide-eyed plastic steer.

I have enough time before the cookoff to tag along with Kendrick on a tour of Lodge Cast Iron. She and her husband run their own small factory in Utah that chrome-plates steel. When we walk onto the dim foundry floor, like something out of Dickens's London, Kendrick inhales the heavy air deeply and says to her husband, "Smell, Ron. That's home." As we follow the tour guide, a slim man with a mustache growing over his lip, Kendrick tells me that Sparrow showed up at breakfast in a chambray shirt with a gingham hanky in her breast pocket. Kendrick was going to go with a gingham motif, she says, but luckily switched to chili peppers.

"I'd really like to beat Diane just once," she says.

The corn bread cookoff is kind of home turf for Kendrick. She knows Lodge's owner, Bob Kellerman, whom she met through the Dutch oven cookoffs. Kendrick also knows her cast iron cookware backward and forward. She can't help feeling she should win.

The cookoff area is in the middle of the festival. Five stoves have been set in a tight circle under a tent, which has been added to prevent any wind off the river from blowing out the pilot lights as it did last year. Bleachers are set up on either end for spectators. The first heat of five cooks is already setting up when Kendrick and I arrive. This includes Moore, who places an arrangement of cut flowers on her table, which makes me think that Kendrick and Sparrow got to her last night. Kendrick and Sparrow are in the second heat, which they see as an advantage. They can find out from Moore how the ovens work.

The only male contestant, Dick Walker, is also in the first heat. Walker, a short, bull-necked man in red suspenders, runs an economic development organization north of Nashville. He is a cookoff first-timer and an enormous clown. He is carrying on as if he's at a chili cookoff. He's making his Grand Slam Cornbread, which is stuffed with a load of sauerkraut, hotdogs, and hot sauce. His wife, a school psychologist, told me that she has eaten so much Grand Slam, she "about threw up." He also talked so much about the cookoff that she threatened to pull the plug on his appearance if he didn't shut up. Now she doesn't have to deal with his competitive corn bread obsession all by herself. Walker has imported a fan club, mostly old friends from his days in the Peace Corps in Central and South America. They nearly fill one of the bleachers and are all wearing Grand Slam ball caps that Walker had custom made. They cheer when he sets out his ingredients and when he cracks the oven door for a look. When Walker lifts a leg and pretends to pee on a nearby hydrant, someone yells, "We're going to be disqualified before we even start."

The four other female cooks look over their shoulders at Walker as they arrange their ingredients. They don't know what to make of him. They didn't have this pegged as a personality contest. One of the judges, Martha Johnston, a redheaded food editor for *Southern Living*, wanders over and strikes up some friendly chitchat, asking contestants about their recipes, where they are from, and so on. Eventually she works her way to Moore, who smiles nervously.

"It's so unusual to talk to a judge. They usually keep us apart," Moore says.

"No one told me I couldn't," Johnston says. "Have you spent a lot of time in the South?"

"No," Moore says, shrugging her shoulders, "but I love corn bread."

"I bet you add sugar to it," Johnston says and turns to another contestant.

❖❖❖❖

Judges are sphinxes to contesters. They consider them inscrutable but can't help trying to decipher them. This is where all the strategizing comes from, as a means to control the uncontrollable. Moore plans to send her dish in first or last, never in the middle. Sparrow wants to get hers in before Kendrick's, before all its hot sauce sears the judges' taste buds together. Kendrick plans to send hers in the middle. She has a chili-patterned pan holder to put on the handle. "It won't make my dish taste any better, but it will help them remember it," she says.

Most of this strategizing is lost on the judges. To them their job is not mysterious. Judging cooking contests is one of those tasks everyone assumes would be fun, and it is, but it's also hard work. Eating is fun, but thinking hard about what you are eating isn't. With every bite a judge contemplates taste, texture, presentation, family appeal, creativity, use of the product, and so on. A seasoned judge, like a wine connoisseur, knows to pay attention to how the taste changes as a morsel moves across the tongue. Obviously, a simple "yum" won't do, especially with thousands of dollars at stake. "You feel very responsible," says Debbie Goldsmith, a food editor at *Better Homes and Gardens* who judged the last National Beef. "It is a huge assignment."

Judges are expected to taste everything, even dishes that look like the garbage disposal coughed them up. A judge at the Bake-Off® contest used her spit cup to avoid swallowing two particularly wretched desserts. The only time judges are let off the hook is when the meat looks dangerously raw. At National Chicken judges are told not to eat any dish that appears undercooked. At Sutter Home a judge asked if he had to eat an essentially bloody burger. The answer was no.

Some contests, especially smaller ones, expect judges to taste too much. One judge had to taste one hundred fruitcakes at a local contest, the boozy vapors filling the room. Even with a spit cup the judge went home with a stomach riled by too much candied fruit and leaden dough. Previously a fruitcake fan, she swore off the holiday loaf for good. At the World Champion Jambalaya Cooking Contest, a team of five judges has the unenviable task of tasting eighty rice-laden jambalayas over two days. No wonder they can have trouble recruiting judges. One champ told me he kept competing to avoid having to judge.

Even at National Chicken, judges can end up overtaxing their taste buds. Judges are divided into three teams to taste fifty dishes, so they are assigned twenty or less, a very manageable number. However, judges are encouraged to taste the rejects from other teams because any judge can rule a dish back into the running. This system means that the fifty are only about halved after the first go-around. Those dishes are tasted by all the judges and roughly halved again, and then the remaining ten to fifteen dishes retasted to choose the winners. So a judge at National Chicken could end up sampling sixty times or more, quite a lot for even a master nibbler. The year Judy Evans, the food editor for the *St. Louis Post-Dispatch*, judged National Chicken the entrée for dinner that night—after a day of contemplating plate after plate of chicken— was, you guessed it, chicken. "I never wanted to eat chicken again," Evans says. "Of course I did."

Like seasoned contesters, seasoned judges have their strategies. All the judges I spoke with say small bites are essential. If you get too full, you don't get to push back from the table. You have to push on like a marathon runner hitting the wall. This is a no-brainer for magazine food editors who regularly work with test kitchens sampling dishes. It's the first-time cooking contest judges, especially men not from a food profession, who usually fill up too quickly. The first year of the Better Burger contest, one of the Sutter Home owners turned green from taking bites that were too big of the then twenty finalists' burgers. At Terlingua my table of judges was instructed not to fill their spoons but to take just a smidgen; otherwise we would be hurting after tasting eleven chilis in about that many minutes. As Evans points out, you need only a small bite anyway to know a dish is not a winner. Judges always say the winners jump out at you, but as I learned at Terlingua, so do the losers.

The other mistake that first-timers can make is skipping breakfast. Carol Haddix, longtime food editor of the *Chicago Tribune*, never judges on an empty stomach. Doing so will make you judge the first dishes higher because you're hungry, she says. You also have to eat as you go to clear your palate. Haddix reaches for an apple slice after tasting an especially salty dish. Evans finds that celery works better than water. A jambalaya judge claimed that a swallow of milk wiped his tongue clean.

Some contests encourage the judges to talk while they evaluate; others require silence so as not to influence one another's opinions. If the judges are evaluating in public, as they do at Gilroy and Better Burger, they have no choice but to do so quietly. At National Beef the judges were told to keep their opinions to themselves until they had completed their score sheets. Once all the score sheets were handed in, then they could talk. It turned out, though, that there wasn't a lot to talk about: All the judges had scored Yee's panfried steak the highest.

Even at contests that ask judges to keep mum during the tasting and scoring, the choice of the winners is usually discussed. This is when judging can get heated. That's where the head judge comes in. Like a jury foreman, she ideally must bring the group around to a unanimous decision that everyone is happy with. If not that, then she must break a tie. Even with a capable head judge, the more verbal and persuasive of the group can rule the day, especially with judging novices. "You just sort of remember that you shouldn't be swayed," says Carolyn Jung, a recent Pillsbury judge. "You have to stick to your guns. You're doing a job there." Jung, however, found herself persuaded by her two fellow judges in the dessert category. Her choice for the $10,000 prize was the Milleniyum Torte, which she thought looked as if it came from a bakery. The two other judges—neither a big fan of chocolate—were for the mini apple pies made with biscuit dough. The pie backers convinced Jung by pointing out that the pies were easier to make and had more family appeal, and kids weren't likely to go for the torte because it had coffee in it.

At the '98 Bake-Off® contest the twelve judges hit a now famous deadlock. It was the war of white chocolate versus couscous, between the future and the past. After eight hours of discriminating munching, the sequestered judges gathered to choose the million-dollar grand prize winner from the four $10,000 category winners. They easily dispensed with Texas Two-Step Slaw, a cabbagey concoction slathered with ranch dressing, and the Tex-Mex Appetizer Tart, a pile of cheese, mayo, roasted peppers, green chilies, and cilantro baked in a refrigerated piecrust. The battle lines were drawn between Salsa Couscous Chicken and Brownie Soufflé Cake. The first was a kind of North Africa meets Tex-Mex sauce over chicken thighs and the tiny pasta created by Ellie Mathews, a writer from Seattle, Washington. The cake, a doctored brownie mix topped with white chocolate and mint-flavored whipped cream, was made by big name contester Edwina Gadsby. In fact, both Gadsbys were there. That was the year Bob made Crab Cakes Italiano.

The judges for the chicken saw themselves as "culinary crusaders," as one put it. They wanted to use their momentary power to push American cooks forward. Handing a million dollars to such an ethnic dish, giving it that kind of cachet, would spur a new open-mindedness in the country's kitchens, they thought. The cake proponents thought couscous would unnerve the ordinary home cook. One spoke of a couscous backlash in her home state. Pillsbury itself had shown a bit of uneasiness over the dish's African roots by changing Mathews's original name, Moroccan Chicken, to Salsa Couscous Chicken, according to press reports. Besides, the cake crew argued, the dessert had broader appeal, and hadn't Pillsbury fans come to expect a gooey grand prize winner?

A first vote showed the judges tipping toward Mathews's chicken, nine to three. After more debate Gadsby's cake picked up a couple of votes. According to the major cake backer, the chicken contingent grew perturbed. A central chicken proponent, a food writer for *The Cleveland Plain Dealer*, wrote that she was mentally prepared to spend the night if she had to. To break the deadlock, the judges read over the recipes. The cake's topping required an hour to cool. That's not quick and easy, the chicken camp cried. Finally, there was only one cake holdout, Sharon Dowell, food editor of *The Daily Oklahoman*. She acquiesced and signed the form Pillsbury required, but she never did actually vote for the chicken.

The next day, as the four finalists stood onstage, the million-dollar dish, covered by a silver dome, was rolled out on a cart. Gadsby says that from the time host Alex Trebeck lifted the cover until she could see what was underneath felt like an eternity. Gadsby could not identify what she saw but knew it wasn't her cake. "You can imagine what chicken and couscous look like after two days. It looked like a glowing orange mass." One reporter wrote that Gadsby looked visibly crushed, while winner Mathews was one of the coolest grand prize winners ever, just wagging her head back and forth.

Gadsby did not know how close she had come to winning until days later when judges began writing stories about their experience. Dowell called Gadsby at home in Montana and told her she had cried over the decision. "It's hard to know that you came that close," Gadsby says. "It wouldn't be so bad if, like years ago, the prize was $40,000. To think you lost $990,000 is, well, yeah, you know, hard."

❧❧❧❧

Most judges I've talked to would rather not lay eyes on the contestants until the winners have been chosen, and that's typically when they do. Jan Hazard, a former longtime editor at *Ladies' Home Journal* and a frequent judge, says no matter how objective you try to be, seeing a contestant, her earnest expression, even her outfit, can't help but color your opinion at least a little. That is why most major contests with big prizes are done blind, with judges tucked away out of sight. At the Pillsbury contest they even send a security guard with a judge who needs to use the ladies' room to avoid any bathroom or hallway chitchat with a contestant. The National Cornbread Cook-off, wanting to strike a friendly, informal note, turns out to be the other end of the spectrum.

At 10 A.M. the contest begins with the announcement "Start your ovens." The judges, having no corn bread to consider just yet, stand off to one side, observing. This worries Sparrow, who is watching the first heat to get a feel for the ovens. "The judges are out here, which would be okay except for this guy," Sparrow says, referring to Walker. He overshadows everyone in his heat with his theatrics. The guy is funny, and some of the judges are laughing. "I've worked on this recipe for years. I weighed 150 pounds when I started this," he tells the cookoff emcee, a local TV anchor, a perky woman in a red blouse who is going from contestant to contestant with a microphone. Walker gets her a Grand Slam hat. His cheering section does the wave for her.

"Let's talk about your recipe, the important stuff," she says.

"The important stuff is Grand Slam, and if you've never had it you'll love it, baby," he crows.

Sparrow elbows me and says, "There's Ruth over by the judges." Sure enough, Kendrick has planted herself right by the judges. She doesn't seem to be talking to them, but Sparrow isn't taking any chances. She walks right over to Kendrick to run interference.

"I'm sure glad we're not competing against old Dick," Kendrick says.

"Did you bring an oven thermometer? The ovens are running slow," Sparrow asks.

Ruth just smiles, then flashes her eyes.

"Ruth," Sparrow squawks.

Applause breaks out behind us. Walker has opened his oven door to peek in, which gets his fan club all riled up. By now the emcee has worked her way over to Moore, who is fielding more questions about life way up north in New Jersey.

"Do they even know about corn bread up there?" the emcee asks her.

~ ~ ~ ~

Moore is the first to send her dish in to the judges: Creamy Seafood Pie with Herbed Cornbread. Just before a runner takes it away, she lays a decorative wooden serving spoon and a spray of fresh herbs across the pan. The ten judges settle down at a large T-shaped table under an open white tent about thirty feet from the cookoff. There are a few newspaper writers and a few local TV personalities. Linda Carman, Martha White's baking expert, a tall, smiley woman, is the head judge. A cookoff worker shows them each dish as it comes in, then cuts and serves them appetizer-sized portions on Styrofoam plates. The judges take bites using white plastic forks and start jotting down numbers on the score sheet. They rate the dish between one and twenty in five categories: taste, creativity, appetizing appearance, ease of preparation, and appropriate use of the product. The group talks casually as they go, but mostly they just eat and scribble.

By the time the first heat finishes, both Sparrow and Kendrick have chosen the stove they want to use. Kendrick wants Walker's stove, which faces the bleachers. She plans to give him a run for his money and play to the crowd. Sparrow wants to be next to Kendrick so she can borrow her oven thermometer. That way she can also keep an eye on Kendrick's timer and be sure to get her dish in first. Sparrow asks a contestant from the first heat to leave that oven on. "I don't know if I'm supposed to do that," she says, looking uncomfortable.

Kendrick sets out a little centerpiece, a toy cowboy, a bowl of Tabasco jelly beans, and the recipe for her Cowboy Cobbler. Sparrow checks it out quickly and then returns to cooking. The emcee and, surprisingly, the judges are still on their lunch break. The cooks work in silence. "Well, this is so exciting. I'm about to have a heart attack," a man in the bleachers behind me says. Kendrick hears him. She picks up the microphone, describes her dish, and gives a brief bio of herself. "I'm going to hand the mike to Diane," Kendrick says and walks toward Sparrow, who shoos her off with a wave of her hands. "She won't take it," Kendrick stammers.

The emcee returns, and the rest of the heat is uneventful. One contestant describes herself as a southern French teacher. She's making Cornbread Cassoulet, which uses a can of diced tomatoes, a can of Great Northern beans, and a can of sliced carrots. She garnishes it with what I guess is a southern French touch: a few rings of raw onion and spoonfuls of yellow-green chow-chow. Another, a grandmotherly woman with poofy white hair pulled into a bun, says she came up with her recipe, Cornbread Gumbo Dinner, to encourage people to eat okra. "To show them it doesn't have to be slippery."

Back at the judging tent, the skillets of corn bread are piling up on a side table like war casualties. Their crusts broken, they ooze their soggy interiors and spray yellow crumbs. The judges eat deliberately, chewing while they contemplate. I sample a few dishes myself while I wait for the judges' scores to be tallied. The cassoulet has that tinny taste of canned food. Kendrick's has a good, solid southwestern flavor, but nothing unusual. Grand Slam gives me bad flashbacks to ballpark food I inhaled in my undiscriminating youth. I don't mind the sauerkraut, which one judge tells me is a polarizing ingredient, but I do mind the chunks of hotdog in hot sauce. Moore's seafood dish is a little bland. The okra in the Cornbread Gumbo is slippery.

I'm a longtime corn bread maker and eater, but I've never really thought hard about the amber loaf before. As I munch, I realize it's one of those simple dishes, like coleslaw, tuna salad, and French toast, that are so easy to get wrong. The bread itself can be stick-to-the-roof-of-your-mouth doughy or dry enough to make you cough crumbs. Even if you bake it correctly, cornmeal can be an ornery ingredient. It has a very distinct flavor and texture that calls for a counterbalance. Otherwise, its roasted, slightly sweet flavor takes over. To my taste buds, beans are not it, nor spinach nor hot sauce. The perfect counterbalance turns out to be blue cheese. Sparrow's dish is the only one to come in with a sauce on the side, which alone makes it stand out, but her simple mix of blue cheese, mayo, plain yogurt, lemon juice, and salt counters the corn bread's sweetness with a nice salty bite.

When the scores are handed to Carman, Sparrow's dish is among the top five. The other four are Kendrick's; another southwestern-style dish, Skillet Chicken Enchiladas; surprising to me, the cassoulet; and Tuscan Stew with Cornbread Topping. Grand Slam hasn't made the grade, although several of the male judges liked it. The scores are very close among the leading five. Now the judges, with Carman mediating, discuss the top three. They quickly begin comparing like to like, which puts Sparrow's dish in a class by itself. Both Tuscan Stew and Cassoulet Cornbread have beans. The male judges prefer cassoulet. The women are for the more sophisticated Tuscan Stew, which uses fontina cheese, spinach, Italian sausage, and, strangely, frozen hash browns. Carman works like a deft counselor, graciously soliciting opinions, prodding with questions, and guiding with her own comments. I want to yell "Ick!" as the male judges lobby for the cassoulet, but Carman just nods and smiles. Eventually the women prevail and talk the male judges into the Tuscan Stew.

Of the two southwestern-style dishes, the judges quickly pick the Skillet Chicken Enchiladas over Kendrick's Cobbler. A male judge criticizes Kendrick's dish for using canned enchilada sauce. The Skillet Chicken Enchiladas used canned sauce as well, but only half as much. That narrows the list to three. Now they have to pick the order they go in. There's a strong contingent for Sparrow to get first place. A features reporter for *The Tennessean* says Sparrow's dish should get it for being such an original idea alone. Everyone loves the blue cheese sauce, but two of the male judges complain that it isn't hot enough. They are reminded that the recipe should have wide appeal, meaning no napalming unsuspecting taste buds. One male judge wants the Tuscan Stew to get first. The *Southern Living* food editor, by far the most articulate and thus the most persuasive in the group, counters, voicing a long-held vegetable prejudice, that she doesn't think a spinach dish has family appeal. The judges are warned they have five minutes before the winner must be announced. The group pulls together and quickly agrees on Sparrow, although a few of the male judges are a little muted in their enthusiasm. Everyone, though, loves Sparrow's sauce, and blue cheese rules the day.

A cast iron skillet crown, the pan combined with a kind of hard hat, is placed on Sparrow's head of curly locks in front of a good-sized crowd at an outdoor stage. Second place goes to the Skillet Chicken Enchiladas, and third to the Tuscan Stew with Cornbread Topping. Sparrow has to hold the crown with one hand to keep it from sliding off. It's the first cookoff she has flat-out won. She is flushed and smiling. As she walks off the stage, she sees Walker look at his wife and stick his finger in his mouth as if to throw up.

While Sparrow talks to reporters, the corn bread eating contest starts on the stage behind her. The contestants are four kids, a teenage girl, and a lanky man. The man essentially puts the entire block in his mouth, pushing it in with the heel of his hand, and then struggles to keep it in as he chews. He even coughs out a few bursts of crumbs. The teenager stretches her neck out like a seal being fed fish, taking a little bite after a little bite as her friends start chanting, "Pack it in. Pack it in." Kendrick looks over her shoulder at Sparrow giving interviews and then, unsmiling, scrapes out the remaining Cowboy Cobbler, a goodly amount, into a trash can. "I should get used to rejection, but it still comes hard."

〰〰〰

Diane Sparrow crossed buffalo wings with corn bread and won the 2002 National Cornbread Cook-off.

BUFFALO CHICKEN CORNBREAD WITH BLEU CHEESE MAYO

1 pound chicken breast tender strips
1/4 cup Louisiana-style hot sauce

1/2 cup mayonnaise
1/4 cup plain yogurt
2 ounces bleu cheese, crumbled
1/2 teaspoon salt
2 teaspoons lemon juice

3 tablespoons butter
1/2 cup chopped red onion
1/2 cup chopped celery
1 package Martha White Cotton Pickin' Cornbread Mix
1/2 cup milk
1 egg

Preheat the oven to 450°F.

Place the chicken tender strips in a bowl. Toss with the hot sauce to coat well. Set aside to marinate for 20 minutes.

In a small bowl, combine the mayonnaise, yogurt, bleu cheese, salt, and lemon juice. Cover and place in the refrigerator until ready to serve.

Melt 1 tablespoon butter in a 10-inch skillet over medium heat. Sauté the onion and celery in the butter until tender. Remove from the pan.

Add the remaining 2 tablespoons butter to the pan. Sauté the chicken tenders in the hot sauce in the butter, stirring constantly, for 5–7 minutes. Combine the Martha White Cornbread Mix with the milk and egg. Stir in the sautéed celery and onion. Pour over the chicken in the hot pan. Place in the oven for 20–25 minutes, or until the corn bread is golden.

Cut into wedges and top each serving with the bleu cheese mayo.

SERVES 6

*

CHAPTER 14

THE TUNNEL OF
FUDGE WOMAN

On an unseasonably hot, humid day even for Houston, I wait in front of one of the city's gleaming downtown hotels, watching cars pull into the turnaround. I breathe as little as possible. All of Houston seems under construction, and the moist air holds the unsettled dust of progress. I stand as still as possible so as not to break any more of a sweat in my suit jacket. A bellhop asks if he can get my bags. A valet asks if he can retrieve my car. No, no, I shake my head. A shiny white four-door pulls into the drive and stops. I forget myself and dash over to the car in my excitement, a drizzle of perspiration beading on my temple.

I'm on my way to meet an American food legend. Her name may not have gone down in the annals of culinary history, but her dish has. I've come to meet the woman behind the cake that changed the country's dessert history. Patricia Gullo, a tall, white-haired beauty with a silky Texan accent I could listen to all day, is my driver. Her husband, Sam, an affable, fit man in his early seventies, sits next to her in the passenger seat.

As we head south, past road construction crews and then a long series of open-air flower shops, I feel my clothes come unstuck as the chill from the air conditioner dries my skin. The flower shops precipitate a cluster of stately hospitals, one next to the other. We cruise past drives marked Emergency Entrance and then turn into St. Dominic's Village, a retirement community that resembles a small college campus, with its low-slung brick buildings woven together with covered walkways across perfect lawns.

We get out of the car, and Gullo and her husband take each other's hand. I follow them into one of the buildings, and we walk down a long, straight hall of uniform doors. The walls are bare. A dried flower wreath hangs on a door here and there. The hall is quiet except for our footsteps. We stop midway down the stretch of doors, and Gullo lightly raps on one. It quickly swings open. My eyes fall upon a short, slight woman with a sweep of white hair piled high on her head. She gives me an enthusiastic smile and extends her pale, slender hand. I smile back and return her grip. I'm shaking hands with the Tunnel of Fudge woman.

≈≈≈≈

Cooking contests strike most people as a goof, just another silly way to express our irrepressible Americanness. That may be, but these contests, wacky or not, have had a real influence on American food. Cooking contests have helped move once unusual ingredients, such as feta and cilantro, into the mainstream. They have produced original recipes that became American classics as well as popularized existing dishes to classic status. For example, according to National Chicken Cooking Contest lore, the 1971 winner provided the inspiration for McDonald's Chicken McNuggets and Americans' love affair with chicken fingers. Even contest sponsors admit this claim is a little dubious. At the least, the winning recipe, Dipper's Nuggets Chicken, popularized this modern twist on the old American favorite, fried chicken. The recipe called for breading slippery pieces of breast meat with flour and sesame seeds, plunging them into a pan of hot salad oil, and then dunking the golden crusted strips in one of three sauces: Nippy Pineapple, Royalty, or Dill. To make Royalty Sauce you heat a 14-ounce bottle of catsup, two tablespoons of cider vinegar, and two tablespoons of butter.

On the downside, cooking competitions have reinforced some of our worst cooking habits, especially our dependency on processed foods in our endless pursuit of cooking as fast as humanly possible. For some reason a nation that can spend hours at the wheel of a car or before a television set turns every stint in the kitchen into a time trial.

Cookoff and recipe contests are essentially offshoots of perhaps the most powerful influence on American twentieth-century cooking: the company test kitchen. When people discuss the major figures that shaped the past one hundred years, Julia Child inevitably comes up, as does James Beard, the Rombauers, Craig Claiborne, and, more recently, Alice Waters and the Silver Palate ladies. The fact is that the nameless, lab-coated home economists toiling away in company test kitchens may trump them all in impact. Throughout the century, food companies flooded the American home kitchen with a deluge of new recipes designed to sell their products. Before the advent of a nationwide advertising system, these recipes were stamped on labels and printed in free pamphlets. They were sent to recipe-hungry magazine and newspaper food editors who dutifully reprinted them verbatim. Cooks copied the recipes off the packages, filed them in their recipe boxes, and then passed them on to friends and relatives, who submitted them to community cookbooks.

These recipes had a ready and willing audience in kitchen aprons. Our grandmothers and mothers did not have a mini cookbook library to turn to that modern-day home cooks do. The avalanche of cookbooks was—is—a late-twentieth-century development. These earlier generations of cooks were accustomed to finding recipes in the world around them, in the newspaper, on the store shelf, from their neighbor. They readily turned to boxes and cans for new ideas, whether it be to learn how to use a new product or how to roast a turkey. When I was a child, my mother used one cookbook, a worn *Good Housekeeping* volume, its black cover splitting from all the loose recipes she stuffed into the pages. My grandmother also owned only one cookbook, which she regularly bypassed in favor of her file filled with clipped and handwritten recipes.

Contest-winning recipes were routed into this casual but effective distribution system. They had something the test kitchen recipes didn't: a personal touch. The recipe, rather than being the product of an anonymous home ec expert, bore the name of a Mrs. Home Cook, U.S.A. This appealed to Americans' ambivalence for experts and the notion that the unschooled may be the true authority. Women used these recipes to see if they really warranted the prize and as means of measuring their own prowess.

These contests put the future of American cooking in the hands of everyday cooks who could change its course for the better or the worse. The latter was the case with Mrs. John Cooke, who in 1905 entered into a Knox gelatin contest a recipe for a molded savory salad of lemony gelatin flecked with red pepper, cabbage, and celery. She called it Perfection Salad. "This salad is especially fine with fried oysters," Mrs. Cooke wrote in her note accompanying her entry. The judges, Fannie Farmer among them, gave Mrs. Cooke third place for her efforts. She won a $100 sewing machine. Knox included the recipe in its next booklet, with this hard sell on gelatin: "It may not be in the highest favor with poorly informed or indifferent housewives, but it certainly is pronounced the best by all the rest."

Home economists had been preaching the gospel of molded salads—they were tidy and a good way to use up leftovers—for almost ten years, but it was Perfection Salad that sold the masses on these shimmying, light-filled concoctions. Maybe the salad appealed to the nation's penchant for sweet-savory dishes. Maybe it was the salad's gimmicky, futuristic appearance, the bits of red and green hovering like confetti in the sunny yellow gel. Whatever the reason, American housewives began throwing everything in the icebox and then the fridge into gelatin with abandon. Most results were far more interesting to look at than to eat, especially when served with a standard pus-like glob of jarred mayonnaise.

Perfection Salad remained a mainstay of the army of molded salads that marched across the country's dinner tables. The Knox company continued to reprint the recipe, updating it over time. It was sometimes called jellied coleslaw. My mother remembers seeing it at church suppers and ladies' luncheons from when she was a kid during the Great

Depression until she was a mother of three during the counterculture of the '60s. By then the gleam was off molded salads, but they have never entirely gone away. The jiggling salads still make regular appearances at institutional cafeterias, community potlucks, and family holiday meals. The newest addition of *Joy of Cooking* contains recipes for four molded salads, one of which, with cucumbers, vaguely resembles Perfection Salad. We have Mrs. Cooke to thank or blame.

Another contest winner, pineapple upside-down cake, has proven a more enduring and tastier American standard than Perfection Salad. In 1925 the Hawaiian Pineapple Company, now the Dole Food Company, held a cooking-with-pineapple contest. The company had only recently begun canning rings of pineapple. The competition was meant to encourage American cooks to experiment with these perfectly shaped rounds of canned tropical fruit. The recipe contest drew a stunning 60,000 entries, 2,500 of which were some kind of upside-down cake.

The winners, including a recipe for upside-down cake, were printed in *Pineapple as 100 Good Cooks Serve It*, a pamphlet disseminated by Dole. The cake was not the down-home dessert cooked in a skillet that it is today. Rather, with its glistening caramel top and sanguine candied cherries, the dessert gave the cook a chance to strut her stuff. It was company food. That there were so many upside-down cake entries is proof enough that the contest did not originate the recipe. Sylvia Lovegren, author of *Fashionable Food*, has found an upside-down cake recipe that predates the contest in a 1924 Seattle charity cookbook. What Dole did was popularize the cake, thus helping to make it a beloved American comfort food.

The long-running Pillsbury Bake-Off® contest, with its legion of finalists, four thousand to date, and its well-tuned publicity machine, has produced some of the most influential and enduring American dishes of any contest, such as the 1960 grand prize winner Dilly Casserole Bread. This egg bread, which uses a cup of cottage cheese and produces a mounded, golden loaf, introduced dill bread to a legion of cooks. Likewise, the 1955 contest begat Open Sesame Pie, which familiarized American cooks with the tiny blond seeds. Dorothy Koteen of Washington, D.C., dotted a refrigerated piecrust with two table-spoons of toasted sesame seeds and then poured in a chiffon filling. Although sesame seeds have been around since antiquity and were used by southern cooks, they were little known to most American cooks. Soon after the pie won the $25,000 grand prize, supermarkets around the country reported a run on the spice. The 1968 grand prize winner spotlighted another tiny seed, the poppy. Phyllis Lidert of Oak Lawn, Illinois, created a lemony pound cake with a ribbon of the black granules woven through the middle. Lidert's cake made for an enduring flavor marriage in American baking: lemon and poppy seeds.

The contest contributed a number of treats that no bake sale worth its brownies could get by without, notably two 1950s entries, Cherry Winks and Peanut Blossoms. In 1950 a Wisconsin woman won $5,000 for adding cornflakes cereal to drop cookie dough and then topping each lumpy round with a waxy red candied cherry. In 1957, Freda Smith of Gibsonburg, Ohio, became one of the Bake-Off® contest's chosen one hundred when she took a chance and pressed a plump Hershey's Kiss into a peanut butter cookie. The judges must not have thought much of her cookies with the jaunty chocolate hat—they sent Smith home empty-handed—but her entry lives on in ovens around America. Over the years, recipes for both of these cookies have continued to multiply in cookbooks and on the Web, white chocolate–dipped biscotti be damned.

None of the Bake-Off® contest winners, though, had the impact of the Tunnel of Fudge. This cake made a diminutive Houston mother of five a celebrity, changed the fortunes of a small company in Minneapolis, and made a little-known European pan a mainstay of nearly every American kitchen.

≁ ≁ ≁ ≁

At eighty-five Ella Rita Helfrich still puts a high price on style. She is dressed for lunch in a snappy black-and-white knit top dotted with small metal studs, black pants, and black pumps. Her fingernails are perfectly manicured. Black rhinestone earrings sparkle on either side of her face. Behind her a hazy light bleeds through a large window over a large wooden bed. She moved to St. Dominic's only this past spring, leaving her small house behind. Patricia Gullo says her mother has a few of the early signs of Alzheimer's foggy advance, including a shaky short-term memory. Before moving to St. Dom's she was easily upset and called Gullo whenever the least little thing went wrong in the house. Gullo and her siblings didn't have an easy time convincing Helfrich to leave her home of more than sixty years. It helped that St. Dominic's would let her bring her own furniture, such as a large dark cabinet filled with family photos, her weighty bed, and her matching couch and loveseat, all of which make her two-room apartment mighty cozy.

"Do you want the three-second tour?" Helfrich asks. I follow her. She has a slightly bowlegged, off-kilter walk, as though old age in its typical cruelty has shrunk one leg a bit more than the other. We go through the small living room, which opens directly onto her bedroom, and then turn into a small hallway leading to the bathroom. Here, tucked into an alcove, is a half-sized refrigerator. This is all the kitchen the Tunnel of Fudge creator has anymore. Above her fridge is a kind of tchotchke-filled shrine to her famous cake and the Bake-Off® contest. There's a crowd of Doughboys, one in the shape of a planter, another a cookie jar. There's a calendar filled with the imp in all sorts of guises: lounging on a croissant, sipping a tropical drink, playfully leaning up against a jack-o'-lantern. A Tunnel of Fudge decorative plate hangs on the back wall. Helfrich carefully removes it to show me. At the center is a Doughboy in relief, again on a croissant, only this time paddling with a spoon. Behind the white asexual blob, a coffee-brown-colored slab of cake oozes forth.

Helfrich was forty-nine when she invented the Tunnel of Fudge. Three of her five children still squeezed into the family's trim white house in The Heights, a nineteenth-century neighborhood just north of downtown Houston. Her husband was a longtime brakeman for the railroad, "a hardworking man who didn't make a lot of money," she says. Helfrich was what we would call today a full-time mom. She was active at her church, All Saints, and was its school's first PTA president. She dabbled in poetry, the kind that rhymes.

She came from a long line of good Cajun cooks, but Helfrich didn't spend much time in the kitchen until she married at twenty-one. Cooking was a problem for Helfrich because she had so many skin allergies. She couldn't peel potatoes. Anything with acid would turn her hands fiery red and her fingernails would even drop off. She had to draft her kids into helping. Skin problems or not, Helfrich never liked routine cooking, the "everyday bacon and eggs." Her kind of cooking was not so predictable. In her "crammed-in kitchen" she preferred to explore terra incognito, especially the unknown corners of chocolate. She'd tweak just about any recipe, but baking, which didn't bother her skin, truly bore the brunt of her sizable creative energies. She still says there are five basic food groups: chocolate, sugar, flour, pecans, and butter.

She'd go on baking binges, throwing an extra egg in here and there, revamping the spices, doubling the amount of chocolate. Helfrich's experimental bent made her an ideal consumer for the processed food industry. As soon as she spotted a new product on the grocery store shelf, she'd snap it up and start messing around with it. Helfrich was dogged. She persisted in her kitchen experiments even though family and friends teased her mercilessly. And like any inventor, Helfrich experienced a fair amount of failure. She still shakes her head, sighs, and holds a hand to her chin over all the food she wasted. Since she couldn't afford to throw anything out, she served her flops.

"A lot of things came out disastrously," she says. "My kids were always saying, 'Oh, Mother, not again.' They suffered."

She read about the Bake-Off® contest and thought, "Well, I poke around in the kitchen." In 1959 she began entering annually. For years she fooled with Pillsbury's boxed dry frosting mixes, stirring them into cake and brownie batters. Eventually and inadvertently, as most discoveries go, these frosting investigations led to the Tunnel of Fudge.

One afternoon Helfrich was expecting her mother and a friend from Oklahoma. "I thought I'd have refreshments," she says. She took a crack at making a chocolate pound cake using a box of Pillsbury's Double Dutch Fudge Buttercream Frosting Mix. Her mistake was to pour too much batter in the pan, a specialty tube pan her kids had given her for Christmas. The cake bubbled like an active volcano, spewing chocolate lava on the oven walls. What was left in the pan cooked up as wet as a pudding. "My mother wanted to taste it, so I got it in a dish and said, 'Want a spoon?'" she says. "My poor mother was used to all my junk."

The dessert was a flop, but it got Helfrich thinking. Several attempts later she had cinched it, a cake with a molten core as if someone had ingeniously piped hot fudge sauce in the middle of it. She used only six ingredients: half a dozen eggs, three sticks of butter, a cup and a half of sugar, two cups of flour, two cups of chopped walnuts, and a box of the frosting mix. There was no milk and no leavening agent other than eggs. The recipe became one of thirty original creations she entered in the 1966 contest. She called it Inside-Out Cake "or Outside-In Cake. I forget," she says.

Pillsbury invited her to San Francisco for the Busy Lady Bake-Off® contest, where the buzzwords were "streamlining" and "up-to-date." This contest championed scratch baking "the Pillsbury shortcutted way." Helfrich's husband wouldn't fly, so Helfrich embarked on her first solo trip, "just little old me," and flew to the West Coast. She was met by her daughter, Patricia Gullo, who was then a twenty-two-year-old newlywed living in San Diego with her FBI agent first husband. For three days Gullo had her beloved mother all to herself, a rare opportunity in a large family. They toured the sights and ate at fancy restaurants, such as the Top of the Mark where they had a Hawaiian breakfast.

It was all a fabulous dream until the day of the contest when Helfrich's G.E. Americana Range went haywire. In the middle of baking her first cake, the stove began "bouncing up and down, shaking, jiggling, shimmying. I thought, 'Here it goes, out the window,'" Helfrich says. Like a rescue squad, a group of contest workers converged on her quaking stove and eventually calmed the appliance. It was already late morning. The Tunnel of Fudge was not a cake to be rushed. By today's quick-and-easy standards, the cake takes a lifetime to make—just a few minutes to mix up but an hour to bake and two hours to cool. Amazingly, the first cake did not fall even though contest workers kept slamming the oven door open and shut while working on the stove.

Helfrich still didn't dare send it to the judges. She kept a cool head, banished that cake to the display table, and stirred up another bowl of batter.

The cake is so moist that Helfrich couldn't check the doneness by pricking it. She had to eyeball it. When the cake got a dry, shiny crust similar to the top of brownies, she yanked the pan out of the oven and set it to cool. Two hours later she sent that Tunnel of Fudge to the judges, took off her Pillsbury apron, and called it a day.

In Houston the next day the nuns at All Saints let one of her teenage daughters go home to watch the awards ceremony on TV with her dad. The nuns watched the program at school. Her son went to the TV section of a department store. A prayer chain of family and friends went to work. Helfrich admits she prayed some, too, but then felt guilty. "I thought there were other things to pray about other than winning a contest," she says.

Clean-cut Pat Boone and former Miss America Marilyn Van Derbur were the emcees that year. He broke with Pillsbury tradition and got the contestants onstage at the awards ceremony to sing a line of the jingle with him. "Nothing says loving like something from the oven, and Pillsbury says it best," the aproned crew crooned in unison. Boone said he thought he heard someone singing off-key and walked over to where Helfrich was standing in the front row, with an extra-high bouffant, darkly penciled eyebrows, and a corsage so big it came up to her earlobe. "I thought it might have been you," he said to Helfrich. Helfrich smiled and blushed. She hadn't even meant to sing, just mouth the words, because she disliked her voice so. When Boone tried to get her to sing the line along with him, she was so flustered that she forgot the words. Suddenly Van Derbur cut in: "What you took from the oven said loving in a big way. From Houston, Texas, our second grand prize winner, Mrs. Carl J. Helfrich."

The $25,000 grand prize went to Mrs. John Petrelli, who wiped away tears, for her Golden Gate Snack Bread, a yeast bread with a cup of processed cheese spread mixed into the dough and a filling of butter creamed with onion soup mix. Helfrich won $5,000, a kitchen full of

General Electric appliances, and, curiously, a tractor. The money bought Helfrich and her husband a car. The couple drove their ancient maroon-and-white Studebaker to a local car dealer and drove home in the first brand-new car they ever owned, a baby blue Chevrolet Impala. They paid for it in full, writing out a check for $3,700. "That was the best part," Helfrich says. The appliances just barely fit into her kitchen at the back of the house. Her husband and son drove the tractor up and down the street in front of their house and then they sold it. "Who wants a tractor?" Helfrich says.

The Bake-Off® contest wasn't through with Helfrich just yet. Newspaper reporters called. Stores asked her to give demonstrations. Strangers from far corners of the country called to congratulate her. Her cake was so popular that grocery stores couldn't keep the frosting mix in stock. Helfrich would hover in grocery store aisles and watch shoppers pluck a box off the shelf and toss the frosting into their cart. The cake had quickly become a regular at parties, especially birthday parties. "I thought the cake was good, but not that good," she says. The Tunnel of Fudge went on to become the most requested recipe in the contest's history. What made it such an instant and enduring hit while Mrs. Petrelli's bread was relatively quickly forgotten? Well, the cake was chocolate, gooey, and had a gimmick, all of which score high with Americans' sizable sweet tooth. The cake was easy and forgiving. It was hard to overbake. And the cake was kid food made sophisticated so that adults could shamelessly indulge. The sophistication of Tunnel of Fudge was supplied by what Helfrich used to baked it in: a Bundt cake pan.

〜〜〜〜

Bundt pans were little known in the 1960s. That was until housekeepers around America paged through the 1966 cookbook of Pillsbury's winning recipes. Right there on pages 44 and 45, the Tunnel of Fudge sat in all its elegant, curvilinear glory, a rococo masterpiece created from chocolate batter. Suddenly a plain old tube pan wouldn't do. Every housewife in the country wanted a Bundt cake pan. The Bake-Off® contest staff fielded thousands of requests from cooks trying to find the unusual fluted pan. When Helfrich wasn't lingering in grocery store aisles, she'd dawdle in department stores eavesdropping on women adding their names to waiting lists for the pans and savoring her newfound effect on the world.

Only one company in the country, Northland Aluminum Products Inc. in Minneapolis, made them. David Dahlquist started the small business in 1946. It was his parents' dream come true. When Dahlquist had been a high school student, his mother would greet him every day by asking, "How's the young entrepreneur this morning?" He managed to finish a degree in chemical engineering, squeezing in all the business courses he could along the way, at the University of Minnesota before sailing off to the Pacific theater of World War II. He was a radar technician on a destroyer. Radar was a new and fragile technology. Each time the boat's huge guns were fired, they knocked out the radar. Dahlquist was one of the men who scrambled to replace the broken radio tubes. He never saw combat. His boat was on the way to Okinawa when the Americans dropped the first of two nuclear bombs on Japan.

Back home in Minnesota, married, a new father, Dahlquist used his savings, a few hundred dollars, to start Northland Aluminum in his brother's basement. Eventually he moved the small business to a forty-by-fifty-foot warehouse in St. Louis Park, a Minneapolis suburb. Dahlquist manufactured what he called Nordic Ware. He made a rosette iron, an ebelskiver pan, and a krumkake iron.

A group of women with what sounded like German accents from the local Hadassah chapter came to his office and asked if he could duplicate a pan one member had inherited from her European grandmother. She called it a *bund* pan, using the German word for "gathering." She handed it to him. It was a heavy tube pan of a sort made of two pieces. The middle was hammered in awkwardly. The outside piece had ridges. "It was a pretty bad specimen," Dahlquist says.

Dahlquist designed his own version, a sleek one-piece cast aluminum number. He added a *t* to bund to come up with his own name, something he could trademark. He began selling the pan in 1950. At first the company sold them just to the Hadassah members, who would send pans to other members around the country. Then Dahlquist got it on the shelves of local department stores, such as Dayton's, and then to stores in Milwaukee, Duluth, and Chicago. In 1960 the *Good Housekeeping Cookbook* had a recipe for a pound cake baked in the pan. Sales for the pan increased but still lagged behind Dahlquist's big sellers: a lamb mold and the Griddle King, a plank of heavy-weight aluminum that stretched over two burners.

Then came the Tunnel of Fudge. Orders for Bundt pans rose, especially in Helfrich's home state. "My shipping manager said, 'What are they doing in Texas with these damn things?'" Dahlquist says. Eventually orders poured in from all fifty states. Dahlquist added a second shift, and then a third. Northland hummed all day churning out fluted cake pans to keep American housewives happy.

Anyone could make a Bundt cake, and they always came out looking plenty fancy, like something in a bakery window. The Bundt cake became a national kitchen craze that kept building steam as home baker after home baker unmolded one for breakfast, lunch, or dinner. The ring cakes made a regular appearance at future Bake-Off® contests: two in 1967, three in 1968, and two more in 1969.

Dahlquist and Pillsbury began secret discussions about joining forces on a line of Bundt cake mixes. Pillsbury needed Dahlquist because he had the pans and the trademark. Dahlquist needed Pillsbury because they had the bucks and the clout. He invited some Pillsbury execs up for a relaxing weekend on clear, cool Lake Superior, four hours northwest of Minneapolis and far from where General Mills spies might lurk. Dahlquist put the Pillsbury execs up in a motel. Each day they cruised through the Apostle Islands in Dahlquist's fifty-seven-foot-long Chris-Craft Roamer while his wife baked Bundt cakes, including the Tunnel of Fudge, in the kitchen belowdecks. As they passed the islands' strange sandstone shores, a brilliant red against the lake's summer blue, the magic smell of blended eggs, milk, butter, sugar, and flour wafted over the deck. "You can imagine being on a boat with those odors," Dahlquist says. "You'd be pretty impressed."

Dahlquist's boating-baking tour produced. In 1970, Dahlquist gave Pillsbury permission to use the trademark. In exchange, Pillsbury agreed to sell his pans with the cake mixes. The only hitch: Pillsbury wanted a guarantee that Dahlquist would produce thirty-thousand pans every day, says Dahlquist. He balked, briefly. His production was half that number. He bought more machinery from California and agreed.

Pillsbury took nearly two years to develop the mixes, Dahlquist says. They went on the shelf in early 1972. A boxed mix and a Bundt pan sold for $1.98. The combo sold well the first year. Nordic Ware's sales jumped from $2 million to between $8 and $10 million. The success, though, was short-lived, thanks to the oil embargo of 1973. The embargo jacked the cost of flour and sugar so high that Pillsbury increased the mix and pan's price by 50 percent. Although $2.98 still seems ridiculously cheap, grocery shoppers began rolling their carts right by the promotion, angry that Pillsbury was trying to gouge them. Sales dropped enough after only two years into the promotion that Pillsbury called it quits. The hundreds of thousands of Bundt pans they had in the warehouse were returned to Dahlquist, he says.

Even though the Pillsbury deal had made the Bundt pan even more popular, the brief alliance nearly proved to be Nordic Ware's undoing. Without the Pillsbury promotion, sales dropped by half. The company struggled through the rest of the decade. The machines that Dahlquist had bought for the Pillsbury deal produced more pans than he could sell. He had to find another use. He used them to make a line of cast aluminum bakeware and cookware. Then in 1978 he saved his company by designing a plastic that could withstand the heat of a conventional oven and, more important, a microwave. Nordic Ware is still best known for the Bundt pan and estimates that there are 45 million in American kitchens. Dahlquist, however, never again laid all his bets on the cake pan.

∿ ∿ ∿ ∿

Neither Dahlquist nor Helfrich is sure whether they ever talked. Each one thinks they may have talked on the phone. Helfrich does remember that back in '66 the company sent her a box of pans to say thanks. "I wish they'd sent me stock," she says. Not too long ago a newspaper story on Helfrich pointed out that she never received any money from Nordic Ware. The family business sent her an apologetic note and another box of pans.

What Helfrich truly wanted was another crack at the Bake-Off®. She entered every single contest from 1966 on. She concocted cheesecakes from frosting mixes that formed their own crust. She tried her luck in other contests as well, winning $10,000 cash plus $2,000 worth of appliances in a Triscuit contest in the '80s. The notice just showed up in the mail one day, Helfrich says, and shrugs.

Gullo and two of her sisters decided it was up to them to get Helfrich back to the Bake-Off® contest. They began entering in '96 and put on a full-court press for the 2000 event, a niece joining that effort, because the cookoff would once again be in San Francisco. Also, with Helfrich in her eighties, the clock was ticking.

Gullo lives with her second husband in Kingwood, a relatively new suburb of Houston. She worked in banking customer service but has been much happier since she went to work in a pediatrician's office in the inner city ten years ago. Gullo's sisters quickly came up with four good recipes while Gullo struggled in the hot Texas summer to reinvent bread pudding. Bread pudding is a very popular dish in the South, Gullo says, and it is a standard in her repertory. Her problem was devising one using Pillsbury products. On the weekends she'd take another crack at alchemizing Pillsbury crescent rolls, a can of coconut pecan frosting, milk, and eggs into something fabulously original. Her attempts always turned out "too sweet. I think the frosting was the problem."

Then one Sunday morning, while sitting in the pew with her husband in the gargantuan Saint Martha's Catholic Church and listening to the priest, her uncle, the recipe for Parmesan Spinach Roll-Ups came to her. The list of ingredients, the measurements, the cooking time, everything. "The Lord did the whole thing," she declares. "I had never used Pillsbury's bread sticks, but that's what the Lord told me to do."

Gullo listened. After church she stopped by a grocery store for the bread sticks, then drove over to her mother's house, made the recipe with "Green Giant spinach and lots of love," typed it up, and sent it in. "This was a gift from God. He wanted my mom to go back."

No wonder the devout Catholic looked beatific in San Francisco. Her ever present, extra bright smile almost overwhelmed her face. Her eyes blazed through her wide glasses. Sometimes she looked happy enough to cry. The two women were nearly as inseparable as they had been in '66. They rode the cable cars again. They peeked into the Top of the Mark. They tried to find the hotel they had stayed in, but couldn't. They sat together at every meal. They were a noticeable pair. Even with her hair stacked à la Marie Antoinette, Helfrich only comes up to her daughter's shoulder. Still, she had a presence that belied her barely five-foot frame and a gracious nonchalance that said, "I belong here."

The timing of Helfrich's return couldn't have been better or more triumphant. Pillsbury had just named her cake to their Hall of Fame. Gullo felt as if she was traveling with a celebrity the way people fussed over her mom. Finalists buzzed about the "Tunnel of Fudge woman" as though they had spotted a Hollywood star. They asked her to sign their cookbooks. They told her stories of family traditions based on the Tunnel of Fudge. They shook her hand. Gullo had her turn in the limelight for once as well. "It gave me a lot of self-confidence that I hadn't had before," she says. However, history did not repeat itself at the awards ceremony. Gullo did not win a prize, but she wasn't surprised. She had never expected a dish with spinach would do well, even with God's help. Her only disappointment was that her husband, Sam, was not allowed to join her and her mother for any of the meals for the finalists, not even the gala dinner or the awards program. The company dictated that a finalist could bring only one guest. Gullo offered to pay for his meal. Pillsbury said no. The Tunnel of Fudge woman's cachet went only so far. Gullo didn't tell her mother until afterward, not wanting to dim the glow of her nostalgic trip. It wasn't the first time Helfrich had been disappointed by Pillsbury.

〰 〰 〰

I return the Tunnel of Fudge plate to Helfrich and tell her I recently made one. "Was the middle soft?" she asks with a worried expression. "Uh," I stammer, "kind of. Well, not exactly," I finally admit. Helfrich looks down at the floor, shakes her head, and moans in her deep Texan drawl. "I hate it. I wish they'd take it off the market."

That would be the current recipe for the Tunnel of Fudge. The cake made possible by progress has been lost to progress. The original cake that graced so many birthday parties and sat proudly at so many potlucks can no longer be made. In the '80s the company phased out its dry frosting mixes, including the one that was integral to the Tunnel of Fudge. The future of frosting lay not in a box but in a can. The new frosting comes ready-made and as soft as whipped butter. To Helfrich the new frosting meant the end of her cake. The Tunnel of Fudge recipe in the 1966 Bake-Off® contest cookbook has a note at the bottom that reads: "Nuts and Double Dutch Fudge Frosting Mix are essential to the success of this unusual recipe." When Helfrich heard that Pillsbury was discontinuing the frosting mix, she bought two cases from her local grocery store.

Pillsbury has revised the recipe several times. One of the early versions had a separate recipe for the filling, undermining Helfrich's stroke of brilliance of creating two textures with one batter. Another version used pudding mix and chocolate chips to create the tunnel. One of the most recent recipes returns to Helfrich's original concept, a single batter, but uses more butter, more sugar, and more flour. The frosting mix is replaced by two cups of powdered sugar and three-fourths of a cup of unsweetened cocoa. Pillsbury has also added a glaze to the revamped cake. The middle comes out moist, but when you cut the cake, the middle does not ooze out. This is what bothers Helfrich. "It should be like fudge, a fudgy sauce."

Helfrich sits us all down in the pastel shades of her pleasant living room for a drink and some chat before lunch. She gets me a small glass of slightly sweet white wine. She and a friend at St. Dom's are known as "the wine sippers," she tells me. A disembodied voice intones, "There's a birthday party at 1:30," over a loudspeaker on the wall that I hadn't previously noticed. Gullo tells the story of stand-up chicken. The first time she cooked for Sam, whom Gullo was bonkers over, she tried a new recipe that called for propping the chicken on a vertical roaster. She forgot to add wine to the pan, so she poured it in when the chicken was already in the oven. Stand-up chicken quickly became na-palm chicken. Sam helped her put out the fire. We all cackle. He brought pizza the next time. "I still don't like stand-up chicken," he says. The phone rings. Gullo answers and then passes it to Helfrich, say-ing, "They want you to play canasta."

Eventually Helfrich fetches her single remaining box of double-dutch frosting, probably the last one in America. It is neatly covered in plastic wrap to keep out bugs. She hands the precious blue box to me. The label reads, "Add fresh butter" and "Not too sweet." The price, thirty-nine cents, is in bold black letters. "You can't buy anything for thirty-nine cents anymore," Helfrich says. Nor can you bake a true Tunnel of Fudge.

~~~~

This is the original and now unmakeable version that won Ella Rita Helfrich of Houston $5,000 and a tractor at the 1966 Bake-Off® contest.

TUNNEL OF FUDGE

1 1/2 cups Land O Lakes butter, softened
6 eggs
1 1/2 cups sugar
2 cups Pillsbury's Best Flour (regular, instant blending, or self-rising)
1 package Pillsbury two-layer-size Double Dutch Fudge Butter Cream
   Frosting Mix
2 cups chopped Diamond walnuts

Cream the butter in a large mixing bowl at high speed. Add the eggs, one at a time, beating well after each. Gradually add the sugar and con-tinue creaming at high speed until light and fluffy. By hand, stir in the flour, frosting mix, and walnuts until well blended. Pour the batter into a greased Bundt pan or 10-inch tube pan. Bake at 350°F for 60–65 minutes. Cool for 2 hours before removing from the pan. Cool com-pletely before serving.

≈ ≈ ≈ ≈

This is the original recipe that won Mrs. John Cooke of New Castle, Pennsylvania, third prize and a $100 sewing machine in Knox's 1905 contest.

PERFECTION SALAD

1/2 package Knox's gelatin
1/2 cup cold water
1/2 cup vinegar
Juice of 1 lemon
1 pint boiling water
1/2 cup sugar
1 teaspoon salt
2 cups celery, cut in small pieces
1 cup finely shredded cabbage
1/4 cup finely cut sweet red peppers

Soak the gelatin in the cold water for 2 minutes. Add the vinegar, lemon juice, boiling water, sugar, and salt. Strain, and when beginning to set, add the remaining ingredients. Turn into a mold and chill. Serve on lettuce leaves with mayonnaise dressing, or cut into dice and serve in cases made of red and green peppers. This is a delicious accompaniment to cold sliced chicken or veal.

CHAPTER 15

COOKING IS AN ERECTION

There is something about the great outdoors and a fire that brings out the cook in a man. Somehow working in the confines of a home kitchen is still a painfully sissifying experience for many men, but firing up the grill outside, snapping a pair of tongs like lobster claws, and wielding an oversized spatula—well, it's the culinary equivalent of hairy chest pounding. It can even bring a he-man to tie on a dainty little apron. The 1950s backyard grilling culture did a number on American men that they may never get over. It naturally follows that men prefer their cookoffs outside and over a hot fire. That's what barbecue, Dutch oven, chuck wagon, and jambalaya cookoffs, all dominated by men, have in common.

In my travels I found a definite cookoff gender split. Speaking broadly, when women dominate, as they do in general cookoffs, the contests are very civilized, sometimes to the point of being bland. There is next to no ribbing, what with all the *support*, more of it than you'd find at a Weight Watchers meeting. However, these feminized contests are comparatively looser when it comes to rules because they stress creativity and originality. When men get involved in big numbers, you have a much rowdier, more blustery affair and a bigger production with pages and pages of rules and a trailerful of gear. Masculine cookoffs are typically about cooking the best of a specific dish rather than creating anything new in the kitchen.

The difference in the cookoffs says a lot about the difference between the sexes, especially when it comes to cooking. In comparison with the less fair sex, women have a far more matter-of-fact relationship with the kitchen; they mostly just cook to the best of their ability. In contrast, men make cooking into a humongous deal. In competition, they turn the preparation of the simplest dish—down-home ribs, for instance—into the equivalent of carving Michelangelo's *David*. They raise the everyday task of cooking to epic heights so as to be worth their important manly attention. When you ask a woman why she cooks competitively, nine out of ten times you'll get a very direct answer: because it's fun. Compare that to the answer I get when I put the same question to a male barbecue warrior in Memphis: "Cooking is an erection. It's a way to brag. You know, my truck is bigger than your truck."

My dime-store gender analysis is based on spring visits to the Memphis in May World Championship Barbecue Cooking Contest and the World Champion Jambalaya Cooking Contest in Louisiana's Cajun country. I got a few ideas as well from the chili cookoffs in Terlingua, where men no longer rule but once did. They left their imprint with the lengthy regulations and all the hubris. Competitive chili, which in the very early days banned women, has evolved into the most gender balanced of the cookoffs, maybe because they use butane stoves, which is neutral territory for the sexes. Women aren't scared off by a Coleman, and men don't find the camp stoves emasculating.

Barbecue and jambalaya are by no means exclusively male domains, but women contestants are few. A black woman, Bessie Lou Cathey, beat out twenty-seven other contestants to take the very first Memphis in May trophy with a bottle of store-bought sauce she doctored. Since then the contest has become a mostly white male club. I found female members of barbecue teams, but typically they were prepping the food, rarely cooking it. I watched as one former champion ordered a female member to cut the veggies for a garnish. Once she had dutifully finished her chopping, he shooed her off and did the actual garnishing. I saw Judy McMichael, nicknamed the Queen Bee and a formidable force behind the Airpork Crew's trophies, do everything but man the grill. She told me when she first joined Airpork Crew, men from other teams wouldn't deign to talk 'cue with her. "It was hard at first. A lot of the other teams have now somewhat accepted me."

During my three days in Memphis, I came across only one team, an all-female team named The Pink Ladies, where women worked the cooker. The team of a dozen women wear more pink than you'd see at a breast cancer benefit and has two female cookers. They were accustomed to cracks from male barbecuers, such as "Who'd y'all hire to cook?" and implications, some subtle, some not, about their sexual orientation.

"People think women can't grill," one of the cookers, Billie Metzcalf, a pink bandana tied over her white-blond hair, yelled at me over "Jungle Boogie" on the team's stereo. "Why can't a woman lift charcoal and light the grill? Why is that so hard to accept?"

At the Jambalaya cookoff in Gonzales this spring, only three contestants out of eighty-seven are women. More important, since the first cookoff in 1968 a woman has never taken the championship golden spoon. When I ask Byron Gautreau, a lanky three-time jambalaya champ, why more women don't enter the cookoff, he thinks a moment, mops the sweat from his brow with a hanky, and looks back at his boiling fifteen-gallon cast iron pot over a bed of chalky white coals. "I guess it's a pretty good little piece of work," he says. "Seems like you'd need some stature to work over the fire."

That may be, but height, specifically her lack of it, wasn't stopping Tootsie Gonzales, a former dirt bike champion and adult tomboy. Gonzales—wife, mother of one, and house cleaner—made the finals last year. Gautreau and others think this might be her year. Why? Gautreau explains by paying her one of the highest compliments in Cajun country: "She can cook."

〜〜〜〜

Some of the biggest differences between boy and girl cookoffs are readily apparent at Memphis in May: the silliness, the epic amounts of gear, and the bottomless drafts of beer. Memphis in May is equal parts frat party, gear exhibit, and cooking contest.

People had told me that I wouldn't believe the cookoff until I saw it, that, as one seasoned competitor told me, "Memphis in May is bigger than life." My first impression walking north toward Tom Lee Park, a strip of mostly treeless grass tucked between downtown Memphis and the Mississippi, is of a great military encampment. Before me stretches a mile of tents precariously pitched along a portion of the southbound river that is so wide it resembles a churning lake. Just now, in late May, the muddy river runs high and fast, like Old Man River might jump its bank any moment and swallow up the mess of barbecuers with one ravenous wet gulp.

As I get closer, the military image fades quickly and the barely controlled chaos becomes obvious: blaring stereos, disco balls twinkling in the fading light, and people strolling about sporting trim, pink rubber snouts secured by elastic. The scale of the wackiness is epic, a kind of piggy-themed Mardi Gras. Booths are decorated with every image of a porker imaginable, from the snarling, frayed boar's head mounted on the end of a shiny Airstream to a wood cutout of an Elvis pig with a black pompadour cresting on his pink scalp. There are pig angels, pig lawn ornaments, pig benches, pig flags, pig everything except for actual live pigs. The team names are an endless porcine play on words: Cotton Pickin Porker, Not Ready for Swine Time Porkers, Piggy Licious, Getting Piggy with It, South Pork, Pork Me Tender, Got Pig?, and my personal favorite, Big Al and the Butt Rubbers.

That men love gear comes as no surprise to me because I'm married to one. However, I've never been anywhere with so many men showing off so much at once. Some contesters may raise an eyebrow over the roller suitcases of kitchen equipment that Diane Sparrow hauls to cookoffs, but she has got nothing on these guys. Memphis in May is a kind of culinary version of a monster truck meet.

First off, few teams content themselves solely with a tent when they can have architecture. Some booths have multistories, full-scale bars, and even landscaped front yards with picket fences. The term "international" alludes to the foreign country that the festival honors each year.

This inspires many an architectural fancy. When Portugal was the chosen nation, a team built a ship with cannons that fired. For India a mini Taj Mahal went up. This year the country is Argentina. The All-Star Ten Pin Porkers have built a mini presidential palace with piggy Peróns on a balcony.

The true pride and joy of each team, though, is its cooker, many of which are trailer-sized and cost in the thousands of dollars. The man who told me that cooking was an erection has a cooker, logically, in the shape of an enormous angry red pig. Stan Peterson's porker has a stiff little crooked tail and a crude-shaped snout. There's a little rectangular door on the pig's right side where the meat is loaded in, and a door in the snout where the wood is inserted.

I come across Peterson on Thursday evening as he busily patches his pig. He towed it from Kansas City, and along the way it got dinged here and there. Peterson is neatly dressed. He has a sharp nose and the emphatic conversational style of a man plagued with few self-doubts. He likes talking about his pig-cooker. He made it out of a 750-gallon fuel barrel. He insulated the barrel with some unknown substance that a plumber friend had gotten him from a nuclear power plant. He covered the barrel with chicken wire and then smeared the goop from his friend like papier-mâché. I wonder out loud if it was toxic. "I don't care if it's toxic," he snaps. "If it was toxic, I'd let my ex-wife do it. You can quote me."

He flips open a roomy plastic toolbox to show me the computer he has installed in the cooker so that he can turn it on and regulate the temperature with his Palm Pilot. That way he can barbecue a three-hundred-pound hog as he drives. He has had it going all day and has used only six pieces of wood. "I brought only thirty-one pieces of wood with me," he brags.

The Memphis in May World Championship Barbecue Cooking Contest, held the third weekend in May each year, is the largest pork-only barbecue contest. There are 262 teams here this year. The cookoff is one of the top three contests on the yearlong circuit, the other two being the bigger American Royal Barbecue in Kansas City and the much smaller Jack Daniel's Invitational in Lynchburg, Tennessee. Everyone I talked to in Memphis had only good things to say about Jack Daniel's and only bad things to say about the Royal. Suffice it to say, at Kansas City they cook beef—in other words, cow.

In Memphis, teams compete in one of three categories: ribs, shoulder, or whole hog. The prizes are nothing to sniff at. A category winner gets $3,000 while the grand prize winner takes home $8,000. Still, that's pocket change compared to most company cookoffs, especially when you consider the costs. Competitive barbecuing is an expensive hobby. Teams pay for everything from gasoline to the hog. Myron Mixon, the head cooker of Jack's Old South, which took the 2002 grand prize, told me he spent an average of $1,100 at each cookoff. Mixon runs a pretty lean operation. Many teams at Memphis in May can spend well over $10,000. Even if you take Mixon's modest average and multiply it by thirty, the number of cookoffs a serious team would typically enter, that's a year's salary going up in hickory smoke. If you don't win regularly, you'll literally pay for it big-time.

I came to realize that there was a river of cash running through Memphis in May that has nothing to do with the prizes. Plenty of teams subsidize their expenses with corporate sponsorship. The companies put up the cash, and the teams cater parties in their booth for them during the week. It's a mixed blessing. Some teams turn a profit. The risk is that they may exhaust themselves barbecuing before the cookoff morning arrives. One barbecuer tells me that last year he got five hours of sleep four nights running and cooked $8,000 worth of meat for his sponsor. By the morning of the cookoff he was a wreck.

The contest makes no distinction between amateur and professional, so you find restaurant crews competing in Memphis as well. If they win, the payoff is a lot of free publicity and hundreds, maybe thousands more customers. That's why Big Bob Gibson's, a family team with two restaurants in Decatur, Alabama, hauls their cooker to Memphis and Kansas City. Their first year out, 1997, the team began picking up state and world titles. Since then the family business has been written up in *Food and Wine, Esquire,* and *The Wall Street Journal,* which has been good for the restaurant and the sales of Big Bob Gibson's sauces. Here in Memphis they went on the *Today* show, which linked its website to their sauce website.

"I don't see stopping anytime soon because it's so good for business," says Don McLemore, the family's gentlemanly silver-haired patriarch. "Some people do it and don't win. Why do they do it?" His voice cracks. "I'm sorry. I'm bragging."

Peterson doesn't own a restaurant, but his big red pig still helps him do business. He owns a computer designing business that works mostly with the airlines. Each year he invites his clients to Memphis to drink beer and gnaw barbecue in his cookoff booth. He pays all their expenses. Last year he spent between $7,500 and $10,000, half of which is tax deductible. During the weekend he snapped up $4 million worth of contracts.

Most barbecue cookoffs are one- or two-day affairs, which is technically true of Memphis. However, teams start setting up on their patch of Tom Lee Park as early as the Sunday before. That leaves teams plenty of time for partying until the Saturday morning cookoff. Until then, stereos pretty much crank around the clock, creating a timeless party zone. Tom Lee Park feels like a strip of open-air bars in a college town with bands of young men on the hunt for beer and booty. I hear a rumor that one team chugged their way through sixteen kegs in three days. During my visit I watch as two men hold a willing young woman upside down by her ankles, her long brown hair splaying on the ground as she sucks beer through a plastic tube. The Pink Ladies tell me the partying got so out of control at one point that spectators, especially women, quit coming. Contest organizers have brought order to the drunken shenanigans with an increasing number of rules. This year the cookoff banned machine-gun-sized water pistols that carousing men were firing at women's chests to create impromptu, unwilling wet T-shirt contests.

All this carrying-on can be misleading because barbecue is a very serious subject in the South. Most of the cooks are in earnest about this much-vaunted tradition of barbecuing, sometimes to a fault. The partying is overdone, and so is the religious-like devotion to what is essentially a humble dish. Just as I grew weary of female contestants glibly belittling their recipes at cookoffs, in Memphis I grow weary of one man after another intoning to me that barbecue "is an art."

Women don't take themselves seriously enough, while men could give it a rest.

This male braggadocio can take on evangelical-like dimensions. The Friday night before the cookoff I sip a martini at the place to be in Memphis, the soaring lobby bar of the Peabody Hotel, and chat about barbecue with a cook who is taking a year off from Memphis. I might as well have been discussing the Gospels with Billy Graham. At one point he says barbecue is "like a calling." I look at him, searching for a hint of facetiousness. He's dead serious, even if he is maybe a little drunk. I gulp my martini to smother a chuckle. Later he says, "It's a fraternal order. God called us to this." I gulp again. Lastly, he orders me not to talk to the cooks during Saturday's competition. "Tomorrow is like hallowed ground." I empty my glass.

〰〰〰

At one point contest organizers became worried that the barbecuers had gotten so serious—between the rigs, the rows and rows of trophies set out in front of booths, and the tribe-sized teams—that they were scaring off your average backyard grillers. They introduced Patio Porkers, a division where smaller teams, especially first-timers, could compete among themselves using their patio barbecuer.

On Friday evening that is where I find a young male ego in training, one who still needs to eat and go to bed on time. Clayton Paschke is a seventh-grade student who doesn't have anything good to say about school except for social studies and PE. He has broad, flat cheeks lightly dotted with red freckles. He has a natural poker face, hardly ever cracks a smile, and is unnervingly calm for an adolescent.

Clayton had driven down from Mt. Carmel, Illinois, with his stepdad and his twenty-five-year-old stepbrother. His mother and sister are due the next day. The name of their team is refreshingly pig pun free: Country Boys Barbecue.

Clayton has brought along his barbecue scrapbook, a spiral ring number we flip through as we look at newspaper clips, judging score sheets, and awards from his short but highly successful barbecuing career. Clayton won a second and then a first in the junior division of Mt.

Carmel's Ribberfest in 1999 and 2000, respectively. The first place knocked him out of the junior division, so in 2001 he took a crack at the adult division, going up against ten teams. He grilled for nearly three straight weeks leading up to the contest. The practice paid off. He won two first places: chicken and ribs. Most of the adult barbecuers congratulated him, but one was so upset about a kid showing up the adults that he called Clayton's stepfather, Tim Griffith, at work. "The guy kept saying he was going to kill me," Griffith says. "Finally, I got tired of it and said, 'Let's meet and have it out,' and the guy backed down."

That hometown win nabbed Clayton a slot in Memphis. The family raised most of the $1,700 they needed from the community. Griffith and Clayton's stepbrother, Gary, built their simple booth with its lattice fence and pop-up tent over a wooden platform. Griffith does some of the cooking. Clayton's mom helped him come up with his recipe. In a nod to his mom's Texas roots, Clayton uses brisket rub on his ribs and cooks with charcoal laced with mesquite. Despite all the help, Clayton is still head of the team. He plans to enter three categories: sauce, chicken, and ribs.

"I'll probably win with sauce," Clayton tells me matter-of-factly.

"He has some self-esteem problems," I say jokingly, looking at Griffith.

"He does," Griffith says, nodding his head vigorously, to my surprise.

A few years ago Clayton's young life threatened to take a wrong turn. Clayton was having trouble adjusting to his parents' divorce and his mother's new marriage. He began getting into trouble at school. He fell in with the wrong kids, Griffith says. When Clayton expressed a bit of interest in the local barbecue cookoff, his mother and stepdad eagerly tied an apron on him. "The last thing these kids are going to want to be around is somebody who cooks," Griffith says.

Clayton's parents' plan worked better than expected. His bad boy friends not only dumped him, but his wins have made Clayton into a bit of a local celebrity. When the local paper wrote a story about his win, a cute girl from school saw it and called Clayton.

So that explains why this devout Christian family from a small town has landed in the middle of party central, to risk Clayton's soul to save his self-esteem. Earlier, when I asked a barbecuer down the way from the family if he'd met them, he said, "They don't poke their head out much." Clayton's previous barbecue cookoffs did nothing to prepare him for this aspect of Memphis in May. "I thought it would be quiet, not a party," he says. Right across from Country Boys Barbecue is one of those party-hearty, two-decker deals with more flags than the United Nations. Clayton, with a blank face, studies the loud music and boogy-ing next door like an anthropologist studying a foreign culture. What impresses him the most is their gear. Next year, he announces, he's bringing a flag.

⟡⟡⟡⟡

Early Saturday afternoon I find myself listening to a barbecue team sing in voices as off-pitch and shaky as an unrehearsed church choir, "Pork is tender, pork is fine, put it on the grill." As they croon these words to the tune of "Love Me Tender," an official judge stands by smiling po-litely.

"Now, that's a little much," a guy near me mutters in disgust.

Memphis in May has formalized all the male boasting and bragging into an actual part of the competition. After the teams turn in their meat in a numbered Styrofoam box, they are visited by three different judges for ten to fifteen minutes each. According to the cookoff, the judges will evaluate the team on cleanliness, their booth and them-selves included, and their presentation of their barbecue. What really goes on is a big sell job that would shame even a car salesman.

At the Airpork Crew's booth, the first judge is due any minute. A team member gently paints sauce on the splayed 130-pound hog, then tenderly tucks curly kale and pineapples around its sunburnt-looking carcass. One member wipes down the hubcaps of the team's trailer. An-other hauls out the trash cans. In the trailer Judy McMichael wipes down the counters and cupboards even though the judge will never see them. One of the cookers, a tall, barrel-chested black man with an un-derbite, squeezes in and dashes behind a curtain in the back to change into clean clothes. "Don't let anybody back here," he calls.

"I'll try to keep the little white girls away," she yells back.

The Airpork Crew is a serious team. They have finished in the top ten highest-scoring teams on the barbecue circuit. Last year they won best booth at Memphis in May. That was before 9/11. All the members work at the Memphis International Airport. "Nine-eleven really hurt us," says head cook Jerry McMichael, the airport's executive vice president and CFO. "Everyone had to put in such long hours at the airport that we haven't been on the circuit." Two years ago they competed in thirty cookoffs. This will be their first contest this year, so the team's hopes aren't as high as usual and their booth, resembling a simple outdoors bistro with hanging ferns, is dressed down.

The team's leitmotif, low and slow, is not original, but McMichael can almost make you believe it is the way he draws it out, nearly singing it. Airpork Crew, he says, is one of the few teams that doesn't use a water pan. The steam from a water pan will keep the meat from burning and allow a team to leave its cooker for a stretch. No water pan means Airpork Crew cannot leave its cooker unattended. Two team members manned the grill last night, keeping themselves awake by playing with an apron that had a nude female physique on it, complete with boobies that squeaked.

"They got squeezed so much, the squeaker broke," the younger cook reports gleefully.

"I didn't touch them, but he fooled with them," the older cook says without cracking a smile.

The team may be out of practice, but they know from experience what the judges will be looking for. As with many serious teams, a good number of the Airpork Crew has gone to barbecue judging school to assist them in getting inside the judges' heads. Judy says women judges like sweeter sauce and older male judges like to have a rib. They also have been to Memphis in May enough so that they actually know a good number of the judges. The ones McMichael doesn't know he'll quickly read, gauging how they like their bullshit, layered on thick or not at all. He and his wife work as a tag team during the presentation. She describes the rub and the sauce. He opens and closes, putting on a good ol' boy show that will make you roll your eyes. Sometimes he tells whoppers, like how the hog slept only on its left side or how his wife fed the piglet with barbecue sauce in a baby bottle.

McMichael notices a bottle cap and bends down on one knee to get it. He orders the tent flap pulled so the trailer is hidden. The others straighten their clothes and put on clean aprons. "Everyone, get pagers, phones turned off," McMichael orders. "Everyone has their fingernails clean? Got aprons? Got gloves?"

The team huddles, puts hands together over their heads, and yells, "One, two, three, team!" The black cook wipes the older cook's mouth with a towel, then puts Chap Stick on himself.

The first judge arrives, a good-natured, roly-poly man. McMichael leads him to the platform of their cooker and lets his inner Bubba loose. "I have two reasons for everything," he croons. He gives a singsongy rundown of Airpork Crew's cooking style: no water pans, burn apple wood, put sweet onions right on the fire. "Try that at home." Then he orders the grill open. I can see the hog's white teeth shining against its amber-red skin. "This hog is named Edna. Edna comes to you today to give you the best hog you can have."

The judge is led to the table where McMichael's wife talks up the rub—"Five kinds of pepper, and the rest of eighteen ingredients remain a secret" and then tells a story about the sauce. While her husband was away, she committed high treason, changing the sauce, using tomato paste and orange blossom honey. Everyone liked it better, so the mutiny was complete. "If you find something floating in there, don't worry because it's pineapple," she says.

Standing off to the side, one of the Airpork Crew members signals with his fingers to McMichael how many minutes are left of the allotted fifteen. A contest volunteer does likewise for the judge. At one point the team member holds up eight fingers when the volunteer holds up nine. She checks her watch.

McMichael comes down with a plate of pork. There is no silverware on purpose. They want the judge to eat with his hands and feel the texture of the meat. As the judge chews, McMichael acts like a convivial host, urging him to have more sauce, asking if he's had enough. He talks about their barbecue style, how they add sauce only during the last two hours, and then ends on a philosophical note: "Only have one hog. If she's bad, she's bad. If she's good, like she is today, she's good. Ain't she pretty?" The team member by the entrance pulls a finger across his throat to signal that time is up.

"It was a presentation as good as I've seen," the judge says and pushes back his chair.

The next judge arrives late, which puts everyone on edge. When he does show, he turns out to be rather humorless. His head is always slightly tilted, which gives him a quizzical look. McMichael launches into his spiel. "I did something special because I thought you might come here. I had my momma send this hog. She fed it nothing but apples." The guy gives him the head tilt and a blank look and says, "Okay."

McMichael dumps the bullshit, and what follows is a more streamlined version of his previous rundown. The judge nods the whole time without smiling. While he's eating, the third judge, an elderly man in a floppy khaki hat, arrives and starts coming into the booth. The team members frantically wave him off. The second judge wordlessly finishes his tasting. Judy holds out a box of wet wipes. The judge reaches to pluck one, but it refuses to come out. I feel the whole team freeze. Judy tries but can't loosen one. Finally, she plunges her hand into the box and jerks out a clump. As soon as the judge leaves, McMichael points to the wipes and says to his wife without smiling, "You need to work on that."

The third judge is ready and waiting, so the team hurriedly regroups for the final round. This judge is affable and talkative, so McMichael lays it on pretty thick, but his energy seems to be slightly flagging. He calls the hog Edna but skips the story about his mother raising it. Judy's presentation is more consistent. The judge wants to watch them cut the pork off the carcass and asks for bacon, which is a little unusual. "Edna will produce," McMichael says.

McMichael isn't the only one whose concentration is waning. One of the team members, the younger cook who squeaked the fake boobies, is losing it like a third-grader who has had to stand quietly in line too long. He's pestering his fellow overnight cook, pushing his hat forward and standing too close to him. The other guy finally cracks and starts choking the pest.

All these hijinks go on behind the judge, who is seated and eating. McMichael has pretty much gone over everything, but his timekeeper holds up four fingers. He has to keep talking. McMichael rambles on about barbecue, southern cooking, and how they don't use a water pan. "As we are closing, apple wood, twenty-two hours, two hundred degrees, last two hours have sauce on."

"I'm honored to have judged here with you," the judge says. Judy holds out the wipes. One pops forth without a hitch.

〜〜〜

I walk to Patio Porkers at the other end of Tom Lee Park, which has taken on the look of an archeological dig, with rib bones smushed into the ground here and there. The muddy road through Patio Porkers is cut deep with ruts and pocked with soupy puddles. There was a monsoon-like rain last night, and even though the sun has shined all day, not one drop of water appears to have evaporated. Barbecuers are watching people like me try to navigate the mud, hopping from one foot to the next, as entertainment. Someone takes pity on me and yells, "Walk on the tire marks."

I had checked on Country Boys Barbecue earlier, and Clayton was very dejected about his ribs. Slumped in a canvas butterfly chair, he told me they weren't any good but wouldn't say why. His teenage sister, Stacey, sat sullenly, squint-eyed in the sun, occasionally glaring at her mother who has brought her here on her seventeenth birthday. "I had like four places to stay," she wailed. Clayton's mother, who has his broad cheeks and almond-shaped eyes, did what she could to brighten her kids' spirits, but they were hopelessly dreary.

When I make my way back, I find the booth overly animated. Even Stacey is up and moving. It turns out that Clayton's ribs made the finals, meaning beyond all expectations he has made the top ten out of fifty-two. A group of judges is due any minute. The two-member team next door leans on their cooker and glowers at the family, which is too busy to notice. Clayton actually smiles. He doesn't show any teeth, but the corners of his mouth are definitely curling. "The Lord works in mysterious ways," his stepdad calls to me over his shoulder as they dash to meet the judges.

Airpork Crew did not have the same luck. The teams that make the finals in their respective categories—shoulder, ribs, and whole hog—are visited one more time by judges, this time a group of them. Teams are only given a few minutes' warning that those judges are on the way. No such warning arrived at the Airpork Crew's booth. The team members all took a seat and had a beer. They were dejected but didn't start tearing down their booth immediately like less graceful losers. In the end, Airpork Crew finished in the top ten out of forty-one teams in whole hog, number seven to be exact. That didn't win them any money, but maintained their reputation as a team to be reckoned with.

As the sun set over the Mississippi, Clayton was called on to a humongous stage in front of a horde of sunburnt, mind-numbed barbecue revelers. The straight-faced redhead had come in third out of thirty-five teams in Patio Porkers, a stunning victory for such a young Memphis in May novice. This time he had really shown up the adults.

〰〰〰〰

A week later and about three hundred miles down the Mississippi, where the flat land hovers above sea level and concrete quays, empty antebellum houses, and chemical plants flank the river, the World Championship Jambalaya Cooking Contest is held every Memorial Day weekend in Gonzales.

Gonzales is a small city about a ten-minute drive from the river, located between New Orleans and Baton Rouge. The city used to be a mostly isolated rural corner, but a highway and then the chemical factories changed that. There's not much of a downtown to Gonzales, although there is a relatively new city hall surrounded by an imaginative park that incorporates the ruins of the old sewage treatment plant. Mostly, though, there is the standard ring of strip development with treeless flats of black tar and speeding cars filled with errand-minded drivers. In this way Gonzales is like most American communities.

What's different about Gonzales is that it has only two seasons, hot and hotter, as someone tells me. There are gators in the bayou, and almost everyone is a Cajun, which means almost everyone can cook, men included.

The word "World" in the cookoff's title is a bit of a misnomer because all the contestants are from Louisiana, from a one-hundred-mile radius or less. Still, the contest is the biggest in a small circuit of jambalaya cookoffs, so it logically follows that whoever wins must be the best in the world.

The cookoff is a huge deal in these parts. The event is a major fundraiser for the community. The jambalaya from the cookoff is sold for $4 a box. Last year they sold two thousand pounds of it. The winner becomes a jambalaya missionary of sorts for his reigning year, crisscrossing the country cooking the Cajun-Creole dish for the unenlightened. As one contestant told me, "This is like our Super Bowl."

To me it looked more like an iron man contest. The World Championship Jambalaya cookoff is a prime example of men making cooking a whole lot harder than it has to be. This cookoff even makes judging incredibly difficult, asking each judge to sample more than one hundred boxes of the rice stew over three days. Byron Gautreau told me he didn't dare stop competing because then the festival would ask him to judge. He'd rather sweat it out over a fifteen-gallon pot.

This year there are a record number of cooks, eighty-seven. There would have been eighty-eight, but one burned himself cooking catfish on a catering job, which then got infected on another catering job, a crawfish boil. All the jambalaya cooks seem to moonlight as caterers, and how many hundreds of pounds of crawfish they recently boiled is a regular topic of conversation.

The cooks have been divided into five three-and-a-half-hour heats. The first three heats will be held on Saturday beginning at 6 A.M. The cooks have to work over open fires in late spring temperatures that easily can top 90 degrees. Each group of cooks stirs its pots under a long, narrow, open-air structure with a metal roof set along the Bayou François, which slinks through the middle of town. The metal awning shades the contestants, but it also traps the considerable heat of fifteen or more fires in a row burning at once, making for quite a sweat lodge. The soupy bayou is only about 20 feet away, but the still green waters do nothing to cool the air.

Last year 1996 champ Wayne Absjore, who everyone calls T. Wayne, took the temperature in the cooking area. His thermometer read 130 degrees. Many of the cooks arrive already dehydrated from a night of partying, and then the cookoff sucks out the few drops of water left in them. No wonder one contestant stumbled over to the bayou last year, lay down, and then couldn't get up because his legs cramped up so badly. It took several days in the hospital to get him pumped full of enough fluids again.

Contestants keep coolers filled with brightly colored sports drinks. They drape white towels around their necks to soak up the sweat and to mop their faces every few minutes. They can't dress for the heat because they have to dress for the fire. So while spectators prance about in tank tops and shorts, the jambalaya cooks don jeans, heavy leather work boots, and even long-sleeved shirts. Gautreau told me he tries to condition himself by getting plenty of sleep leading up to the cookoff and spending time outdoors in the heat. His air-conditioned office job, though, pretty much foils that training. "It's getting to it wears me down," Gautreau says.

When I arrive Friday evening for the Champ of Champs cookoff, I find Wally Taillon, a heavyset man with gray hair, ruddy cheeks, and a constant, small, bemused smile on his face, absolutely soaked through his blue shirt with sweat. He looks as though he bent over and dunked his torso to his waist in the bayou. Taillon began competing in 1979 and finally won in 1993. Like many of the contestants, he followed a male relative into the cookoff. His uncle was one of the founders. "The smoke is killing me," Taillon says, blinking his eyes and tipping his head back as he guzzles what looks like a bottle of window cleaner.

The Champ of Champs is what it sounds like: a cookoff between past champions. If you participate in it in addition to the major cookoff, as Taillon, Gautreau, Absjore, and a few others are, you could end up sweating it out over jambalaya three times for a total of fourteen hours over the weekend. That may explain the curse of the Champ of Champs champ. No one who has won the Champ of Champs has ever gone on to win the central cookoff. They're just too sweated out.

Taillon admits that most Cajuns don't cook jambalaya in hot weather. It's much more of a cold weather dish, a regular on the dinner table at hunting camps in the fall. But festival season, even in Louisiana, falls in the summer. The cookoff was originally in the middle of June, which could get over 100 degrees, so the organizers made a small allowance for the limits of human heat tolerance and pushed it back a few weeks, to Memorial Day weekend.

Jambalaya is a standard dish at church dinners and other social functions, of which there are many in Cajun country. It is tasty and filling. It is also relatively easy to make. But you wouldn't know that from the cookoff, which insists on a very particular, local way of making jambalaya. The contest has laden this simple rice dish with so many rules that the cooks might as well be making five-course haute cuisine dinner for twenty. Let's just say more than one man during my two days in Gonzales said to me, "Jambalaya making is an art."

Like chili, jambalaya breaks down into eating jambalaya and competitive jambalaya. The latter is concerned with cooking the rice to perfection, which is signaled by the appearance of the grain's vertical seam, something I didn't even know rice had. "If it's not showing, that means you didn't cook it right, either too fast or without enough water," Taillon says. If the jambalaya comes out too dark, that little hairline won't be visible to the naked eye. A rich amber is ideal, but if the color goes more brown or gold, you're in trouble. Contestants used to have an easier time getting the color right when Worcestershire sauce was allowed, but the contest raised the bar by excluding the watery brown stuff. One way that cooks cheat, I was told, is to rub the inside of their pot with Worcestershire.

The other major difference between eating jambalaya and competitive jambalaya, at least in Gonzales, is that the cooks can use only chicken—to be more specific, hen on the bone. The contest uses mature chicken because the meat is more likely to cling to the bone and not fall away into the rice. Jambalaya judges don't like seeing bits of chicken meat kicking around. In fact, the judges purposely taste only the rice. As Taillon explains, you want good chicken flavor, but you don't want the chicken.

When most people think of jambalaya, they think of a kind of fun, free-form dish, one you could toss some leftovers in or let your imagination run a little loose with. Not here. The contest severely limits the ingredients: Each contestant pays a $150 entry fee and in return gets fifteen pounds of rice, forty-five pounds of hen on the bone, fifteen pounds of onions, and all the green peppers, garlic, celery, salt, and black and cayenne pepper he likes. A cook can eliminate ingredients but not add. The cooks bring only their pot, lid, and paddle. Even the oak logs, stacked in loose piles along the bayou, are supplied by the contest.

Judges score each dish in four equally weighted categories: appearance, rice texture, chicken flavor, and overall taste. Notice that only half of the scoring has to do with the actual taste. That may explain why the head judge tells me, "I've seen a jambalaya win that we couldn't sell."

Tonight at the Champ of Champs cookoff, the contestants can use sausage and pork meat in their jambalaya as well. The technique is the same, though, so Taillon shows me how to make a competition jambalaya. Taillon's helper tonight is Chad Decoteau, the cookoff's current president. Decoteau is decked out like most the Cajun men here, with a pair of wraparound sunglasses, a cell phone in a belt holster, and his shirt neatly tucked into his clean blue jeans.

Before I arrived, Taillon had browned his meat in vegetable oil. Next he added the chopped onion. Some cooks sauté the onions in the bottom of the pot, but this is how many jambalayas go wrong because the cooks scorch the onions. That is why Taillon threw his onions on top of the meat to cook. Taillon added three gallons of water, one for every five pounds of rice, stoked the fire, and brought the pot to a boil. Now he and Decoteau rake the fire out from under the pot with quick pulling motions. As the watery stew cools, the grease floats to the top. Using a big spoon Taillon skims off the pools of fat and, with a flick of his wrist, dumps them on the grass. He leaves a little to give the rice flavor. "It's how you take care of your pot," he says. "It don't take but a couple of minutes and it's gone."

The two men build the fire back up under the pot, bringing the pot's contents to a low boil. Taillon adds garlic, salt, and pepper. He has a strong aversion to anything green and so does not use celery or green pepper. The twosome poke some more wood into the fire, arrange two rounded pieces of metal from an oil barrel to reflect the heat, and kick the boil up hard. Then Taillon adds or "dumps" his fifteen pounds of rice all at once. For seven minutes Taillon boils the rice so hard that it sputters into the air. He stirs the cooking rice until all the water is gone.

The fire is pulled out from under the pot one last time. Taillon runs the back of a large spoon over the rice, flattening it out, and covers the pot. He leaves the jambalaya alone for ten minutes, then "bleeds" it. All the water left in the pot pools on top of the rice. Taillon gently plies the rice with his paddle, parting the grains so that the water will seep back down to the bottom of the pot where he wants it. He's careful not to wedge the paddle in too deep and disturb the gratin, the caked layer of rice and onion that is sure to have formed along the bottom. The lid goes on, and he leaves the pot alone for twenty to twenty-five minutes. While he waits, he dabs his face with a towel and drains sports drinks.

Once the jambalaya is done, he pokes and jabs at the rice, digging out bits here and there and loading them into a Styrofoam box for the judges. "You'd think the rice was all cooked the same, but there are pockets better cooked," he says.

Taillon loads a box of his jambalaya for me. I carry it off like a precious gift and duck into the nearby school auditorium, which is the festival's air-conditioned dining room for the weekend. The jambalaya is fabulous, full of smoky, earthy flavor. There's enough for four, and I almost polish off the box.

Taillon does not win the Champ of Champs, which is good news in a way. The winner, Absjore, his ball cap pulled low, steps onstage to say a few words to the crowd. "It's a bad jinx. It's a bad history. I thank the judges for picking me. That's all I have to say."

～～～～

On Saturday morning I find Tootsie Gonzales, red-faced and smiley, splashing Florida water on her neck, a feminine touch that stands out amid the ball caps and low-belted jeans. She is a small, strong-looking woman with bright eyes. She is cooking in the first heat near Taillon, whom she calls Mr. Wally. Rather than drive the thirty minutes from their house, she, her husband, and young daughter spent the night in their RV in a nearby lot along the bayou. That gave her an extra half hour to sleep.

At around 8 A.M. the heat is the most bearable it will be all day, but many of the cooks have sweated through their shirts, especially Taillon. Most of the spectators are cooks scheduled for later heats, such as Absjore, who has a large boyish face and tells me proudly that he's the first ever jambalaya champ from the western side of the Mississippi. He's here, standing in front of Gonzales's station, to check out the cook stations and to see if "the hens hold together." The word is that the onions are dry.

"What do you think? Is she going to take it this year?" a man in the standard wraparound sunglasses stops to ask him.

"I'm surprised she didn't win last year," Absjore says. "She's a good, consistent cook."

If a woman was to win the cookoff, it would be a major break in tradition in a tradition-bound event. That doesn't seem to bother any of the male contestants I speak with. It seems like a natural evolution, that a woman should be able to vote, have her choice in career, and reign as the World Jambalaya Champ.

This is Gonzales's fourth year in the cookoff. She made the finals for the first time last year. Her mother, a woman with near translucent skin, says Gonzales didn't care for sewing as a girl. She took ag instead of home ec. She won loads of Presidential Fitness awards. "The boys came and asked if she could play hardball with them."

Gonzales does love cooking, but that's a gender-neutral activity in these parts. She sets the broad, flat lid on her pot, then taps it with her foot as she walks by and nearly stumbles. Now she has to wait the thirty minutes for her jambalaya to set. As she cracks a bottle of Gatorade, I ask if she thinks being a woman in this male cooking bastion gives her any kind of edge. She nods her head as she swallows. She measures her ingredients, a basic kitchen technique that the male contestants typically ignore. She also uses a timer. Now some of the men bring along measuring cups and spoons, even timers. Another thing: "I observe a lot," she says. "Men aren't observant."

For example, she has noticed that the cook next to her began by making stock with his hen. She is trying something new today as well but won't tell me exactly what. She just hints that it has got to do with her ratio of water to rice. Any little difference that makes a jambalaya stand out could win the contest, she says.

"Oh, I would love to win," she says, her eyes widening. "It's time for the winner to be a woman. I don't know how the guys would feel about it, but I think they'd be okay with it."

If she does win, it will be unusually hard won. The World Championship Jambalaya contest is in some ways the most unfair contest I've seen. Four finalists are picked from each heat. That means a contestant's jambalaya is not judged against the entire field but just his heat. This can work to a contestant's favor if you end up in a heat with a lot of first-timers. It can also work to a contestant's disadvantage if you end up in a heat packed with serious contenders. That's the case with Gonzales. There are a number of former champions in her time slot.

When Gonzales's jambalaya is finished, she takes the big lid off and squats by the pot. A contest worker will come by soon and spoon out portions of the jambalaya. Gonzales intends to make sure they spoon out the best rice in her pot. Using a spoon she pokes at pockets of rice, examining the grains, taking a tad here, a full spoonful there. She's digging out the rice with the best color and seams. She dishes it into a big green bowl in her other hand. Then she uses the back of her spoon to create a well in the middle of the pot and carefully loads the contents of the green bowl. This strikes me as possibly cheating, but she's doing it right here in front of everybody.

"They're gonna come and stir it up," someone yells from the crowd and then laughs.

All sixteen boxes, each numbered, go to the judging table on a stage. The five judges sit facing the audience, chewing and chewing, their lips moving in slow, unsmiling rotations while Gonzales's chatty mayor rambles on over the mike. Eventually the Jambalaya Queen, a teen in cutoffs and a tiara, is called onstage to read the four winning numbers.

She reads them very, very slowly and as people around here say, "nasty."

Sometimes history just refuses to be made. Each time the queen finally spits out one of the winning numbers, Gonzales remains quiet. Instead, a hairy arm shoots up or a male voice hoots in response. Gonzales has no time to reflect. She's a helper for a cook, a first-timer, in the second heat. She pulls on her yellow ice vest and heads back to the fires.

The first heat over, the festival finally has some jambalaya to sell. I grab a box and head into the cool of the air-conditioned school auditorium. The room is filling up quickly with people holding Styrofoam boxes. On the stage a gaggle of elderly people stand in a small semicircle too far back from a microphone and sing patriotic songs in high, breathless voices. I open my box of jambalaya and am met with a slightly discouraging sight: a few pieces of scrawny-looking chicken atop a mound of rice. The chicken is too stringy to eat. The rice is dry but tastes mostly of greasy chicken fat. However, I can see the seams on the rice kernels.

A woman in dark glasses down the long table from me is having a similar experience. She complains loudly that she doesn't like her jambalaya. It's too dry. Her friend hushes her.

"That's how they do it in competition."

CHAPTER 16

STATE FAIR

Summer is a slow season for the contesters. There's not too much on the horizon cookoffwise other than Gilroy, and a number don't even bother with that contest because the $1,000 grand prize is so slim. Entries for Better Burger's $20,000 grill-off aren't due until the end of August. National Chicken closes mid-October. There's a reasonable list of recipe contests, but only a few have prizes totaling more than $500. Hellmann's will shower five thousand greenbacks over the cook who invents a WrapWich. Velveeta will ship a family of four to Florida for a knockout dish that uses a half-pound chunk of the shiny processed cheese. Mostly, all there is to do is sit around the kitchen table and wait for the *Southern Living* Cook-Off to anoint its fifteen finalists.

That is, unless you are Norita Solt.

The last time I saw Solt was at the Post Selects Cereal cookoff in New York City where she won second place for her Creole Banana Nut Crunch Bread Pudding. Back then her husband had just lost his accounting job, and Solt worried she'd have to return to the full-time work world. She hardly had time to fill out an application. Every day she drove nearly two hundred miles round-trip to visit her ninety-nine-year-old aunt Gy who lay dying slowly in a hospital in Macomb, Illinois.

Since then Aunt Gy has passed, and Solt's accountant husband landed a job with what looks like the most secure employer he's had in years—a bank. That has left Solt ample time to indulge her obsession: the Iowa State Fair. Since 1997 she has devoted the first two weeks of August to her fair mania. She has the ribbons to show for it. Last year alone she entered seventy-seven dishes and won thirty-nine ribbons (fourteen blue, three overall) and more than $2,000 in cash and prizes, her best year ever. This year she hopes to do even better.

"Welcome to kitchen hell," Solt says, meeting me at her front door with her shih tzu, Lily, barking at her feet.

Solt has dove gray, naturally poofy hair cut into a bob that closes in tight around her face, and big round glasses. It is a cut that makes her vaguely resemble her little dog. She has a high little-girl voice that she never has liked even though it has deepened a note now that she is fifty-six. Her youthful voice is matched by an ebullience most people lose before they are out of their twenties. She speaks of her life as one filled with endless possibilities. She also can swear a mean streak, says what she thinks, and has a good sense of humor. On a recent trip to Mexico with her husband and his new coworkers, Solt rode the mechanical bull in a bar, one hand raised above her head like a rodeo cowgirl.

She lives in a circular maze of new houses with gargantuan garages in suburban Bettendorf, one of the Quad-Cities that hugs the Mississippi River as it snakes between Iowa and Illinois. She leads me through the dim light of her foyer and den to her kitchen, which is like coming upon a sunny courtyard with its expanse of pristine white cupboards. "This is too much house for us, but we bought it for the kitchen," Solt says. There are brass knobs, a sweep of sea-green-colored Corian counters, and an island. It's the classic New American kitchen that millions of middle-class women dream about every night.

Solt was not exaggerating about the hell element. The pantry and cupboards appear to have exploded, blowing all their contents onto the counters, floor, island, and kitchen table. Solt clears a stack of paperwork and books off a chair for me to sit down, then pushes aside legal pads, tape dispensers, fair entry tags, and cardboard cake disks so I can squeeze my notebook onto the kitchen table. A round, golden onion tart sits amid the table's chaos. Near me on the floor, a teetering stack of bakeware threatens to give. When I look across the kitchen to where Solt has returned to whipping egg whites for an angel food cake, I can't see her over the dry goods on the island.

"Are they supposed to be shiny?" she says to herself. "I have no idea what the batter is supposed to look like. Aunt Gy, if you're out there, help me."

Solt is making her first ever angel food cake, using her Aunt Gy's recipe. The cake is a kind of memorial to tiny Aunt Gy, pronounced Jie. She taught Solt to cook. Solt's mother did not have the patience to teach her and was painfully slow at the stove. The featherlight cake is one of the dozen or so entries she plans to ferry 180 miles to the Iowa State Fair in Des Moines early tomorrow morning. She hopes to enter seventy-five or more dishes over the fair's two weeks of cooking and baking contests.

"Oh, shit, I thought I left the oven on," Solt says, holding a tube pan filled with the frothy cake batter in one hand and propping the oven door open with the other. A TV plays soap operas in the woody den off the kitchen. Radio is too distracting, but the soft murmur of a television helps Solt focus.

Before me is the seventeen-page schedule Solt has crafted for herself. It's a dizzyingly elaborate horizontal chart that lists times, divisions, classes, the recipe she plans to enter, and prizes. She has even left room on the right side for notes. For example, to the far right of the bread machine category she has typed "entire loaf must be baked in machine."

Solt started working on the fair six months ago when she began jotting down recipe ideas on her computer. This year she has compiled a total of 301 pages of recipes, most of them original, some not. Once the premium book came out in June, she began crafting the organizational feat I now hold in my hands. According to her schedule, Solt will have dishes in competition every day. She will accomplish this by commuting round-trip to Des Moines four to five days a week. When not on the road, she will cook like a fiend. Over the past few weeks she has cooked and frozen some dishes ahead, but most of the kitchen work happens in the heat of fair time. Needless to say, Solt does the state fair as a total immersion experience. She even loses five to ten pounds during the two weeks because she rarely pauses to sit down for a meal. In those thirty minutes another winning zucchini bread could be mixed up.

Saturday she stayed up to 1:30 A.M. baking. She got up at 4:30 A.M. to drive over seven yeast breads, four quick breads, a pita bread, an Armenian soup, and the exotic-looking Walk on the Wild Side Cake. The remains of it are tucked into the current kitchen detritus. The chocolate maple marble cake has tiger stripes in the batter, iced leopard spots on the side and iced zebra stripes on the top. She won two first places, three second places, three third places, and an honorable mention. Sunday she got in bed by midnight but was up at 5 A.M. to rush back to Des Moines on Monday.

Today is Tuesday, a stay-at-home and cook-like-mad day. Tomorrow she'll enter twelve categories. More important, tomorrow there are three contests, one of which Solt has her heart set on winning: garlic, onion, and legendary recipes. This isn't about cash. Each winner of those three divisions receives a handmade ceramic plate, a must-have for any hard-core fair entrant. "I want one of those plates," Solt says.

She figures with four entries she'll leave with one carefully tucked under her arm. For the legendary contest she has made a round, plump loaf of Ukrainian Easter bread, which she'll serve with pashka, a kind of spreadable cheesecake. That contest requires a written description of the food tradition, and Solt's notes say the pashka recipe came from Olga Wright, Frank Lloyd Wright's third wife. She has made a Cajun garlic dressing and a garlic bread pudding for the garlic contest. For onions she's made Cold Onion Picnic Deep Dish Pye, which sits on the table before me.

The other onion entry carmelizes on the stove. While the chopped onions sizzle, Solt considers a piecrust made with olive oil that lays empty in a tart pan, looking pale and wan. "It's like bread," Solt says, tasting it. I take a nibble. The crust has decent flavor but is much too chewy. She's not sure whether to finish off the tart or put her efforts into a more winning dish. The timer goes off, and she pulls the angel food cake from the oven.

"Oh, it did puff," she says. "Maybe Aunt Gy is watching over it."

She hangs the cake in its pan upside down on an oversized bottle of vinegar and then turns back to the stove. "Well, garlic never hurt anything," she says, adding a few cloves to the onions. She pulls down a huge new jar of mayonnaise, one of the few things that seems to actually be still in a cupboard, sets it down near the cake, and begins to unscrew the top.

"Oh, no," she cries.

I jump and turn to look. At first glance I think the mayo jar has belched its white contents onto the counter, but it's the angel food cake. It slid from the pan into one foamy, slumped, ruined heap. There's a big smear of cake on the mayo jar.

Solt is fearless in the kitchen and does not dwell on her mistakes. When other cooks might stomp on their kitchen towel or have tears streaming down their flour-dusted cheeks, Solt charges ahead. She pinches off a wad of the disastrous cake and pops it into her mouth. She turns to the pan of onions and adds a packet of grated cheese and a big blob of mayo. As Solt watches, the fats begin to separate, oozing into slick puddles atop the onions. "That looks totally disgusting," she says.

I expect her to pitch the whole mess. Rather, she spoons the onions out into a bowl and drains the fat out of the pan. She caramelizes more onions and adds them to the original batch. Then she puts the whole pile in a small baking dish, tops it with some slivered almonds, and pops the dish into the oven. She strolls over to her computer to edit the original recipe, deleting the water chestnuts and wine she left out. "That's the other thing that happens during the fair," she trills. "What I call serendipity."

It's nearly 6:30 P.M. She brings up from the basement the pashka, wrapped in cheesecloth and tucked into a chinois. She unmolds it and unwinds the cloth. A perfect creamy cone emerges. She still has to make a tart with the olive oil crust, decorate the pashka with almond slices, and paint an elaborate Ukrainian egg.

"Poor pitiful thing," Solt says, using her hands to pile the angel food cake into a heap on the counter. "Help yourself."

~~~~

If you think Solt sounds extreme or obsessed or if she strikes you as some kind of anomaly in the state fair world, you're wrong. Solt is just one of about fifty hard-core competitors at the Iowa State Fair. There's Louise Piper, the pie and bread lady, and Joy McFarland, the cake lady. Then there are the generalists like Solt, who is known for her creative flair, and Marion Karlin, a retired psychologist who drives 120 miles from Waterloo most fair days with her car stuffed with entries. Karlin entered more than three hundred dishes at last year's fair.

There are the full-time workers who take their summer vacation at fair time. Twenty-eight-year-old Charles Duke stops painting houses for three weeks so he can enter about one hundred dishes. Sally Kilkenny takes off from her job in the insurance industry and spends the day in the food exhibition building with her adolescent daughter. Chris Montalvo, a telecommunications system designer in Des Moines, spends her vacation each year cooking up seventy entries. "It's the same thing as going on a golfing vacation," she says. "Golf doesn't produce anything. I have to produce something. I want something for my efforts."

They've been known to finish dishes in their parked cars. One woman works out of a camper for the duration of the fair. They've timed the fastest routes from their front door to the fair's food arts building. They cut their nightly dose of sleep in half. Solt gets so wrapped up in the fair that she bawls the first day and the last day.

Joyce Agnew, who runs company-sponsored contests at state fairs around the country, has come across hard-core fair entrants everywhere. Diane Roupe, a roving state fair judge and author of the *Blue Ribbon Cookbook*, has found them at fairs around the Midwest. "It's not people who say I'm too tired to cook and eat pizza out three times a week," says Roupe. "These people are in life. They are with it." Arlette Hollister says there have been hard-cores as long as she has been running the food exhibits at the Iowa State Fair, sixteen years. Their numbers have increased, she says, from a handful to a roomful. Now about fifty entrants each haul more than fifty dishes to the fair each year.

In Iowa the hard-cores appear on the winners' list regularly, if only because with so many entries the odds are much better that they'll win something. Hollister thinks it's more than that, that they generally are very good cooks. She says they raise the bar for all the entries, pushing the average fair entrant to try that much harder.

State fairs are the ground zero of competitive cooking. The oldest form of competitive cooking, they are truly open to all comers. Here, cooks compete not for big money or national attention, or exotic trips, but for ribbons. There are the beautiful blue ribbons that class winners take home. Then there are the bouquet-sized, rainbow-colored overall ribbons, what they call "big ass ribbons" in Iowa, won by the best dish in a whole division. No one minds red ribbons for second place or the green ribbons for third place, either.

The fair rewards prowess first and foremost. You don't have to be Einstein in the kitchen, rethinking soufflé theory, to score a blue ribbon. Imagination can't hurt, though, because some of the contests do call for original recipes, but ingenuity is not a must. The state fair is essentially about separating the good cooks from the bad cooks and holding them up for all to see.

The beauty of state fair cooking contests is that there are so many of them, one right after the other, like horse races. Over the course of a day a cook can have as many chances at winning as she can make dishes. It's like gambling, and I think that is what is so addicting about it. If you lose with a pie, you can turn your sights on the cake decorating class. If you have a ribbonless day, hit the kitchen that night and try with meat loaf tomorrow.

〜〜〜〜

The Iowa State Fair has the most contests and the biggest purses of any fair in the country, thus its nickname "The Big One." There are 168 divisions, with some 900 classes. The purse in Iowa totals $55,000. No wonder 771 people entered more than 10,000 dishes in 2001. This year the fair expects more than 800 contenders and more than 11,000 dishes. Consequently, the contests—or exhibitions, as they are called— have mushroomed beyond the fair's ten-day-run. They start four days before the fair gates even officially open.

The tremendous size, scope, and level of competition at the Iowa State Fair food exhibits is due to a woman whose only D in college was in home ec. Hollister, a former English and speech teacher, was asked to take over the fair's food department in 1985 when the purse totaled $6,000 and there were only twenty-five divisions. Hollister ascribes her success to what she calls PEP: "persistence, enthusiasm, and persuasion." She signed up new sponsors and added such contests as Tofu Cooking; Squash! Squash! Squash!; and Cooking with Scented Geraniums. She added cash prizes to the ribbons. Most of the cash prizes range from $25 to $200. And then there is the $3,000 grand prize for the cinnamon roll contest. She recruited judges from *Better Homes and Gardens* and other Meredith publications, which is based in Des Moines, giving the blue ribbons just an extra touch of cachet.

The number of people who enter dishes has risen every year under Hollister's watch. Gone are the days when farmwives took their county fair winners on to the state fairs, Roupe says. Now farm, suburban, and city people, some with no family connection to agriculture, enter the state fair directly. More men are entering, especially in the canning and bread baking divisions, and more young cooks are competing.

The upshot of the changing demographics is that the entries have become more sophisticated. People who travel and eat out began bringing dishes inspired by meals they'd had in restaurants. When Roupe began entering the Iowa State Fair contests in the late '80s, cakes were not decorated, just simply iced. During the '90s the decorations got more and more baroque. "Some of the old-time entrants rebelled," Roupe says. "Presentation to them was not important. Sometimes there were complaints on how fancy the cake looked."

Hollister is as surprised as anyone that in an age when the majority of American women have jobs, she gets the deluge of fair entries that she does each year. "I don't understand it," Hollister says. "I think what it is is that women and men work all day. This is something completely different than what they are doing. When women were home all day, they cooked all day. Now this is an outlet, a kind of a hobby."

"Because they don't have to do it three times a day, 365 days a year, they have discovered the fun of cooking," Roupe says. "They also go into a higher grade of cooking."

As food hobbies go, entering the fair demands a compulsive-like attention to detail. Rules change from contest to contest, so you have to read them carefully. Edible garnishes may be allowed in one cake contest and not in another. Solt says a fracas erupted last year when a woman put her cookies on a plate rather than the required cardboard disk. Then there's paperwork worthy of a tax accountant. Each entry has to come with its form carefully filled out and attached to the bottom of the plate. A typed or printed (no cursive) copy of the recipe in ink (no pencil) on a three-by-five card is required, but some contests also call for a second copy on an 8 1/2 by 11 sheet of paper. If it's a company-sponsored contest, you'll need to attach a proof of purchase, too. If any of these fall off, your dish will be disqualified. If you have directions for how the dish should be stored until the contest, you'll need to write those on a Post-it. Good luck getting it to stick to plastic wrap.

All this food must be loaded into a car and driven to the fair. This is where a lot can go wrong. Stories are legion about how quick braking or rough turns have sent cakes flying into laps, hitting the dashboard, or kerplopping to the floor. Solt tells me about the year Joy McFarland had a car accident on the way to the fair with twenty cakes. It was a cake massacre, smashed layers and icing smeared everywhere. McFarland wanted to salvage a layer or two and go on to the fair, but the police called to the scene would not let her.

When I arrive at Solt's at 5:45 A.M., she is still in her pale pink nightie and robe. In bare feet she rushes around the kitchen grabbing boxes, shuffling papers, and opening and closing the refrigerator. Her eyes are big, anxious. I ask if there's something I can do. "No," she says, unsmiling. Her husband, Ron, stands safely out of range. As Solt rushes upstairs to get dressed, he pours a cup of coffee and tells me his rules of survival during fair time: "Get out of her way. Don't ask if she needs help. If she asks, that's okay."

Solt reappears in jeans and gym shoes. She asks her husband to help her load the car, a wide four-door with an ample trunk and backseat. They carry out two coolers and several boxes. Within minutes we are backing out with a cargo of Quick Beef Provençal, Savory Onion and Raisin Spread, Baked Onion Dip, Cajun Garlic Salad Dressing, Garlic Bread Pudding, Ukrainian Easter Bread and Paskha, Pineapple Banana Nut Bread, and Cold Onion Picnic Deep Dish Pye. She gave up on painting the Ukrainian egg but stayed up until 11:30 transforming the wan olive oil piecrust into Sour Cream Apple Tart, also in the car. Solt lets out a huge sigh. It's 6 A.M. and the August sun already shines brightly, etching silos, the yellow fronds of corn stalk, and the cattle hunkered down in fields. This whole deep-green world of farms seems to stand still as Solt and I zip west at seventy-five miles per hour across the nation's bread basket toward Des Moines and the promise of blue ribbons.

Solt and I talk all the way to Des Moines. She's an only child. Her hair was so black when she was a baby, Aunt Gy asked her mother if maybe the nurses hadn't accidentally switched her with an American Indian infant. She wishes she could have been a hippie but was born too soon. She wanted to be a choreographer but became a legal secretary. "I fell in love, and the rest is history." She married at eighteen against her parents' wishes. She was a cheerleader. He was a football player. She spent the next thirteen years thinking of leaving her husband until she finally did. She met Ron through friends. They each had two kids.

Iowa pretty much looks all the same as we sail across I-80, an endless horizon of cornfields interrupted by neat farmhouses and barns. Not until we get much closer to Des Moines does the well-mannered land act up, the fertile flats giving way to hills and little valleys. We never see the Des Moines skyline. Solt's route takes us over the city, then dips south through residential neighborhoods to avoid fair traffic. When we pull onto the fairgrounds, all is deliciously quiet. This is the fourth day of food competitions, but the rides don't start twirling and the corn dogs frying until tomorrow. As we pull into the lot behind the nondescript Maytag Family Center, Solt points to a woman rushing across the parking lot holding a plate in front of her with both hands and says, "Here's one of the little regulars."

We hurriedly unpack the contents of Solt's car, enough food for a dinner party for twelve, and fill up a long table near the front door. The hallway is abuzz with white-haired women in wire-rimmed glasses dashing here and there with plates of food. Solt sighs, then pops the tart out of its pan, plops a cherry tomato on the garlic bread pudding, and arranges crackers around the dip. A woman walking by pauses and asks "How many things do you have?"

"Twelve," Solt says.

"Oh, my God," she says and walks off.

While Solt sorts out her garnishes and paperwork, I duck into the display room, which turns out to be a kind of de facto museum of American baking. All the winners of the past four days have been stashed in lighted cases that glow in the dim room. I stroll past corn-flakes wreath cookies, thumbprint cookies, caramel balls of Cheerios, biscuits, butterscotch bars, brownies, drop sugar cookies, and Rice Krispie bars. Some dishes look appetizing, some look appalling. There are golden corn breads and anemic corn breads, plump biscuits and biscuits as wizened as an old woman.

The display reflects the crossroads that American cooking is at just now. I spot gourmet touches, such as dried cranberries, macadamia nuts, and even white chocolate. Then there are the dreaded minimarshmal-lows and bursts of multicolored jimmies. There's a division called "Lard: The Other Baking Ingredient." In this case there's a zucchini bread that looks like a wedge of black earth with grubs burrowing through it.

I notice lots of the ribbons belong to Charles Duke and Joy McFar-land. Duke cleaned up in the lard category, pulling in seven blue rib-bons. McFarland won a second place in the Greatest Cocoa Cake division with her Hershey's Supreme and another second in the much vied for Softasilk contest with her Chocolate-Raspberry Sensation. This is where I find a slice of Solt's Walk on the Wild Side Cake, which won an honorable mention.

As I stroll through the Junior Division, I see ample proof of how we Americans start our young cooks early thinking that food is a big joke. In the trick-or-treat category the winner made cookies in the shape of long-dismembered fingers with slivered almonds for fingernails. Then there are the dirt cakes, which amount to a kind of baking freak show. These single-layer cakes are topped with what looks like crumbly topsoil and a wriggling mass of gummy worms. The blue ribbon winner used worms coated with crystallized sugar.

Solt has turned in all her dishes and now can devote the day to watching the judges and hanging out with her peers. I follow her into one of two overly air-conditioned theaters where banana bread judging has already begun. Contestants, some with friends and family in tow, are seated in creaking folding chairs. They look down on the judges as if they are watching a play. The judges nibble away on banana bread and whisper their responses to note takers seated next to them. One weighs banana breads with fruit. The other sizes up banana breads with nuts. The third has just plain banana breads. The breads are ferried back and forth from two long tables.

We find Marion Karlin, the retired psychologist. She has ginger-colored hair and the voice of a 1930s gangster moll. Like Solt, she also enters national contests and has been to National Beef and the National Oyster Cook-off. She has far trumped Solt in the number of entries. She brought forty-two today. "Mine is the Loch Ness Monster," she says pointing to her bread on the judges' table. "It had a deep crack in it, so I stuffed banana chips in."

Karlin began entering the fair after she retired from counseling, a profession she seems a little dubious about now. She tells me about how she had people write the reasons they shouldn't smoke and then attached them with a rubber band to a pack of cigarettes. She shakes her head at the ridiculousness. She also tried to help people lose weight to no avail. Cooking is a more rewarding pursuit for her. "It's a passion. Passions are good. Addictions," she says, wagging her finger at me, "are bad."

There are about thirty people in the auditorium, most just sit quietly observing the judges. It's not much to watch, at least to the uninitiated.

Karlin explains to me that she studies the judges' faces: "If their mouth turns down, that's not good." Karlin and Solt also track where their breads go once the judges have tasted them as an indication of how their entries fared. This is maddening because each judge uses a different system, so all the theorizing about placement is just that, theorizing. Solt notices that her bread, after being judged, is back on one of the long tables, at the far end. Solt reads this as a bad sign. "It's probably too sweet." Karlin's Loch Ness Monster is still on the judging table.

"Do you plan to taper off?" Solt asks Karlin.

"Taper off?" Karlin squeaks, holding her hand to her chest.

A judge of one of the banana bread classes stands up and takes hold of a mike. This is the educational part of the competitions. The judges always explain why they picked the winners. In doing so they pass on tips, offer examples of well-executed dishes, and dispel out-of-date notions. In fact, fairs are the front lines of teaching Americans how to improve their cooking. Every entry even receives a written critique from the judge. The assembled will use this information specifically to improve their entries for next year and boost their cooking skills along the way.

This judge clears her throat as if to deliver bad news. "We opened quite a few that were undercooked," she says. "I've never refused to judge so many before."

"Uh-oh," somebody in the audience says.

The judge recommends using smaller pans, not using vegetable spray, and not so much beating, which makes for tunnels. "Are there questions about my lecture?" she asks. No hands go up. The audience sits forward in their seats, waiting for the winners' names. Neither Karlin nor Solt scores a ribbon. Their friend Louise Piper, the pie lady, does earn a blue ribbon in Banana Bread (no nuts), which makes them happy. Piper had to put her husband in a rest home this spring, they tell me. Everyone wants her to do especially well at the fair this year. They turn their attention to the next contest, Cookies for Karlin, Raisin Creations for Solt.

Solt and I while away the afternoon. We scrutinize judges' expressions. The raisin judge makes a face when she tastes Solt's spread. We gossip with other hard-cores. Martha Stewart's visit to the fair last year is a favorite topic. She threw out a gift box of Iowa products, right on the fairground, one woman says. Louise Piper says Stewart was very nice to her. The group ignores Piper's comment. She wouldn't sign autographs, someone offers. They all harrumph.

I find these women down-to-earth, funny, even bawdy. There's an ease about them I haven't found at other contests, probably because there's no huge sums of money at stake and they aren't making art. They're very serious but not one lick pretentious. They love recounting stories about kitchen disasters, batter hitting the ceiling, and ovens left on. They guffaw over some of their wins.

"I got a first for my popcorn pudding," Sally Kilkenny says, laughing, as she charges up the steps in a judging room.

"It's gross," says her leggy daughter, trailing behind her.

Kilkenny tells me how she tries out her recipes on "the funeral ladies" at her church. She gives them the food to serve at funerals, then they tell her what they think. They said her honey cake was too dry. They liked her pineapple upside-down cakes so much that the funeral ladies ate all the cakes themselves. One woman, trim and in stylish red glasses, tells me about catering a party in a barn in the middle of the summer when it got so hot and humid that her skirt stretched out and she had to hike it over her "boobs." "My legs got so sweaty that when I went to the bathroom, I couldn't get my panties up."

Charles Duke remains aloof. He occasionally sits nervously at the back of the theater, but mostly he hovers in the hall with his teenage brother. He looks younger than his twenty-eight years, has a button nose, wide-set eyes, and a constant smile. When his chicken curry wins a blue ribbon, a judge asks over the mike, "Is Charles here?" Someone runs out into the hall to find him.

Duke appears but stands tentatively just inside the door as the judges sing the praises of his dish. Then he is gone again like a phantom. "He gets so hyper, he can't stand to be in here," Solt tells me. When he wins back-to-back blue ribbons, this time for his fudge nut pie, someone is sent into the hall again to find him.

～～～～

"Do you have to go to the potty?"

Solt is talking to me. It's been so long since I've been asked this question, I'm speechless. This question doesn't strike the women sitting around me as strange. They all look at me, waiting for an answer. The judging for onion, garlic, and legendary is about to begin, and Solt plans to stay in her seat while the state fair gods decide whether she gets one of those handmade ceramic plates this year. Solt doesn't want to be off escorting me to the fair's far-flung bathroom in another building. "No," I finally sputter.

Kilkenny says she has one, maybe two plates. Another hard-core volunteer says she has one. "I want one," Solt says, staring down at the two judges, a husband and wife who look disturbingly alike. They will judge the two onion classes, appetizers and entrées. They will pick a first in each class and then the best overall of those two. That cook gets the plate.

They begin by sampling the dozen appetizers. I can't read the man's face, but the woman's poker face brightens for a split second whenever she likes something, opening a little as it does when she tastes Solt's dish, the slippery onion dip that she salvaged yesterday. In between, the couple talk and even argue in urgent, low voices. When they are done with the dozen or so entries, they have three dishes sitting in front of them. Solt's dip sits right in front of them. "Looks like I got third," Norita says dejectedly.

She has read the dish placement wrong. In fact, she gets first. She's in the running for a plate. She sits upright on the end of her seat and stares as the judges munch and quietly argue their way through the main dishes, including Solt's cold onion pie. In short order the judging couple gives her another first. Two firsts for Solt means she's won the overall. The plate is hers. "Oh, my God," Solt exhales and throws herself across several chairs.

"Well, you are fancy, girl," Kilkenny crows.

Having gotten one plate, Solt is now hungry for another. She comes close. She wins a first in the garlic salad dressing and a second with her Garlic Bread Pudding. The overall prize and plate, though, goes to

Kilkenny for her Garlic Raisin Spread. In the legendary recipes the judge goes on and on about how good Solt's pashka is, how beautiful the round of egg bread is, hinting that it would be first place but for the missing Ukrainian egg. "I know, I know," Solt cries. "I hard-boiled it on Sunday but ran out of time last night to paint it." She gets second place.

That brings the day's take to four blue ribbons, two red ribbons, two honorable mentions, a second place overall, and the plate. That brings the total of cash she's won so far at the fair to $365. We rush out, leaving by 4 P.M. Tonight she'll make sixteen jumbo cinnamon rolls, Cajun shrimp bisque, Cajun shrimp pasta, pasta fagiole, and a sourdough bread. Tomorrow might just be another blue ribbon day.

CHAPTER 17

LURCHING TOWARD

CONTESTING

So maybe by now you've begun to feel a few drops of contester blood running through your veins. You've rifled through your recipe box, pulling out a card or two on which you've penciled a quasi-original pizza or a relative's carrot cake that you revamped. You've mentally picked apart a restaurant dish or two, analyzing spicing and texture, while your spouse recounts the stages eight through ten of the Tour de France. While waiting at the dentist's office you've scribbled a hasty, obtuse note that says something like "pumpkin bread plus corn bread" and tossed the brainstorm into the vacuum known as your purse.

That is how it started with me. I never expected to catch the bug, but I picked it up sometime around the National Cornbread Cook-off. Actually, there was an earlier sign that I might succumb. I signed up for a chili cookoff after I ventured to Terlingua. With chili, though, I could use a cookbook. Now for the first time I was considering creating my own recipes. This would be a big stretch for me, a devout recipe follower. When I returned from Chattanooga, I set my sights high, on the *Southern Living* Cook-Off. The contest allowed food professionals, which I ostensibly am, so I went to work. I had a distinct advantage: nearly a year's worth of advice from big-league contesters, judges, and contest organizers ringing in my head. Here's the basic tip sheet I worked from, just in case you feel yourself succumbing.

DO YOUR HOMEWORK This move truly sets contesters apart. Look up the past winners. Check out the recipes on the company's website. Page through food magazines and cookbooks. Study restaurant menus. Keep tabs on the winners of all major cookoffs and recipe contests, even ones you didn't enter. Here's what you should discern from all this research.

Past winners of the contest you are considering are a guide to what might score the next go-around. For starters, they indicate how complicated or simple a contest likes its recipes to be. If winners tend to have short, straight-ahead ingredients lists, no-nonsense cooking instructions, and the mass appeal of a Disney movie, think likewise for your entry. If the winners have ingredients lists the length of a Russian novel and directions complex enough to create a nuclear device, follow suit and let your inner Julia Child out. These latter contests, which include the Gilroy's Great Garlic Cook-Off and Sutter Home's Build a Better Burger, are few and far between.

Consider the style of the winning dishes. If you read over recent winners of Better Burger, it seems clear that an elaborate topping, whether it be salsa, aioli, or chutney, is a must. Contesters have duly noted that the '99 and '01 National Beef winners both crossed steak with fruit. The next contest is sure to have many entries featuring like-minded combos. However, after Asian-style dishes took first and second prizes at the '99 National Chicken, everyone expected that cuisine to fare well again in 2001. There wasn't an Asian dish among any of the winners.

The Bake-Off® contest is a maddeningly difficult contest to get a read on. Almost everyone assumes a chocolatey dessert is the magic key. It's true that sweets have won most at the contest, but chocolate desserts have taken only nine grand prizes, or nearly 25 percent. The problem is these one-in-four odds prompt thousands upon thousands of home bakers to fixate on heavy chocolatey desserts, making it an intensely competitive category. Of the one hundred final recipes there's room for only twenty-five or so desserts, and they can't all be chocolate. That is exactly why the recent winner, Denise Yennie, did not enter anything chocolate or sweet. She knew her chances of being named one of the one hundred were better if she thought savory. That's why she focused on the three savory categories.

If you look at the main dish and appetizer categories, you see another trend. In the recent competition, three of the four $10,000 prizes as well as the G.E. Innovation award went to chicken dishes. In general, chicken, specifically white meat, is a regular winner in contests of all kinds. Pork shows up occasionally, as does fish. Beef is often a no-show in the winners' circle. When in doubt, go with America's favorite bird— that is, unless you're entering National Beef.

The company's own recipes, if they have them, will also give you an idea what might make a winner. These recipes are developed in the test kitchen, and they indicate how the sponsors like to use their products. The test kitchen cooks already know how the product works best, so let them guide you with their concoctions. Also, these cooks are likely to screen entries if not test them as well. If you are inspired by the company recipes, remember that imitation is the greatest form of flattery. Too much imitation, though, will get your recipe stamped unoriginal. Bye-bye.

Magazines, cookbooks, and menus will keep you up on the most current trends. Asian, Thai specifically, Mediterranean, Southwestern, and updated American comfort food have fared well in the food media and likewise in contests in recent years. There have been anomalies. Janice Elder has won with some southern-style dishes. Greek- and Caribbean-influenced dishes pop up here and there. Now Latino and Spanish, even Swedish, are all on the upswing in contests.

With all this information, a contester has amassed something like a racing form. How she sizes up her culinary bet is, of course, very subjective.

I did not play it safe. I had my reasons. This was the first year of the *Southern Living* Cook-Off, so there were no past winners to research. The magazine has run many contests over the years, but I didn't bother with them because this cookoff seemed like an altogether different bird. From talking to contesters I knew many were shying away from the category called Taste of the South, which the website described as "new twists on Southern classics." I figured in that category I might be going up against serious southern cooks, but at least I wouldn't have to contend with the big guns: the contesters.

I decided to put a new twist on the South by pulling it north. In my New England kitchen I reworked a southern classic with Yankee ingredients. I added cranberry and pumpkin to corn bread. I used pecans and a cast iron pan to tilt the balance of the dish to the South. I pulled the blue and gray concoction together with a nod to my midwestern German roots. I created a corn bread coffee cake.

RULES This is where more than half of contest entries go wrong. If you make one mistake, such as forget to fill in your zip code or leave out the recipe title, your entry will be tossed. The urge to zip off a recipe and post it on the fly should be strongly resisted. That is why so many entries arrive without the number of servings marked or even the contestant's name.

Read, reread, and then reread the rules again. Use a highlighting pen to mark crucial information. For example, some contests ask you to list ingredients in the order they are used.

Southern Living has an online form that I used to guide me through the process to some degree. During a practice run, whenever I screwed up the form, it refused to be sent. However, the form would not detect mistakes I made in the recipe, which should include the number of servings, size of cookware used, cooking times, and temperature.

USE PRODUCTS PROMINENTLY When there is a qualifying ingredient, make it the star of the dish. For example, the Gilroy Garlic Cook-Off requires a minimum of seven garlic cloves. That was just a starting point for Roxanne Chan and her Florentine Frittata Salad. She used garlic in the frittata and in the dressing, and then tossed one cup of sliced cloves over the salad. She used so much garlic that she lost count of the cloves. Kristine Snyder used only one tablespoon of Sutter Home Sauvignon Blanc in her winning Soy-Glazed Salmon Burgers with Ginger-Lime Aioli, but in the recipe she advised the cook to sip a glass while grilling.

The *Southern Living* Cook-Off has so many qualifying ingredients—over thirty—that it was hard to come up with a recipe that didn't use one. The more serious contesters crafted recipes that used a number of qualifying ingredients in one dish. Pat Harmon devised a dish that used four. I heard that someone had managed eight. A newbie, I cut myself some slack. I picked Domino sugar as my one and only qualifying ingredient. My coffee cake called for three-fourths of a cup, not exactly prominent but not too shabby, either.

CATCHY NAMES Almost as much energy can be expended on naming your culinary prodigy as in creating it. In the early years of contesting, contestants liked them short and snappy, like advertising jingles. Consider these finalists from the 1953 Bake-Off® contest: By Cracky Bars, Cloud-topped Cakettes, Candy Lasses, Orange Upsidaisies, Surprise Zookies, and Blushing Beauty Dumplings. There were also your plain Janes such as Garlic Cheese Toast, Liver and Onion Dinner, and Cheese Nut Loaf, void of sexual innuendo or alliteration but still short.

Currently there are two schools of thinking on recipe titles. One believes in simplicity. Chan is of this mind, as some of her winners with short titles and staccato rhythms make clear: Chili Chicken Rice Casserole, Thai-Style Pumpkin Soup, and Asian Style Slaw. She did show a little flourish with a hot sandwich featuring Havarti blue cheese and crab that she dubbed Fisherman's Wharf Grilled Cheese. She uses alliteration when possible but doesn't fuss.

The other school believes in something far more extravagant, titles packed with alliteration, cultural references, and, taking their cue from restaurant menus, laundry lists of ingredients. The point here is to grab the judge's attention. One judge told me that this technique can work. Other judges don't care what a recipe is called. Sometimes the judges don't even see the dishes' names.

Beautiful and talented Camilla Saulsbury is in this camp with titles that trip off the tongue and could double for band names, such as Calypso Crab Cakes with Fresh Mango-Papaya Relish or Shangri-la Shrimp Salad with Hot Mango-Lime Vinaigrette. This approach is harder than it appears and requires a soft touch. If you try too hard, you can produce a real doozy, such as the long-winded cultural mishmash of Nuevo Cubano Chicken Kiev with Mango Mustard Sauce, that will only prompt a perplexed "Huh?" from the judge.

The cultural and geographic references can get pretty loose. There's hardly anything Tuscan about Bob Gadsby's Tuscan Chicken Cakes with Tomato-Basil Relish, but Mediterranean is all the rage. No one goes with just plain old Italian, too spaghetti and meat balls. Instead you get Siciliano or Florentine. And rather than Mexican you get Creamy Cancun Roasted Garlic Soup with Fiery Garlic Shrimp or Baja Chicken Salad with Taco Vinaigrette. For some reason people don't tend to tweak the Asian label too much, except perhaps Pacific Rim. One snynonym stretch produced the colonial throwback Siam Phyllo Chicken, a 2001 National Chicken entry with instructions fit for origami.

I vacillated between both schools of thought without success. It seems that a writer ought to be able to think of a recipe title, but I froze, just as I do at the Scrabble board. I tossed out This Ain't Your Momma's Cornbread. Too smart-alecky, I decided. I tried to work with the whole North meets South thing to no avail. I meditated on my own dilemma, a midwesterner who sounds suspiciously southern to most New Englanders, in an attempt to divine the name of my cross-regional creation. I came up with Where Are You *From?* Coffeecake. My husband suggested I just call it Amy's Cornbread Coffeecake. "You don't understand," I wailed.

With the deadline encroaching, I used a hybrid approach that resulted in the straightforward but lengthy and utterly boring Cranberry Pumpkin Cornbread Coffeecake with Pecan Streusel. My cake deserved better, but I was out of time.

LOTS OF ENTRIES Contesters don't hold back. When they enter a contest, the entry forms fly. Chan entered more than thirty recipes to *Southern Living*. Diane Sparrow sent nineteen. Janice and Larry Elder entered about a dozen between them. Especially in contests with categories, like *Southern Living,* your chances improve dramatically the more entries you send in. When Ruth Kendrick pressed Terry Ann Moore for her secret for getting into the Bake-Off® contest, Moore answered, "Lots of entries." Moore, who has been three times, never sent in less than a dozen and managed eighty for one contest.

I didn't have a trove of original recipes to work with. I zigzagged to cookoffs all spring. Now the long days of a precious Maine summer were upon me. This is when all the state's population, after the shut-in months of winter and then the bruising insult of mud season, give into a blissful, sun-drenched mania to be outdoors every possible waking second. Indoor activities—laundry, watching TV, work, sleeping, cooking—are cut to the barest minimum.

Had I an outdoor kitchen—something so frivolous in Maine that the natives might stone you for it—I could have managed more than one entry. As it was, my coffee cake entry nearly killed me. In May, between trips to Houston and Memphis, I pulled out the stained copy of my favorite corn bread recipe, a version from a dairy-free cookbook that I had added buttermilk to. I cracked a Shaker cookbook to the page with my favorite pumpkin bread recipe. I meshed the two, threw the cranberries into the batter, and made a streusel topping from brown sugar and pecans. I baked the cake in a 10-inch cast iron skillet. The first test was promising but not perfect. The cake was too heavy and too thick.

Over a month later, on a Sunday afternoon, June 30, the very last day that entries could be sent in, I made my second and final testing of my coffee cake for friends visiting from Vermont. I cooked it longer, at a lower temperature, and in a 12-inch skillet. Bingo. While my guests, a family of four outdoorsy redheads, munched the cake for brunch, I rushed upstairs to my computer to fill out the online entry form. I read over my recipe one more time, clicked on the send button, and then raced back downstairs to go to the beach with my guests, husband, and two dogs.

The import of the moment was lost on those around me, who busied themselves stuffing towels into beach bags, searching for missing thongs, and slicking white sunscreen on their pale complexions. Regardless, there was no denying what had just happened: I had entered my first cooking contest.

~ ~ ~ ~

CRANBERRY PUMPKIN CORNBREAD COFFEECAKE
WITH PECAN STREUSEL

STREUSEL TOPPING

1/2 cup unbleached all-purpose flour
1 cup coarsely chopped pecans
1/2 cup light brown sugar
1/4 teaspoon nutmeg
5 tablespoons unsalted butter, melted

BATTER

3/4 cup sugar
3/4 cup light brown sugar
1 cup (2 sticks) unsalted butter, melted
2 large eggs
1 can prepared pumpkin
1 1/2 cups cornmeal
1 1/2 cups unbleached all-purpose flour
2 teaspoons baking powder
1/2 teaspoon baking soda
1/2 teaspoon salt
1 teaspoon cinnamon
1 teaspoon cloves
1 teaspoon nutmeg
1 1/2 cups dried cranberries

1. Preheat the oven to 400°F. Coat a 12-inch cast iron pan with Pam.

2. To make the topping: Toss together the flour, pecans, brown sugar, and nutmeg. Pour in the melted butter and stir until the mixture is moistened and crumbly. Set aside.

3. To make the batter: In a bowl, beat the sugar, brown sugar, and melted butter to blend. Beat in the eggs, one at a time, and continue beating until light and fluffy. Mix in the pumpkin. In a separate bowl, mix the cornmeal, flour, baking powder, baking soda, salt, cinnamon, cloves, and nutmeg. Add the dry ingredients to the wet ingredients gradually, stirring until completely incorporated. Mix in the cranberries.

4. Pour the batter into the cast iron pan and spread evenly. Crumble the streusel topping over the top. Bake for 35 minutes, or until a cake tester inserted in the middle comes out clean. Cool on a rack. Serve at room temperature.

MAKES 10 TO 12 SERVINGS

EPILOGUE

In the spring I called and emailed Barbara Morgan, the contesting doyenne in California, without reply. Morgan was living history for me. Off the top of her head she could talk about thirty years of contesting. Also, no one had a better sense of humor about competitive cooking than Morgan. I was blatantly looking for more funny quotes.

I found out secondhand that Morgan had become very ill and had been quickly moved to a nursing home. I tracked down the number for the nursing home and left a message on a Friday. Monday morning an email awaited me. Morgan had died the night before. According to Diane Sparrow, when Morgan was asked if she had any final words for her contesting friends, she replied, *"Bon appétit."*

Meanwhile, Cindy Schmuelling, the Pillsbury first-timer who arrived home to a hopeless prognosis for her cancer, was given a reprieve. Having given her a death sentence, the doctors changed their minds. They blasted her with chemo and then cut out the tumor in her left lung and the other in her liver. She spent the summer in her new house recovering and began dreaming of the next Bake-Off® contest.

Ruth Kendrick was named a finalist at the Gilroy Great Garlic Cook-Off. She served her Shrimp and Crab Garlic Spring Rolls with Spicy

Garlic Dipping Sauce on the Asian-style Pottery Barn plates she had bought for Sparrow to use at Gilroy the year before. She came in second, as Sparrow had the previous cookoff. A new rising star, Beth Royals of Richmond, Virginia, took first with Garlic-Scented Seafood Cakes with Citrus Salsa and Chipotle Aioli. Roxanne Chan told me she was surprised by how much canned stuff the winners used, "even canned crab" in Royals's winner. Chan worried that Gilroy was losing its gourmet edge.

Sutter Home, in a maneuver to open the contest to Californians, teamed up with the American Culinary Federation, the largest association of professional chefs and cooks in the country. The ACF is based in New York City, which, Sutter Home believed, freed the contest from the California state law that precluded residents from entering. Chan could enter the contest again. None of her three entries made the cut, but the recipes of two other Californians did. When I called Mathew Botting, the chief counsel for the state's Department of Alcoholic Beverage Control, he had just heard about Sutter Home's end run. To Botting's thinking the contest was still under the purview of California law. He was looking into it.

Sparrow, who longed for another shot at the grill, only managed to send in a couple of entries for Better Burger. All her creative energies had been spent on her son's epic do-it-yourself summer wedding. She made as well as served pulled pork sandwiches, pasta and crab salad, Buffalo chicken wings, sweet onion dip, fruit salad in carved watermelon bowls, and black bean tortilla roll-ups for more than four hundred guests. She crafted a three-tiered apricot cheesecake for the wedding cake, not to mention a chocolate ganache groom's cake. She stitched five formal vests for the ushers, the flower girl's dress, and a quilt for all the wedding guests to sign. She also cooked the rehearsal brunch. The mother of the bride contributed the coffee cakes for that meal. Not long after the nuptial blowout, Sparrow's third son, Nick, announced his engagement. He and his fiancée's guest list quickly ballooned to 430.

In the summer Bake-Off® contest organizers got the go-ahead from

General Mills to start planning the 2004 contest. There was no public announcement, so legions of Bake-Off® contest devotees continued to wait nervously and hope. The fate of the rule that knocked three-time finalists out of the competition remained uncertain, keeping the hopes of Pat Harmon and others alive.

At the end of August, *Southern Living* announced the fifteen finalists, selected from a staggering forty thousand entries. The list included five contesters: Camilla Saulsbury, Bob Gadsby, Beth Royals, Lori Welander, and Steve Bradley, the contesting son of a longtime contester. Then two weeks later Alex DeSantis, husband of longtime contester Shirley De-Santis, joined the list. Someone had dropped out. It was Bradley. His mother had just won $400 in the *Better Homes and Gardens* monthly contest. Her prize-winning Ribeyes with Chipotle Butter, published in the magazine's August issue, was ruled too similar to Bradley's *Southern Living* entry. He was disqualified, and one contesting family's loss became another's gain.

During the last weekend in September the chosen fifteen gathered in Orlando, Florida, at the tony Gaylord Palms Resort. The magazine planned to create an awards program as a cooking television show with Al Roker as the MC. Susan Dozier, executive food editor at *Southern Living*, told me she thought this modern format would trump even the Bake-Off®'s televised awards program.

On Friday the contestants had an hour and a half to prepare their dishes. While the judges deliberated, the contestants rehearsed for the next day's taping. On Saturday the contestants demonstrated their dishes for the camera in groups of three. Then the winner was announced: Pecan Pie Cheesecake. Ginnie Prater, a young southern mother eight months pregnant with her second child, cut a Mrs. Smith Pecan Pie into twenty thin slices, set those slices in a pie shell, and poured a cheesecake batter over the top. The pie was one of five qualifying ingredients that Prater used in her dessert. She had entered cooking contests before but had never made it to a cookoff. Her cake was horrifyingly sweet but a stroke of genius nonetheless.

The recipe was quickly posted on the magazine's website. A virtual catfight ensued. Readers could size up the winning recipe on the website. They had at it. Clearly few were baking the hybrid dessert before taking a swipe with sharp claws fully extended. For example:

"I can't imagine what this beat out to win the contest. Cake from the day-old rack?"

"Although I do recall the name being the *'Southern' Living* cooking contest, a true southern woman would never, ever use a store-bought pie as part of her recipe."

"You not only did a disservice to everyone who entered 'true' recipes, but you have made the winner a target of embarrassment. This so-called winner is a laugh."

"I guess the winner can't believe her own luck since she must have sent her recipe as a joke. Good for her, though; it's nice that sometimes untalented people get some attention and money."

"Shame on you, *Southern Living.* I'm not surprised, though. My daughter recently moved to the Carolinas. After visiting her, we find that no one in the South can cook, so maybe store-bought is the way to go! Come to Vermont. We will teach you how to cook."

Then the backlash commenced. The battle lines broke down between North and South, proud scratch bakers and harried convenience cooks, women who work and women who don't, people who read the rules and people who didn't.

"This was amazing!! I'm sorry so many people were offended at a store-bought pie, but it was delicious. I work sixty-five hours a week and do not have a lot of time to bake from scratch."

"I haven't tried this recipe yet, so it's not fair to rate it. I think it's unfair of some southern 'cooks' to suggest that those of us born in the northern part of this country aren't as talented in the kitchen."

"Boy, what a bunch of sad people. Your recipe was fine. I guess they have all day to cook. Well, with a job and four kids, I take shortcuts."

The war raged on. By Tuesday morning there were 204 postings that filled 34 pages. Most gave Prater's winning cake one or no stars. Even with the counteroffensive, the $100,000 cake rated a measly two stars.

I called Dozier to see what the magazine staff thought. Dozier told me she was crushed when she first read the petulant postings. Then once she thought it over, the fracas made sense. She didn't think it was a North versus South dispute. It was intra-gender warfare. The food fight was, as is often the case, more complicated than just who was the better cook. It was over who was the better woman, the wage earner or the stay-at-home.

"People use food as a tool to express their superiority," Dozier sighed. "In this politically correct climate, food is one of the last tools left."

She recalled a similar controversy breaking out over a white cake on the magazine's December cover. It used a cake mix as a base, "so people would have more time to decorate. We got some incredible hate mail."

The magazine, Dozier explained, has a core group of readers who do not work and devote a lot of time to cooking. For women who work, cooking is a sideline creative activity. For these full-time homemakers, cooking is a defining aspect of their personalities, Dozier said. A store-bought pie winning $100,000 was a personal affront to this latter group. It said, "What you're doing doesn't matter." In other words, get a job.

"Something threatens people when a convenience product produces good culinary results," Dozier said.

The irony was that a full-time mom had crafted the winning recipe. Dozier said the magazine would leave the comments up. They took down only a few really hateful ones, such as the posting about burning a cross soaked in rum on the winner's front lawn. Dozier was discouraged but not deterred. The annual cookoff would go on to its second year.

In the fall Pat Harmon noticed Wolfgang Hanau's name on another winners' list. The chef's name popped up in the monthly What Do You Do with Your Pace? Contest. He was the April winner for his Seared Pacific Coast Sea Bass with Fruity Mango Salsa. It turns out he wasn't the only food pro working the amateur contests and winning. Harmon got wind that the grand prize winner in the Rice Federation's Rice to the Rescue contest was a food writer. The rumor was true. Jan Curry, a freelance food columnist for the *News and Observer* in Raleigh, North Carolina, had won the $5,000 grand prize. She'd also recently picked up a first place in cookies with her Toffee Brown Butter Shortbread in the T-Fal Perfect Bake Contest. Both contests specifically list food writers as ineligible. Harmon notified Pace and the Rice Federation. She didn't relish playing watchdog.

"I know that some contesters think this complaining discourages sponsors from sponsoring contests, but I believe rules need to be followed," she wrote me in an email. "After all, there are a lot of big money prizes at stake here for us amateurs."

Down south that river of cash running through Memphis in May washed Jerry McMichael, head cook of the Airpork Crew, right out of his job. The Memphis International Airport, where McMichael had been vice president and CFO, had largely financed the team, considering it a marketing tool. That changed after 9/11. McMichael was ordered to spend no more than $1,600 for the team's 2002 Memphis in May appearance. He went a tad over budget. A story in the *Commercial Appeal* reported that McMichael spent more than $27,000. The airport president fired him in October 2002. The team disbanded.

An audit uncovered further evidence that McMichael had deposited airport funds into the team's checking account and then siphoned off more than $90,000 for his own use. The U.S. attorney's office was considering criminal charges. I pictured McMichael rolling a barbecued hog into a courtroom and working his mojo on a federal judge. "Now, your honor, my momma specially raised Edna just for you."

As for the fate of my Cranberry Pumpkin Cornbread Coffeecake with Pecan Streusel, it obviously did not make the grade for the *Southern Living* Cook-Off. When the finalists were announced, I didn't gnash my teeth over the ineptitude of the contest judges or fume over how they had passed over the most incredible coffeecake recipe known to man. I knew exactly why I was not a finalist, and it had nothing to do with the quality of my cake.

About twenty-four hours after sending in my entry, a good twenty hours after the deadline had passed, I was sitting at my desk scribbling a to-do list. From my jumble of thoughts a four-word sentence suddenly emerged clear as day. I forgot the pumpkin. *The Pumpkin.*

I had made the classic newbie mistake. Pumpkin was in the title.

Pumpkin was mentioned in the directions. But the can of pumpkin was *not* in my ingredients' list. I put my head down on my desk. I emailed Sparrow about my great failing. "Bet you never do that again," she wrote back.

My first impulse was never to enter another contest again. Obviously, I wasn't up to it. Truth be told, though, I was still inordinately proud of my coffee cake recipe. My ego had swelled when I pulled my concoction out of the oven and looked down at its lovely amber top. I didn't say anything to anyone, but I really thought I had a winner. Briefly, the cranberry-studded cake had opened doors to another world, a world where I might be $100,000 richer and celebrated for my genius in the kitchen. Even without the promises of riches and fleeting fame, inventing a coffee cake had been surprisingly rewarding, as much as writing a particularly difficult article or skiing a tricky slope. The high of it took me off guard. For God's sake, it was only a coffee cake. But it was *my* coffee cake.

I wanted to feel that buzz again. I set about creating a burger for Sutter Home, toying with the idea of an Asian-style cheeseburger. I began looking for other contests to enter my coffee cake in while I tweaked the recipe in my mind. What if I put the streusel filling in the middle of the cake? I thought. Or created a savory filling from blue cheese? I could use the fresh thyme in my garden.

Another contester was born.